CW00541423

Multilingual Learning an Language Supportive Ped in Sub-Saharan Africa

This edited collection provides unprecedented insight into the emerging field of multilingual education in Sub-Saharan Africa (SSA). Multilingual education is claimed to have many benefits, amongst which are that it can improve both content and language learning, especially for learners who may have low ability in the medium of instruction and are consequently struggling to learn. The book represents a range of Sub-Saharan school contexts and describes how multilingual strategies have been developed and implemented within them to support the learning of content and language. It looks at multilingual learning from several points of view, including 'translanguaging', or the use of multiple languages – and especially African languages – for learning and language-supportive pedagogy, or the implementation of a distinct pedagogy to support learners working through the medium of a second language.

The book puts forward strategies for creating materials, classroom environments and teacher education programmes which support the use of all of a student's languages to improve language and content learning. The contexts which the book describes are challenging, including low school resourcing, poverty and low literacy in the home, and school policy which militates against the use of African languages in school. The volume also draws on multilingual education approaches which have been successfully carried out in higher resource countries and lend themselves to being adapted for use in SSA. It shows how multilingual learning can bring about transformation in education and provides inspiration for how these strategies might spread and be further developed to improve learning in schools in SSA and beyond.

Elizabeth J. Erling is an educational research consultant who has worked in international education and English language teaching initiatives at the Open University, UK, the University of Graz and the University of Vienna, Austria.

John Clegg is a freelance education consultant and occasional researcher at the Graduate School of Education, University of Bristol, UK.

Casmir M. Rubagumya is a professor of Language Education at St. John's University of Tanzania, Tanzania.

Colin Reilly is a senior research officer in the Department of Language and Linguistics at the University of Essex, UK.

Routledge Series in Language and Content Integrated Teaching & Plurilingual Education
Series Editors: Angel M. Y. Lin and Christiane Dalton-Puffer

Scaffolding Language Development in Immersion and Dual Language Classrooms
Diane J. Tedick and Roy Lyster

Soft CLIL and English Language Teaching
Understanding Japanese Policy, Practice, and Implications
Makoto Ikeda, Shinichi Izumi, Yoshinori Watanabe, Richard Pinner and Matthew Davis

Multilingual Learning and Language Supportive Pedagogies in Sub-Saharan Africa
Edited by Elizabeth J. Erling, John Clegg, Casmir M. Rubagumya and Colin Reilly

For a full list of titles in this series, please visit:
www.routledge.com/Routledge-Series-in-Language-and-Content-Integrated-Teaching--Plurilingual-Education/book-series/CITPE

Multilingual Learning and Language Supportive Pedagogies in Sub-Saharan Africa

Edited by
Elizabeth J. Erling, John Clegg,
Casmir M. Rubagumya and
Colin Reilly

Routledge
Taylor & Francis Group
LONDON AND NEW YORK

First published 2022
by Routledge
2 Park Square, Milton Park, Abingdon, Oxon OX14 4RN

and by Routledge
605 Third Avenue, New York, NY 10158

Routledge is an imprint of the Taylor & Francis Group, an informa business

© 2022 selection and editorial matter, Elizabeth J. Erling, John Clegg, Casmir M. Rubagumya and Colin Reilly; individual chapters, the contributors

The right of Elizabeth J. Erling, John Clegg, Casmir M. Rubagumya and Colin Reilly to be identified as the authors of the editorial material, and of the authors for their individual chapters, has been asserted in accordance with sections 77 and 78 of the Copyright, Designs and Patents Act 1988.

With the exception of Chapter 3, no part of this book may be reprinted or reproduced or utilised in any form or by any electronic, mechanical, or other means, now known or hereafter invented, including photocopying and recording, or in any information storage or retrieval system, without permission in writing from the publishers.

Chapter 3 of this book is available for free in PDF format as Open Access from the individual product page at www.routledge.com. It has been made available under a Creative Commons Attribution-Non Commercial-No Derivatives 4.0 license.

Trademark notice: Product or corporate names may be trademarks or registered trademarks, and are used only for identification and explanation without intent to infringe.

British Library Cataloguing-in-Publication Data
A catalogue record for this book is available from the British Library

Library of Congress Cataloging-in-Publication Data
A catalog record has been requested for this book

ISBN: 978-0-367-46353-3 (hbk)
ISBN: 978-0-367-67752-7 (pbk)
ISBN: 978-1-003-02838-3 (ebk)

DOI: 10.4324/9781003028383

Typeset in Galliard
by Newgen Publishing UK

This volume is dedicated to the parents, teachers, activists, and academics who tirelessly advocate for change and work towards improving education systems so that all children, wherever they may be, are able to access and flourish within education through a language they understand.

Contents

Figures

Tables

Contributors

Gladys Y. Aponte is a doctoral student in Urban Education at The Graduate Center, City University of New York. Prior to pursuing a doctoral degree, Gladys was a dual language bilingual teacher in New York City public schools. As an adjunct instructor and CUNY-NYSIEB Research Assistant, Gladys collaborates with educators to plan and implement translanguaging pedagogies. She holds a BA in Elementary Education from Hunter College, and an MSEd in Dual Language Bilingual Education and Childhood Special Education from Bank Street College.

Angeline M. Barrett (PhD) is an associate professor in Education at the University of Bristol, where she is co-Director of the Centre for Comparative and International Research in Education in the School of Education. She is also Deputy Director of the South West Doctoral Training Partnership. Her main research interests are in teacher professionalism and pedagogy within formal education, which she studies in relation to issues of international policy agendas, social justice and sustainability. Angeline has researched education in Tanzania almost continuously over the last 20 years and prior to this taught science and mathematics in schools and with colleagues in Tanzania, Uganda and England.

Angela Becker is a language and education consultant with SIL International. She has an EdD in Educational Psychology from Regent University, an MEd in Teaching and Curriculum from Pennsylvania State University, and a BS in Early Childhood and Elementary Education from Grove City College. Angela began her career as an early-level elementary teacher in the US and then joined the SIL Africa team in Kenya where she worked to promote literacy and language development in minority language communities with a focus in literacy-learning material development, curriculum writing and research. While remaining connected with SIL through part-time consultation, Angela now works as an assistant professor in Education at Lancaster Bible College.

Carole Bloch (PhD) directs PRAESA (Project for the Study of Alternative Education in South Africa), a non-government multilingual language and literacy organisation (www.praesa.org.za) and is Associate Professor in Early

Language and Literacy at the University of the Western Cape. Since 1992, Carole's focus has been on exploring and sharing ways to transform children's opportunities to learn to read and write meaningfully in multilingual settings using holistic, story-based approaches. She has conducted research into young children's literacy and biliteracy learning in African settings, facilitated training for teachers and teacher trainers as well as the publication of several storybooks for children of all ages in many African languages and English. In 2012, with colleagues in PRAESA, Carole co-founded and led the first four years of the Nal'ibali national Reading-for-Enjoyment Campaign (www.nalibali.org) in South Africa. She is a member of the Reading Hall of Fame (www.readinghalloffame.org/) and is serving as a vice president of IBBY International 2018–20 (www.ibby.org/).

John Clegg worked formerly at the University of West London and is now a freelance education consultant, specialising in education in a second language. He has worked for 35 years in curriculum evaluation, materials design, teacher education and research in English-medium education in Africa mainly on projects which develop education through a second language, bilingual and language supportive learning materials and primary teacher-education for the Molteno Project. He has also been active in Content and Language Integrated Learning in Europe. He is co-author of *Putting CLIL into Practice* (Oxford University Press) and has written several articles on teaching and learning in a second language.

Mats Deutschmann is Professor in English at the School of Humanities, Education and Social Sciences at Örebro University, Sweden. His main fields of research interest lie in sociolinguistics and language politics in post-colonial contexts, and the Seychelles is of special interest since he grew up there and experienced the school system first hand. He is currently leading two projects on language and stereotyping where the Seychelles context is also included.

Elizabeth J. Erling (PhD) formerly Professor of English Language Teaching Research and Methodology at the University of Graz and senior lecturer in International Education and ELT at the Open University, UK, is an independent research affiliated with the University of Vienna. She has been involved in several teacher education and research initiatives in Sub-Saharan Africa, South Asia and Europe. Her research focuses on beliefs about English and their relation to pedagogy and policy.

Ivana Espinet is an assistant professor at Kingsborough Community College. She holds a PhD in Urban Education from the CUNY Graduate Center and an MA in Instructional Technology and Education from Teachers College, Columbia University. She is a former project director for CUNY New York State Initiative on Emergent Bilinguals. She is interested in the use of multimodal and collaborative methodologies to learn about emergent bilinguals in school and in out-of-school programmes.

Cornelius Wambi Gulere was a senior lecturer in the Faculty of Education of Uganda Christian University in Uganda during the time of this study and is now Education Secretary, Uganda Orthodox Church Schools. His area of interest is knowledge creation through translation, riddle performance and social discourses. He holds a PhD in Literature from Makerere University, and has written and published many children's stories while helping others to write in their African languages.

Alexandra Holland is Academic Development Manager at Aga Khan Academies, a growing network of bilingual schools situated in Africa, the Middle East and South and Central Asia, educating students through the medium of English and a national language. She supports teachers in Kenya, India and Mozambique in building International Baccalaureate continuum programmes which are relevant to students in the developing world, and which prepare students to use their education to improve quality of life in their local communities, and has supported teachers in developing a translanguaging approach within the IB primary years and middle years programmes.

Zawadi Richard Juma (PhD) is Acting Dean of the Faculty of Humanities and Education at St John's University of Tanzania. She is an experienced science educator, curriculum developer and teacher educator. Her main research interest relates to the design of secondary school science curricula that develop of socio-scientific skills and knowledge relevant to students' daily lives in Tanzania. Since 2016, she has been a Coordinator of the Language Supportive Teaching and Textbook (LSTT) project in Tanzania.

Annukka Kinnaird is a literacy and education consultant working with SIL. She has an MA in English and a BA in Education from the University of Oulu, Finland, as well as certificates for teaching primary school and English in secondary schools, as well as SIL's training in Anthropology and Applied Field Linguistics. She has worked in Cameroon since 1992, spending 21 years in a small village where she has worked on the language analysis and orthography of two local languages, creating primers and other literacy materials for them, training local literacy teachers and leading a mother tongue-based multilingual education pilot project. She now continues with her literacy and community development work remotely from Scotland.

Kevin Kezabu Lubuulwa is a lecturer in the Faculty of Education of Uganda Christian University in Uganda. Kevin's research interests are in Educational Action Research, African Literature and Environmental Education. She holds a PhD in Education from the University of Tasmania.

Sive Mbolekwa is a literacy activist and storyteller who has worked and trained young people and teachers in early literacy strategies through storytelling. In 2017, he joined PRAESA as a Storyplay Mentor, before which he worked in primary school early literacy programmes and curated a literacy festival for the Zithulele area of the Eastern Cape Province. He has also enabled and supported young people's informally structured literacy learning in a community literacy club and has a deep interest in sharing a culture of thinking critically about our social conditions with children.

Megan Sutton Mercado has been a language and education specialist with SIL International since 2017. Her consulting work includes African-language adult literacy projects in Kenya, Tanzania, Malawi and Namibia. Her current research interests include the impact of mother tongue education programmes, the creation of instructional materials, and the ways in which technology facilitates or impedes the use of non-dominant languages.

Lizzi O. Milligan (PhD) is a reader in the Department of Education at the University of Bath. Her research focuses on issues of social and epistemic justice and educational quality in the Global South. Current projects explore these in relation to English Medium Instruction and girls' education in Rwanda and different forms of justice in secondary education in Uganda, Nepal and Peru.

Jesse Julius Ndabakurane is a linguist and currently works with the University of Dodoma, Tanzania in the Department of Foreign Languages and Literature. He has recently (2020) completed his PhD in linguistics at the University of Dodoma. His research interest lies in language and education as well as language and health. Currently, he works as a research assistant in Language Supportive Teaching and Textbooks (LSTT) project, a collaboration between the University of Dodoma, St. John's University of Tanzania and Bristol University that aims to facilitate content learning and learning through English in secondary schools.

Kepha Obiri is the translanguaging and Kiswahili support teacher at the Aga Khan Academy Mombasa. After joining the Academy in 2015, through its unique Teacher Preparation Programme, he has been at the centre of the implementation of the translanguaging model of bilingual education. In this role, he has supported the growth of the Bilingual programme in the IB primary years programme, working to develop bilingual teaching and learning in Grades 4 and 5. Prior to joining the Academy, Kepha worked in the Kenyan public education system as a teacher of English and Literature.

Colin Reilly (PhD) is a senior research officer in the Department of Language and Linguistics at the University of Essex and a Teaching Associate in the School of Education at the University of Glasgow. His research focuses on linguistic ethnography, multilingualism and language policy, particularly within Sub-Saharan Africa. Since 2017 he has been Secretary of the British Association for Applied Linguistics Language in Africa Special Interest Group.

Casmir M. Rubagumya (PhD) is Professor of Language Education at St John's University of Tanzania. He formerly taught at the University of Dar es Salaam and the University of Dodoma, both in Tanzania. His research interests are in teaching English as a second/foreign language, language policy in multilingual settings and language and power. He is editor of *Language in Education in*

Africa (1990) and *Teaching and Researching Language in African Classrooms* (1994). He has published chapters in edited books as well as articles in peer-reviewed journals such as *International Review of Education, International Journal of Educational Development, Language, Culture and Curriculum* and *Journal of Multilingual and Multicultural Development.* He has also done consultancy work on language in education for clients such as the Canadian International Development Research Centre (1996), Tanzania Ministry of Education (1997, 1998) and The World Bank Institute, Human Development Group (2000).

Kimberly Safford is a senior lecturer in Education at the Open University, UK, where she authors courses and contributes to teacher education programmes in Africa and India. She is co-editor of *Learning and Teaching Around the World: Comparative and International Studies in Primary Education* (Routledge).

Maite T. Sánchez is Assistant Professor of Bilingual Education at Hunter College of the City University of New York (CUNY). She was CUNY-NYSIEB's Project Director from 2012 to 2017 and currently serves as Advisor. Maite holds a PhD in education from Boston College, an MEd in education from Northeastern University and a BA in psychology from Pontificia Universidad Católica del Perú (Lima, Peru). Her research focuses on language education policy and practice, translanguaging pedagogy and the experiences of novice bilingual education teachers entering the profession. Further information can be found on her website: www.maitesanchez.org

Eliakimu Sane (PhD) is a linguist working in the Department of Foreign Languages and Literature at the University of Dodoma, Tanzania. He received his PhD in linguistics in 2016 from the University of Dodoma. His interest is in language and culture as well as language and education. He currently serves as the assistant coordinator of the Language Supportive Teaching and Textbooks Project, which is a collaboration amongst the University of Dodoma, St. John's University of Tanzania and Bristol University and financed through the Partnership to Strengthen Innovation and Practice in Secondary Education.

Leila Schroeder has been a senior consultant for SIL international since 2008. She lived and worked in Kenya from 1991 to 2016, writing literacy curricula, planning and promoting multilingual education programmes and training teachers. She has also done orthography consulting since 2004. She has advised literacy programmes in Liberia, Ethiopia, Mozambique, Ghana, Tanzania, Kenya, Mali, South Sudan and Nigeria. Her publications have focused primarily on writing systems and curricula, reflecting linguistic contexts and applying pedagogical principles to them.

Monica Shank Lauwo is a PhD candidate in Language and Literacy Education at the University of British Columbia. She is the founder and director of Cheche Community Library, a multilingual learning centre in Northern Tanzania embracing learners' linguistic and cultural resources as the foundations of learning and knowledge production. She has extensive experience as an educator in diverse contexts in Tanzania and Kenya. Her research interests include translanguaging, multiliteracies, critical literacy, identity and language ideologies, particularly in East Africa.

Barbara Trudell (PhD) is the Director of SIL Africa Learning & Development. She has lived and worked in Sub-Saharan Africa since 1993, carrying out literacy programme facilitation, research, consulting and alliance-building with concerned individuals and institutions around issues of language and education. Barbara's research experience includes work in Cameroon, Burkina Faso, Senegal, Kenya, Uganda, Nigeria and South Africa. She has carried out consultancies for agencies such as USAID, UNICEF, Save the Children, RTI, FHI360, GIZ and the British Council. Recent publications have focused on language policy formation and implementation, reading and culture, community processes of language development, and issues related to the use of African languages in formal and nonformal learning contexts.

Fritz Makafui Tugli is a graduate of the University of Cape Coast, Ghana, and a former teaching assistant at the Department of Mathematics and Statistics. He is keenly interested in issues affecting the teaching and learning of mathematics. He was a research assistant on the British Council-Education Development Trust-Open University project on *Multilingual Classrooms: Opportunities and Challenges*. He still works as a research assistant, copy-edits mathematics textbooks, and is making plans to pursue postgraduate studies in mathematics.

Francis William (PhD) is a senior lecturer in education at the University of Dodoma, where he is a Coordinator of Research Publications and Consultancy. He is an experienced science and teacher education. His main research interests lie within curriculum issues including material design and evaluation within all educational sectors. Since 2016, he has been a coordinator for language supportive teaching and textbooks (LSTT) project in Tanzania.

Justin Zelime (PhD) is currently senior lecturer of English at the University of Seychelles. He started his career as a secondary school teacher in the Seychelles and has also worked several years for the Ministry of Education. He holds a BA in Modern English Studies from the University of Wales, a Postgraduate Certificate in Education from the National Institute of Education, Seychelles, an MA in English Language Teaching from the University of Warwick, and is currently finalising his PhD at Umea University, Sweden. His main research interest is in language in multilingual contexts like the Seychelles and the impact of education policy on teaching and learning.

Preface

Ever since I started doing research on language in education in the African context way back in the 1980s, the question of the language of instruction in Sub-Saharan Africa has been generating a lot of heat but very little light. Trappes-Lomax (1990) asked an important rhetorical question 30 years ago: can a foreign language be a national medium? The answer is definitely NO! He gave three predictable consequences of the continued use of international languages for education in SSA: First, the objectives of education will not be achieved because you cannot learn in a language you do not understand. Second, those who may have privileged access to the language of instruction will have an unfair advantage over everybody else; i.e. the majority. In Sub-Saharan Africa there is already an emerging minority elite whose first language is English; the so-called Afro-Saxons (Rubagumya, 2004). This group can have access to well-resourced private schools both inside their countries in SSA as well as abroad. What happens to the majority is none of their business. A colleague at the University of Dar es Salaam, asked why his children do not speak Kiswahili, responded "*watoto wangu hawaongei lugha za kishenzi*" (my children do not speak barbaric languages). And he was saying this in a 'barbaric language'! Third, the cost of failure of the language of instruction to deliver quality education will be felt in every domain, economic, social and political.

These consequences have, by and large, been manifesting themselves in many Sub-Saharan African countries and there is enough research evidence to show this (e.g. Ndayipfukamiye, 2001; Batselelwang and Kamwendo, 2013; Brock-Utne et. al., 2010). There seems to be no end to the problem. What is clear is that the kind of policies being pursued in most SSA countries cannot achieve their intended objective, which is that the education system should support learners to become competent in the language of instruction. Worse still, learners face a double disadvantage because they cannot access content because they are constrained by the very language that is supposed to facilitate learning.

It is within this context that this book is written. It is sobering to see contributions in this volume that give hope to possibly see some light at the end of the tunnel. This is because these contributions are not only about theory, they are also about best practices in different SSA countries. These best practices suggest to us that all is not lost. Even within the constraints of current language policies in SSA countries, something can be done by different education stakeholders like teachers and researchers to ensure that meaningful learning takes place inside classrooms in SSA. There is substantial ground covered in the volume ranging from documenting what research tells us about multilingual learning in SSA, implementing the use of African languages in early literacy, ways to enhance content learning at primary and secondary school levels and resources development (see Introduction).

That said, I think the question of changing the language of instruction in SSA from English (or French, or Portuguese) to indigenous African languages cannot be swept under the carpet. It needs attention and we have to confront it sooner or later. The contributions in this volume are motivated by the desire to see learners in SSA engaged in meaningful education, official language policy constraints notwithstanding. They start from the assumption that the official language of instruction in many SSA countries under discussion will probably remain English, at least in the near future. I think the contributors are right to make this assumption, but this does not mean the fundamental question should not be asked: when are African countries going to change to indigenous African languages as their official languages of education? All the reasons given against using African languages in education have been refuted by research evidence and this is not the place to repeat them. Suffice it to say that those opposed the use of African languages in education often confuse two issues, learning a foreign language and using it as a language of instruction. The latter does not necessarily improve the former. There is also the fear that African languages are so many and therefore divisive, and so, the argument goes, we need a 'neutral' international language. This argument would only make sense if all African countries had 'so many languages'. Somalia, Rwanda and Burundi are virtually monolingual countries, so the question of 'so many languages' does not arise. In any case the histories of these countries do not suggest they have been the most politically stable, even with a single official language. Furthermore, English is not a neutral language in SSA. It creates another 'tribe'– a very powerful one – of an elite who control both material and symbolic resources.

To my mind, this volume has gone a long way in convincing the doubting Thomases that African languages are not a problem; they are useful resources needed for meaningful learning to take place and African children, like all other children in the world, have the right to use their languages in education. There is obviously a glaring need to trial multilingual approaches to learning; there is also a fairly open field for experimentation – the educational space is not filled with established practices; and there is also a market for published materials. If even a single country were to openly embrace and start using multilingual pedagogies experimentally in schools, new effective practices could easily be developed which could be seen not only to fulfil the needs of multilingual learners in SSA, but also to attract political and academic interest from all over the world. The objective of embracing African languages and multilingual learning approaches in SSA may not be achieved today, but I believe that, over time, the powers that be will see reason and allow the necessary changes to take place. As we say in Kiswahili, *TUTAFIKA* (WE WILL GET THERE)!

Casmir M. Rubagumya
Dodoma, Tanzania

References

Batselelwang, J. and Kamwendo, G. (2013) Language policy and practice at secondary school in Botswana: a multi-layered onion. In Shoba, J.A. and Chimbutane, F. (eds) *Bilingual Education and Language Policy in the Global South.* New York: Routledge.

Brock-Utne, B. Desai, Z. Qorro, M. and Pitman, A. (2010) *Language of Instruction in Tanzania and South Africa: Highlights from a Project.* Rotterdam: Sense.

Ndayipfukamiye, L. (2001) The contradictions of teaching bilingually in Burundi: from nyakatsi to maisons en etages. In Heller, M. and Martin-Jones, M. (eds) *Voices of Authority: Education and Linguistic Difference.* London: Ablex.

Rubagumya, C.M. (2004) English in Africa and the emergence of 'Afro-Saxons': globalization or marginalization? In Baynham, M., Deignan, A. and White, G. (eds) *Applied Linguistics at the Interface.* London: Equinox/BAAL.

Trappes-Lomax, H. (1990) Can a foreign language be a national medium? In Rubagumya C.M. (ed) *Language in Education in Africa: A Tanzanian Perspective.* Clevedon: Multilingual Matters.

Acknowledgements

We are grateful to Christiane Dalton-Puffer and Angel Lin for seeing the potential in this volume and considering it essential to a series on Language and Content Integrated Teaching & Plurilingual Education. We also thank our colleagues across the world who gave their time and expertise to provide critical feedback on various aspects of this volume, including: Liz Chamberlain, Tracey Costley, Gibson Ferguson, Sarah Jane Mukherjee, Goodith White, Eddie Williams and Elvis Yevudey. Special thanks must go to Melanie Wiener who provided invaluable support in editing and referencing for the volume.

As editors, we must also sincerely thank all the authors who have contributed their work to this volume, provided critical feedback on other contributions and have patiently worked with us through cycles of revisions. We all undertook this work alongside a range of personal and professional challenges, which then intensified during the COVID-19 pandemic. These challenges only made it feel more urgent to see this book in print. We are also grateful to each other, for the variety of experience and expertise each of us brought to the volume, and for generally being wonderful people to work with.

1 Introduction

Multilingual learning and language supportive pedagogies in Sub-Saharan Africa

Elizabeth J. Erling, John Clegg, Casmir M. Rubagumya and Colin Reilly

Introduction

The starting point of the volume is that multilingual learning offers a means of achieving both better learning outcomes in Sub-Saharan African schools and social justice in education (García & Wei, 2013; Heugh, 2015; Kerfoot & Simon-Vandenbergen, 2015; McKinney, 2017). We conceive of multilingual learning as the practice of welcoming and using students' entire language repertoire as a resource for learning, with this repertoire consisting of linguistic varieties, dialects, discursive genres, registers, styles or accents, gesture, multimodal language practices, at whatever level of proficiency (Blommaert, 2010). This position entails an understanding of multilingualism as a resource (Cenoz & Gorter, 2015; Chimbutane, 2018; Weber, 2014). We take the view that using multilingual approaches offers the potential to improve both content and language learning, especially for learners who may have low ability in the official language of instruction (LOI) and are consequently struggling to learn. Whether in a strictly balanced form of bilingual education in which two languages have official status, or in a context where only one language is prescribed as the official LOI, multilingual learning has the potential to facilitate the transition from learning in a familiar language to learning in one which is less familiar.

The volume focuses on contexts in Sub-Saharan Africa (SSA), following the United Nation's classification of referring to the 46 countries that are fully or partially located below the Sahara. This region is the one in which most of the global poor live and which hosts 27 of the world's 28 poorest countries, all with a poverty rate above 30% (Patel, 2018). Multilingualism has often been framed as a problem obstructing the provision of indigenous language education, national and regional cohesion and economic development (Arcand & Grin, 2013; Brock-Utne & Mercer, 2014). Although there are many commonalities between countries in the region, these national contexts are variable in many respects that have a bearing on education: with regard to sociolinguistic diversity, national wealth, presence of a private school sector, political stability, labour markets, analytical capabilities of Ministries of Education, degree of urbanisation and history of

DOI: 10.4324/9781003028383-1

ethnic tensions. Not able to deal with the diversity of situations between countries in SSA in their entirety, the volume covers many of these aspects in contributions from Cameroon, Ghana, Kenya, Rwanda, the Seychelles, South Africa, Tanzania and Uganda.

The volume focuses on formal education at the pre-primary, primary and secondary levels, in SSA. While many of the findings and implications have relevance in contexts where any international language serves as the language of education (whether English, French or Portuguese), this volume primarily deals with contexts in which English is the dominant official LOI in the state education system. Many of these countries are former British colonies, with English being a legacy of colonialist educational policies. However, the volume also includes examples from countries which have transferred from having other international post-colonial languages playing the dominant role in education to English. This includes Rwanda, which transferred from French medium to English medium after the 1994 genocide and the Seychelles (the African country with the smallest population), which was also previously French medium. While there cannot be a one-size-fits-all solution for all of these contexts, we point to similar educational challenges in the region that might be mediated by multilingual education.

The contexts in SSA described in this volume can be considered 'low resource', as capacity constraints around resources – for individuals, schools and communities – inhibit the quality and equity of learning and teaching. In these contexts, LOI, while central to academic success, is just one of a number of challenges facing education, with others being situations in which learners are unable to effectively engage with education due to malnutrition, school buildings lacking appropriate infrastructure, an absence of adequate textbooks and learning materials, and a substantial shortage of teachers (Moon, 2013). For the teachers in place, many also live and work with limited resources and are unable to access quality professional development. The implementational tasks of Ministries of Education are formidable and to a considerable extent a matter of allocating scarce resources between competing priorities. Not wishing to be naïve about the many obstacles for so many people 'to do and be what they have reason to value' (Sen, 1999), we attempt in this volume not to take a deficit approach to language and education in SSA by focusing only on the many obstacles, but to draw attention to the ways in which multilingual education is both possible and necessary to be implemented in such contexts. This volume provides examples of promising practices which are already taking place within SSA, highlighting what can be done to produce more positive and beneficial learning experiences within these contexts of limited resource. It provides inspiration for how these practices might spread, be scaled up and be further developed to improve learning in schools in SSA and beyond.

In the first part of this chapter, we provide a general overview of the challenges for learning in schools in SSA and how they are related to languages of instruction. Without pretending to provide a comprehensive overview, we explore some of the key issues influencing the formulation and delivery of language-in-education policies in SSA and point to some of the reasons for their failure. In the second part of this chapter, we explore the theoretical positionings of multilingual learning that underpin the chapters in the volume. We close this chapter by introducing the themes and chapters that follow, which offer explorations of multilingual classroom practices, resources and teacher education initiatives that have been found to enhance content and language learning.

Context and background

With most of the global poor living in SSA (Patel, 2018), every collection about education in the region starts by citing the high levels of poverty, the large number of people living on less than $2.00 a day (ca. 413 million people, or 41% of the population) and the low literacy rates (an average of one-third of the population cannot read or write) (World Bank, 2020). Despite considerable economic progress (IMF, 2018), poverty in SSA is multidimensional and widespread, and likely to have been made far worse by the economic crisis ensuing from COVID-19 (Gerszon et al., 2020).

Education is generally recognised as having the potential to contribute to the post-colonial development of countries across SSA, with indigenous languages playing an important role (Alexander, 2009; Djité, 2008; Erling & Seargeant, 2013). What has been called 'mother tongue education', which is education in the languages that children speak in their homes and local communities, has been promoted by organisations like UNESCO since the 1950s (1953, 2003, 2008) as a means to enhance the effect of early schooling and literacy development. This is in line with international research undertaken in other contexts which has repeatedly found that the prolonged use of children's home languages in early schooling is critical for cognitive development (e.g. Cummins, 2000; Kosonen, 2005) and can enhance a later switch to bilingual education and education in an additional language. There is widespread recognition of the centrality of the quality of classroom interaction in achieving educational quality, and the role of indigenous African languages in promoting this (Alexander, 2015; Tikly & Barrett, 2011). Scholars investigating various educational contexts in SSA have reinforced these calls for the use of indigenous African languages in education and a large number of studies evidenced that their use can enhance school achievement (Alidou & Brock-Utne, 2011; Rubagumya, 1986, 1994; Smith, 2011; Smits et al., 2008). Using children's home languages in education has also been found to decrease attrition and increase the likelihood of family and community engagement in the school – all factors that contribute to the effectiveness of students' learning at school (Trudell, 2016a). Moreover, it has been found to support community cohesion, participation in society, improved access to health, skills development and the growth of the economy (Coleman, 2010; Hanushek & Woessman, 2008). Studies also suggest that the use of international languages in education severely limits students' abilities to develop foundations for learning – with children from the least developed districts, poor and rural households and ethnic minorities being most likely to be affected (Babaci-Wilhite, 2015; Pflepsen, 2015; Pinnock & Vijayakumar, 2009; Trudell, 2016b). Williams (2014) has convincingly argued that such policies are not only responsible for depressing educational achievement but also contribute to reducing skills development and low economic performance in the region. The high costs of providing education in indigenous languages is regularly cited as a reason limiting implementation; however, studies have estimated that multilingual policies need not be prohibitively expensive, especially when one considers the long-term costs of educational failure due to the provision of education in an international language (Grin, 2003; Heugh et al., 2007).

While language-in-education polices as they exist in SSA are largely failing learners, there is increasing evidence globally of dual language and multilingual education initiatives that serve linguistically diverse learners well. Influential research by Thomas and Collier (2002) compares a range of ways of educating minority language users in the United States. 'Submersion' – the unsupported education of English learners – and early exit transition programmes were found to be the least effective. Dual language bilingual education (aiming often at a 50–50% split between the use of two languages in the curriculum) over a lengthy period of time, proved the most effective. Following from this work have been an increasing number of studies that demonstrate the value of dual language programmes in terms of higher cognitive development, assessment results and student engagement, as well as enhanced social relationships and valuing of students' diversity and multiple languages (Collier & Thomas, 2017; Thomas & Collier, 2012). Moreover, research suggests that an extended period of home language learning enhances additional language learning, including English (Cummins, 1991; Ginkel, 2014).

With the weight of this evidence in mind, it is difficult to understand why there has not been wider recognition of the importance of language and multilingual education approaches in achieving quality education in SSA, and why the struggle to implement indigenous language-in-education policies endures. In the following, we explore some of the key reasons for the dominance of international language policies, which include the failure of global education initiatives to put language at the centre of quality education; and the inadequacy of early exit language-in-education policies and their implementation. These aspects will be explored below before presenting the spaces of possibility in multilingual learning that have arisen despite these obstacles.

Education initiatives in SSA and their failure to put language at the centre of quality education

The importance of language in learning has often been overlooked in global education initiatives. Education for all, for example, a UNESCO-led global movement started in 2000 aimed to make quality basic education accessible to all children and significantly reduce illiteracy. This need was especially present in SSA, where at the beginning of the twenty-first century, literacy levels were relatively low (only 58% of adults) and barely one in two children completed primary school (UNESCO, 2014). Initiatives undertaken within this movement prioritised increasing access to education, but in doing so neglected to focus on teaching and learning quality, and the role of language therein (Alexander, 2015; Ferguson, 2013; Romaine, 2013; UNESCO, 2015). As a result, in the sustainable development goals (SDGs), a follow-on set of global targets to be achieved by 2030, the stand-alone education goal, SDG 4, states the intention to 'Ensure inclusive and *equitable quality education* and promote lifelong learning opportunities for all' (United Nations, 2015, our emphasis). Although there is now an increased focus on achieving equitable quality in education, there remains a lack of focused attention to the key role which language has in achieving this. This includes a lack of explicit mention of the role of language policies in supporting quality (Marinotti, 2017) as well as failure within the sustainable development community more broadly to recognise the importance of language within global development (Footitt et al., 2018; Taylor-Leech & Benson, 2017). Despite decades of research on 'Language and Development', the field still 'lacks status as an academic discipline' (Coleman, 2017, pp. 443–444) and there is little serious interdisciplinary engagement concerning language issues within development. The multilingual realities of societies in SSA are often ignored and development initiatives continue to be dominated by former colonial, European languages (Bamgbose, 2014).

While change has been slow to happen, education systems around the world are having to respond to multilingualism and diversity in twenty-first century classrooms (Taylor-Leech & Liddicoat, 2014). Also in SSA, there is growing recognition of the fact that so many children are required to learn through a language that they are still learning, and that there is an urgent need for further support for the use of students' home languages in education so that they are enabled to access learning more easily. Several studies have reported on the implementation of indigenous languages in education in SSA and noted, amongst difficulties, that strides have been made in terms of implementing and financing them (e.g. Alexander, 1995; Awopetu, 2016; Chimbutane & Benson, 2012; Diallo, 2011; Kioko et al., 2014; Mokibelo, 2014; Nikiema, 2011; Nyati-Saleshando, 2011; Okebukola et al., 2013; Orwenjo et al., 2014). Amongst this work is UNESCO's Policy Paper entitled 'If you don't understand, how can you learn?', clearly stating the organisation's position, underpinned by a wealth of international research, that quality education depends on the delivery of education in a language that students' speak at home and in their communities. The report also highlights that when home and school languages differ, there is an adverse impact on students' test scores. It provides examples of good practice, guidelines for education policies that recognise the importance of teaching children in their home language and recommendations for making teaching and assessment more inclusive of learners' languages (UNESCO, 2016b).

Such publications indicate that some challenges in implementing indigenous language policies are being met and spaces of possibility are emerging in SSA and globally. Increasingly embraced in international initiatives are models of mother tongue-based multilingual education (MTB-MLE) – an approach which begins education in the language with which learners are most familiar and speak most fluently. Additional languages, such as national lingua francas and international languages, are introduced and gradually take their place alongside the mother tongue (Mackenzie & Walker, 2012; UNESCO, 2018, Wisbey, 2016). Critics have argued that speakers of indigenous languages are not always better served in such initiatives (Cruz & Mahboob, 2012; Tupas, 2015; Weber, 2014), but if these initiatives truly draw on students' actual language resources for learning and implement measures to counter the inequities facing particular language speakers, they offer potential for transformation. This volume highlights some of the contexts in which good practice in MTB-MLE has developed.

The inadequacy of early exit indigenous African language policies and their implementation

As implied above, a further reason why multilingual education has been slow to take root in SSA relates to a widespread failure to recognise the inadequacy of existing 'early exit' indigenous African language policies. 'Early exit' is the term used to describe the school language policy widely used in SSA whereby learners start early primary school learning in an indigenous African language (preferably the children's home language) and transfer after a short period to learning in what we call here the second language (L2), which in most cases is a former colonial/international language, such as English, French or Portuguese. The period of indigenous language instruction in the majority of school contexts in SSA normally spans three years (from Primary Grades 1–3), during which time the international language is taught as a subject. Education through the international language beginning at the start of Primary Grade 4, at which point indigenous languages get reduced to a subject in the curriculum (Heugh, 2011; Trudell, 2016b).

A significant drawback of early exit policies is that they do not provide enough time to equip learners with the level of ability in the international language which they need in order to access the content of the curriculum (Dutcher, 2004; Heugh, 2009; Pflepsen, 2015). Three initial years of schooling at three or four lessons per week cannot prepare learners to learn complex curricular content through a new language in any language-learning programme, much less those that face the resource constraints as experienced in SSA. Merely teaching the grammar, vocabulary, communicative functions and elementary discourse structures of social language would take longer. To teach the beginnings of the academic variety of language which learners use when they learn content within this timeframe is simply not possible, nor necessarily desirable given the role of early primary education in easing the transition from home to school.

Objections to the existing early exit model rely on the work of Cummins (2000) and others who have shown that sufficient cognitive academic language proficiency (CALP)[1] needs to be developed in order to learn content through an additional language. This work finds that learners need between six and eight years to learn the language of education before they can learn at school through this language. It also reveals that it is best to make as much use as possible of learners' full language repertoires and their out-of-school knowledge and experience during these six to eight years. Early exit policies neither allow for enough time for sufficient learning of the international language nor do they allow for enough CALP skills to develop in the indigenous language which could then be transferred to the international language. Moreover, the use of international languages in education has been found to strongly discourage the use of local content in learning, which is essential for connecting with students' out-of-school experiences and learning (Kerfoot & Simon-Vandenbergen, 2015; Makalela, 2015b). Such policies clearly represent a severe barrier to content learning and carry much of the responsibility for the limited levels of school achievement which are evident in SSA, with Heugh (2009, p. 108) even persuasively arguing that their 'design guarantees educational failure' (cf. Ginkel, 2014 and Clegg, this volume). Despite this, a number of educational systems in SSA are stagnating in early exit policies, or even returning to providing education in the international language only.

Not even insufficient early exit indigenous language policies get implemented

Studies mentioned above have found that when indigenous language policies are implemented, benefits in learning can be detected (Heugh et al., 2007; Rosekrans et al., 2012; Trudell, 2016b). However, learners are unlikely to reach the desired grade-level competence in content and language through the implementation of early exit policies. Studies have also found that classroom practice often does not conform to three-year indigenous language policies (Nyaga & Anthonissen, 2012; Trudell, 2016b). This means that even the policies that are known to be insufficient to transform learning in schools in SSA are not given a chance to achieve some effect. The continued reliance on international languages in education substantially limits the potential of far from ideal indigenous language policies and contributes to perceptions that they are inadequate, which – in turn – results in some commentators promoting a return to international language-only policies.

No support for the transition to education through the international language

If early exit language policies were actually implemented in the initial levels of primary school, another factor which would increase their effect is if the transition from one language to another were supported. In SSA a range of options have been proposed to ease the shift, including a gradual transition or a staged introduction to the new language in certain subjects (Alexander, 1995; Luckett, 1995; Macdonald, 1991; Schmied, 1991). The international language could be proposed for use only in subjects that are considered to be less linguistically demanding and hence easier to understand (e.g. movement education), more readily supplied with visuals (e.g. geography), or closer to the learner's personal experience (e.g.

social studies). Proposals for these transitional patterns have, however, largely been theoretical with the 'sudden change' version of transition tending to persist. In order for any polices promoting the use of indigenous languages in education to take effect, transition to the use of international languages for learning must be managed and supported. Language teaching before, during and after the transition should focus on the language demands of the curriculum, both subject-specific and cross-curricular. The fact that this does not occur in most contexts ensures that these insufficient policies have limited effect.

Lack of resources in indigenous languages

Additional necessary requirements for the success of indigenous language policies are sufficient high-quality texts and instructional materials in the many indigenous African languages that learners use in their homes and communities. Such resources, however, are often sparsely available in early exit programs in SSA, and when they exist it is often in only a selection of languages (Clegg & Simpson, 2016; Erling et al., 2016; Opoku-Amankwa et al., 2011). Reasons provided for the lack of resources include too many indigenous languages to choose from, a shortage of writers and teachers proficient in the languages of the school, these languages not having sufficient written development, and limited interests from publishers to produce resources in these languages in view of the wide availability of textbooks in international languages (Opoku-Amankwa et al., 2015). As there is often too little funding allocated to textbooks in any language, many students across SSA at all levels either lack books altogether or are required to share them extensively with others (UNESCO 2016a). Thus there is a reliance on textbooks in international languages. Ministries do not normally assess materials for their readability or commission materials for learners who have not yet developed sufficient ability in the international language, which means that whatever materials exist are often far too difficult for learners in SSA to use (see Clegg, this volume; Clegg & Milligan, this volume). The resulting loss of access to the curriculum is considerable, as is the waste of money involved (Clegg, 2019).

Here too, the picture is not only bleak: some strides have been made in creating resources in indigenous languages that can be used in education (Chiatoh, 2011; Owen-Smith, 2010), including the development of The African Storybook Project (www.africanstorybook.org/) – a collection of digital, open access picture storybooks in African languages and Nal'ibali (www.nalibali.org/). These are high-quality, pedagogically well thought-through multilingual stories which can be used throughout the continent and further afield. The Molteno project has also made significant contributions both to the codifying of African languages and the publication of early years reading materials in them. Both the African Academy of Languages (ACALAN) and the Centre for Advanced Studies of African Society (CASAS) have been working towards unifying the orthographies and harmonising the written forms of indigenous African languages so that they can be better used as languages of education (Bamgbose, 2007; Brock-Utne & Mercer, 2014). In addition, solutions have been developed for using less developed languages as resources in education (Trudell & Young, 2016) and models are being explored for reducing the production costs of textbooks and making them more widely available (UNESCO, 2016a).

While increasingly more resources in indigenous African language are being produced, materials which embody multilingual learning are not common anywhere. The situation suggests an urgent need for more accurate and equitable teaching resources that allow for students' multilingual language practices. This volume provides examples of how such further developments can be resourced and sustained.

Need for a longer period of indigenous language education

An extended period of schooling in the language most widely used in the community – the norm in many parts of the world – is no doubt what is required in SSA, and six to eight years of indigenous language instruction has been recommended (Alidou & Brock-Utne, 2011; Erling et al., 2017). In some countries in SSA, indigenous language schooling lasts for longer than three years, for example, in Ethiopia and Tanzania. It has been shown that eight years of indigenous language schooling has positive effects in Ethiopia, such as improved access to, and quality of, primary education, including high teacher and student language proficiency, improved classroom interaction and better student performance in all subjects (cf. Heugh et al., 2007).

In Tanzania, Kiswahili is the LOI for seven years and English-medium education begins in Grade 8 at the beginning of secondary school. However, after a seven-year period of schooling in Kiswahili, learners are not obviously either better educated in content nor more able to use English for learning in secondary school (Brock-Utne et al., 2004). This implies that, on its own, extended indigenous language schooling is unlikely to add the educational value which it sometimes promises. One factor that may play a part in the relative lack of success of longer use of Kiswahili relates to what Rubagumya (2003) has pointed out – that Kiswahili is not the home language for many learners in schools, and so does not support their learning but presents further obstacles. Increasing attention is being paid to quality conditions which extended indigenous language education must fulfil in order to enable learners to achieve in languages and subjects with evidence-based investigations of what these conditions might be and how they are effectively applied in certain contexts increasingly necessary (see Piper et al., 2018; Schroeder et al., this volume).

Lack of teachers and teacher education that prepares teachers for teaching in indigenous languages

Even when resources in indigenous languages exist, schools need teachers who share their students' language repertoires. Teacher deployment policies often do not take into consideration whether a teacher can speak the language of the area, resulting in teachers and students not always speaking the same languages (Benson

& Plüddemann, 2010; Kamwendo, 2015; Yevudey & Agbozo, 2019). There is thus a need for both further learning of African languages and teacher education on how to teach through these languages, and also how best to develop students' abilities in the relevant international language. Teachers need to know that it is not only legitimate but also beneficial to teach their students in the language(s) that they understand. They require full awareness of the successes of using African languages in education and the evidence undergirding the intentions of policies (Kioko et al., 2014).

As is the case in publishing, teacher education in SSA has a tendency to treat the training of teachers as if learners were fluent in the international LOI. Approaches to teaching subjects using multilingual education strategies are not common topics. Teacher education institutions are not pushed to develop appropriate practices and training does not, by and large, focus on either the teaching of subjects to learners with limited L2 abilities or on multilingual education (Heugh et al., 2007). This book, however, describes the work of a group of initial training institutions in Tanzania to spread good practice in the language supportive teaching of subjects (Barrett et al., this volume; Rubagumya et al., this volume). In-service teacher education, on the other hand, has a fairly good record of offering training which is appropriate in SSA. Language supportive pedagogies (LSPs) have been promoted widely both by local providers and international agencies, for example the Molteno project. Trudell (2018) gives an overview of language-related projects involving in-service teacher education in Nigeria alone. Centres of international quality exist, such as the Project for the Study of Alternative Education in South Africa (PRAESA) at the University of Cape Town, which have successfully promoted multilingual learning especially in the early years (Bloch & Mbolekwa, this volume). Individual multilingual projects have provided professional development to in-service teachers and trainers as well as to projects which use the indigenous African languages as the language of schooling, such as the successful Ife Six-Year Primary Project in Nigeria. Chapters in this book describe a variety of such initiatives which indicate that SSA has the capacity to be a locus of developing practices in multilingual education.

Theoretical positionings of multilingual learning

Without pretending to undertake a thorough overview of this work, in this section we provide an introduction to the theoretical positionings underlying the approaches to multilingual learning put forward in this volume. These rely most strongly on content and language integrated learning (CLIL), LSP and translanguaging pedagogies.

Before going into the detail of these concepts, some initial terminology needs to be defined. As has been noted elsewhere, notions such as first language, mother tongue and second language do not account for the complex translingual discourse practices in many African contexts (Makalela, 2016). In this volume, we attempt to avoid the terms 'mother tongue' and 'L1', preferring instead the term indigenous African language or local language to refer to the languages that are spoken in homes and communities in SSA. We use the term international language to refer to the post-colonial languages that dominate the official language policies of most schools in SSA: English, French and Portuguese. We recognise that it is not appropriate to suggest a sequential view of language learning in SSA by using the terms L1 and L2. Despite this, some contributions use the term L2 as a shorthand to refer to the additional languages that serve as the languages of school, and which many learners first learn when entering school or start to learn after they have developed competence in their home and community languages. In such cases, the LOI might be the second, third, fourth or more language that these children are learning. Finally, many contributions employ the term LOI to describe the medium prescribed in policy to teach the content of the curriculum. Many of the chapters in the volume address the issue of implementing multilingual learning strategies in school contexts whose polices are overwhelmingly monolingual, promoting the sole use of English as the only LOI. Others, however, address issues in bilingual education programmes – for example in Kiswahili and English in Kenya or Spanish and English in the United States. In these contexts, however, other languages are part of students' repertoires and must also be considered in teaching and learning.

CLIL and LSP

The chapters in the volume provide insight into multilingual education strategies that have been developed and implemented to support the learning of content and languages. These strategies include both those which have arisen in the context of SSA, those that draw on concepts from CLIL as developed primarily in Europe and those which have their roots in other contexts such as minority education in, for example, North America, the UK or Australia.

CLIL is a way of teaching and learning subjects in a second or foreign language that was developed in Europe in the 1990s to help fulfil the European Union's need of creating multilingual citizens and is now widely used across the continent and beyond (Ball et al., 2015; Coyle et al., 2010; Dalton-Puffer, 2011; Lin, 2016). In CLIL, there is a dual focus on content and on language, each ideally being interwoven, even if the emphasis is greater on one or the other at a particular time. CLIL is closely related to and shares some elements and a range of educational practices with bilingual education and immersion (Lyster, 2018). It also shares some basic theories and practice with English as an additional language practices developed for language minorities in English-dominant contexts in North America (e.g. Echevarria et al., 2013; Gibbons, 2009) or language-sensitive educational approaches in contexts where other languages serve as the LOI (e.g. German as an additional language, cf. Budde, 2012). CLIL pedagogies are grounded in constructivist and cognitive theory, and so should be inherently student-centred and active. In CLIL, a key aspect of pedagogy is supporting the learning of academic content by becoming a user of appropriate context-specific text types. Students are scaffolded through tasks in which they need to make sense of and form their own ideas about subject content, while also being introduced to (language) learning strategies, so that they gradually become more independent learners who rely increasingly less on the teacher as the main holder of content knowledge (van Kampen et al., 2017).

Because CLIL is often associated with contexts of elite bilingual education in Europe (Cenoz et al., 2014), and because it has not often been recognised that the majority of learners in SSA learn through a second or foreign language, the term has not often been used in relation to teaching and learning in SSA. More common is the term LSP, which is increasingly used in relation to educational practice in SSA which takes into account that learners need additional linguistic and cognitive support when working through a second language (Clegg & Simpson, 2016; Milligan et al., 2016). Use of this term indicates a recognition that learning in a second language can make reading, writing and talking about content – as well as listening to the teacher – difficult because learners may not have the vocabulary to understand and express concepts, the grammar to generate sentences and the discourse ability to follow and construct texts. LSP (explained in detail in Chapters 7 and 11) was developed to account for the fact that students expend cognitive capacity in focusing attention on matters of form and deplete the cognitive assets which they need in order to acquire new curricular content. The principal aim is to reduce the demands of an unfamiliar L2 on learners and thus allow and encourage them to deploy as many of their cognitive resources as possible towards learning new concepts.

Published mainstream language supportive subject materials are uncommon in any context, and, as argued above, there are hardly any mainstream subject L2-medium materials designed for African learners with their specific early L2-medium abilities. Thus included in this volume is a focus on the development of language supportive textbooks and resources that enable multilingual students to make deeper meaning while also legitimising their language practices, as well as teacher education initiatives which support these practices (Clegg & Milligan, this volume; Rubagumya et al., this volume).

The theory of translanguaging and translanguaging pedagogies

Central to the language supportive practices of promise explored in chapters are translanguaging pedagogies, in which learners' full multilingual repertoires can be legitimately used as resources for learning (García & Wei, 2013). The theory of translanguaging views speakers' languages as part of a single unitary system on which they draw selectively and strategically to navigate communicative contexts (Wei, 2018). In this view, the idea that a language has a separate code that distinguishes it from other languages is less important than an overarching concept of 'languaging' in which identity, culture, community as well as social, emotional and cognitive development can be expressed in multiple languages, varieties, genres and different levels of fluency. This theory resonates particularly well in SSA, where recent research suggests that multilingualism has always been the norm: in peri-urban and urban areas, multilingualism is pronounced due to widespread migration to these centres of local and national commerce

(Wolff, 2000). Projects like Crossroads (https://soascrossroads.org/research/the-project/) provide nuanced understandings of multilingualism in rural areas (Lüpke, 2016). Such work suggests a need to recognise that speakers 'employ meta-discursive regimes that are versatile, mobile and fluid in response to transnational mobility and blurring of boundaries between nation states in the 21st century' (Makalela, 2016, p. 187). Speakers' repertoires consist of some – if not all – of the following named languages: international/post-colonial languages; national languages which serve as lingua franca; local, indigenous African languages of homes and communities; and African Urban Youth Languages (e.g. Chibrazi, Sheng, Totistaal), which are increasingly coming under the spotlight of linguists and sociolinguists across SSA, who are investigating their relationship to standard and/or vernacular varieties and considering their use in education (see Hurst-Harosh, 2018). A restricted understanding of African multilingualism has prevented stakeholders in education from recognising the range of learners' language resources and ultimately from using multilingualism as a productive resource for learning (Lüpke et al., forthcoming; Makoe & McKinney, 2014).

While there are certainly contexts in SSA – particularly in rural areas – where the majority of students share the same home language (Trudell, 2016b; Yevudey & Agbozo, 2019), in others, a limited understanding of the linguistic situation has meant that the languages promoted in policy do not match the actual languages of learners and may actually be another language in which they have little or developing proficiency. The promotion of indigenous African languages in education often fails to recognise the rich multilingual repertoires of learners, simplistically putting forward one language for schooling where community members are more linguistically diverse. In Zambia, for example, depending on the region, one of seven officially designated regional languages, out of a possible 72, will be prescribed for use in early primary education regardless of the repertoires of children and communities (Banda & Mwanza, 2017). A further example comes from Tanzania, often hailed as one of the best language-in-education policy examples in SSA, as Kiswahili is the medium of instruction for the first seven years of school. However, this policy ignores that, given more than 120 ethnic community languages in the country, most children entering primary school, especially those in rural areas, have little or no proficiency in Kiswahili and are generally not enabled to use their home languages for developing competence in Kiswahili. For many children across SSA, particularly those in migrant families, it can be difficult to identify a single 'mother tongue'. The following example, taken from Erling et al.'s fieldwork in Ghana (reported on in their chapter in this volume) well illustrates this point: in one of the schools in which data was collected the official language of the school was Ga, which was the language spoken by people indigenous to the area and is still the language used by community leaders. Because the school is in a market area, to which people from all over the country migrate, Twi functions as the lingua franca of the community. While Twi is one of the 11 languages that can be used in education, it was not the official language of the school in this case – despite there being very few proficient Ga-speakers at the school – because of the political pressure to maintain the historical dominance of

Ga. There were also a number of other languages used in the area, as many children from migrant families who speak the languages of the rural areas where they originate from and return to on occasion. Many children have some proficiency in all of these languages (the language of the mother, the father, the community and the clan), as well as English, and it is difficult to determine what are these children's 'mother tongues' and which language they are going to be most comfortable with for acquiring literacy and learning the content of the national curriculum (Erling et al., 2017; Makalela, 2016). In such cases, policies promoting the use of a single 'mother tongue' in education might have limited effect (cf. Piper et al., 2018). Conclusions are then sometimes drawn that such indigenous language policies are ineffective, which lead to their abandonment, when in fact, the use of learners' actual language resources in education has never taken place. Contributors to this volume illustrate how translanguaging pedagogies can allow students to draw on their entire language repertoires for learning, even when the teacher does not have competence in all of these languages and resources do not exist in them.

Promoting translanguaging pedagogies in education

A growing number of scholars and practitioners suggest that a way to raise outcomes of students who may not have full access to the LOI is through mobilising their full language repertoire as a resource for learning through translanguaging (Cummins, 2010; Duarte, 2019; García & Kleyn, 2016; García & Sylvan, 2011). Translanguaging pedagogies entail languages being used flexibly in education, so that students can improve their competence in all of their languages. The idea is to maximise learners' abilities to draw on the wide range of linguistic resources that they have developed both in- and outside of school to benefit content and language learning, rather than limiting the students by requiring them to rely only on their emergent competence in the LOI. Inviting students' full language repertoires into the classroom not only has the potential of amplifying learning of content and language without necessarily disrupting students' abilities in other languages, but also of legitimising students' identities (García-Mateus & Palmer, 2017; García & Wei, 2013). If students are able to engage in translanguaging talk about a reading passage or while composing a written text in the LOI, the resulting level of language use is often higher. Learners who translanguage to learn also often have higher learning motivation, are more psychologically centred and are more embedded in their culture and their community (García et al., 2017). This is because the approach entails teachers regarding students' multilingualism as a benefit rather than a disadvantage, which is more likely to allow the learner and the school as a whole to connect with the community.

While practical strategies for translanguaging in classrooms are still being developed, they are on the increase (Celic & Seltzer, 2011; Conteh, 2018; García et al., 2017; Hamman et al., 2018). Ofelia García and team at the City University of New York-New York State Initiative on Emergent Bilinguals (CUNY-NYSIEB) have actively pursued a set of definable, trainable strategies. In some contexts, equal roles can be given to two or more languages in teacher talk, learner talk, learner writing, reading passages and assessment (García et al., 2017). In others, preference may be given to one language – perhaps the official LOI, while allocating supportive roles to others. Recent research has also recognised the particular value of translanguaging in CLIL contexts, both in terms of its affective and cognitive value, and therefore should be further promoted in bilingual learning situations (Nikula & Moore, 2019).

Translanguaging research and practice in SSA

In SSA, there is a significant literature that has explored the grassroots common-practice of code-switching in classrooms that many teachers use to support the learning of content (e.g. Arthur, 1996; Chimbutane, 2013; Clegg & Afitska, 2011; Mafela, 2009; Makgato, 2014; Mokgwathi & Webb, 2013; Ncoko, Osman, & Cockcroft, 2000; Ndlangamandla, 2010; Setati & Adler, 2000). In such work, the use of indigenous languages is observed to happen in differing forms, primarily unofficially. Many teachers express negative attitudes towards code-switching and tend to avoid it if possible, especially when pressured by official policy. Others 'smuggle' it into the classroom when learning through the official language fails (Probyn, 2009). Such studies have uncovered that code-switching is often conceived of as a pedagogically unplanned and spontaneous strategy which teachers use to ensure a minimum degree of understanding in the classroom.

In contrast to this, the translanguaging literature puts forward the idea that the use of students' full language repertoire for learning does not represent a deficit, only to be used when learning through the L2 fails, but should be something that teachers explicitly plan for, welcome and facilitate. Calls for the use of translanguaging and other LSPs to enhance content learning are increasingly heard across SSA. The majority of research within this area has emerged from, and focuses on, South Africa (Guzula et al., 2016; Kerfoot & Simon-Vandenbergen, 2015; Makalela, 2015a; McKinney, 2020; Probyn, 2015). Translanguaging and education are increasingly discussed across numerous countries in SSA, including Botswana (Bagwasi, 2017), the Democratic Republic of Congo (Gandara & Randall, 2019), Ghana (Sherris et al., 2018; Yeveudey, 2015); Kenya (Crisfield et al., 2021; Kiramba, 2016; Mwaniki, 2016), Malawi (Reilly, 2021), Mali (Lüpke, 2020), Namibia (Mwinda & Van der Walt, 2015), Rwanda (Andersson et al., 2012), Senegal (Goodchild & Weidl, 2018), Tanzania (Shank Lauwo, 2018), Zambia (Banda & Mwanza, 2017) and Zimbabwe (Charamba, 2019). While learning in multiple languages is still often regarded with suspicion, some studies suggest that translanguaging is being increasingly used in classrooms (Yevudey& Agbozo, 2019). Translanguaging has been found to be offering new opportunities to bridge the gap and achieve more effective learning and therewith disrupting existing power and status gaps between languages. When outcomes of multilingual education improve, more positive attitudes towards the use of indigenous languages education can be noted. Makalela (2016) suggests that conceptualising language use through a translanguaging perspective is particularly apt for the African context and has introduced the concept of Ubuntu Translanguaging as a framework for understanding the complexity of multilingual communication while valorising a continuum as well as an interdependence of human cultures and communication systems. He also outlines some of the ways in which translanguaging pedagogies can be integrated into teacher education programmes in SSA while also extending student teachers access to and abilities in indigenous African languages (Makalela, 2015a).

The language supportive and translanguaging pedagogies described in this volume are appropriate for their contexts and necessary for their learners. They are full of promise and potential for education in diverse societies and the debate which surrounds them can be animated and vigorous. However, they are not well codified or widespread in their application. Actual examples of pedagogy, materials and teacher education are in short supply all over the world. It is hardly surprising that SSA has been slow in developing these practices; it has not been easy to see them working elsewhere. For this very reason, however, SSA could take the lead in developing versions of multilingual and language supportive learning which are adapted to its own specific requirements. This volume represents a step in this direction.

Themes and contributions to the volume

This volume gives additional weight to already existing evidence that using indigenous languages in education is beneficial to learners and provides teachers and other education stakeholders in SSA insights into what works and what they can do to help their learners. It describes existing research and promising practices which are already taking place within SSA, highlighting what can be done to produce a more positive and beneficial learning experience within these contexts. It provides inspiration for how multilingual learning might be scaled up and further developed to improve education in SSA and beyond. In order to develop appropriate policy for low-resource contexts, the volume includes some insights from how multilingual education has been successfully carried out in the higher resource multilingual context of the United States (e.g. Espinet, Sanchez and Aponte, this volume). The contributions make clear what can be achieved using the resources which are available to educators, including the multilingual linguistic resources of students. While there is great traction in the pedagogical strategies proposed in this volume, they are put forward with full recognition of the challenges of implementing them. Alongside the successes and positive outcomes, contributors discuss challenges to multilingual learning. They discuss how they have been addressed within individual projects and highlight continuing structural challenges within this work. Authors are aware that limited progress has been made.

Types of contribution

The volume includes a wide range of contributors – from scholars who have spent their careers promoting the use of indigenous African languages in education to those newer to this field who have benefited from their work. Authors range from those based in universities and educational organisations in SSA to those working in partnerships with them in the Global North. Some of the chapters address specific contexts; others present an overview. The volume features traditional academic contributions drawing on established literature grounded in theory and empirical research, arising both in SSA and in contexts elsewhere in the world as well as vignettes, which are shorter, more discursive and reflective pieces describing lessons learned and tips for successful implementation from experienced practitioners, or insights from early phases of research.

Chapter summaries

The volume is presented in three sections, which explore: (1) What research tells us about the status of multilingual learning in SSA; (2) Lessons learned for implementing multilingual learning in pre-primary, primary and secondary schools in SSA; and (3) How multilingual resources and changes in teacher education can be developed.

Part 1: What does research tell us about the status of multilingual learning in SSA?

The volume begins with Schroeder, Mercado and Trudell providing an overview of research into multilingual learning in SSA. Their wide-ranging research synthesis includes discussion of programmes using indigenous African languages in Ethiopia, Mali, Nigeria, Burkina Faso, Cameroon, Malawi and Kenya. They highlight that, while evidence clearly indicates that use of international languages in education leads to poor learning outcomes, there must be more in-depth assessment of learning outcomes within African language initiatives to enable practitioners to sufficiently understand what types of programme are most effective. This section continues with Deutschmann and Zelime's discussion of language-in-education policy in the Seychelles. Their research studies that have examined a wide range of aspects of indigenous language policy implementation highlight the inequity which arises from a policy situation in which, despite the majority of the population sharing a language – Kreol Seselwa – a monolingual English-only language-in-education policy is adopted from Grade 3. They find that negative language ideologies towards Kreol Seselwa are a major factor in the marginalisation of the language within classroom language practices, which in turn disproportionately advantages students with English language proficiency. They close with recommendations for further research and practice, suggesting, for example, that the focus should shift away from LOI and towards pedagogical practices and knowledge attainment. This section closes with a chapter by Erling,

Stafford and Tugli, which illustrates what might be described as a 'typical' classroom context in Ghana. Here we find amongst teachers a limited awareness of multilingual pedagogies coupled with beliefs that use of English in the classroom is best for students (cf. Erling & Seargeant, 2013). This results in a situation in which English is the dominant language of the classroom and students are afforded few opportunities to contribute, in any language, to classroom talk. This chapter demonstrates the need for the multilingual and LSPs that are described in the section that follows.

Part 2: Multilingual learning in pre-primary, primary and secondary schools: lessons learned

This section explores key issues in using multilingual pedagogies in pre-primary, primary and secondary schools. Bloch and Mbolekwa focus on the development of literacy at the pre-primary level in South Africa, arguing that children must be given strong literacy foundations and a joy in reading in learning, in order that they can be successful at school. They argue that the current framing of literacy issues in multilingual South Africa must be problematised and transformed to offer new, contextually relevant opportunities for children to develop oral and written literacy, emphasising a holistic, meaning-focused, participatory pedagogy. Kinnaird and Becker provide insight into the preschool and primary education levels in Cameroon and Kenya, reporting on approaches used within SIL partnerships which aimed to mobilise indigenous languages as part of education projects. They note that the inclusion of indigenous languages was a central factor in the acceptance of education initiatives in communities. These contributions suggest that early literacy is essential to get right in terms of transforming education in SSA. However, the approaches described therein that promote joy in reading and embrace indigenous African languages as valuable literacy resources should extend far beyond early stages of education.

Clegg's contribution highlights issues which stem from the large gap between the language demands of the primary school curriculum and the language repertoires of learners, proposing extending indigenous African language-medium and multilingual learning for up to eight years as a solution. This, along with the explicit introduction of language supportive pedagogies (LSPs), he argues, would enable more effective learning and teaching. Rubagumya, Sane and Ndabakurane discuss the introduction of LSPs within selected teacher training courses and provide an overview of the principles underlying the approach as well as a selection of the activities currently being adopted in Tanzania. They highlight that, despite positive outcomes and support from teachers and students, LSP has not yet been approved by the Ministry of Education. Thus, further work needs to be done to ensure the sustainability of such initiatives.

Espinet, Sánchez and Aponte report on work being undertaken by educators in New York City to promote translanguaging spaces for their diverse, multilingual students. They provide a blueprint for activities which can be used to promote critical inquiry amongst multilingual students using minimal resources: a community walk with students adopting the role of 'bilingual ethnographers', the construction of linguistic family maps, and multimodal analysis and sharing, all of which would work well in other contexts, including SSA. Drawing on approaches that were developed in New York City, Obiri and Holland provide an example of a translanguaging space that is being carved out in primary school in Kenya. They describe the development of a bilingual unit of work in Kiswahili and English and illuminate the important role that local communities can play in influencing student attitudes towards the value of their languages.

Part 3: Multilingual resource development and teacher education

This section provides examples of how multilingual resources and teacher education initiatives supporting them can be and have been developed, both in SSA and in other international contexts. Clegg and Milligan describe how English-medium subject textbooks are designed with the assumption that students possess a high degree of reading fluency and, when students are unable to effectively read their textbooks, this acts as a major impediment to learning. They then present resources created for Primary Grade 4 science subjects in Rwanda, illustrating that resources can be created which, adopting multilingual LSP, can be more appropriate and accessible for learners in SSA.

Shank Lauwo presents findings from an action research project which centred on the development of a community library in Tanzania. She discusses how specific processes such as reading and writing multilingual books and traditional storytelling can be utilised within pedagogies of translanguaging and multimodality to enable transformative approaches to multilingual education. Gulere and Lubuulwa focus on the creation of multilingual resources as part of teacher education in Uganda. They report on the successes and challenges of a collaborative project in which student teachers have created 2,000 storybooks in Ugandan languages using the Storyweaver and African Storybook platforms.

This section closes with a contribution from Barrett, Juma and William, who report on the Language Supportive Teaching and Textbooks project described by Rubagumya et al., focusing on the steps and challenges in implementing LSP at scale and within teacher training programmes. All of the contributions in this section highlight how sharing learning globally with regard to the development of multilingual resources and teacher education can foster educational transformation.

Conclusion

Much work is still to be done in terms of transforming language-in-education policies in SSA, through promoting multilingual and LSPs, supporting professional learning in teacher education practices and facilitating the production of multilingual and language supportive resources. Changes in language education practices, while greatly desirable, are no panacea for other challenges in providing quality education for all. However, this volume provides unprecedented insight into how some of these transformations are coming about and provides inspiration for how they might be further developed and sustained to improve learning in SSA and beyond.

Note

1 While the notion of CALP has been criticised by some for positioning academic language as a set of objective linguistic features that can and must be mastered and for marginalising and stigmatising the fluid linguistic practices of multilingual racialised communities (Flores & García, 2020; Flores & Rosa, 2015), the need to develop academic language skills for accessing new concepts and content in the official languages of SSA schools is acute. That the standards of academic language – particularly in an international language that a large number of learners have limited access to – perpetuate inequalities cannot be denied (cf. Lippi-Green, 2012). However, as Cummins (2017, p. 405) suggests, additive, multilingual approaches to education have the potential to challenge historical and societal power relations that devalue and exclude the language and cultural practices of learners who are disadvantaged by official language policies.

References

Alexander, N 1995, 'Models of multilingual schooling for a democratic South Africa', in K Heugh, A Siegrühn & P Plüddemann (eds), *Multilingual Education for South Africa*, Heinemann, Johannesburg, pp. 79–82.

Alexander, N 2009, 'The impact of the hegemony of English on access to and quality of education with special reference to South Africa', in W Harbert & S McConnell-Ginet (eds), *Language and Poverty*, Multilingual Matters, Bristol, pp. 53–66.

Alexander, R 2015, 'Teaching and learning for all? The quality imperative revisited', *International Journal of Educational Development, 40*, pp. 250–258.

Alidou, H & Brock-Utne, B 2011, 'Teaching practices – teaching in a familiar language', in A Ouane & C Glanz (eds), *Optimising Learning, Education and Publishing in Africa: The Language Factor – A Review and Analysis of Theory and Practice in Mother-Tongue and Bilingual Education in Sub-Saharan Africa*, UNESCO, Hamburg, pp. 159–163 https://uil.unesco.org/literacy/multilingual-research/optimising-learning-education-and-publishing-africa-language-factor.

Andersson, I, Kagwesage, A & Rusanganwa, J 2012, 'Negotiating meaning in multilingual group work: A case study of higher education in Rwanda', *International Journal of Bilingual Education and Bilingualism, 16*, pp. 1–15, DOI: 10.1080/13670050.2012.695771.

Arcand, JL & Grin, F 2013, 'Language in economic development: Is English special and is linguistic fragmentation bad?', in E Erling & P Sergeant (eds), *English and Development: Policy, Pedagogy and Globalization*, Multilingual Matters, Bristol, pp. 243–267.

Arthur, J 1996, 'Code switching and collusion: Classroom interaction in Botswana primary schools', *Linguistics and Education, 8*(1), pp. 17–33. https://doi.org/10.1016/S0898-5898(96)90004-2

Awopetu, AV 2016, 'Impact of mother tongue on children's learning abilities in early childhood classroom, *Procedia - Social and Behavioral Sciences, 233*, pp. 58–63.

Babaci-Wilhite, Z 2015, 'Zanzibar's curriculum reform: Implications for children's educational rights', *Prospects*, *45*(2), pp. 181–195. https://doi.org/10.1007/s11125-015-9341-6

Bagwasi, MM 2017, 'A critique of Botswana's language policy from a translanguaging perspective', *Current Issues in Language Planning*, *18*(2), pp. 199–214.

Ball, SJ, Kelly, K & Clegg, J 2015, *Putting CLIL into Practice*, Oxford University Press, Oxford.

Bamgbose, A 2007, 'Multilingualism and exclusion: Policy, practice and prospects', in P Cuvalier, T Du Plessis, M Meeus & L Tech (eds), *Multilingualism and Exclusion*, Van Shaik, Pretoria, pp. 1–21.

Bamgbose, A 2014, 'The language factor in development goals', *Journal of Multilingual and Multicultural Development*, *35*(7), pp. 646–657. https://doi.org/10.1080/01434632.2014.908888

Banda, F & Mwanza, D 2017, 'Language-in-education policy and linguistic diversity in Zambia: An alternative explanation to low reading levels among primary school pupils', in M Khulupirika & M Banja (eds), *Selected Readings in Education*, University of Zambia Press, Lusaka, pp. 109–132.

Benson, C & Plüddemann, P 2010, 'Empowerment of bilingual education professionals: The training of trainers programme for educators in multilingual settings in southern Africa (ToTSA) 2002-2005', *International Journal of Bilingual Education and Bilingualism*, *13*(3), pp. 371–394. https://doi.org/10.1080/13670050903373899

Blommaert, J 2010, *The Sociolinguistics of Globalization*, Cambridge University Press, Cambridge.

Brock-Utne, B & Mercer, M 2014, 'Using African languages for democracy and lifelong learning in Africa: A post-2015 challenge and the work of CASAS', *International Review of Education*, *60*(6), pp. 777–792. https://doi.org/10.1007/s11159-014-9448-7

Brock-Utne, B, Desai, Z & Qorro, M 2004, *Researching the Language of Instruction in Tanzania and South Africa*, African Minds, Cape Town.

Budde, M 2012, *Über Sprache reflektieren: Unterricht in sprachheterogenen Lerngruppen*, Kassel University Press, Kassel, viewed 20 March 2020, www.uni-kassel.de/upress/online/frei/978-3-86219-260-1.volltext.frei.pdf.

Celic, C & Seltzer, K 2011, 'Translanguaging: A CUNY-NYSIEB guide for educators', *CUNY-NYS Initiative on Emergent Bilinguals*, www.cuny-nysieb.org/wp-content/uploads/2016/04/Translanguaging-Guide-March-2013.pdf.

Cenoz, J & Gorter, D 2015, 'Towards a holistic approach in the study of multilingual education', in J Cenoz & D Gorter (eds), *Multilingual Education: Between Language Learning and Translanguaging*, Cambridge University Press, Cambridge, pp. 1–15.

Cenoz, J, Genesee, F & Gorter, D 2014, 'Critical analysis of CLIL: Taking stock and looking forward', *Applied Linguistics*, *35*, pp. 243–262. https://doi.org/10.1093/applin/amt011

Charamba, E 2019, 'Translanguaging: Developing scientific scholarship in a multilingual classroom', *Journal of Multilingual and Multicultural Development*, *41*, pp. 1–18, DOI: 10.1080/01434632.2019.1625907.

Chiatoh, BA 2011, 'Sustaining mother tongue medium education: An inter-community self-help framework in Cameroon', *International Review of Education*, *57*, pp. 583–597.

Chimbutane, F 2013, 'Codeswitching in L1 and L2 learning contexts: Insights from a study of teacher beliefs and practices in Mozambican bilingual education programmes', *Language and Education*, *27*(4), pp. 314–328. https://doi.org/10.1080/09500782.2013.788022

Chimbutane, F 2018, 'Multilingualism and education in Sub-Saharan Africa: Policies, practices and implications', in A Bonnet & P Siemund (eds), *Foreign Language Education in Multilingual Classrooms*, John Benjamins, Amsterdam, pp. 57–75.

Chimbutane, F & Benson, C 2012, 'Expanded spaces for Mozambican languages in primary education: Where bottom-up meets top-down', *International Multilingual Research Journal, 6*(1), pp. 8–21. https://doi.org/10.1080/19313152.2012.639278

Clegg, J 2019, 'How English depresses school achievement in Africa', *ELT Journal, 73*(1), pp. 89–91.

Clegg, J & Afitska, O 2011, 'Teaching and learning in two languages in African classrooms', *Comparative Education, 47*(1), pp. 61–77. https://doi.org/10.1080/03050068.2011.541677

Clegg, J & Simpson, J 2016, 'Improving the effectiveness of English as a medium of instruction in Sub-Saharan Africa', *Comparative Education, 52*(3), pp. 359–374. https://doi.org/10.1080/03050068.2016.1185268

Coleman, H 2010, *The English Language in Development*, British Council, London, viewed 21 March 2020, www.teachingenglish.org.uk/article/english-language-development.

Coleman, H 2017, 'Milestones in language planning and development aid', *Current Issues in Language Planning, 18*(4), pp. 442–468, DOI: 10.1080/14664208.2017.1351113.

Collier, VP & Thomas, WP 2017, 'Validating the power of bilingual schooling: Thirty-two years of large-scale, longitudinal research', *Annual Review of Applied Linguistics, 37*, pp. 1–15.

Conteh, J 2018, 'Translanguaging as pedagogy – A critical review', in A Creese & A Blackledge (eds), *The Routledge Handbook of Language and Superdiversity: An Interdisciplinary Perspective*, Routledge, London, pp. 473–487 https://doi.org/10.4324/9781315696010

Coyle, D, Hood, P & Marsh, D 2010, *CLIL: Content and Language Integrated Learning*, Cambridge University Press, Cambridge, viewed 14 May 2020, https://assets.cambridge.org/97805211/30219/excerpt/9780521130219_excerpt.pdf.

Crisfield, E, Gordon, I, Holland, A 2021, 'Translanguaging as a pathway to ethical bilingual education: An exploratory case study from Kenya', in B Paulsrudd, Z Tian & J Toth (eds), *English-Medium Instruction and Translanguaging*, Multilingual Matters, Bristol.

Cruz, P & Mahboob, A 2012, 'Critiquing mother-tongue-based language in education policies: A focus on the Philippines', in I Martin (ed), *Re-Conceptualizing English Education in a Multilingual Society*, Springer, Amsterdam, pp. 47–65.

Cummins, J 1991, 'Interdependence of first- and second-language-proficiency in bilingual children', in E Bialystok (ed), *Language Processing in Bilingual Children*, Cambridge University Press, Cambridge, pp. 70–89.

Cummins, J 2000, *Language, Power, and Pedagogy: Bilingual Children in the Crossfire*, Multilingual Matters, Clevedon.

Cummins, J 2010, 'Instructional conditions for trilingual development', *International Journal of Bilingual Education and Bilingualism, 4*(1), pp. 61–75. https://doi.org/10.1080/13670050108667719

Cummins, J 2017, Additive approaches legitimate? *Harvard Educational Review, 87*(3), pp. 404–426.

Dalton-Puffer, C 2011, 'Content-and-language integrated learning: From practice to principles?', *Annual Review of Applied Linguistics, 31*(2011), pp. 182–204. https://doi.org/10.1017/S0267190511000092

Diallo, I 2011, 'To understand lessons, think through your own languages. An analysis of narratives in support of the introduction of indigenous languages in the education system in Senegal', *Language Matters*, *42*(2), pp. 207–230. https://doi.org/10.1080/10228195.2011.585655

Djité, P 2008, *The Sociolinguistics of Development in Africa*, Multilingual Matters, Bristol.

Duarte, J 2019, 'Translanguaging in mainstream education: A sociocultural approach', *International Journal of Bilingual Education and Bilingualism*, *22*(2), pp. 150–164. https://doi.org/10.1080/13670050.2016.1231774

Dutcher, N 2004, *Expanding Educational Opportunity in Linguistically Diverse Societies*, 2nd edition, Center for Applied Linguistics, Washington, DC.

Echevarria, J, Vogt, M & Short, DJ 2013, *Making Content Comprehensible for English Learners: The SIOP Model*, Pearson, New York.

Erling, EJ, Adinolfi, L & Hultgren, AK 2017, Multilingual Classrooms: Opportunities and Challenges for English Medium Instruction in Low and Middle Income Contexts, Education Development Trust, Reading, viewed 20 March 2020, http://login.ezproxy1.lib.asu.edu/login?url=https://search.proquest.com/docview/2155984127?accountid=4485%0Ahttps://arizona-asu-primo.hosted.exlibrisgroup.com/openurl/01ASU/01ASU_SP?genre=report&atitle=&author=Erling%2C+Elizabeth+J.%3BAdinolfi%2C+Lina%3BH.

Erling, EJ, Adinolfi, L, Hultgren, AK, Buckler, A & Mukorera, M 2016, 'Medium of instruction policies in Ghanaian and Indian primary schools: An overview of key issues and recommendations', *Comparative Education*, *52*(3), pp. 294–310. https://doi.org/10.1080/03050068.2016.1185254

Erling, EJ & Seargeant, P 2013, *English and Development: Policy, Pedagogy and Globalization. English and Development: Policy, Pedagogy and Globalization*, Multilingual Matters, Bristol.

Ferguson, G 2013, 'The language of instruction issue: Reality, aspiration and the wider context', *Multilingual Education in Africa: Lessons from the Juba Language-in-Education Conference*, British Council, London, pp. 17–22.

Flores, N & García, ES 2020, 'Power, language, and bilingual learners', in NS Nasir, CD Lee, R Pea, & M McKinney de Royston (eds), *Handbook of the Cultural Foundations of Learning*, Routledge, New York, pp. 178–192.

Flores, N & Rosa, J 2015, 'Undoing appropriateness: Raciolinguistic ideologies and language diversity in education', *Harvard Educational Review*, *85*(2), pp. 149–171.

Footitt, H, Crack, A & Tesseur, W 2018, *Respecting communities in international development: languages and cultural understanding*, INTRAC, Oxford, viewed 2 March 2020 www.intrac.org/resources/respecting-communities-international-development-languages-cultural-understanding/listening_zones_report_-en/.

Gandara, F & Randall, J 2019, 'Assessing mathematics proficiency of multilingual students: The case for translanguaging in the Democratic Republic of the Congo', *Comparative Education Review*, *63*(1), pp. 58–78.

García, O & Kleyn, T (eds) 2016, *Translanguaging with Multilingual Students: Learning from Classroom Moments*, Routledge, London.

García, O & Sylvan, CE 2011, 'Pedagogies and practices in multilingual classrooms: Singularities in pluralities', *Modern Language Journal*, *95*(3), pp. 385–400. https://doi.org/10.1111/j.1540-4781.2011.01208.x

García, O & Wei, L 2013, *Translanguaging: Language, Bilingualism and Education*, Palgrave, London. https://doi.org/10.1057/9781137385765

García, O, Johnson, SI & Seltzer, K 2017, *The Translanguaging Classroom: Leveraging Student Bilingualism for Learning*, Caslon, Philadelphia.

García-Mateus, S & Palmer, D 2017, 'Translanguaging pedagogies for positive identities in two-way dual language bilingual education', *Journal of Language, Identity & Education*, *16*(4), pp. 245–255. https://doi.org/10.1080/15348458.2017.1329016

Gerszon, D, Mahler, B, Laknerr, C, Aguilar, AC & Wu, H 2020, 'The impact of COVID-19 (Coronavirus) on global poverty: Why Sub-Saharan Africa might be the region hardest hit', The World Bank, Washington, DC, viewed 20 April 2020, https://blogs.worldbank.org/opendata/impact-covid-19-coronavirus-global-poverty-why-sub-saharan-africa-might-be-region-hardest.

Gibbons, P 2009, *English Learners, Academic Literacy and Thinking: Learning in the Challenge Zone*, Heinemann, Portsmouth.

Ginkel, AJ 2014, Additive Language Learning for Multilingual Settings, US Aid, Washington, DC, viewed 12 April 2020, pdf.usaid.gov/pdf_docs/PA00JW1R.pdf.

Goodchild, S & Weidl, M 2018, 'Translanguaging practices in the Casamance, Senegal: Similar but different – two case studies: Exploring urban, rural and educational spaces', in A Sherris & E Adami (eds), *Making Signs, Translanguaging Ethnographies*, Multilingual Matters, Bristol, pp. 133–151, DOI 10.21832/9781788921923-011.

Grin, F 2003, 'The economics of language policy implementation: Identifying and measuring costs', in N Alexander (ed), *Mother Tongue-based Bilingual Education in Southern Africa. The Dynamics of Implementation*, Proceedings of the Symposium at the University of Cape Town, Cape Town, pp. 11–25.

Guzula, X, McKinney, C & Tyler, R 2016, 'Languaging-for-learning: Legitimising translanguaging and enabling multimodal practices in third spaces', *Southern African Linguistics and Applied Language Studies*, *34*, pp. 211–226.

Hamman, L, Beck, E & Donaldson, A 2018, 'A pedagogy of translanguaging', Language *Magazine*, viewed 23 March 2020, www.languagemagazine.com/2018/09/10/a-pedagogy-of-translanguaging/.

Hanushek, EA & Woessman, L 2008, 'The role of cognitive skills in educational development', *Journal of Economic Literature*, *46*(3), pp. 607–668. https://doi.org/http://dx.doi.org/10.1257/jel.46.3.607

Heugh, K 2009, 'Literacy and bi/multilingual education in Africa: Recovering collective memory and expertise', in T Skuttnab-Kangas, R Phillipson, AK Mohanty & M Panda (eds), *Social Justice through Multilingual Education*, Multilingual Matters, Bristol, pp. 103–124.

Heugh, K 2011, 'Theory and practice – language education models in Africa: Research, design, decision-making and outcomes', in A Ouane & C Glanz (eds), *Optimising Learning, Education and Publishing in Africa: The Language Factor*, UNESCO/ADEA.

Heugh, K 2015, 'Epistemologies in multilingual education: Translanguaging and genre – companions in conversation with policy and practice', *Language and Education*, *29*(3), pp. 280–285. https://doi.org/10.1080/09500782.2014.994529

Heugh, K, Benson, C, Bogale, B & Yohannes, M 2007, *Final report study on medium of instruction in primary schools in Ethiopia*, The Human Sciences Research Council, Pretoria, http://hdl.handle.net/20.500.11910/6273

International Monetary Fund (IMF) 2018, *Regional Economic Outlook: Capital Flows and The Future of Work*, IMF, Washington, DC, viewed 14 March 2020, www.imf.org/en/Publications/REO/SSA/Issues/2018/09/20/sreo1018.

Kamwendo, G 2015, 'The straight for English policy in Malawi: The road not to be taken' in L Miti (ed), *The Language of Instruction Question in Malawi*, CASAS, Cape Town, pp. 29–40.

Kerfoot, C & Simon-Vandenbergen, AM 2015, 'Language in epistemic access: Mobilising multilingualism and literacy development for more equitable education in South Africa', *Language and Education*, *29*(3), pp. 177–185. https://doi.org/10.1080/09500782.2014.994522

Kioko, AN, Ndung'u, RW, Njoroge, MC & Mutiga, J 2014, 'Mother tongue and education in Africa: Publicising the reality', *Multilingual Education*, *4*(1), p. 18. https://doi.org/10.1186/s13616-014-0018-x

Kiramba, L 2016, 'Translanguaging in the writing of emergent multilinguals', *International Multilingual Research Journal*, *11*(2), pp. 115–130. DOI: 10.1080/19313152.2016.1239457.

Kosonen, K 2005, *Education in Local Languages: Policy and Practice in Southeast Asia. First Languages First: Community-based Literacy Programmes for Minority Language Contexts in Asia*, Bangkok.

Lin, A 2016, *Language Across the Curriculum & CLIL in English as an Additional Language (EAL) Contexts: Theory and Practice*, Springer, Amsterdam.

Lippi-Green, R 2012, *English with an Accent: Language, Ideology and Discrimination in the United States* (2nd Ed). Routledge, London.

Luckett, K 1995, 'National Additive Bilingualism: Towards a Language Plan for South African Education', in K Heugh, A Siegrühn & P Plüddemann (eds), *Multilingual Education for South Africa*, Heinemann, Johannesburg, pp. 73–78.

Lüpke, F 2016, 'Uncovering small-scale multilingualism', *Critical Multilingualism Studies*, *4*(2), pp. 35–74.

Lüpke, F 2020, 'The writing's on the wall: Spaces for language-independent and language-based literacies', *International Journal of Multilingualism*, *17*(3), pp. 382–403. DOI: 10.1080/14790718.2020.1766466.

Lüpke, F, Biagui, A, Biai, L, Diatta, J, Mané, A, Preira, G, Weidl, M forthcoming, 'LILIEMA: Language-independent literacies for inclusive education in multilingual areas', in P Harding-Esch & H Coleman (eds), *Language and the sustainable development goals*, British Council, London.

Lyster, R 2018, *Content-based Language Teaching*, Routledge, London.

Macdonald, C 1991, *Eager to Talk, Learn and Think: Bilingual Primary Education in South Africa*, Maskew-Miller Longman, Cape Town.

Mackenzie, P & Walker, J 2012, *Mother-Tongue Education: Policy Lessons for Quality and Inclusion*, Global Campaign for Quality Education, Johannesburg, viewed 5 May 2020, www.campaignforeducation.org/docs/reports/GCE%20Mother%20Tongue_EN.pdf.

Mafela, L 2009, 'Code-switching in Botswana history classrooms in the decade of education for sustainable development', *Language Matters*, *40*(1), pp. 56–79. https://doi.org/10.1080/10228190903055568

Makalela, L 2015a, 'Moving out of linguistic boxes: The effects of translanguaging strategies for multilingual classrooms', *Language and Education*, *29*(3), pp. 200–217. https://doi.org/10.1080/09500782.2014.994524

Makalela, L 2015b, 'Translanguaging as a vehicle for epistemic access: Cases for reading comprehension and multilingual interactions', *Per Linguam*, *31*(1), p. 15. https://doi.org/10.5785/31-1-628

Makalela, L 2016, 'Ubuntu translanguaging: An alternative framework for complex multilingual encounters', *Southern African Linguistics and Applied Language Studies*, *34*(3), pp. 187–196.

Makgato, M 2014, 'The use of English and code switching in the teaching and learning of technology in some schools in eastern cape province, South Africa', *Mediterranean Journal of Social Sciences*, *5*(23), pp. 933–940. https://doi.org/10.5901/mjss.2014.v5n23p933

Makoe, P & McKinney, C 2014, 'Linguistic ideologies in multilingual South African suburban schools', *Journal of Multilingual and Multicultural Development*, *35*(7), pp. 658–673.

Marinotti, JP (ed) 2017, 'Language, the sustainable development goals, and vulnerable populations; Final Report', United Nations, New York, viewed 23 April 2020, www.languageandtheun.org/symposium2017report.html.

McKinney, C 2017, *Language and Power in Post-Colonial Schooling: Ideologies in Practice*, Routledge, London.

McKinney, C 2020, 'Decoloniality and language in education', in JA Windle, D De Jesus & L Bartlett (eds), *The Dynamics of Language and Inequality in Education: Social and Symbolic Boundaries in the Global South*, Multilingual Matters, Bristol, pp. 155–132.

Milligan, LO, Clegg, J & Tikly, L 2016, 'Exploring the potential for language supportive learning in English medium instruction: A Rwandan case study', *Comparative Education*, *52*(3), pp. 328–342. https://doi.org/10.1080/03050068.2016.1185258

Mokgwathi, T & Webb, V 2013, 'The educational effects of code-switching in the classroom-benefits and setbacks: A case of selected senior secondary schools in Botswana', *Language Matters*, *44*(3), pp. 108–125. https://doi.org/10.1080/10228195.2013.839734

Mokibelo, EB 2014, 'The national language as a language of instruction in Botswana primary schools', *Language and Education*, *28*(5), pp. 421–435. https://doi.org/10.1080/09500782.2014.892126

Moon, B (ed) 2013, *Teacher Education and the Challenge of Development: A Global Analysis*, Routledge, London.

Mwaniki, M 2016, 'Translanguaging as a class/lecture-room language management strategy in multilingual contexts: Insights from autoethnographic snapshots from Kenya and South Africa', *Southern African Linguistics and Applied Language Studies*, *34*(3), pp. 197–209, DOI: 10.2989/16073614.2016.1250357.

Mwinda, N & van der Walt, C 2015, 'From "English-only" to translanguaging strategies: Exploring possibilities', *Per Linguam*, *31*, pp. 100–118. DOI: 10.5785/31-3-620.

Ncoko, SOS, Osman, R & Cockcroft, K 2000, 'Codeswitching among multilingual learners in primary schools in South Africa: An exploratory study', *International Journal of Bilingual Education and Bilingualism*, *3*(4), pp. 225–241. https://doi.org/10.1080/13670050008667709

Ndlangamandla, SC 2010, 'Multilingualism in desegregated schools: Learners' use of and views towards African languages', *Southern African Linguistics and Applied Language Studies*, *28*(1), pp. 61–73. https://doi.org/10.2989/16073614.2010.488444

Nikiema, N 2011, 'A first-language-first multilingual model to meet the quality imperative in formal basic education in three "francophone" West African countries', *International Review of Education*, *57*, pp. 599–616.

Nikula, T & Moore, P 2019, 'Translanguaging in CLIL', *International Journal of Bilingual Education and Bilingualism*, *22*(2), pp. 237–249. http://dx.doi.org/10.1080/13670050.2016.1254151

Nyaga, S & Anthonissen, C 2012, 'Teaching in linguistically diverse classrooms: Difficulties in the implementation of the language-in-education policy in multilingual Kenyan primary school classrooms', *Compare*, *42*(6), pp. 863–879. https://doi.org/10.1080/03057925.2012.707457

Nyati-Saleshando, L 2011, 'An advocacy project for multicultural education: The case of the Shiyeyi language in Botswana', *International Review of Education*, *57*, pp. 567–582.

Okebukola, PA, Owolabi, O & Okebukola, FO 2013, 'Mother tongue as default language of instruction in lower primary science classes: Tension between policy prescription and practice in Nigeria', *Journal of Research in Science Teaching*, *50*(1), pp. 62–81. https://doi.org/10.1002/tea.21070

Opoku-Amankwa, K, Brew-Hammond, A & Kofigah, FE 2011, 'What is in a textbook? Investigating the language and literacy learning principles of the "gateway to English" textbook series', *Pedagogy, Culture and Society*, *19*(2), pp. 291–310. https://doi.org/10.1080/14681366.2011.582264

Opoku-Amankwa, K, Edu-Buandoh, DF & Brew-Hammond, A 2015, 'Publishing for mother tongue-based bilingual education in Ghana: Politics and consequences', *Language and Education*, *29*(1), pp. 1–14. https://doi.org/10.1080/09500782.2014.921194

Orwenjo, DO, Njoroge, MC & Ndung'u, RW (eds) 2014, *Multilingualism and Education in Africa: The State of the State of the Art*, Cambridge Scholars Publishing, Newcastle.

Owen-Smith, M 2010, 'The language challenge in the classroom: A serious shift in thinking and action is needed', *Focus: Journal of the Helen Suzman Foundation*, *56*, pp. 31–37, viewed 3 June 2020, https://hsf.org.za/publications/focus/focus-56-february-2010-on-learning-and-teaching/the-language-challenge-in-the-classroom-a-serious-shift-in-thinking-and-action-is-needed.

Patel, N 2018, *Figure of the Week: Understanding Poverty in Africa*, Brookings, Washington, DC, viewed 21 November 2019, www.brookings.edu/blog/africa-in-focus/2018/11/21/figure-of-the-week-understanding-poverty-in-africa/#:~:text=As of 2015%2C

Pflepsen, B 2015, *Planning for Language Use in Education: Best Practices and Practical Steps to Improve Learning Outcomes*, US Aid, Washington, DC, viewed 14 May 2020, https://globalreadingnetwork.net/eddata/planning-language-use-education-best-practices-and-practical-steps-improve-learning-outcomes.

Pinnock, H & Vijayakumar, G 2009, *Language and Education: The Missing Link. How the Language Used in School Threatens the Achievement of Education for All*, UNESCO, Paris, viewed 20 May 2020, www.unesco.org/education/EFAWG2009/LanguageEducation.pdf.

Piper, B, Zuilkowski, SS, Kwayumba, D & Oyanga, A 2018, 'Examining the secondary effects of mother-tongue literacy instruction in Kenya: Impacts on student learning in English, Kiswahili, and mathematics', *International Journal of Educational Development*, *59*, pp. 110–127. https://doi.org/10.1016/j.ijedudev.2017.10.002

Probyn, M 2009, '"Smuggling the vernacular into the classroom": Conflicts and tensions in classroom codeswitching in township/rural schools in South Africa', *International Journal of Bilingual Education and Bilingualism*, *12*(2), pp. 123–136. https://doi.org/10.1080/13670050802153137

Probyn, M 2015, 'Pedagogical translanguaging: Bridging discourses in South African science classrooms', *Language and Education*, *29*(3), pp. 218–234. https://doi.org/10.1080/09500782.2014.994525

Reilly, C 2021, 'Malawian universities as translanguaging spaces', in B Paulsrudd, Z Tian & J Toth (eds), *English-Medium Instruction and Translanguaging*, Multilingual Matters, Bristol.

Romaine, S 2013, 'Keeping the promise of the Millennium Development Goals: Why language matters', *Applied Linguistics Review*, *4*(2), p. 219. https://doi.org/10.1515/applirev-2013-5001

Rosekrans, K, Sherris, A & Chatry-Komarek, M 2012, 'Education reform for the expansion of mother-tongue education in Ghana', *International Review of Education*, *58*(5), pp. 593–618. https://doi.org/10.1007/s11159-012-9312-6

Rubagumya, C 2003, 'English medium primary schools in Tanzania: A new "linguistic market" in education', in B Brock-Utne, Z Desai & M Qorro (eds), *Language of Instruction in Tanzania and South Africa*, E&D Limited, Dar es Salaam.

Rubagumya, CM 1986, 'Language planning in the Tanzanian educational system: Problems and prospects', *Journal of Multilingual and Multicultural Development*, *7*(4), pp. 283–300, DOI: 10.1080/01434632.1986.9994245.

Rubagumya, CM. (ed) 1994, *Teaching and Researching Language in African Classrooms*, Multilingual Matters, Clevedon.

Schmied, JJ 1991, *English in Africa*, Longman, New York.

Sen, A 1999, *Development as Freedom*, Oxford University Press, Oxford.

Setati, M & Adler, J 2000, 'Between languages and discourses: Language practices in primary multilingual mathematics classrooms in South Africa', *Educational Studies in Mathematics*, *43*(3), pp. 243–269. https://doi.org/10.1023/A:1011996002062

Shank Lauwo, MS 2018, 'Power, literacy engagement, and polyphonic identities: Translanguaging in a Tanzanian community library', *Southern African Linguistics and Applied Language Studies*, 36(2), pp. 133–146, DOI: 10.2989/16073614.2018.1495569.

Sherris, A, Schaefer, P & Aworo, SM 2018, 'The paradox of translanguaging in Safaliba: A rural indigenous Ghanaian language', in A Sherris & E Adami (eds), *Making Signs, Translanguaging Ethnographies: Exploring Urban, Rural, and Educational Spaces*, Multilingual Matters, Bristol, pp. 152–169.

Smith, M 2011, 'Which in- and out-of-school factors explain variations in learning across different socio-economic groups? Findings from South Africa', *Comparative Education*, *47*(1), pp. 79–102.

Smits, J, Huisman, J & Kruijff, K 2008, *Home Language and Education in the Developing World*, UNESCO, Paris, viewed 26 March 2020, http://unesdoc.unesco.org/images/0017/001787/178702e.pdf.

Taylor-Leech, K & Benson, C 2017, 'Language planning and development aid: The (in)visibility of language in development aid discourse', *Current Issues in Language Planning*, *18*(4), pp. 339–355. https://doi.org/10.1080/14664208.2017.1360690

Taylor-Leech, K & Liddicoat, AJ 2014, 'Macro-language planning for multilingual education: Focus on programmes and provision', *Current Issues in Language Planning*, *15*(4), pp. 353–360.

Thomas, WP & Collier, VP 2002, 'A national study of school effectiveness for language minority students' long-term academic achievement', *Center for Research on Education, Diversity & Excellence*, *96*, pp. 1–351.

Thomas, WP & Collier, VP 2012, *Dual Language Education for a Transformed World*, Dual Language Education of New Mexico-Fuente Press, Albuquerque, NM.

Tikly, L & Barrett, AM 2011, 'Social justice, capabilities and the quality of education in low income countries', *International Journal of Educational Development*, *31*(1), pp. 3–14. https://doi.org/10.1016/j.ijedudev.2010.06.001

Trudell, B 2016a, 'Language choice and education quality in Eastern and Southern Africa: A review', *Comparative Education*, *52*(3), pp. 281–293. https://doi.org/10.1080/03050068.2016.1185252

Trudell, B 2016b, *The Impact of Language Policy and Practice on Children's Learning: Evidence from Eastern and Southern Africa*, United Nations International Children Emergency Fund, New York, viewed 19 April 2020, www.unicef.org/esaro/UNICEF(2016)LanguageandLearning-FullReport(SingleView).pdf.

Trudell, B (2018). *Language and Education in Nigeria: A Review of Policy and Practice.* British Council, London, viewed 30 November 2020 www.britishcouncil.org.ng/sites/default/files/j149_language_and_education_nigeria_final_web.pdf

Trudell, B & Young, C (eds) 2016, *Good Answers to Tough Questions in Mother Tongue-Based Multilingual Education*, SIL International, Dallas, viewed 18 May 2020, www.sil.org/literacy-education/good-answers-tough-questions-mother-tongue-based-multilingual-education.

Tupas, R 2015, 'Inequalities of multilingualism: Challenges to mother tongue-based multilingual education', *Language and Education*, *29*(2), pp. 112–124. https://doi.org/10.1080/09500782.2014.977295

UNESCO 1953, *The Use of Vernacular Languages in Education*, UNESCO, Switzerland.

UNESCO 2003, *Education in a Multilingual World (Education Position Paper)*, UNESCO, Paris.

UNESCO 2008, *Mother Tongue Matters: Local Language as a Key to Effective Learning*, UNESCO, Paris, viewed 15 April 2020, http://unesdoc.unesco.org/images/0016/001611/161121e.pdf.

UNESCO 2015, *Fixing the Broken Promise of Education for All: Findings from the Global Initiative on Out-of-School Children.* UNESCO, Montreal, https://doi.org/10.15220/978-92-9189-162-7-en

UNESCO 2016a, Every Child Should Have a Textbook, Global Education Monitoring Report. Policy Paper 23, https://en.unesco.org/gem-report/every-child-should-have-textbook

UNESCO 2016b, *If you don't understand, how can you learn? Global Education Monitoring Report. Policy Paper 24*, https://en.unesco.org/gem-report/if-you-don't-understand-how-can-you-learn.

UNESCO 2018, *MTB MLE Resource Kit. Including the Excluded: Promoting Multilingual Education*, UNESCO, Bangkok.

UNESCO 2014, *Education for All in Sub-Saharan Africa: Assessment Report*, viewed 9 March 2020, https://unesdoc.unesco.org/ark:/48223/pf0000232658.

United Nations 2015, *The Sustainable Development Goals*, United Nations, New York, viewed 12 May 2020, www.un.org/sustainabledevelopment/sustainable-development-goals/.

van Kampen, E, Meirink, J, Admiraal, W & Berry, A 2017, 'Do we all share the same goals for content and language integrated learning (CLIL)? Specialist and practitioner perceptions of "ideal" CLIL pedagogies in the Netherlands', *International Journal of Bilingual Education and Bilingualism*, *23*(8), pp. 855–871, DOI: 10.1080/13670050.2017.1411332.

Weber, J.-J 2014, *Flexible Multilingual Education: Putting Children's Needs First*, Multilingual Matters, Bristol.

Wei, L 2018, 'Translanguaging as a practical theory of language', *Applied Linguistics*, *39*(1), pp. 9–30. https://doi.org/10.1093/applin/amx039

Williams, E 2014, 'English in African politics of education: Capital or capital illusion?' *International Journal of the Sociology of Language*, *225*, pp.131–145.

Wisbey, M 2016, *Mother Tongue-based Multilingual Education: The Key to Unlocking SDG4 – Quality Education for All*, UNESCO, Bangkok.

Wolff, EH 2000, 'Language and society', in D Heine & B Nurse (eds), *African Languages. An Introduction*, Cambridge University Press, Cambridge, pp. 298–347.

World Bank 2020, 'Literacy rate, adult total (% of people ages 15 and above) – Sub-Saharan Africa', World Bank, Washington, DC https://data.worldbank.org/indicator/SE.ADT.LITR.ZS?end=2010&locations=ZG-1W-Z4-8S-Z7-ZJ&start=2010&view=bar.

Yevudey, E & Agbozo, GE 2019, 'Teacher trainee sociolinguistic backgrounds and attitudes to language-in-education policy in Ghana: A preliminary survey', *Current Issues in Language Planning*, *20*(4), pp. 338–364. https://doi.org/10.1080/14664208.2019.1585158

Part 1

What does research tell us about the status of multilingual learning in SSA?

2 Research in multilingual learning in Africa

Assessing the effectiveness of multilingual education programming

Leila Schroeder, Megan Sutton Mercado and Barbara Trudell

Introduction

Research on multilingual learning in the Global South is not lacking; a great deal of descriptive work has been done in multilingual classrooms across Africa, Asia and Latin America. The evidence from such work is clear that (1) the use of a non-L1 language as the language of instruction is not resulting in acceptable learning outcomes (Kioko et al., 2014; Glewwe et al., 2009, p. 112; Skutnabb-Kangas & Dunbar, 2010) and (2) the use of a local language of instruction produces dramatic improvements in learning outcomes (Kim et al., 2019; Taylor & von Fintel, 2016; UNESCO 2016; Wagner, 2017, p. 129). Quantitative work on the topic is less common; such work that has been done often requires extensive interpretive context in order to be understood well. More rare, however, are conceptually complete, data-driven understandings of what is required for optimal learning in the multilingual classroom of the Global South: the necessary processes and timing of transition of language medium; the necessary teacher competencies for successful transition of language medium; the impact of the linguistic features of both the first language (L1) and the additional language (L2) on language learning; and a clear definition of second language acquisition outcomes. In this paper, we examine the existing research evidence regarding multilingual learning in low-resource contexts of Sub-Saharan Africa, specifically in the context of mother tongue-based multilingual education (MTB MLE) models being implemented in African countries. A number of studies on MTB MLE programming in Africa are analysed and compared, in order to provide insights regarding whether and when L1-medium instruction can be seen to support effective transition to secondary school. Finally, some suggestions are offered regarding research topics that would help fill knowledge gaps in the field.

DOI: 10.4324/9781003028383-3

Limitations of the existing evidence

Where research on MTB MLE programming in Africa is concerned, producing – and finding – accurate assessments of learning outcomes is a significant challenge. This is due to at least two features of such programming:

- The ideological discourses surrounding MTB MLE research and pilot programmes, related to linguistic rights, maintenance of indigenous and local cultures and inclusive education. These discourses are powerful and compelling; however, they do not necessarily prioritize tracking the kinds of learning outcomes needed in an MTB MLE programme for successful transition to secondary school in an L2. This in turn makes comparative assessment of such learning outcomes a challenge.
- A lack of rigorous assessment of learning outcomes at key points in the programme, such as year-end testing, end-of-programme testing and relevant national examinations. Such assessment can certainly be challenging; interpreting the results can be difficult as well due to factors beyond programme planners' control. Nevertheless, without this level of assessment, actual learning outcomes are difficult to specify.

These two features help to explain the relatively small number of MTB MLE programmes that could be identified in this study as 'effective' or 'ineffective' with any measure of clarity. The weak documentation of the impact of most of the MTB MLE programmes reviewed, and our focus on determining long-term programme impact on secondary school success, limited both the number of programmes chosen here and the consistency and rigor of the measures used by the researchers on each programme. Assessments of student readiness for secondary were difficult to find, and they varied in terms of the skills they assessed and whether they used national exams or programme-specific assessments.

Features of the study

The geographical range of this study is Sub-Saharan Africa; this focus is supported by the clear need for reliable research findings on what actually works in African classrooms, which feature "the world's lowest enrolment rates and highest dropout rates" (Spaull, 2015, p. 139). The study looks at the research evidence available on programmes featuring some kind of L1-medium instruction, in the context of MTB MLE programming. Multilingual education programming in which two or more non-L1 languages are used in primary-grade classrooms is not under study here. The literature review was carried out in 2019, based on multiple searches of electronic and hard-copy resources available through several academic libraries. Specifically, we were looking for studies of MTB MLE programmes that could provide reasonable evidence of a long-term effect on children's learning. More than 50 studies were identified and assessed for such evidence.[1]

What does the research say regarding L1-medium instruction programming that effectively supports successful transition to secondary school?

The question guiding this study has to do with the effectiveness of using the child's first language as language of instruction in primary school, 'effectiveness' being determined based on the likelihood of the learner's successful transitioning to the secondary school level. It is understood that in nearly all cases in Africa, an international language is the language of instruction in secondary school curricula. Thus, this measure of effective L1-medium learning in primary grades assumes that not only curricular content, but L2 fluency as well, have been mastered adequately enough to sustain the learner in the L2-medium learning environment of secondary school. The choice to define the effectiveness of primary-grade MLE instructional programming in this way is based on the view of primary school as a first step in the learner's educational trajectory, rather than a stand-alone learning experience. It is true that L1-medium learning in the early grades also has significant community and sociocultural benefits, especially for minoritized language communities.[2] Not only so, but Trudell (2012, p. 372) notes that even a few years of L1-medium learning give children an academic advantage over their peers in L2-medium primary schools, since "just learning to read, write and calculate in their own language puts children ahead of those who are taught only in a language they do not understand." However, the evidence is that these benefits of L1-medium learning in the early grades do not necessarily translate into successful transition to L2-medium secondary school.

Assessment of the MTB MLE programmes under study had two components:

1. We looked for research evidence on learners' performance at the end of the primary cycle. Quantitative, end-of-primary school testing outcomes were accepted as the best indicators of performance; secondary school testing outcomes were also sought. However, such measures were not consistently available in the research; as a result, in some cases comparison figures and qualitative assessment are also cited as evidence.
2. From the literature on language and education, we identified seven MLE programme features that can be linked to a high likelihood that instruction in the primary grades will result in learners' success in secondary school, where instruction is typically carried out in the L2. The MLE programme research studies were then assessed for the presence of these features:
    - **Years of L1-medium instruction:** A minimum of six years of learning through the L1 (Heugh, 2011, pp. 120–121; Baker, 2006, p. 173; Walter, 2013, p. 275).
    - **L1 language of instruction across the curriculum**, with the possible exception of oral L2 learning (Mkandawire, 2018; Benson, 2013, p. 291).
    - **Teacher training:** The programme includes at least one year of formal teacher training, *or* a minimum of three weeks of in-service training

spread over a school year, with coaching provided as well (Piper et al., 2018a; Piper & Kim, 2018; Kim et al., 2016, pp. 51–54).

- **Textbooks in L1:** All subjects (except oral L2) have L1 textbooks, allowing learners to read to learn, and to practice L1 reading for several hours daily. Textbooks for L2 acquisition are also available (Walter, 2013, pp. 272–279; Fafunwa et al., 1989, p. 11).
- **L1 reading is taught for at least four years:** Reading is taught in the L1 for at least four years. L2 reading is introduced once the oral vocabulary and phonological skills to support it have been acquired (Krashen, 2002, p. 143; Baker, 2006, p. 333).
- **Systematic oral L2 skills development for all subjects in the school system:** The scope and sequence for oral L2 learning is in place for the length of the programme, taking into account vocabulary and grammar which will be used later in English-medium textbooks (Alidou & Brock-Utne, 2011, pp. 166–167).
- **The L1 is used for examinations:** If L1 content areas are taught using L1 textbooks, exams are also given in the L1 (Ouane & Glanz, 2011, pp. 35–36; Alidou & Brock-Utne, 2011, p. 168; Benson, 2013, p. 288).

Based on these two components, nine programmes were found to have enough research data to indicate their degree of effectiveness in leading to successful student transition to secondary school. Four of the nine programmes were assessed as effective by the criteria listed above, and five of the nine programmes were assessed as ineffective by these same criteria. The sections below describe both sets of programmes. Each individual programme description begins with a tabular assessment of the presence of the seven MLE programme features described above, as found in the research on that programme (Tables 2.1, 2.2, 2.4, 2.5, 2.6, 2.7, 2.8, 2.9 and 2.11). A table of all the programmes and their assessment for the seven MLE programme features can be found in Appendix 2.1. Additional notes on these assessments, especially those of the effective programmes, can be found in Appendix 2.2.

Effective programmes: high likelihood of the learners' successful transitioning to secondary school

Four Africa-sited MTB MLE programmes were found to qualify as effective in terms of enabling successful student transition to secondary school: a late-exit MLE programme in Ethiopia, Bambara-medium MLE programming in Mali, Yoruba-language late-exit MLE programming in Nigeria and the *Écoles Bilingues* programme in Burkina Faso.

Ethiopia: late-exit (six to eight years) transition programme

While the national policy of Ethiopia has supported the use of the mother tongue in education since 1994 (Benson et al., 2010, p. 40), each region of the country

Table 2.1 Research findings on Ethiopia 6-8 year programmes

Years of L1-medium instruction	*6–8*
L1 used as language of instruction across the curriculum	yes
Teacher training 1+ year of formal training or 3+ weeks of in-service training over a school year	yes
Textbooks in L1 for all subjects, plus textbooks for acquiring L2	yes
L1 reading taught for 4+ years	yes
Oral L2 skills development for all subjects	no
L1 is used for examinations	yes

chooses the extent to which the regional language is used in schools. As a result, comparison of exam results across regions has enabled researchers to analyse the effects of various lengths of time of L1-medium instruction. The post-primary national exams were given in three subject areas, plus English. They were maths, biology and chemistry in 2002; Physics was added in 2004 (Heugh et al., 2010, p. 292).

In 2000, 2004 and 2008, Heugh et al. examined the effects of learning outcomes in various regions of Ethiopia. The study concluded that

> Overall, across the three systemic assessments, students who have eight years of [mother tongue medium] and who are assessed in their [other tongue] outperform students who switch to English medium earlier.
>
> (Heugh et al., 2010, p. 292)

Both the 2000 and 2008 assessment data showed that generally, students who had had eight years of L1-medium learning had the highest scores[3] – high enough to predict successful entry into secondary school (Heugh et al., 2010, p. 295). The next highest scores were from students with six years of mother tongue-medium learning, along with some subjects taught in the L1 in Grades 7–8 (Heugh et al., 2010, pp. 295–305).

The Ethiopian assessment authority divided student achievement into three bands: below basic, basic and proficient, shown in Figure 2.1 (Heugh et al., 2012, pp. 252–253). The surprising evidence revealed in Figure 2.1 is that the Tigray, Oromia and Amhara regions had the highest proportion of students in the proficient or basic categories. These regions were not the most urban or privileged, but they dedicated extensive time to L1 learning, which appears to have improved their students' outcomes (Benson et al., 2012, pp. 40–43).

Analysis

This research provides solid confirmation of the value of late-exit MLE. It is true that challenges to nationwide implementation of the programme were noted by

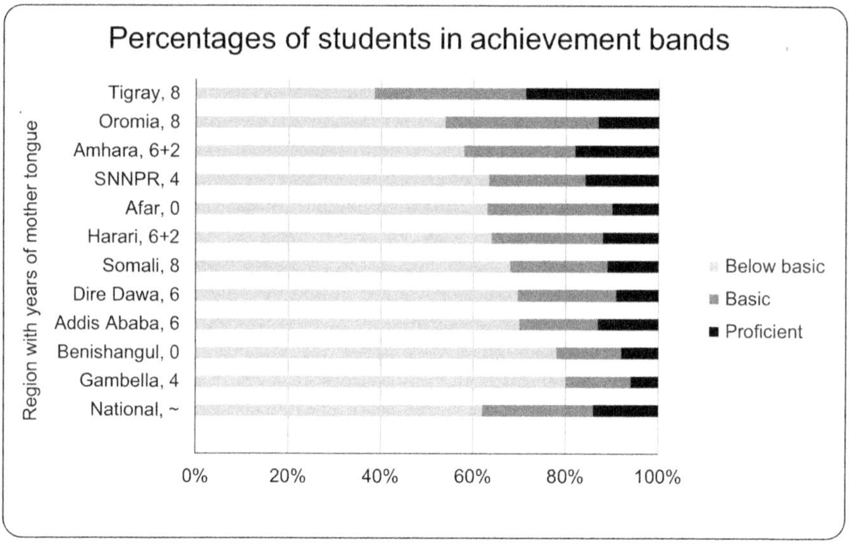

Figure 2.1 Harari and Amhara, with 6 + 2 years, offered L1 instruction through Grade 6, with some L1 support in Grades 7 and 8 (Heugh et al., 2012, p. 247). Although schools in Dire Dawa and Addis Ababa use Amharic for six years, the language is an L2 for about 50% of students (ibid., p. 249).

Heugh et al. (2010, pp. 294–295) and Smith et al. (2012, p. 2). Even though L1-medium textbooks had been developed for all the L1 languages, they recommend better distribution of those textbooks and teachers' guides, the development of clear, measurable skill-based curricular outcomes, teacher training which includes reading pedagogy and English-acquisition textbooks which are aligned with the techniques that teachers have been trained to use. Despite these implementation flaws, however, test scores indicate that the late-exit programmes were more effective than the early-exit programmes. This is further evidenced by the National Organization for Examinations' (NOE) *ANOVA* test Grade 8 data from 2004 which showed a statistically significant difference between the overall performance scores of students learning through their home languages vs. students learning through English (Benson et al., 2010, p. 56).

Mali: Bambara-language Pédagogie Convergente *programming*

Mali's *Pédagogie Convergente* programme provides another example of effective MLE programming. *Pédagogie Convergente* began in 1979, with adult literacy classes in the Bambara language. The programme evolved into a Bambara-language children's education programme in 1987, though it was not generally seen to have much promise; Bender (2002, p. 2) notes that educators "sent children they didn't think could succeed". However, by the end of the primary cycle, the students' exam results convinced parents, teachers and the Malian government to implement the programme more widely, which is why from 1994 to 2005, the programme was gradually extended to involve 2,050 public schools and 11 national languages (Bühmann & Trudell, 2008, p. 10).

In 2000, the first student generation in the extended *Pédagogie Convergente* programme reached Grade 7. Regional results for the entrance exam also showed that these students performed better overall, with an average of 16.23 points higher than students in the French-medium schools (Bühmann & Trudell, 2008, p. 11). All tests were in French and were identical for both experimental and control groups. Table 2.3 below lists the average Grade 7 entrance exam scores for each region (ibid., pp. 10–12).

By 2002, *Pédagogie Convergente* had spread to more than 1,000 Malian primary schools. Students in the programme were performing "significantly better in French and mathematics than their counterparts in French-only schools" (ibid., p. 12).

Table 2.2 Research findings on Mali Bambara programme

Years of L1-medium instruction	*6*
L1 used as language of instruction across the curriculum	yes
Teacher training 1+ year of formal training or 3+ weeks of in-service training over a school year	yes
Textbooks in L1 for all subjects, plus textbooks for acquiring L2	yes
L1 reading taught for 4+ years	yes
Oral L2 skills development for all subjects	yes
L1 is used for examinations	no

Table 2.3 Average Grade 7 entrance exam scores in *Pédagogie Convergente* schools and French-medium schools, 1994–2000 Ministry of Education, Mali

Average seventh grade entrance exam scores by region, 2000			
Region	*Pédagogie convergent schools*	*Monolingual French schools*	*Difference in score averages*
Kayes	68.1	49.04	19.06
Koulikoro	92.9	61	31.9
Sikasso	65.1	46.03	19.07
Ségou	46.69	45.12	1.57
Mopti	79.22	51.03	28.21
Tombouctou	62	62.01	-0.01
Gao	59.56	53.51	6.05
Bamako	75.54	56.75	18.79
National	68.57	52.34	16.23

Source: Bühmann and Trudell (2008), p. 11.

In a less formal perspective on the programme's learning outcomes, one researcher relates that her attempt to study the programme's long-term results was impeded because the programme's former students were absent from the community, attending secondary schools. In contrast, students who had attended the traditional French-medium school in the area had not continued on past primary school but were still farming in the local community (Bender, 2019, personal communication). While this distinction does not imply the superiority of one life choice over another, it does demonstrate the effectiveness of the *Pédagogie Convergente* programme as defined in this study. Eventually *Pédagogie Convergente* became available in 11 out of 13 national languages (Bühmann & Trudell, 2008, pp. 10–11).

Analysis

It is likely that the effectiveness of the *Pédagogie Convergente* programme in facilitating transition to secondary education had much to do with the time given to the mastery of reading: children practiced reading in their L1 for the entire primary cycle, using L1 textbooks to study all content areas. Though L1-medium instruction was given for six years, increasing time was given to French each year after Grade 1. Oral French began to be taught as a subject in Grade 2 across Mali. Math and French reading began to be taught via the L2 in Grade 3, getting 50% of reading lesson time (Youssuf Haidara, personal communication, 15 May 2019), though use of the L1 also continued.

Another factor in the effectiveness of the programme was the child-friendly approach that teachers were trained to use (Bender, 2002, p. 2), enabling the children to communicate with the teacher and one another. Other language-related factors in the effectiveness of the programme include: the regularized, documented spelling rules for Bambara; the use of only the Bambara language exclusively throughout Grade 1, with oral French instruction added in Grade 2; and the development of technical vocabulary in Bambara for use in teaching content areas. In addition, the Malian government provided significant institutional support for the programme.

Nigeria: Yoruba-language experimental (late-exit transition) programme

One of the best-known MTB MLE studies in Africa is the 1970–1976 Yoruba language-medium programme (Fafunwa et al., 1989; Trudell, 2018). The programme included innovations in curriculum development and teacher training, as well as differential use of Yoruba as language of instruction. All of these programme features contributed to the significance of the findings of the study.

It is important to note that both the experimental and the "control" classes in the programme were characterized by innovative practices, and many curricular features were the same in both the experimental and control schools. The primary difference between the two groups was the number of years the L1 was used as language of instruction: the experimental group of students

Table 2.4 Research findings on Nigeria, Ife: six-year programme

Years of L1-medium instruction	*6*
L1 used as language of instruction across the curriculum	yes
Teacher training 1+ year of formal training or 3+ weeks of in-service training over a school year	yes
Textbooks in L1 for all subjects, plus textbooks for acquiring L2	yes
L1 reading taught for 4+ years	yes
Oral L2 skills development for all subjects	yes
L1 is used for examinations	yes

followed a late-exit model with six years of L1-medium instruction, while the "control" group used an early-exit model with only three years (Grades 1–3). In both the early-exit and late-exit cohorts, the entire curriculum – literacy skills, mathematics, social and cultural studies and science – were taught in the Yoruba language. Both groups, a total of 820 students, studied English as a subject. All the teachers (Fasokun, 2000, p. 5) in the programme received the same training in the use of the pedagogical materials. Students in both the experimental and "control" groups performed significantly better than students not in the programme. The primary evidence of this was seen in their respective dropout rates: less than 10% among the experimental group and 30% among the control group, compared to a national average of 40–60% dropout at the time (ibid., p. 5).

With the primary difference between experimental and "control" groups being the number of years in L1-medium instruction, the experimental group showed exceptional longitudinal results, compared to the control group (Fafunwa et al., 1989, p. 11; Fasokun, 2000). The researchers created assessments to examine the students' performance in social studies, science, mathematics, Yoruba, oral and written English.

- From primary Grade 5 onward, the experimental classes outperformed the "control" classes in mathematics, social and cultural studies and science.
- Primary Grade 6 examination results showed significantly higher scores among the experimental group for the subjects of science, mathematics, Yoruba language and English language (Fasokun, 2000, p. 5).
- Pass rates among the experimental group were higher than those of the "control" group. In fact, all students in the experimental group passed the end-of-primary school First School Leaving Certificate Examination in 1975, while a number of students in the control classes failed (Aaron, 2018, p. 155).
- The programme showed post-secondary results as well: of the intake of students in the later experimental schools in 1973, more than one third were found by 1987 to have finished university studies – a higher than average proportion (Fasokun, 2000, p. 5).

Analysis

The strong performance of both the three-year control group and the six-year, L1-medium experimental group was supported by several programme features. In addition to those mentioned above, these included:

- extensive training of Yoruba-speaking teachers on how to make their teaching more child-friendly
- in-service teacher workshops to introduce new pedagogical materials (ibid., p. 68), and
- Yoruba-language textbooks and teachers' guides that were developed by the University of Ife and other Nigerian universities, as well as the Institute of Education (ibid., pp. 9–29).[4]

In addition, the 25 Yoruba titles were developed a year in advance of their use in Grade 1, giving teachers time to be trained to use them. This array of programme features demonstrates the value of supporting L1-medium instruction with other education best practices. However, even though both groups of students benefitted from these positive practices, the studies clearly show that the six years of Yoruba as language of instruction made the critical difference between the two groups.

Burkina Faso: *Écoles Bilingues*

The *Écoles Bilingues* programme was one of several formal and non-formal education initiatives begun in Burkina Faso in the 1990s and 2000s, featuring the use of local languages (Trudell, 2012). The *Écoles Bilingues* programme took children through an accelerated five-year bilingual programme, transitioning the learners to the use of French as the sole language of instruction by Grade 6 (see Table 2.5). Longitudinal results were dramatically positive, based on examination scores as well as dropout and pass rates (Ilboudo, 2010, p. 20). The programme included 12 recognized national languages[5] and French; the relative percentage of class instructional time in the national language and in French began with 90% national language/10% French, and was modified each year to reach 10% mother tongue/90% French by Grade 5 (ibid., pp. 70–77). Because the extensive use of their L1 allowed children in the experimental programme to learn relatively quickly, they were able to progress through the national curriculum faster than those in traditional French-medium schools. As a result, the curriculum was accelerated in the experimental schools, to cover six years of national curriculum topics in five years (ibid., p. 69).

The most powerful impact of this late-exit transition programme was seen in exam results and pass rates. The first cohort of *Écoles Bilingues* students took the standard, French-language end of primary school examination in 1998. After their five years of instruction in the experimental schools, these students performed better than their counterparts who had had six to seven years of

Table 2.5 Research findings on Burkina Faso programme

Years of L1-medium instruction	5
L1 used as language of instruction across the curriculum	yes
Teacher training 1+ year of formal training or 3+ weeks of in-service training over a school year	yes
Textbooks in L1 for all subjects, plus textbooks for acquiring L2	yes
L1 reading taught for 4+ years	yes
Oral L2 skills development for all subjects	yes
L1 is used for examinations	no

instruction in French. In 2002, 85.2% of the *Écoles Bilingues* students successfully passed the end of primary school examination, compared to a national average of 61.8% (Brock-Utne & Alidou, 2011, p. 198). Ilboudo (2010, p. 111) notes that

> In total, 1,960 students from bilingual schools took the CEP exam over the period concerned, with an average pass rate of 78.16%. The average pass rate at national level over the same period was 65.69%. Aside from test scores, other areas of programme impact included lower dropout rates, increased pass rates, the development of preschool programmes attached to the programme schools, and increased enrolment and literacy rates for females in particular.

Analysis

Despite the programme's success, Ilboudo mentions several issues which hindered its effectiveness, including the facts that examinations are only given in French and that teachers are rarely monitored (ibid., pp. 131–132). The extensive linguistic and pedagogical challenges involved in translating textbooks into the languages of the children (ibid., p. 133) are also noted by Ilboudo, who called them "national languages". Nevertheless, the results of this programme are impressive. Particularly significant are the findings that the children in this programme were able to move faster through the curriculum than their counterparts in the traditional French-medium schools, and to do well on the French-language examinations as well (ibid., p. 134).

Ineffective programmes: little likelihood of the learners' successful transitioning to secondary school

Review of the research also identified five ineffective Africa-language-medium programmes, for which there is evidence that they did not produce students who were able to successfully transition to secondary school: the Kom Education Pilot Project in Cameroon, the Yoruba-language early-exit programme in Nigeria, the four-year L1-medium programme in Ethiopia, the four-year Chichewa-medium programme in Malawi and programmes following the three-year L1-medium policy in Kenya.

Cameroon: Kom Education Pilot Project

The Kom Education Pilot Project was initiated in 2007 (Laitin et al., 2019, p. 240). Students in 12 schools in the rural Kom-speaking area of Cameroon were taught using the Kom language as the language of instruction for the first three years of primary school (ibid., p. 240), with oral English taught as a subject in Grades 1 and 2 and English-language literacy learning begun in Grade 3 (Trammell, 2008, p. 4). After Grades 1, 3 and 5, researchers evaluated these students and a matched control group of students in 12 schools that used only English as the language of instruction. Each time, both groups were given tests for English and mathematics proficiency, with the mathematics evaluation administered in English (Laitin et al., 2019, p. 240).

In the tests conducted after Grades 1 and 3 of the Kom programme, students strongly outperformed their counterparts in the English-medium schools. In Grade 3, Kom students averaged 45% and control students 22% on independent assessments of English and mathematics. By Grade 5, however, the English and mathematics exam performance of the Kom-medium programme graduates had dropped, averaging 28% with control students at 24% (Laitin et al., 2019, p. 240).

Analysis

The low Grade 5 outcomes from the Kom project are in some ways surprising, given the positive practices used in the first 3 years of schooling, shown in Table 2.6. These practices included:

- support for the use of Kom across the curriculum, with the provision of Kom-language materials for science, civics and mathematics (Trammell, 2008, p. 9)

Table 2.6 Research findings on Cameroon Kom programme

Years of L1-medium instruction	*3*
L1 used as language of instruction across the curriculum	yes
Teacher training 1+ year of formal training or 3+ weeks of in-service training over a school year	yes
Textbooks in L1 for all subjects, plus textbooks for acquiring L2	yes
L1 reading taught for 4+ years	no
Oral L2 skills development for all subjects	yes
L1 is used for examinations	no

- teacher training before and during the programme, with coaching visits as well (ibid., pp. 17–19)
- instruction in English as a subject that progressed from oral skills to literacy skills (ibid., p. 17).

Given these positive practices in the Kom project, the fact that students showed little advantage over English-medium students by Grade 5 could be related to the inherent limitations of the early-exit transition model. The programme indicates that three years of L1-medium instruction is not enough time to gain literacy and academic skills, learn sufficient L2 reading and vocabulary, and transfer academic skills into the L2.

Nigeria: Yoruba-language early-exit "control" groups

As noted above, the Yoruba experimental programme of 1970–1976 included both experimental and "control" groups which received much the same programme support. As shown in Table 2.7, the "control" group's schools followed the three-year model for MLE, with Yoruba language-medium instruction for three years followed by a transition to English-medium instruction in Grade 4 (Aaron, 2018, p. 155; Fafunwa, 1989, p. 20). As noted above, the learning materials and teacher training were nearly identical to those of the late-exit experimental group.

The researchers created subject tests specifically for the project, which in Grades 4–6 were administered in Yoruba for the experimental students and in English for the control students (Fafunwa, 1989, pp. 109–112). In these exams, the children in the late-exit experimental group scored significantly higher, even in English (ibid., pp. 117–125). The researchers also gathered information from the primary school leaving certificate exams and common entrance exams for secondary school (ibid., p. 102), as well as the experimental and control students' performance in secondary school (ibid., p. 131).

While Fasokun provided little comparative data regarding those exams, he did explain that the dropout rate in the six-year group was 10%, compared to a higher

Table 2.7 Research findings on Nigeria Ife: three-year programme

Years of L1-medium instruction	*3*
L1 used as language of instruction across the curriculum	yes
Teacher training 1+ year of formal training or 3+ weeks of in-service training over a school year	yes
Textbooks in L1 for all subjects, plus textbooks for acquiring L2	yes
L1 reading taught for 4+ years	no
Oral L2 skills development for all subjects	yes
L1 is used for examinations	yes

dropout rate of 30% among the three-year students. However, both of these rates were lower than the national average of 40–60%, showing that the three-year students benefitted somewhat from the programme, but at a much lower level than the six-year students (Fasokun, 2000, p. 5).

Analysis

Both the "control" and the experimental groups of students were provided with well-supported L1-medium instruction. However, a sizable number of students in the three-year L1-medium group failed the First School Leaving Certificate, while all of the students in the six-year L1-medium group passed, indicating that – at least in this case – the effectiveness of the programme was strongly linked to the number of years in which the learner receives instruction in the L1.

Ethiopia: four-year L1-medium programmes

Research indicates that the regions of Ethiopia that offer four years of L1-medium instruction achieve less effective student transition to secondary school than those regions offering eight years, regardless of how the programmes are implemented. The Southern Nations, Nationalities and Peoples' Region (SNNPR) offered L1-medium instruction in the first six years of school, for languages that qualified[6] until 2004 when its policy changed to offering L1-medium instruction only in the first four years of school (Heugh et al., 2010, p. 298). In the Gambella Region, four years of L1-medium instruction were offered over that same period. In 2008, students in SNNPR averaged 36% on their Grade 8 national assessment exams in the subjects of English, mathematics, biology, chemistry and physics, while students in Gambella averaged 31% (ibid., p. 298). Both of these scores were lower than those of regions with eight years of L1-medium instruction (ibid., p. 249); by the researchers' assessment, the scores were also too low to predict successful entry into secondary school (Heugh et al., 2010, p. 295).

Table 2.8 Research findings on Ethiopia four-year programme

Years of L1-medium instruction	*4*
L1 used as language of instruction across the curriculum	yes
Teacher training 1+ year of formal training or 3+ weeks of in-service training over a school year	yes
Textbooks in L1 for all subjects, plus textbooks for acquiring L2	yes
L1 reading taught for 4+ years	yes
Oral L2 skills development for all subjects	no
L1 is used for examinations	no

Analysis

The regional approaches taken by the SNNPR and Gambella to MLE programming differ in some important ways. The SNNPR has provided support for the development of many languages, with high parent and community participation. In Gambella region, on the other hand, fewer of its languages have been developed for use in schools (Heugh et al., 2012, p. 255); this means that more children are learning in a language other than their home language. Additionally, the SNNPR curriculum includes teaching the L1 as a subject until the end of primary school, while all L1 support in Gambella ends after year four (ibid., p. 250). Nevertheless, neither of these four-year, L1-medium programmes prepares students adequately to score high enough on the end-of-primary school exams that will allow them to enter secondary school (Heugh et al., 2010, p. 295; Benson et al., 2010, p. 47).

Malawi: four-year Chichewa-medium programme

Both Malawi and Zambia are home to significant numbers of speakers of the Chichewa or Chinyanja language, spoken in Malawi and Zambia respectively (Trudell, 2016, p. 44). Research by Williams (1998) used the linguistic similarity between Chichewa and Chinyanja to evaluate the impact of different instructional practices in the two countries. During the period of the study, Malawi's language policy mandated Chichewa as the language of instruction for the first 4 years of primary school, with English taught as a subject. In Zambia, the policy directed that English should be the language of instruction throughout primary school, with local languages taught as subjects. In 1992 and 1994, Williams administered reading tests in English and Chichewa/Chinyanja to students in Grades 3–6 in both countries; the results are summarized in Table 2.10.

Table 2.10 shows that L1 reading scores in Malawi were much higher than those in Zambia, as would be expected given the different curricular choices of the two countries. However, in both countries, only 48% and 47% (in Malawi and Zambia, respectively) of the tested students in Grade 6 were able to read in English. This study thus indicates that neither the four-year Malawian primary

Table 2.9 Research findings on Malawi Chichewa programme

Years of L1-medium instruction	4
L1 used as language of instruction across the curriculum	yes
Teacher training 1+ year of formal training or 3+ weeks of in-service training over a school year	no
Textbooks in L1 for all subjects, plus textbooks for acquiring L2	no
L1 reading taught for 4+ years	yes
Oral L2 skills development for all subjects	no
L1 is used for examinations	Yes

Table 2.10 Average reading scores, Malawi and Zambia, 1992 and 1994

Average scores	*Malawi*	*Zambia*
1992 English reading, Grade 6	48%	47%
1992 Local language reading, Grade 6	77%	37%
1994 English reading, Grade 5	43%	40%
1994 local language reading, Grade 5	67%	13%

Source: Williams (1998), pp. 19, 23, 27, 30.

school programme nor the full L2-medium primary school programme in Zambia resulted in strong English reading skills. Williams notes that the English reading skills of most of the students in both countries were inadequate for its use in learning other subjects (ibid., p. 58), leading to likely failure to transition well to the English-medium secondary school.

Analysis

The reading skills gained by Malawian students during four years of L1-medium instruction led Williams to conclude that if resources are scarce, students are more likely to gain literacy skills through a known language than an unknown one (ibid., p. 62). The Zambian children, taught in L2-medium throughout primary school, did not show significant reading skills in any language. However, despite the literacy skills acquired by Malawian students in the L1, the data indicate that four years of L1-medium instruction in Malawi were still not enough time to reach the level of English proficiency required for successful transition to English-medium secondary school.

Kenya: programmes following the three-year L1-medium policy in Kenya

The national language policy of Kenya directs that children be taught in the "language of the catchment area" for the first 3 years of school (Trudell, 2016, p. 36; Trudell & Piper, 2014). No particular languages are named in this policy. This policy directive is well founded: research demonstrates that many primary-grade Kenyan students struggle to learn through the medium of English. In one study, 72% of students were unable to read the English-language textbooks provided to them (Glewwe et al., 2009, pp. 23–24). Additionally, Piper et al. (2016a, p. 143) report that in tests of reading comprehension, rural Grade 3 students scored up to 800% higher when tested in their L1s than when tested in English. This evidence notwithstanding, the common practice in Kenyan primary schools is to use English as the language of instruction from Grade 1 (Trudell, 2016, p. 36). Teaching and learning materials in the L1 are not provided to teachers (Wangia et al., 2014, p. 17; Piper et al., 2018b, p. 117), nor are teachers trained to teach the L1 as a subject or use it as the language of instruction (Commeyras & Inyega, 2007, p. 265).

Table 2.11 Research findings on Kenya programmes

Years of L1-medium instruction	*0*
L1 used as language of instruction across the curriculum	no
Teacher training 1+ year of formal training or 3+ weeks of in-service training over a school year	no
Textbooks in L1 for all subjects, plus textbooks for acquiring L2	no
L1 reading taught for 4+ years	no
Oral L2 skills development for all subjects	no
L1 is used for examinations	no

Recently, comparative data on L1-medium learning was gathered as part of the *Primary Math and Reading* (PRIMR) initiative (Piper et al., 2016b, pp. 776–783). This intervention was designed primarily to improve children's oral reading fluency and comprehension in English and Kiswahili in the first 2 years of primary school. However, one L1 element was also incorporated into the programme. From 2013 to 2014, all schools in the PRIMR group received teacher training, coaching and printed materials, to support reading instruction in English and Kiswahili. A smaller intervention, called *PRIMR-MT*, was carried out among learners in Kikamba- and Lubukusu-speaking areas (ibid., p. 783). This latter group also received L1 reading textbooks, and teachers received two days of training in how to teach reading in the L1.

After a year of instruction, PRIMR-MT students performed significantly better than the PRIMR students on assessments of L1 oral reading fluency and reading comprehension (ibid., p. 796). The researchers hypothesized that this was because PRIMR-MT students received explicit instruction and exposure to relevant vocabulary, which students in the PRIMR programme did not receive (ibid., p. 798). The researchers also evaluated whether L1-medium reading instruction showed benefits for the learning of other subjects (Piper et al., 2018b, p. 110). In tests of Grades 1 and 2 students, no significant differences were found between the PRIMR and PRIMR-MT groups in English and Kiswahili literacy, although the Grade 1 Kiswahili listening comprehension scores of the PRIMR-MT group were significantly lower. In mathematics, the L1-reading group scored lower on two out of six subtests, while other differences were not significant (ibid., p. 115).

Analysis

These findings are consistent with those already mentioned: brief and limited use of children's L1 as language of instruction does not increase proficiency in their L2. The extreme brevity of the L1-medium instruction component in the PRIMR-MT programme actually made the failure of the programme very predictable; the L1 was little used in subjects other than literacy (Piper et al., 2018b, pp. 116–117), and students were tested after only one year of the intervention.

Such limited L1 use is the norm in Kenyan primary classrooms. Its use is actively discouraged (Wangia et al., 2014, pp. 13–18; Mutiga, 2014, p. 221); teachers are neither encouraged nor trained to teach the L1 as a subject, nor to use it as the language of instruction (Commeyras & Inyega, 2007, p. 265). With such minimal instructional time in the L1, poor results for L1-medium learning are to be expected.

Discussion

Research on these nine MLE programmes has provided a range of useful information on what makes for effective MTB MLE programming in Africa, in terms of preparing students for successful transition to L2-medium secondary school learning. (See Appendix 2.1 for a tabular comparison of all seven features in all nine programmes.) Of the four programmes determined to be effective, the most prominent common feature is the practice of L1-medium instruction for at least six years, with eight years being more effective in Ethiopia. The five programmes which proved ineffective had many of the same features as the effective programmes; however, in the effective programmes, students were given more time to consolidate their learning and transfer knowledge gained in the L1 to L2 learning contexts. Other common features of the four effective programmes include the presence of L1-medium student textbooks for all subjects, as well as pedagogical materials for L2 acquisition. Teacher training was also an important component of the effective programmes; they were also likely to employ explicit strategies for L2 acquisition.

The five ineffective programmes studied indicate that limiting L1-medium instruction to the first 3–4 years of primary school results in unsuccessful student transition to secondary school. In that amount of time, students in the five programmes were unable to adequately transfer their L1 knowledge and reading skills to the L2. The transfer of literacy skills requires children to have strong L1 literacy skills, as well as an adequate mastery of the L2 (Baker, 2006, p. 154). The five programmes demonstrate that three years is not enough time for students to gain strong L1 reading skills, nor to build adequate proficiency in the L2; this makes the needed transfer of their L1-medium skills to the L2-medium secondary school environment very unlikely. The short timeframe allowed for L1-medium instruction in the ineffective programmes also implies a relatively weak institutional commitment to the use of African languages in the education system. The investment required for implementing L1-medium learning with teacher training, materials development and other supports of learning was notably absent in these cases.

Further research

The findings of this study raise many questions that merit further study, including the following:

Pedagogical questions

- What indicators can be developed to assess learners' readiness for transition to secondary school, where an L2 will be the language of instruction? As one example, more follow-up studies should be done to identify the frequency and density of all English vocabulary used in Grade 9 subject textbooks in a given country (see Walter, 2005).
- What pedagogical approaches are being used in the L1–L2 transition reading strategies of current primary-grade programmes, and what are the results in terms of students' ability to read and understand L2-medium subject textbooks and their domain-specific vocabulary?
- To what extent could learning be enhanced by using diglot textbooks that teach specialized vocabulary in the L2 along with subject content in the L1?
- Which reading methods are most effective in African-language learning contexts, and are they the same for both the L1 and the L2?

Linguistic questions

- What could be done to help L2 readers adjust to significant orthographic differences between the L1 and the L2 as they begin to read L2 subject textbooks?
- What are the effects of corpus planning in the L1 on student performance in L2 content subjects in secondary school? Does enhanced subject vocabulary in the L1 lead to better learning in the L2-medium secondary school?

Programmatic questions

- What are the best ways for teachers to help students learn from the L2 textbooks being used at the beginning of L2-medium instruction?
- How would an L1 maintenance model (featuring equal use of the L1 and an L2 as languages of instruction by the end of primary school) compare in results to a late-exit transition model (featuring the exclusive use of L2-medium instruction by the end of primary school)?

Policy questions

- What factors are influencing the common national government policy choice of early-exit MLE after three years of L1-medium instruction?
- Given the prevalence of pro-local language of instruction policy in Africa, why is its implementation so rare?

Conclusion

This study of the research on MTB MLE programming in Africa yields some important findings, despite the difficult assessment context of the research we have reported on. As noted above, the difficulty in producing and finding accurate assessment of learning outcomes in research on MTB MLE programming in Africa is related to factors such as the ideological discourses surrounding MTB MLE research and pilot programmes, and a lack of rigorous assessment of learning outcomes at key points in the programme. These factors help to explain the relatively small number of MTB MLE programmes that could be identified in this study as effective or ineffective with any measure of clarity. Nevertheless, African parents and students do aspire to a successful schooling experience, not only in primary school but also beyond. Enabling such aspirations means that MTB MLE programme designers, implementers and advocates must understand which programme features facilitate strong learning outcomes, and which do not. Clear determination of programme effectiveness is crucial if children in African communities are to move beyond primary school and succeed academically in post-primary education.

Notes

1 This search and assessment process focused only on research studies of programs in which both L1 and L2 are written in Latin script. This choice was made because script transition processes have a number of features unique to the linguistic context, and are not readily comparable to transition processes between languages that use the same script.

2 Chimbutane and Benson (2012) describe a range of significant, non-academic benefits of using home languages as languages of instruction in Mozambican MLE programming, including enhanced parental involvement in their children's school experience and a greater acknowledgement of the value of Mozambican cultures and languages.

3 Some regional variation was noted, however; Gambella region was unable to participate in the study, so no comparison could be made for a 4-year program that year (Heugh et al., 2010, 296).

4 For the first three years, both experimental and control groups used these Yoruba-language textbooks, with the experimental group continuing on through Grade 6.

5 The term *langue nationale*, as used in francophone Africa, refers to local African languages.

6 Writing systems for some languages in SNNPR were still being developed at this time, and others were being developed to teach as subjects (Benson et al., 2012, p. 42).

References

Aaron, MJ 2018, 'The Feasibility of Sustainable Obolo Bilingual Education in Nigeria', PhD Thesis, University of Reading. http://centaur.reading.ac.uk/82043/2/21803694_Aaron_thesis_redacted.pdf.

Alidou, H & Brock-Utne, B 2011, 'Teaching Practices – Teaching in a Familiar Language', in A Ouane & C Glanz (eds), *Optimising Learning, Education and Publishing in Africa: The Language Factor*, Association for the Development of Education in Africa, UNESCO Institute for Lifelong Learning, Tunisia, Germany, pp. 159–186.

Baker, C 2006, *Foundations of Bilingual Education and Bilingualism*, Multilingual Matters Ltd, Buffalo.

Bender, P 2002, *Language of Instruction Seminar Series: Notes from the Presentation on Mali*, World Bank, Washington, DC.

Benson, C 2013, 'Towards Adopting a Multilingual Habitus in Educational Development', in C Benson & K Kosonen (eds), *Language Issues in Comparative Education*, Springer, Amsterdam, pp. 283–299.

Benson, C, Heugh, K, Mekonnen, Y & Bogale, B 2010, 'Ethiopia: A Study and Its Implications for Multilingual Education', in K Heugh & T Skutnabb-Kangas (eds), *Multilingual Education Works: From the Periphery to the Centre*, Orient BlackSwan, New Delhi, pp. 30–83.

Benson, C, Heugh, K, Bogale, B & Mekonnen, Y 2012, 'Multilingual Education in Ethiopian Primary Schools', in K Heugh & T Skutnabb-Kangas (eds), *Multilingual Education and Sustainable Diversity Work: From Periphery to Center*, Taylor and Francis, New York, pp. 33–61.

Brock-Utne, B & Alidou, H 2011, 'Active Students – Learning through a Language They Master', in A Ouane & C Glanz (eds), *Optimising Learning, Education, and Publishing in Africa: The Language Factor*, Association for the Development of Education in Africa, UNESCO Institute for Lifelong Learning, Hamburg, pp. 187–216.

Bühmann, D & Trudell, B 2008, *Mother Tongue Matters: Local Language as a Key to Effective Learning*, UNESCO, Paris. https://afrikaansetaalraad.co.za/wp-content/uploads/2017/09/Mother-tongue-matters_Local-language-as-a-key-to-effective-learning-2008.pdf.

Chilora, HG 2000, "Language Policy, Research and Practice in Malawi." Paper presented at the Comparative and International Education Society 2000 Conference. San Antonio, TX. https://pdf.usaid.gov/pdf_docs/pnack274.pdf.

Chimbutane, F & Benson, C 2012, 'Expanded Spaces for Mozambican Languages in Primary Education: Where Bottom-up Meets Top-down', *International Multilingual Research Journal*, vol. 6, pp. 8–21. DOI: 10.1080/19313152.2012.639278.

Commeyras, M & Inyega, HN 2007, 'An Integrative Review of Teaching Reading in Kenyan Primary Schools', *Reading Research Quarterly*, vol. 42, pp. 258–281. DOI: https://doi.org/10.1598/RRQ.42.2.3.

de Hoop, J 2010, *Selective Secondary Education and School Participation in Sub-Saharan Africa: Evidence from Malawi*, Tinbergen Institute and VU University, Amsterdam. DOI: https://dx.doi.org/10.2139/ssrn.1590126.

Fafunwa, AB, Macauley, JI & Funnso Sokoya, JA 1989, *Education in Mother Tongue: The Ife Primary Education Research Project (1970-1978)*, University Press Limited, Ibadan, https://eric.ed.gov/?id=ED350120.

Fasokun, TO 2000, *Aliu Babatunde Fafunwa*, UNESCO: International Bureau of Education, Paris. www.ibe.unesco.org/sites/default/files/fafunwae.pdf

Glewwe, P, Kremer, M & Moulin, S 2009, 'Many Children Left Behind? Textbooks and Test Scores in Kenya', *NBER Working Paper Series 13300*, National Bureau of Economic Research, Cambridge, MA. www.nber.org/papers/w13300.

Heugh, K 2011, 'Theory and Practice – Language Education Models in Africa: Research, Design, Decision-Making, and Outcomes', in A Ouane & C Glanz (eds), *Optimising Learning, Education and Publishing in Africa: The Language Factor*, Association for the Development of Education in Africa, UNESCO Institute for Lifelong Learning, Hamburg, pp. 105–155.

Heugh, K, Benson, C, Yohannes, MAG & Bogale, B 2010, 'Multilingual Education in Ethiopia: What Assessment Shows About What Works and What Does't', in K Heugh & T Skutnabb-Kangas (eds), *Multilingual Education Works: From the Periphery to the Centre*, Orient Black Swan, New Delhi, pp. 287–315.

——— 2012, 'Implications for Multilingual Education: Student Achievement in Different Models of Education in Ethiopia', in K Heugh & T Skutnabb-Kangas (eds), *Multilingual Education and Sustainable Diversity Work: From Periphery to Center*, Orient Black Swan, New Delhi, pp. 239–262.

Ilboudo, PT 2010, *Bilingual Education in Burkina Faso: An Alternative Approach for Quality Basic Education. African Experiences – National Case Studies*. Association for the Development of Education in Africa, Tunisia.

Kim, GY, Boyle, HN, Zuilkowski, SS & Nakamura, P 2016, *Landscape Report on Early Grade Literacy*, USAID, Washington, DC, www.air.org/resource/landscape-report-early-grade-literacy.

Kim, GY, Lee, H & Zuilkowski, SS 2019, 'Impact of Literacy Interventions on Reading Skills in Low- and Middle-Income Countries: A Meta-Analysis', *Child Development*, vol. 91(2) pp. 1–23. DOI: https://doi.org/10.1111/cdev.13204.

Kioko, A, Ndung'u, RW, Njoroge, MC & Mutiga, J 2014, 'Mother Tongue and Education in Africa: Publicising the Reality', *Multilingual Education*, vol. 4 (18), pp. 1–11 www.multilingual-education.com/content/4/1/18.

Krashen, S 2002, 'Developing Academic Language: Early L1 reading and Later L2 reading', *International Journal of the Sociology of Language*, vol. 155/156, pp. 143–151.

Laitin, DD, Ramachandran, R & Walter, SL 2019, 'The Legacy of Colonial Language Policies and Their Impact on Student Learning: Evidence from an Experimental Program in Cameroon', *Economic Development and Cultural Change*, vol. 68, pp. 239–272. DOI: https://doi.org/10.1086/700617.

Mkandawire, SB 2018, 'Literacy Versus Language: Exploring Their Similarities and Differences', *Journal of Lexicography and Terminology*, vol. 2(1) pp. 37–55.

Mutiga, J 2014, 'Value Addition and Attitude Change in Language Revitalization: The Case of Kitharaka', in D Orwenjo, M Njoroge, R Ndung'u & P Mwangi (eds), *Multilingualism and Education in Africa: The State of the State of the Art*, Cambridge Scholars Publishing, Cambridge, pp. 204–225.

Ouane, A & Glanz, C (eds) 2011, *Optimising Learning, Education and Publishing in Africa – the Language Factor*, Association for the Development of Education in Africa, UNESCO Institute for Lifelong Learning, Hamburg.

Piper, B & Kim, GY 2018, 'Cross-Language Transfer of Reading Skills: An Empirical Investigation of Bidirectionality and the Influence of Instructional Environments', *Reading and Writing*, vol. 32, pp. 839–871. DOI: https://doi.org/10.1007/s11145-018-9889-7.

Piper, B, Schroeder, L & Trudell, B 2016a, 'Oral Reading Fluency and Comprehension in Kenya: Reading Acquisition in a Multilingual Environment', *Journal of Research in Reading*, vol. 39, pp. 133–152. DOI: https://doi.org/10.1111/1467-9817.12052.

Piper, B, Zuilkowski, SS & Ong'ele, S 2016b, 'Implementing Mother Tongue Instruction in the Real World: Results from a Medium-Scale Randomized Controlled Trial in Kenya', *Comparative Education Review*, vol. 60, pp. 776–807.

Piper, B, Simmons Zuilkowski, S, Dubeck, M, Jepkemei, E, & King, SJ 2018a, 'Identifying the Essential Ingredients to Literacy and Numeracy Improvement: Teacher Professional

Development and Coaching, Student Textbooks, and Structured Teachers' Guides', *World Development*, vol. 106, pp. 324–336. DOI: https://doi.org/10.1016/j.worlddev.2018.01.018

Piper, B, Zuilkowski, SS, Kwayumba, D & Oyanga, A 2018b, 'Examining the Secondary Effects of Mother-Tongue Literacy Instruction in Kenya: Impacts on Student Learning in English, Kiswahili, and Mathematics', *International Journal of Educational Development*, vol. 59, pp. 110–27. DOI: https://doi.org/10.1016/j.ijedudev.2017.10.002.

Sampa, F 2005, *Zambia's Primary Reading Programme (PRP): Improving Access and Quality Education in Basic Schools.* (African Experiences – Country Case Studies 4), ADEA, Paris, http://clearinghouse.adeanet.org/en/zambias-primary-reading-program-prp-improving-access-and-quality-basic-schools

Skutnabb-Kangas, T & Dunbar, R 2010, 'Indigenous Children's Education as Linguistic Genocide and a Crime against Humanity? A global view', *Journal of Indigenous Peoples' Rights*, vol. 1, pp. 1–128 www.e-pages.dk/grusweb/55/.

Smith, C, Stone, R & Comings, J 2012, *Literacy Policy and Practice in Ethiopia: Building on the TELL Program and EGRA Results, Field Study Report*, Center for International Education, Amherst, MA, www.air.org/sites/default/files/downloads/report/TELL_Field_Study_-_Literacy_Policy_and_Practice_in_Ethiopia_0.pdf.

Spaull, N 2015, 'Schooling in South Africa: How Low-Quality Education Becomes a Poverty Trap', in A De Lannoy, S Swartz, L Lake & C Smith (eds), *South African Child Gauge*, Children's Institute, Cape Town, pp. 34–41, www.ci.uct.ac.za/ci/child-gauge/2015.

Taylor, S & von Fintel, M 2016, 'Estimating the Impact of Language of Instruction in South African Primary Schools: A Fixed Effects Approach', *Economics of Education Review*, vol. 50, pp. 75–89. DOI: https://doi.org/10.1016/j.econedurev.2016.01.003.

Trammell, K 2008, 'Mother-Tongue/Multilingual Education Kom Education Pilot Project', Unpublished Programme Report, SIL, Cameroon.

Trudell, B 2012, 'Of gateways and Gatekeepers: Language, Education and Mobility in Francophone Africa', *International Journal of Educational Development*, vol. 32, pp. 368–375.

Trudell, B 2016, *The Impact of Language Policy and Practice on Children's Learning: Evidence from Eastern and Southern Africa*, UNICEF, New York, www.unicef.org/esaro/UNICEF(2016)LanguageandLearning-FullReport(SingleView).pdf.

Trudell, B 2018, *Language and Education in Nigeria: A Review of Policy and Practice*, British Council and UNICEF, Abuja, www.britishcouncil.org.ng/sites/default/files/language_and_education_nigeria.pdf.

Trudell, B & Piper, B 2014, 'Whatever the Law Says: Language Policy Implementation and Early-Grade Literacy Achievement in Kenya', *Current Issues in Language Planning*, vol. 15, pp. 4–21.

UNESCO 2016, *If You Don't Understand, How Can You Learn?* Global Education Monitoring Report, Policy Paper 24, UNESCO, Paris, https://en.unesco.org/gem-report/if-you-don%E2%80%99t-understand-how-can-you-learn.

Walter, SL 2013, 'Exploring the Development of Reading in Multilingual Education Programs', *Language Issues in Comparative Education*, vol. 1, pp. 265–281.

Wagner, DA 2017, 'Children's Reading in Low-Income Countries', *Reading Teacher*, vol. 71, pp. 127–33. DOI: https://doi.org/10.1002/trtr.1621.

Walter, K 2005, 'The Eritrean English Curriculum: Assessing Academic Readiness', Unpublished MA thesis, The University of Texas at Arlington, Arlington, TX.

Wangia, JI, Furaha, M & Kikech, B 2014, 'The Language of Instruction Versus Learning in Lower Primary Schools in Kenya', in D Orwenjo, M Njoroge, R Ndung'u & P Mwangi (eds), *Multilingualism and Education in Africa: The State of the State of the Art*, Cambridge Scholars Publishing, Cambridge, pp. 8–23.

Williams, E 1998, *Investigating Bilingual Literacy: Evidence from Malawi and Zambia. Education Research Paper*, Education Research 24. Department for International Development (DFID), London, https://eric.ed.gov/?id=ED419222.

Appendix

APPENDIX 2.1 MLE PROGRAM FEATURES LINKED TO EFFECTIVE LEARNING OUTCOMES

Presence or absence of features that increase likelihood of successful student transition to secondary school for each MTB-MLE program studied.

	Ethiopia 6+ year	*Mali Bambara*	*Nigeria Ife: 6 year*	*Burkina Faso*	*Cameroon Kom*	*Nigeria Ife: 3 year*	*Ethiopia 4 year*	*Malawi*	*Kenya*
Years of L1-medium instruction	6–8	6	6	5	3	3	4	4	0
L1 used as medium of instruction across the curriculum	**yes**	**yes**	**yes**	**yes**	**yes**	**yes**	**yes**	**yes**	no
Teacher training 1+ year of formal training or 3+ weeks of in-service training over a school year	**yes**	**yes**	**yes**	**yes**	**yes**	**yes**	**yes**	no	no
Textbooks in L1 for all subjects, plus textbooks for acquiring L2	**yes**	**yes**	**yes**	**yes**	**yes**	**yes**	**yes**	no	no
L1 reading taught for 4+ years	**yes**	**yes**	**yes**	**yes**	no	no	**yes**	**yes**	no
Oral L2 skills development for all subjects	no	**yes**	**yes**	**yes**	**yes**	**yes**	no	no	no
L1 is used for examinations	no	no	**yes**	no	no	**yes**	no	**yes**	no

APPENDIX 2.2 ADDITIONAL NOTES ON SCORES IN APPENDIX 2.1

Notes on the effective programmes

Ethiopia six-year-plus programmes

Years of L1-medium instruction. Heugh et al. (2010, p. 292) concluded, "Overall, across the systemic assessments, students who have eight years of MTM (mother tongue medium) and who are assessed in their MT outperform students who switch to English medium earlier." The assessments were conducted in 2000, 2004 and 2008.

Teacher training. Teachers needed more training time (Smith et al., 2012, p. 21) than they were given, lacked subject matter knowledge, familiarity with reading pedagogy, and skills in using the English language (Smith et al., 2012, pp. 20–24, 43).

L1 textbooks for all subjects. Despite the development of L1 textbooks, researchers recommended distribution of a larger quantity of textbooks and teachers' guides, development of clear, measurable skill-based curricular outcomes (Smith et al., 2012, pp. 4–5).

L1 as LoI across curriculum. Across Ethiopia's regions with late-exit policy, there is an exception in the Harari region, where math and science were taught starting with Grade 7 (Heugh, 2010, p. 296).

Oral L2 skills development. This was a weak area for teachers and had poor outcomes for many students (Smith et al., 2012, pp. 20–41). Smith et al. point out the phonological gaps between Ethiopian languages and English and between Ethiopian Roman orthographies and that of English (ibid., pp. 12–13).

Mali** Pedagogie Convergente **programme

Years of L1-medium instruction. Though L1 instruction was given for six years, more time was given to French each year after Grade 1. Oral French began to be taught as a subject in Grade 2. Math and French reading began to be taught via L2 in Grade 3. French reading began in Grade 3, getting 50% of reading lesson time (Haidara, personal communication, 15 May 2019).

L1 as LoI across curriculum. Eleven subjects taught via the L1, with the exception of math beginning in Grade 3 and science in Grade 5 (Haidara, personal communication, 15 May 2019).

Nigeria six-year programme

L1 as language of instruction across the curriculum. Learners were given six continuous years of L1 learning, except for the subject English (Fafunwa, 1989, pp. 1, 189).

Teacher training. Yoruba-language teachers' guides were developed by the University of Ife and other Nigerian universities, as well as the Institute of Education (Fafunwa, 1989, pp. 19–20, 21–22, 29, 67–71; Aaron, 2018, p. 154).

Reading taught in L1 for 4+ years. Yoruba reading was taught first in all of the experimental programme groups, then for the late-exit programmes English reading was directly taught in Grades 5 and 6. English reading pedagogy was developed and used during those two years. It included using passages with comprehension and language exercises as well as pattern drills (Fafunwa, 1989, pp. 57–59; Aaron, 2018, p. 154).

Oral L2 skills development. Well-planned L2 vocabulary and conversational development, plus listening skills and student books as well as teachers' guides (Fafunwa, 1989, pp. 55–66).

Burkina Faso

L1 as language of instruction across the curriculum. This applies to the first 2 years, followed by three years of gradually reduced exposure to L1 learning. Textbooks were developed for the following content areas: history, math, science and geography as well as teachers' guides for all of these (Ilboudo, 2010, p. 116). Over 50 "high-level" specialists were involved in the development of the textbooks and other materials (Ilboudo, 2010, p. 118).

Teacher training. First- and second-year teachers were given six-week training courses (Ilboudo, 2010, pp. 86–87). A weakness of the early programmes (ibid., p. 114) was the serious lack of qualified teachers who spoke the languages of the students and who were experts in the assigned content areas, but pre-service training was developed and used (ibid., p. 122). Amount of training given is unknown, but Ilboudo (p. 128) identifies more than 1,000 teachers, 300 inspectors and 50 trainers trained for these programmes.

Reading taught in L1 for 4+ years. Mother tongue reading was taught for the first 4 years, with L2 reading introduced in year three (Ilboudo, 2010, p. 88).

L1 used for examinations. A hindrance to effectiveness when Ilboudo was gathering data was the exclusive use of French for all examinations (Ilboudo, 2010, p. 134). This has now changed.

Notes on some of the ineffective programmes

Ethiopia four-year programme

SNNPR and Gambella, the two regions implementing four years of mother tongue medium education, are linguistically diverse. Several languages in the region were in the midst of developing orthographies and educational resources at the time of the study. This meant that L1 instruction and textbooks were available for some students, but not for all.

Malawi

L1 used as language of instruction across the curriculum. The Malawian programme depicted in this column went beyond Chichewa literacy to its use as a language of instruction. More recent programmes have used the L1 only for reading, so they are not depicted (Sampa, 2005, p. 31).

L1 textbooks. These were intended for use in schools, but their distribution was inadequate so many students did not have them (Williams, 1998, p. 14; Chilora, 2000, p. 3).

Teacher training. It is estimated that more than 30% of the participating teachers did not receive teacher training or were completely unqualified for teaching (Chilora, 2000, p. 7).

L1 used for examinations. Examinations during the time of Williams' research were primarily given in English, with Chichewa regarded as a subject rather than a language of instruction: "The PSLCE tests students on 5 subjects: Chichewa, English, mathematics, science, and social studies" (de Hoop, 2010, p. 8).

3 Researching Kreol Seselwa and its role in education in the pursuit of educational equity in the Seychelles

Mats Deutschmann and Justin Zelime

Introduction

As the smallest and least populated country in Africa, Seychelles offers an accessible context for research into matters regarding language-in-education policies. Its small size allows depth of insight into the challenges faced by many nations in Sub-Saharan Africa (SSA). Although unique in many ways, the Seychelles shares several of the central language challenges common to the postcolonial conditions of the region. As most nations in the region, the Seychelles inherited a school system based on that of former colonial powers (Britain and France), and with this also a mindset which sees the colonial languages as the given carriers of knowledge. In spite of concerted efforts to raise the status and role of the first language[1] (hereafter L1), Kreol Seselwa (hereafter KS), in education after independence, English remains the primary language of instruction (hereafter LoI) from primary three onwards, and secondary education is largely steered by the curriculum dictated by the structures of the British International General Certificate of Secondary Education (IGCSE). Good knowledge of English is thus a primary deciding success factor for all students in the system, something which also affects educational equity in various ways.

The Seychelles stands out as regards educational in/equity in SSA. On the one hand, it scores very highly on literacy ratings with literacy rates over 90%, and truly has free education for all. Schools are relatively well funded. On the other hand, there is a lot of inequity in the system, e.g. the Seychelles had the largest within-school variation in reading achievements among the 14 investigated nations included under the Southern and Eastern Africa Consortium for Monitoring Educational Quality (SACMEQ). Here the factor of whether English is spoken at home or not (a clear class marker in the Seychelles) and gender differences are particularly striking, something which indicates "huge inequity between pupils" (Hungi & Thuku, 2010, p. 92). Arguably, this is a consequence of the language-in-education situation in the Seychelles.

Like many countries in SSA, the Seychelles has adopted an early-exit *transitional* bilingual (or partly trilingual) model of education, where all subjects except

DOI: 10.4324/9781003028383-4

English, French and Mathematics are taught in the L1 (KS) for the first two years of education. KS is then replaced completely, and quite abruptly, by English, resulting in a model which in practical terms is more or less monolingual. This sudden change of the language situation in the classroom has serious implications for the learner, and as Clegg and Simpson (2016) point out, learning is lost in the absence of carefully planned and supported transition (see also Heugh et al., 2007). Not only is there a risk that students have difficulties in understanding the teacher, but they may also experience difficulties in communicating their own knowledge and understanding in a language that they are not entirely familiar with. As Clegg (2005, p. 42) puts it: "if we assess children in a second language it may not tell us what they know". Current policies also affect the content of curricula. English as a LoI means that many of the learning materials used in school are produced elsewhere, and the "local context" is often overlooked. In addition, since the current system follows the IGCSE curriculum in the final grades, the local context is of secondary importance. Overall, current policies have negative implications for the status of the L1, and by extension local identity and self-esteem. While the above description could fit many SSA contexts, Seychelles is unique by its small size. Not only can problems be investigated systematically, but given the will, changes can also be implemented with relative ease. Informing such moves in the Seychelles is one of our ambitions.

This chapter addresses two major questions related to the above. Based on five studies carried out between 2015 and 2018, we examine the consequences of the current language policies for young learners in the Seychelles. Second, we address the question of why a nation where the vast majority of the school population have the same mother tongue (KS) should adhere to strict L2 LoI policies. In our final discussion, we will point to potential alternatives to the current policy.

The evidence put forward in this chapter comes mainly, but not exclusively, from five studies of various aspects of the Seychelles education system that we have conducted which examine:

1. current language-in-education policy documents (Zelime & Deutschmann, 2016)
2. students' attitudes towards the languages used in education (Deutschmann & Zelime, 2015)
3. teacher attitudes and practices regarding LoI (Zelime & Deutschmann, 2018)
4. how language of assessment affects student performance in the subject of Social Studies (Zelime, Deutschmann & Rijlaarsdam, 2018)
5. how choice of language affects students' ability to write about local contexts (Zelime & Deutschmann, 2019).

In addition, we provide an historical background on the Seychelles language situation, aiming to give an informed evaluation of how the current system affects the learning situation of young Seychellois. We relate our findings to Spolsky's Theory of Language Policy (2004, 2019), in order to explore the question of why the current system is the way it is. Finally, we propose productive pathways forward by suggesting potential adaptations of the current system which take the many different factors and interests that may affect such processes into account and by striking a balance between them.

Theoretical framework

Spolsky (2004) asserts that there are several coexisting, but often conflicting, factors that motivate a country's language-in-education policies. These are divided into three main domains in his framework: language practices, language beliefs and "any specific efforts to modify or influence that practice by any kind of language intervention, planning or management" (Spolsky, 2004, p. 5). He argues that the language policy of any independent nation state will reveal the complex interplay of these "interdependent but often conflicting factors" (2004, p. 133). Spolsky (2019, p. 326) maintains that this is a "complex and chaotic non-hierarchical system", which more traditional bottom-up/top-down models are unable to capture. Instead, each level within a system can have its own logic, and each domain can influence and be influenced by all the other domains. According to Shohamy (2008, p. 364), Spolsky's (2004) framework:

> introduces a broader concept of language policy, one that incorporates ideology, ecology and management, arguing for a complex relationship among these components and thus providing a fuller and more comprehensive understanding of what language policy really is.

Spolsky's framework puts focus on the *interplay* between different aspects such as national ideology, the role of English as a global language, a nation's sociolinguistic situation, political interests, economic interests, language beliefs as shaped by history, as well as micro level factors such as language practice at home and elsewhere outside school. The Seychelles is particularly interesting to research from this perspective. As a very small nation with a population of less than 100,000 inhabitants, various "actors" and their role in shaping current policies can quite accurately be identified. "Actors", in this context, may refer to human individuals, but also other entities such as global politics, new technological developments and economic interests.

Background: the Seychelles

The Seychelles are situated four degrees south of the equator in the western Indian Ocean. The islands have no indigenous population and are inhabited by people with a creole mix of African, European and Asian descent. The pillar of the economy is tourism, closely followed by the fisheries industry. The Seychelles boasts the highest nominal per capita GDP in Africa, and it has a high Human Development Index (see United Nations Development Programme, 2019). However, poverty remains a widespread problem due to the high level of economic inequality (World Bank, 2020).

The Seychelles education system is based on a comprehensive policy of education for all (Ministry of Education, 2004). It consists of 11 years of compulsory schooling (generally from the age of 6 to 16), preceded by two years of early childhood education (generally ages three-and-a-half to five-and-a-half) which are not compulsory, but which most children attend (Ministry of Education, 2000; 2004). The system is closely steered and monitored by the Ministry of Education, and highly exam oriented. Final exams in the compulsory system take place in secondary Grade 5, when the most promising students sit their IGCSEs exams, given by Cambridge International. In addition to state schools, there are four private schools on the islands, three of which conduct their teaching entirely in English and one which is based on the French system.

History

In the eighteenth century, when the islands were first colonized by the French, the practice of "deculturation" (Chaudeson, 2001, p. 91) meant that African languages and cultural expressions were forbidden. As a consequence, a new language, KS, emerged within a generation or two as the initial simple French pidgin developed into the mother tongue of the majority through the process of creolization (see Bickerton, 1977 for further details). The Seychelles became a British colony in 1815. However, French kept its role in religious practice, high culture and in education until the 1940s, when the church-owned schools were replaced by more formal and organized state schools based on the English system. Now English also became the sole LoI (Fleischmann 2008, p. 74). During the entire colonial period, KS remained a low status language, confined to informal discourse and completely banned from schools. Students were punished for using KS in school and such punishments could include "writing lines", formal rituals designed to bring ridicule to the "offender", and even corporal punishment (Fleischmann, 2008, p. 141).

The language situation in the Seychelles during this historical period is a direct reflection of the pre-independence power structures on the islands: the British were the formal administrative rulers, while the francophone elite still retained considerable economic power and influence. A prerequisite for access to positions of power (within the fields of administration, law, religion and education, for example) among the general Creole-speaking population (94% according to Moumou (2004, p. 46)) was a mastery of English, and to a lesser extent French. In spite of this, KS survived as the everyday language of the majority, regardless of class or race, arguably a result of its role in signalling the Creole identity that distinguished the local population from the colonial cultures.

Post-independence era: the recognition of KS

With independence in 1976, and the subsequent left-wing coup d'état in 1977, the status of KS improved, and it began its journey towards becoming an official language with a role in politics, culture and education. The establishment of KS as an official national language played a key role in the nation-building process. It was a way of marking a break with the colonial past and the establishment of a new cultural and linguistic autonomous identity (Ivanov, Deutschmann & Enever, 2015). However, the elevation of KS to a formal language was not given, even among its speakers. During the late 1970s and early 1980s, there were intense status and corpus planning efforts (Baldauf & Kaplan, 2005) to raise the status of KS (see Fleischmann, 2008, pp. 58–67 for further details of this process). Not only did this process involve the formalization of orthography, grammar and lexicon, but also included several translations of key works of literature into KS, and other efforts in the cultural sector. Most importantly, KS was given a role in education, both as LoI and as an academic subject. The implementation of KS in education also meant that learning materials had to be produced, and above all, teachers had to be trained for the task of teaching KS. In spite of these challenges, the Seychelles became the first Creole-speaking nation in the world to implement a creole language as a LoI in education in January 1982 (Siegel, 2005).

KS was initially introduced as LoI from primary Grade 1 to Grade 4 and was also taught as a separate subject until primary Grade 6. In addition, KS became the sole LoI throughout the compulsory grades of schooling in the subjects of Social Education, Physical Education, the Creative Arts and Religion. KS thus formed part of a trilingual policy where English remained the LoI in "academic" subjects after primary Grade 4, where KS was the LoI up to primary Grade 4 but had a primary role in more practical subjects, and where French was taught as a foreign language from primary Grade 1 (Campling, Confiance & Purvis, 2011; Purvis, 2004). Instructing young children in their mother tongue had highly positive effects. Comparisons of the last classes to be taught in English and the first classes taught under the new system showed that the latter outscored the former in almost every subject, including French and the sciences. Interestingly, the children who had been taught in KS also performed as well in the subject of English as the previous groups, who had been taught exclusively in English (Bickerton, 1990, p. 48). In addition, literacy rates went up radically (Campling, Confiance & Purvis, 2011, p. 51). Note that these findings were based on data from the entire primary Grade 6 cohorts in the country, and therefore have important implications for the SSA region as a whole.

Recent setbacks and challenges

As the previous section illustrates, KS was given a lot of attention and corpus planning in the Seychelles, a state of affairs somewhat unique in SSA contexts. Despite this, KS's role in education and elsewhere has suffered serious setbacks over the last decades. After concerns were raised by the Language Policy Review Committee report in 1994, a study based on interviews with teachers, parents and the general public, KS's role as LoI was reduced to primary Grades 1 and 2 in 1996. There were several motivations for this: policymakers argued that with increased exposure to English in popular media (television for example), children were better equipped to handle an earlier switch to English as LoI. Further, teachers reported finding the transition from one LoI to another challenging, claiming that they had to "re-teach" children basic concepts after primary Grade 4 as they failed to grasp these in English. Lack of resources was also seen as another primary obstacle for further promoting KS in schools. Producing textbooks to cover all the subjects on all levels was perceived as not feasible in a country with a population of less than 100,000, and it was also challenging to meet the demand for teachers trained in KS (Ivanov et al., 2015). Although legitimate, we would argue that many of the points of critique raised in the 1994 report could have been overcome had there been a will. There were however other, more ideologically oriented factors, that probably contributed to the weakened role of KS in education.

The changed status given to KS in education, and elsewhere, is also likely to have been affected by the political changes that took place in the republic during the early 1990s. In 1993, the so-called "Third Republic" was declared, and the Seychelles became a multi-party democracy with free elections. From this time onward, the Seychelles also gradually moved from a relatively centrally state controlled planned economy (highly dependent on aid from the former Soviet Union and its allies) to a more open liberal economy, where "solidifying old and soliciting new ties with some of the world's most influential powers abroad" became increasingly important in the bid to join the global economic community (Laversuch, 2008, p. 377). According to Laversuch, language policies propagating the use of English and French at the expense of KS were largely economically motivated in order to "assist the country in gaining a foothold in other foreign markets where English and/or French are used as the primary/exclusive language(s) of government and business" (2008, p. 378). It is also feasible that the ruling party wanted to dissociate itself with some of the more radical reforms that had taken place after it seized power in 1977 in order to appeal to a greater proportion of the general electorate; the introduction of KS in education was considered by many to be one such radical reform.

Whatever the reasons, from 1996 to date, the role of KS in education has become increasingly limited. It is now only used as LoI during primary Grades 1 and 2 and ceases to be a subject at school after primary Grade 6. Many argue that it should be abandoned altogether as LoI, and in fact this has already happened in the subject of Mathematics, which is now taught entirely in English from primary one onwards. Another issue of concern is the role of KS as "language of support" in the current system, i.e. a language into which teachers can switch for the purpose of increasing understanding of concepts. Although it is clearly stated in the National Curriculum Framework (NCF) (Ministry of Education, 2013) that KS can be used in this capacity throughout the education system, there are indications that this is becoming less and less acceptable (see Zelime & Deutschmann, 2016).

Current studies

The studies on which we draw our evidence in this chapter are part of a greater project, where the ambition has been to survey the state of the current language-in-education situation in the Seychelles, and how things have changed since the 1996 reforms. In this chapter, however, our focus lies on an analysis of the impact of the specific findings from the studies that relate to how language policies, at various policy levels (from management to practice), affect the role of KS in the system and educational equity (or lack thereof). In order to show how various aspects (expressed language policies, belief systems and practice) contribute to the current language-in-education situation in the Seychelles, we have used Spolsky's framework of *language practices*, *language, beliefs* and *values*, and language *planning* and/or *management*. This choice of method is motivated in order to provide the "bigger picture", and an overall understanding of the language-in-education context of a country which is relatively unfamiliar to most readers. We refer those interested in more specific details to the original articles.

The main aim of Study One (Zelime & Deutschmann, 2016) was to investigate the intentions of the declared trilingual language-in-education policy in the Seychelles NCF, and how overarching ideologies expressed in this document were (or were not) translated into directions for specific implementation and intended practice in other steering documents, and in the three-language subject curricula, namely KS, English and French. Our findings revealed that there were large discrepancies between the overarching principles expressed in the NCF and those evident in the specific subject curricula. In the NCF all three national languages are given central roles and equal status, and if anything, the role of KS is highlighted. The NCF clearly states that any of the three languages can be used as "support languages" throughout the system in the pursuit of providing quality, goal oriented, individualized and student-centred education for "all", regardless of social class or gender. There is a strong emphasis on literacy in all the three languages (KS, English and French). A weakness in the document, however, is that there are very few practical guidelines about the specific role of each language in teaching and examination.

While the status of the three languages is equal in the NCF, clear differences in the power and functions of the languages emerge in the subject curricula. From the descriptions, it is evident that the role of KS is peripheral and mainly serves as a transition language, which is used to develop basic learning skills and thereby help young children to enter the more complex cognitive universe of the ex-colonial languages. In contrast, English is described as instrumental for knowledge acquirement and academic success. The peripheral role of KS is also evident from the time allocated to this subject in the curriculum. From primary Grade 3 to Grade 6 KS is allocated five weekly slots in the timetable, and it ceases to be a school subject after primary Grade 6. In contrast, English is allocated seven weekly slots and is also the LoI. Similarly, while the use of KS as support language is advocated in the NCF, this is actively discouraged in practical guidelines to teachers produced by the Ministry of Education as evidenced from the following quote:

> [...] the prescribed medium of instruction has to be respected by teachers and greater emphasis has to be placed on more effective curriculum

> implementation. This is due to the fact that 80% of inspectorate reports revealed a high degree of code-mixing during the delivery of lessons.
>
> (*Education Sector Medium-Term Strategic Plan*, Ministry of Education, 2014, p. 47)

The practice of using KS as support language (which presupposes "code-mixing"), a central principle in the NCF, is questioned and positioned as deficit practice.

Study Two (Deutschmann & Zelime, 2015) explored language attitudes of learners regarding the three school language subjects, KS, English and French among students in primary and secondary schools in the Seychelles. These attitudes were then correlated with students' performance in these subjects in the primary six national assessments. Questionnaires were distributed to approximately 400 learners, from primary Grade 1 to secondary Grade 3, to capture their attitudes towards the four basic language skills (reading, writing, listening and speaking) in the three languages.

The results clearly showed that students of all ages were very positive towards KS. These positive attitudes were particularly noticeable in the primary Grades where KS was favoured over English and French in all four literacy skill domains. These attitudes were also mirrored in the primary six national assessments, where KS was the subject students performed best in. There was, however, a clear change in attitudes towards writing and reading (but not listening or speaking) in KS once students entered the secondary level. Secondary students were significantly more negative towards reading and writing in KS. The more negative attitudes towards KS as a written language seem to be a reflection of KS ceasing to be an academic subject after primary Grade 6. Further, negative attitudes towards English were particularly evident among primary school boys. These attitudes were also mirrored in their primary six exam results, where girls massively outscored boys in English.

Study Three (Zelime & Deutschmann, 2018) investigated the language beliefs, attitudes and classroom practices of primary school teachers. Findings were based on questionnaire answers from 142 teachers in 22 primary schools (almost all primary schools in the Seychelles), coupled with classroom observations and teacher interviews. Findings revealed that while the vast majority (98%) of teachers used KS for everyday oral communication, they were, on the whole, quite negative to its role in education. None of the respondents were positive to its potential use as LoI from Grade 3 onwards, and a striking 96.5% of the respondents would have liked to see English introduced as LoI even earlier in system (even at preschool level) (p. 139). Teachers were thus far more positive towards English as a LoI. Even in very locally contextualized subjects such as Social Studies, very few thought that students would perform better if taught in KS. Further, a substantial number of the teachers believed that English-only practice should be used when teaching (i.e. KS should not be used as support language). A clear majority of the teachers thought the advantages of teaching in English outweighed the disadvantages in the current system. KS was generally viewed as a less prestigious language than English, in particular in professional contexts. For example, very few of the teachers were of the opinion that a good knowledge of KS was advantageous on the job market.

Results from the classroom observations of six primary Grade 6 school teachers supported the findings from the questionnaires. KS was used very frequently by the majority of learners, but hardly ever by the teachers. For instance, KS was used extensively by students during group work, when the teacher was out of earshot. Further, many learners answered questions that the teachers posed to them in English using KS, for example, when struggling to express themselves in English. Overall, teachers did not encourage this and responded to such utterances in English, and also insisted that students use English. This practice also meant that those students who were reasonably proficient in English were given disproportionate amounts of floor space. In some lessons, for example, one or two learners did almost all the talking because they were clearly proficient in oral English. The insistence on English-only communication also meant that there was very little exploratory talk (Barnes, 1976; 2008), i.e. less formal and more dialogic communication where the teacher and learners interact to explore new concepts. This was partly due to the fact that in spite of their insistence on English, many of the teachers were themselves sometimes struggling to express themselves in this language. As a result, over 90% of the teacher–student discourse was made up of teacher-centred pre-prepared plenary talk (Hardman, 2008), or short question response-type dialogues, where the focus lay on transmission rather than construction of knowledge. In our interviews with teachers, it was clear that they recognized that many learners had difficulties in understanding what was being taught and needed support. However, it was also clear that the teachers lacked strategies to deal with this problem, something which some teachers reluctantly acknowledged.

Study Four (Zelime, Deutschmann & Rijlaarsdam, 2018) explored how the language of assessment affected students' opportunities to communicate their knowledge, and the impact of this on their academic performance. A within-groups experimental design was implemented, and 151 primary Grade 6 students (11 to 12 years) from three different schools wrote a short test in both KS and English, in a counterbalanced design. The theme of the test was fishing, a topic in the Social Studies curriculum which is based mostly on local contextual knowledge, and which is taught in English. The tests were marked by three independent graders for content in both languages. In our analysis of results, we also compared results between "high-performing" students and "low-performing" students, as defined by the local class streaming practice (upper and lower streams where the former are defined as high performers).

The main finding showed that the participants scored significantly higher in this specific Social Studies test when they received instructions and were allowed to write in KS as opposed to English. This effect constituted approximately a 13% improvement based on the total score. In this particular study, we could not show that there were any significant differences in the magnitude of the difference between English and KS test scores among upper- and lower-stream students. Thus, the study implies that the use of English as test language leads to a general performance loss affecting all students, irrespective of class level (upper- and lower-stream). Note here, however, that in an exam-oriented system with distinct pass and fail levels, a 13% loss of performance will be more serious for a weaker student than a high performer.

Finally, Study Five (Zelime & Deutschmann, 2019) investigated the extent to which the choice of language was a factor influencing primary Grade 6 students' writing and their opportunities to incorporate their own knowledge, person, experiences and world views in their school knowledge production. The evidence was based on findings from the corpus of 308 written texts, produced in Study Four above. In our analysis, we included text length and compared aspects of the ideational and interpersonal dimensions (see Halliday, 1994) in students' texts written in L2 (English) and L1 (KS). The study investigated the degree of code switching, i.e. the interpolation of KS words/phrases into the English text and vice versa, and the use of first person pronouns (since we wanted to investigate identification with the topic) in the two sub-corpora, and how differences could be accounted for qualitatively. We also compared texts of high-performing and low-performing students with respect to the above.

The results showed that the texts written in KS were longer than those written in English. Further, there were far more examples of code switching in the English texts, and this was particularly the case for texts written by the "weaker" lower-stream students. To try to deal with language shortcomings, lower stream students drew on KS to explain what they meant. The Kreol words that appeared in the English texts typically described local objects and phenomena (fish names, local fishing methods, places and food). Fish names were particularly common in the code-switching data, and it is evident from the results that children in the Seychelles possess a very rich vocabulary to describe this semantic domain in KS. This was not the case in English. The use of English words in the KS texts was relatively rare, and restricted to the phenomena that children learn about in school, for example words such a *fish factory*, *cannery*, *purse seiners* and *foreign exchange*. Finally, the use of the first person pronouns in the KS texts was almost twice as frequent as in the English texts. The difference in frequency of usage of these pronouns in English texts and KS texts was greatest among lower-stream students. First person pronouns primarily referred to aspects related to local and national identity: *our country, our economy*, etc. In addition, and especially in the KS texts, personal pronouns were also often used to signal inclusiveness with the activities described: "***nou** servi kazye pou attrap pwason; **nou** lapes" etc.* (we use fish traps to catch fish, we fish, etc.). These pronouns were often replaced by *they* in the English texts (the fishermen) signalling a greater distance and less identification with the topic.

In summary, the intentions of the NCF are reasonably clearly stated: in the pursuit of educational equity, all languages have an equal role to ensure individualized education which takes the prerequisites of each learner into account. As the results from the five studies taken together show, however, the intentions of the NCF do not translate well into practice. One important factor in this is arguably teacher attitudes, which are generally very negative towards the role of KS in the system, and which also seems to be highly influential when it comes to practical implementations of policy intentions. The overall result is a system where the role of the mother tongue in education is marginalized, and this has negative effects on the learning situation of all learners, but particularly for those who have limited access to English.

Discussion

In the following, we explore why policies and classroom practices differ so much and what happens to the NCF's principles in the stages between the planning and implementation. To do so, we draw on Spolsky's framework, which suggests that such differences occur when there are conflicting interests at work. We identify some of the conflicting interests, ideologies and practices working in the Seychelles system regarding the role of KS and, ultimately, educational equity. Figure 3.1 gives insight into some of these factors, including local politics, historical factors, global factors, economic factors, foreign language interests and practical circumstances in the field. We then discuss potential models of change to counteract current trends (i.e. the belief systems and practice models indicated by dotted lines in Figure 3.1 below).

Local and outside influences

Laversuch (2008) points to the forces of economics and globalization in the diminishing role of KS in the Seychelles education system, and this is partly confirmed through interviews with senior Curriculum Officers (see Ivanov, Deutschmann & Enever, 2015). With the increased importance of tourism, combined with a more global context afforded through social media and increased

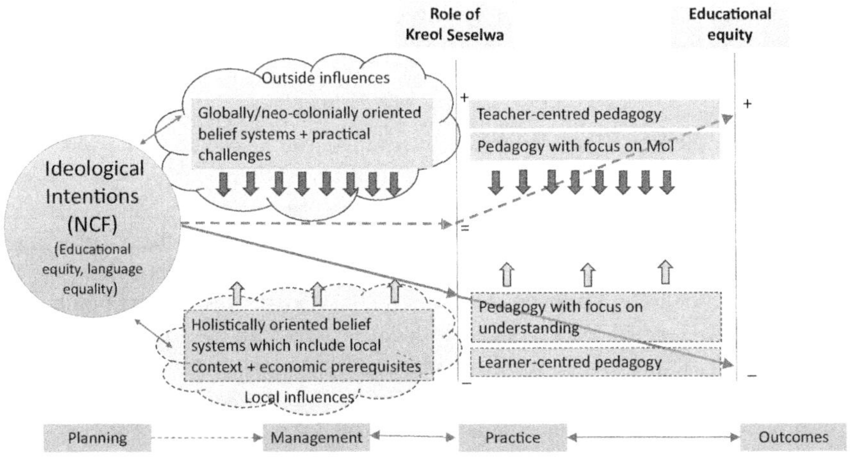

Figure 3.1 Influences affecting the intentions of the National Curriculum Framework.

travel, English has become increasingly important. Study Two evidences that pragmatic considerations such as employability are key motivating factors for teachers' negative perceptions of the role of KS in education (see also Fleischmann, 2008). Teachers cannot see the point of propagating a language which is only locally relevant.

This negative view of KS is also strengthened by historical factors. According to Mahoune (2000), a "colonial hangover" makes it hard for Creoles to accept their own language as one equal to others. English is still the language of administration in the Seychelles, and although KS was given strong political backing in the 1980s and early 1990s, a majority of the population still associate success and development with English (and to a lesser degree French). Many of today's decision makers owe their success to the old colonial and/or private school systems where KS had/has no role. Further, among this social class, English or French-only private schools are becoming an increasingly popular alternative for their children's education, and this adds to the myth that English and/or French is a recipe for academic success. Such forces can essentially be viewed as neocolonial (see Figure 3.1 above), reinventing old colonial ideals, and/or examples of *elite closure*, i.e. when "the elite successfully employ official language policies [...] to limit access of nonelite groups to political position and socioeconomic advancement" (Myers-Scotton, 1993, p. 149).

Given these circumstances, KS's role in education is politically sensitive, and the current government are well aware of the delicate balancing act the language issue in education involves. Giving too much emphasis to English as LoI would potentially alienate parts of the electorate, while the reverse risks irritating others. Avoiding specific directives regarding the role of specific languages in the NCF is arguably a way of playing it safe by committing to a trilingual language policy in principle, without specifying the practicalities. Unfortunately, this strategy comes at the expense of leaving teachers and students without clear guiding principles for language practice at school. This opens up possibilities for variation in practical implementation, driven by different ideologies. In this process the teachers and their ideologies are key factors.

As evidenced from our studies, teachers are generally quite negative towards KS in education (see also Fleischmann, 2008). Teachers are also very influential: for example, the 1996 reforms reducing the role of KS in education were largely motivated by teacher opinions. Further, since the Ministry of Education is largely made up of former teachers, teacher ideologies are largely reflected in their practice-oriented management policies. Moreover, the Seychelles is a small country, and many of the public servants in the Ministry are former colleagues of the teachers they are monitoring. Teachers are, just like the rest of the population, influenced by colonial/neocolonial ideals and current global trends, but there are also other factors that contribute to teachers' negative attitudes towards KS.

The Seychelles education system is currently facing a number of challenges affecting teachers' work environment. Lack of discipline in schools has long been an issue. After a number of incidents of violence, many secondary teachers feel personally threatened. There has also been a general decline in academic achievement over the past 10 to 15 years, and it has become increasingly difficult to recruit new teachers to the profession. A common opinion among teachers is that there has been a general "moral decline" in the country, and that "things were better before". Many incorrectly blame progressive reforms, such as the abandonment of corporal punishment and the introduction of KS, for the current state of affairs. Further, there is a general lack of resources for aspects such as infrastructural investments and vocational training to meet current challenges. These factors have led to the system experiencing a negative spiralling effect, and quite incorrectly KS is seen as part of the problem, a situation which is probably mirrored in many SSA contexts.

Language practice

As Spolsky (2004) points out, language, beliefs and values are intrinsically interwoven with practice, and current LoI practice has highly negative pedagogic consequences. Our classroom observations show that teacher-oriented pedagogy in combination with strict English-only practice means that many learners are unable to access what is being taught. Further, as shown by Study Four, current assessment practices also mean that learners are unable to express what they know adequately. This is reflected in exam results, where a large proportion of the primary Grade 6 students fail in key subjects such as English and Maths. In addition, the exclusion of KS means that learners are denied the opportunity to express themselves and relate their everyday experiences to their school knowledge, and the local context is thus marginalized (as shown in Study Five). This is just one illustration of what Spolsky (2009) refers to as a serious gap between the L1 and the L2, where children will be convinced that their local knowledge and languages are in some way deficient and irrelevant.

Teacher-centred pedagogy coupled with an exam-oriented system, and a strict monolingual practice as regards LoI, lead to an increase of inequity in the system. As Study Two shows, individuals who understand what is being taught are given more teacher time and do relatively well, while those who cannot follow what is going on are isolated and left with little support and fail. This, we would argue, is one of the reasons for current disciplinary issues in the Seychelles schools today. Many students feel abandoned by the current system and react negatively. As Erling (2017, p. 388) points out, English language skills might enhance opportunities for individuals, but they also reinforce embedded inequalities and thereby do not necessarily contribute to the overall well-being of societies.

This is certainly the case in the Seychelles. While some learners manage to negotiate the system and get good enough grades to enter post-secondary education and university, and thereby secure good jobs, a larger section of learners leave school with no qualifications whatsoever. This is reflected in current labour statistics (see Seychelles National Bureau of Statistics): there is a general lack of skilled labour (particularly in tourism and construction) and the Seychelles houses approximately 22,000 expatriate workers, while unemployment remains an issue among the local population.

Potential models of change

In any model of change, we argue that the merits of all the languages in the current system should be recognized as potential contributors to communication and understanding. In this pursuit we would argue that additive multilingual models represent a way forward. Such models recognize the use of the L1 plus official/foreign language/s as dual/multiple media of instruction to the end of school. In the additive education model, the mother tongue is never removed as a LoI, even if its role gradually may be reduced as learners become more proficient in the L2 LoI. The advantage with such models is that they encourage a high level of proficiency in the mother tongue *in addition* to a high level of proficiency in the official/foreign language.

There has been much research carried out in SSA that speaks for the promotion of additive models in all stages of primary, secondary and tertiary education in order to maximize the quality of education (see Wolff, 2011 and Heugh, 2011, for example). Perhaps more so than in other SSA contexts, such a system is highly feasible in the Seychelles, and there are many local factors that speak in favour of successful implementations. For example, the Seychelles is a small country and it is reasonably easy to reach all practitioners for training. Further, the Seychelles has a relatively uncomplicated language situation where KS is spoken by the vast majority. There are thus no arguments speaking in favour of favouring English as a neutralizing lingua franca in a complex ethnic situation, as is the case in many SSA countries. In addition, KS has been standardized, and formal orthography, grammar, lexicon, etc. are already in place. The biggest hurdle to changes in the current practice, as we see it, are current belief systems that resist the expanded role of KS in education.

In line with Spolsky, we argue that, in order to be successful, any potential future language policy has to acknowledge current language ideologies, where the beliefs of key actors like teachers are of primary importance. Consequently, we maintain that new LoI models that are based on different language ideological frameworks than current ones will not succeed unless teachers are thoroughly introduced to the thinking behind these new frameworks (in teacher training or vocational training). Models for change also have to acknowledge and respect current ideologies and practices, even when, at first sight, these may seem to be in conflict with the pursuit of educational equity.

One of the main problems in the Seychelles context is that there has been a history of setting language belief systems against each other in the interest of political pursuits. The colonial powers diminished the local language and culture in order to elevate and justify their own systems, and similarly the colonial systems and languages were discredited in post-coup d'état nationalist pursuits of the 1980s, which in turn led to a backlash after 1996. This has created a polarized situation where belief constructs are either for or against KS/English in education, and where the practitioners largely are in favour of English. This practice of equating specific languages with educational successes/failures is, we would argue, not constructive. Rather than fronting the role of a specific LoI in the educational system, emphasis should instead be placed on the role of communication and understanding of ideas and knowledge, regardless of language. In this pursuit, pedagogy (rather than language) needs to be the focus of attention.

It is also here that we see that major efforts need to be made in order to better inform teachers, and the general public, of the merits of multilingual education. In such efforts, focus on understanding and knowledge attainment need to be primary, and LoI secondary. For example, it is not important what language is used to teach basic mathematical concepts. What is important is that students understand them. Further, the implementation of an additive model should not be seen to threaten current assessment standards such as IGCSEs. KS should be presented as a way of helping knowledge development, while at the same time recognizing the importance of the global context. It is simply not realistic that Seychellois citizens would accept an abandonment of international systems given its small and rather isolated position.

Conclusion

In conclusion, this study of the Seychelles illustrates a general dilemma in postcolonial contexts such as SSA: in the bid to align education with international standards and content (IGCSEs for example), and to prepare for engagement in a global community, systems adopt a more or less monolingual approach. Such changes are often made easier due to language ideologies that linger on from colonial times. While such policies do in fact open up international opportunities for a limited group, they also shut the door for large sections of the population, who are not able to negotiate the linguistic hurdles. What is more, such policies also come at a cost – the inability of indigenous languages and cultures to develop and contribute to development. In reversing such tendencies, we would argue for models which emphasize pedagogy and learning as opposed to being fixated with LoI as a way forward in SSA.

In the pursuit of such models, informed research plays a critical role. Much research to date has pointed to the shortcomings of current transitional models in SSA, and how these lead to educational inequity (see for example UNICEF, 2016 for a comprehensive overview). Our own research reveals similar flaws in the Seychelles. Arguably, there has been enough research conducted for us to say that we know that language issues lie at the heart of many of the challenges facing pupils and teachers in the SSA region today. Nevertheless, systems based on former colonial languages as sole LoI persist. Radical changes seem to be politically inconceivable, something which in turn may be a result of a postcolonial mindset and so-called elite closure (Myers-Scotton, 1993). Here we would argue that research which demonstrates how indigenous African languages can play an important supportive role within current systems in order to improve learning is extremely important. Controlled intervention studies and action research with the aim to develop and test various additive language models and measure their effects on learning are essential in the pursuit of educational improvements. Such studies could give concrete evidence that there are real alternatives to current

LoI practices that still accommodate the demands of international systems based on former colonial languages such as English and French. In short, such evidence based on research is a key component in disarming arguments against strengthening the role of indigenous languages in schools in the SSA region.

Note

1 The term *first language* (L1) is used in this chapter synonymously with *mother tongue*, and refers to the language that a person first is exposed to and acquires in early childhood because it is spoken in the family and/or is the language of the region or community where the child lives.

References

Baldauf, RB & Kaplan, RB 2005, 'Language-in-education policy and planning', in E Hinkel (ed), *Handbook of Research in Second Language Teaching and Learning*, Erlbaum, Mahwah, NJ, pp. 957–970.

Barnes, D 1976, *From Communication to Curriculum*, Penguin Books, Harmondsworth.

Barnes, D 2008, 'Exploratory talk for learning', in N Mercer & S Hodgkinson (eds), *Exploring Talk in School: Inspired by the Work of Douglas Barnes*, Sage, London, pp. 1–16. http://dx.doi.org/10.4135/9781446279526.n1

Bickerton, D 1990, 'Instead of the Cult of Personality', *Notes on Linguistics*, vol. 49, pp. 47-50.

Bickerton, D 1977, 'Pidginization and creolization: Language acquisition and language universals', in A Valdman, (ed), *Pidgin and Creole Linguistics*, University Press, Bloomington, IN, pp. 49–69.

Campling, L, Confiance, H & Purvis, M 2011, *Social Policies in Seychelles. Social Policies in Small States Series*, Publication Section Commonwealth Secretariat, London.

Chaudeson, R 2001, *Creolization of Language and Culture*, Routledge, London.

Clegg, J 2005, 'Moving towards bilingual education in Africa', in H Coleman (ed), *Language and Development: Africa and Beyond Proceedings of the 7th International Language and Development Conference*, British Council, Addis Ababa, pp. 40–50.

Clegg, J & Simpson, J 2016, 'Improving the effectiveness of English as a medium of instruction in sub-Saharan Africa', *Comparative Education*, vol. 52, pp. 359–374.

Deutschmann, M & Zelime, J 2015, '"I used to like writing in Kreol but now I only use English": An exploratory study of language attitudes and examination performance among primary and secondary school students in the Seychelles', *Island Studies*, vol. 1, pp. 36–45.

Erling, EJ 2017, 'Language planning, English language education and development aid in Bangladesh', *Current Issues in Language Planning*, vol. 18, pp. 388–406.

Fleischmann, CT 2008, *Pour Mwan Mon Lalang Maternel i Al avek Mwan Partou – A Sociolinguistic Study on Attitudes towards Seychellois Creole*, Peter Lang, Bern.

Halliday, M 1994, *An Introduction to Functional Grammar*, Edward Arnold: London.

Hardman, FC 2008, 'Teachers' use of feedback in whole-class and group-based talk', in M Neil & H Steve (eds), *Exploring Talk in Schools: Inspired by the Work of Douglas Barnes*, Sage, London, p. 131.

Heugh, K 2011, 'Theory and practice – language education models in Africa: Research, design, decision-making and outcomes', in A Oane & C Glanz (eds), *Optimising*

Learning, Education and Publishing in Africa: The Language Factor – A Review and Analysis of Theory and Practice in Mother-Tongue and Bilingual Education in sub-Saharan Africa, UNESCO, Hamburg, pp. 105–156.

Heugh, K, Benson, C, Bogale, B & Mekonnen, A 2007, *Study on Medium of Instruction in Primary Schools in Ethiopia*, Ministry of Education, Addis Ababa, Ethiopia.

Hungi, N, & Thuku, F 2010, 'Variations in reading achievement across 14 Southern African school systems: Which factors matter?', *International Review of Education*, vol. 56, pp. 63–101.

Ivanov, S, Deutschmann, M & Enever, J 2015, 'Researching language-in-education policies: Evidence from the Seychelles, Russia and the European Union', in E Lindgren & J Enever (eds), *Researching Language Teaching and Learning*. Department of Language Studies, Umeå University, Umeå, pp. 85–101.

Laversuch, IM 2008, 'An unequal balance: The Seychelles' trilingual language policy', *Current Issues in Language Planning*, vol. 9, pp. 375–394.

Mahoune, JCP 2000, 'Seychellois creole development & evolution', *IIAS Newsletter*, vol. 22, p. 21.

Ministry of Education 2000 *Education for a Learning Society-Policy Statement of the Ministry of Education*, Ministry of Education, Mahé, Seychelles.

Ministry of Education 2004, *Education Act-Non-Formal Early Childhood Education Centre*, Ministry of Education, Mahé, Seychelles.

Ministry of Education 2013, *The Seychelles National Curriculum Framework*, Ministry of Education, Mahé, Seychelles.

Ministry of Education 2014, *Education Sector Medium-Term Strategic Plan 2013-2017 and Beyond*, Ministry of Education, Mahé, Seychelles.

Moumou, M 2004, 'Preparing our students for the future: Critical literacy in the Seychelles classrooms', *English Teaching: Practice and Critique*, vol. 3, pp. 46–58.

Myers-Scotton, C 1993, 'Elite closure as a powerful language strategy: The African case', *International Journal of the Sociology of Language*, vol. 103, pp. 149–164.

Purvis, M-T 2004, 'Education in the Seychelles: An overview', *Seychelles Medical and Dental Journal*, vol. 7, pp. 46–51.

Seychelles National Bureau of Statistics 2019, *Economic Statistics*. Victoria, Mahe, Seychelles www.nbs.gov.sc/

Shohamy, E 2008, 'Language policy and language assessment: The relationship', *Current Issues in Language Planning*, vol. 9, pp. 363–373.

Siegel, J 2005, 'Literacy in pidgins and creole languages', *Current Issues in Language Planning*, vol. 6, pp. 143–163.

Spolsky, B 2004, *Language Policy*, Cambridge University Press, Cambridge.

Spolsky, B 2009, *Language Management*, Cambridge University Press, Cambridge.

Spolsky, B 2019, 'A modified and enriched theory of language policy (and management)', *Language Policy*, vol. 18, pp. 323–338.

United Nations Development Programme 2019, Human Development Report: *Beyond income, beyond averages, beyond today: Inequalities in human development in the 21st century*, UNDP, New York http://hdr.undp.org/en/2019-report

UNICEF 2016, *The Impact of Language Policy and Practice on Children's Learning: Evidence from Eastern and Southern Africa*, UNICEF, Paris www.unicef.org/esaro/UNICEF(2016)LanguageandLearning-FullReport(SingleView).pdf.

Wolff, E 2011, 'Background and history – Language planning in Africa', in A Oane & C Glanz (eds), *Optimising Learning, Education and Publishing in Africa: The Language*

Factor – A Review and Analysis of Theory and Practice in Mother-Tongue and Bilingual Education in sub-Saharan Africa, UNESCO, Hamburg, pp. 49–100.

World Bank 2020, *GINI-index (World Bank estimate)*. The World Bank, Washington, DC, https://data.worldbank.org/indicator/SI.POV.GINI

Zelime, J & Deutschmann, M 2016, 'Revisiting the trilingual language-in-education policy in the Seychelles National Curriculum Framework and subject curricula: Intentions and practice', *Island Studies*, vol. 3, pp. 50–59.

Zelime, J & Deutschmann, M 2018, 'Conflicting ideologies: When the ideological meets the perceived and operational – A study of primary teachers' attitudes, perceptions and practice of Seychelles Creole (Kreol Seselwa) and English as mediums of instruction in the Seychelles primary schools', in K Smith (ed), *Norsk og internasjonal lærerutdanningsforskning: Hvor er vi? Hvor vil vi gå? Hva skal vi gjøre nå?*, Fagbokforlaget, Norway, pp. 129–151.

Zelime, J & Deutschmann, M 2019, 'Communicating local knowledge in a foreign language – A comparative study of ideational and interpersonal aspects of primary school pupils' L1 and L2 texts in the Seychelles', *L1-Educational Studies in Language and Literature*, vol. 19, pp. 1–28.

Zelime, J, Deutschmann, M, & Rijlaarsdam, G 2018, 'The effect of the language of testing on second language learners' academic performance in Social Studies: The case of Kreol Seselwa and English in the Seychelles classrooms', *L1-Educational Studies in Language and Literature*, vol. 18, pp. 1–22.

4 Classroom talk in Ghanaian upper primary schools

Understanding English-only, teacher-dominant practices

Elizabeth J. Erling, Kimberly Safford and Fritz Makafui Tugli

Introduction

Research undertaken in schools in SSA has long recognized that learners learn best in languages that they know best (Brock-Utne, 2001; Pinnock & Vijayakumar, 2009; Rubagumya, 1994; Trudell, 2016). This understanding was also the conclusion of a Global Education Monitoring Policy Paper, which emphasizes the need for students to be taught in a language that they understand well, posing the important question, 'If you don't understand, how can you learn?' (UNESCO, 2016). Indeed, receptive skills for understanding in a language, for instance being able to listen to the teacher and read the textbook, are essential for classroom learning to take place. However, the productive skills of writing and speaking in the language of instruction are also central to cognitive and language development. This chapter focuses on the role of what we call 'productive classroom talk' in learning in classrooms in Ghanaian upper primary schools, where English is the official language of instruction and students, highly proficient in their home and community languages, have only emergent proficiency in English.[1] We draw on conceptions of dialogic and scaffolded learning developed by Alexander (2008), Littleton and Mercer (2013) and Vygotsky (1978), to define 'productive classroom talk' as teachers and students using talk to think and reason together for the purpose of developing knowledge and language.

There is a large body of evidence demonstrating that productive classroom talk engages students' attention and participation, enhances understanding, accelerates learning and raises achievement in formal examinations (Alexander, 2015; Hattie, 2009). Productive classroom talk differs from more traditional, hierarchical classroom talk, which is strongly teacher-centred and teacher-controlled, and often focuses on students reproducing small units of memorized factual knowledge (Veen, Wilt, Kruistum, Oers & Michaels, 2017). A rigorous review of research on pedagogy and teaching practices in low-resource contexts such as those found in SSA established that productive classroom talk is enabled through 'inclusive and supportive communications', which include varied teacher questioning,

DOI: 10.4324/9781003028383-5

informative feedback, building on student responses, student questioning, the use of local languages and code-switching (Westbrook et al., 2013). However, enabling such talk, while challenging in all contexts, is particularly difficult when students are developing competence in the language of instruction. While the language-in-education policy in Ghana promotes the use of local languages in lower primary education, there is an official switch to English at the upper primary level, when students are around nine to ten years old. As the majority of upper primary students do not yet meet the curriculum learning outcomes for this level of schooling (Darvas & Balwanz, 2013; UNESCO, 2014), this policy has been cited as one of the key reasons behind student underachievement in English and across all curriculum subjects in Ghana (Erling et al., 2016).

While productive classroom talk is largely recognized as being central to learning, it has rarely been explored empirically in the context of classrooms in SSA. Seeking to fill this gap, this chapter presents and discusses findings from research that examined classroom talk in four Ghanaian government primary schools, where two researchers (Safford and Tugli) in a research project led by Erling observed 15 lessons at the upper primary level and interviewed 25 teachers and other stakeholders in the state education system about the opportunities and barriers arising from Ghana's language-in-education policy. Classroom observations sought to capture evidence of 'inclusive and supportive communications' (Westbrook et al., 2013) and multilingual pedagogic practice to support productive classroom talk and the development of content and language learning.

Analysis of the classroom observation data reveals that lessons were highly transmissive, with two aspects of classroom practice and language use being significant and persistent:

1. Teachers use English as the language of virtually all classroom activity and there was very limited use of local languages, despite teachers' awareness of students' emergent proficiency in English and teachers' beliefs that students learn better using local languages.
2. Teachers use a limited repertoire of pedagogies, giving students few or no opportunities to speak in any language, even during those occasions when they created an inclusive and supportive atmosphere in the classroom.

The interview data provide insight into two factors influencing these dominant classroom practices. The first is that teachers believe that they are acting in their students' best interests by using English only, because they think this is the best way for students to develop English proficiency. This was the case whether teachers did or did not share the same local languages as their students. The second is that teachers have limited awareness of multilingual pedagogies that support the development of content-related classroom talk, or, if they are aware, they feel unable to enact such pedagogies. In interviews, teachers seem to feel that Ghana's language-in-education policy provides them with no 'implementational space' to draw on multilingual pedagogies to support content and language learning. In light of these findings, this chapter considers recommendations for policy and practice to encourage productive classroom talk, within the constraints of limited resources in Ghanaian government primary schools.

Learning outcomes and language-in-education policy in Ghana

Ghana is a medium-size country in the western part of SSA. Due to developments in its economy, democratic political system and education system, it was reclassified as a middle-income country by the World Bank in 2011. Achieving universal primary education has been a key goal of educational initiatives in the country, which has been achieved, with 72% of students continuing to secondary school (UNESCO, 2019). Low student achievement, however, remains a national concern, and high levels of student failure within the education system seem to be language related (see Amfo & Anderson, 2019).

Like most countries in SSA, Ghana is ethnically and linguistically diverse, with the number of languages recognized by the government commonly cited as 79 (Opoku-Amankwa, Edu-Buandoh & Brew-Hammond, 2015). Most people regularly use two or more indigenous Ghanaian languages, and in urban areas English functions as a major lingua franca alongside Krio, Hausa and the Akan languages (e.g. Twi), which are mutually comprehensible varieties spoken by around half the population (Kerswill, 2017). English is also the country's official language, maintained as such when the country became independent from Britain in 1957, and is used by government, the law courts and the media.

English has long functioned as the main language of education in most grades, in all school types across the country. However, as in many other countries in SSA, policy now stipulates that local languages are used as the language of instruction at the lower primary level (Grades 1–3) and English is to be taught as a subject in this stage of education. In Ghana, there are 11 government-sponsored Ghanaian languages designated for this purpose (Asante Twi, Akuapem Twi, Dagbani, Dangme, Dagaare, Ewe, Fante, Ga, Gonja, Kasem and Nzema). According to policy, the ratio of local language to English decreases in Grades 1–3, with English incrementally increasing from 20% to 50% over time, to prepare for its sole use as the language of instruction from Grades 4 to 6 and beyond. The Ghanaian local language, which was previously the language of instruction, continues to be taught as a subject from Grade 4 and beyond, and, in some schools, an additional Ghanaian language may be added at the upper primary level.

Ghana's current language-in-education policy for primary education is not achieving its intended aim of ensuring access to learning in local languages and in English for all students. This is evidenced in assessments of students' levels of English, which show that only around a third of students are able to achieve minimum competency in English when they transition to English-only language of instruction in Grade 4, with more than a third failing to achieve the appropriate literacy levels for their educational grade (Darvas & Balwanz, 2013; MoE, 2016; UNESCO, 2014). This result remains relatively unchanged at the end of primary school in Grade 6 (see Figure 4.1).

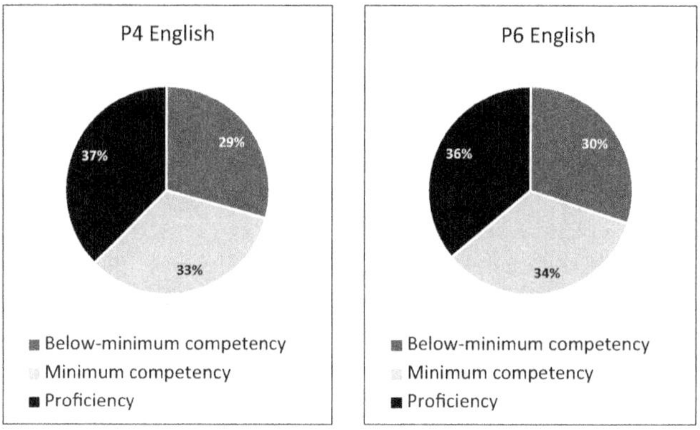

Figure 4.1 Minimum competency and proficiency results in English, Grade 4 and Grade 6.

Furthermore, assessment evidence indicates that the majority of students who complete primary school are doing so without having attained proficiency in the core subject areas (English, mathematics, integrated science and social studies), with the situation being significantly worse in rural and economically deprived areas.

Investigating classroom talk in Ghanaian primary schools

Given the underachievement of learning outcomes in Ghana, the research reported on in this chapter was designed to investigate current practices for classroom talk in Ghanaian upper primary classrooms (Grades 4–6), after the policy-mandated switch to English has occurred, in order to better understand how talk may be facilitating or hindering learning for students with emergent proficiency in English. We wanted to explore in particular the extent to which teachers were aware of and taking account of their students' emergent English proficiencies and what strategies they drew on, including inclusive, supportive and multilingual communications, to support the development of content learning. For data collection, a team of researchers – one UK-based and one Ghana-based – undertook fieldwork in upper primary classrooms in four government primary schools in the Greater Accra Region of Ghana over a period of ten days in September 2016. The fieldwork consisted of visits to schools which included observations of a range of lessons, in the context of the wider language-in-education policy of the school and community. Classroom practices and how they are influenced by the current language-in-education policy were discussed in interviews with the teachers observed, as well as their head teachers and state and district education officials. The research was funded through a collaboration between the British Council, Education Development Trust and the Open University, UK and led by Erling (see further Erling, Adinolfi & Hultgren, 2017). Ethical protocols followed the structured framework of the Open

University's Human Participants and Material Ethics Committee[2] and were informed by the British Association for Applied Linguistics Recommendations for Good Practice in Applied Linguistics[3], recognizing also the complexity of conducting research in low- and middle-income countries (Hultgren, Erling & Chowdhury, 2016). In order to gain access to the participating schools, Tugli, the Ghana-based researcher established initial contact, making visits and follow-up calls to inform the head teacher about the project and to develop rapport with teachers, find out their schedules and prepare for the data collection. Each participant was briefed orally about the research and provided an information sheet, and returned a signed informed consent form. Participation was treated in strict confidence, with the identities of teachers and schools involved in the study being anonymised and protected so they could speak honestly about their views and experiences.

Research contexts and data collection

The fieldwork involved four school visits to primary schools for students from kindergarten to the end of upper primary (Grade 6). Tugli and Safford visited two schools each in two districts, the first being primarily urban and the second more rural and on the outskirts of the Greater Accra Region. The inclusion of this more rural district provides a glimpse into the particular challenges of implementing the language-in-education policy in the most remote and hard-to-reach areas of the country, which were not included in the study as they are difficult to access for research purposes.

Schools 1 and 2 are in District A, a densely populated, cosmopolitan and multilingual trading area. The official language of the part of the district where the schools are located is Ga, the language spoken by the people indigenous to the area. Ga is also the official language of the schools in this district, even though it is not widely spoken by the students. While chiefs and elders with traditional influence in this community promote the use of Ga in education, because of vast migration from other areas of Ghana, the majority of teachers and students at the school use Twi. The teachers in this district come from all over the country and therefore speak a number of Ghanaian languages, which means that not all students have teachers who speak their language (particularly those students from migrant and ethnic minority families). For all of these reasons, selecting a single Ghanaian language as a medium of instruction at the lower primary level can be a problem, and many participants noted that this contributes to a reliance on English.

Schools 3 and 4 are in District B, which is technically part of Greater Accra, but is peri-urban and much more rural and remote than District A in the heart of Accra. Many parts of District B are inaccessible in the rainy season. Attendance and punctuality at the two schools are poor, with many students helping their families with farming or nomadic livestock. Unlike District A, District B is fairly linguistically homogeneous, with the majority of people using the Dangme language[4], which is also the officially recognized local language of instruction for Grades 1–3. However, most teachers in the district come from other parts of the country and are more likely to be proficient in languages such as Twi and Ewe. In general, Dangme speakers are under-represented in the teaching workforce. According to interviews with district officials, many teachers in District B are not able to conduct lessons in Dangme nor use existing bespoke resources which have been provided for local language teaching and learning at the lower secondary level (see Rosekrans, Sherris & Chatry-Komarek, 2012), which makes it very challenging to implement the language-in-education policy in the majority of schools in the district.

Classroom observation

Across the four schools, a combination of 15 different lessons were formally observed by two researchers, both English language lessons and other subject lessons in upper primary Grades 4–6. The observation schedule was designed to capture how teachers enacted language policy in the classroom and how students responded to this, and to explore the extent to which teacher practices supported students who were learning through a language in which they had emergent competence. Drawing on previous studies investigating inclusive, supportive and multilingual classroom practices (e.g. Bunyi, 2005; Ferguson, 2003; Macaro, 2005; Probyn, 2015), the schedule documented the following variables:

1. The ratio of teacher talk to student talk.
2. The percentage of talk in English and in other languages.
3. Activity types (reading, writing, speaking and listening).
4. Activity configuration (e.g. pair or group work, choral reading, independent work).
5. Teacher's classroom practices for inclusion and participation (e.g. the use of local resources, drawing on students' background, questioning and feedback).
6. Teacher's language-supportive practices (e.g. recasting, allowing student response time, using local languages, code-switching and translanguaging).
7. Teacher's use of language for non-academic purposes (classroom management, explaining rules, praise and disciplining).

Before the observation, teachers were asked to teach the class as they normally would, using the language(s) and activities that were usual routines for them. Being aware that the presence of a UK-based researcher might cause the teachers to speak more English than they normally would, the Ghana-based researcher was influential in reassuring teachers that use of local language would be understood. The researchers sat together at the back of the classroom where they were least likely to disrupt classroom teaching, and each researcher completed an observation schedule. Lessons were videoed with a small device, only to provide an *aide memoire* when checking that the observation schedule had been filled in appropriately. When the observation was completed, one researcher compared the two different schedules and clarified any differences in data capturing. The data from the classroom observation schedule were then entered into Statistical Package for Social Sciences, with descriptive statistical tools, such as frequency tables, charts and cross tabulations employed to elicit more information about the relationship between the seven variables listed above. The two lessons which stood out as having the highest number of teacher–student interactions after the statistical analysis were then transcribed for further qualitative analysis, to identify more specifically what kinds of student–teacher language interactions were taking place.

The observations were followed by interviews, undertaken in English with the Ghana-based and UK-based researcher, with each of the participating teachers, as well as their head teachers and local education officials linked to each of their schools. The interviews were intended to include teachers' perceptions of their classroom practice and other stakeholders' awareness of and attitudes to the language-in-education policy. All the interviews were recorded and transcribed by the Ghana-based researcher, representing the local variety of English. Transcript samples were independently coded by two other members of the wider research team in order to establish consistency in coding practices. Results from the first round of coding were compared, and from this exercise, themes were developed, refined and applied to all the transcripts. Excerpts from interviews with these multilingual speakers of English appear verbatim in this chapter to support interpretations of the classroom practices observed.

Findings

Data from the classroom observations and interviews revealed the following two tendencies: first, teachers use English as the language of almost all classroom activity and there was very limited use of local languages, despite teachers' awareness of students' emergent proficiency in English and teachers' beliefs that students would learn better using local languages. Second, teachers use a limited repertoire of pedagogies, giving students few or no opportunities to speak in any language, even during those occasions when they created an inclusive and supportive atmosphere in the classroom. These two tendencies, and the factors revealed in interviews which appear to be influencing them, are discussed below.

Teachers' use of English and students' emergent proficiency

The classroom observations document that English was the main language teachers used for all classroom activities. In all 15 upper primary lessons observed, teachers delivered all their explanations solely in English. Even for aspects of teaching that previous research has established commonly occur in local languages, such as establishing rapport and enhancing motivation (cf. Ferguson, 2003; Macaro, 2005), and despite findings elsewhere which report regular use of translanguaging in lower primary classrooms (Yevudey & Agbozo, 2019), the observations found that English was used for all such purposes: when the teachers praised students' efforts, encouraged or disciplined them, or made links to their experiences, they always used English to do this. Only four teachers were observed to use a local language during a lesson: one teacher in District A told a joke with a Twi punchline; he also made fun of his shoe in Ga ('Alatsa'). His class was lively and the students were engaged, but these are the only instances when he used local languages in the lesson. Two teachers in District B used Dangme (in singular instances) to check students' understanding (one of the two teachers also used Dangme again to bring students to attention). Finally, one teacher gave an individual student feedback in Twi (the teacher mentions this in the interview); otherwise, this lesson was carried out entirely in English. While the presence of a UK-based researcher may have influenced the use of English in the classroom, the fact that its use was so dominant and persistent, observed in many other less formal classroom observations experienced by the researchers and openly justified in teacher interviews, as explained below, adds reliability to these findings.

While the teachers relied solely on English for teaching purposes, the observations of students in lessons and scrutiny of their written work suggested that the majority of them had what the researchers classified as 'limited competence' in English. The research team estimated that students had limited proficiency in 85% of classes (n = 10). In 15% (n = 2) of the classrooms (which were in Grades 5 and 6 in School A), students were estimated to be 'fairly competent' in spoken English (see Table 4.1), though no estimates were made about their abilities to access the curriculum in English.

The interviews confirmed that teachers were aware of their students' emergent levels of English, with all teachers stating that having to teach in English slowed down teaching and learning considerably. Such sentiments are well demonstrated in the following excerpt:

> I think the language policy is somehow a barrier – to our work – in the sense that, you see, not all children can speak the English language but we are asked – and forced – to teach in the language. ...
>
> (Teacher 8, School 2)

Several teachers, especially those from District B, reported that students are more proficient in the local languages than in English, e.g.:

Table 4.1 Students' competence in spoken English by school

	Very limited competence	*Limited competence*	*Fairly competent*
School 1 (n = 3)	0	1	2
School 2 (n = 4)	1	3	0
School 3 (n = 3)	0	3	0
School 4 (n = 3)	0	3	0
Total (n = **13***)	**1**	**10**	**2**

Note: * Two classes were observed twice because they were taught by a different teacher, meaning that there were 15 observations, but only 13 classes.

> ... they can express themselves better in the local language because that one, that's what they use in their everyday activities ... because they have that one at home, during everything, their thoughts and their thinking in that one, too, is better. ...
>
> (Teacher 13, School 4)

While this was by no means the norm, there was one lesson – a Grade 6 Mathematics lesson – that featured a District A teacher using a local language (Twi) to translate an English term, as part of feedback to an individual student. When asked in the interview about this use of Twi, the teacher explained:

> ... we asked for the common – the least – value ... and the child who [answered had] given a wrong answer. I was trying to explain to him what 'the least' or when you say the lowest, what you're referring to.
>
> (Teacher 3, School 1)

The excerpt reveals that the teacher is aware of the potential benefit of using the local language to enhance students' content knowledge, clear up misconceptions and/or check understanding. However, in observed lessons, the technique of checking understanding was limited in any language. The most common means of checking understanding was brief: asking the class if they had understood, to which the students responded with a resounding 'yes'. In 60% of the lessons ($n = 9$) the teachers checked their students' understanding in this way (two in the more linguistically homogenous District B repeated this check in Dangme). When asked about other ways to check understanding, three teachers reported that they primarily did this by looking at their students' faces, and by marking their exercise books. There seemed to be little awareness of other strategies to check or support understanding, e.g.: classroom discussions, listening to students talk in pairs or groups or having them present information. This is reflected in the limited range of teaching repertoires observed in the lessons, discussed further below.

Factors influencing the persistent use of English

The interview data indicate two main factors influencing teachers in their persistent use of English as the sole language of instruction despite their awareness of students' emergent proficiency. The first is that many of them do not share another language with their students. As is often the case in Ghanaian schools, many teachers come from other areas of the country and do not have proficiency in the local languages used in school (Owu-Ewie & Eshun, 2019). This was the case for the majority of the teachers in District B. One teacher reported that she was trying to learn the local language (Dangme), while others reported strategies that they had developed, such as calling in a student from another class to help, translate or explain. In District A, most of the teachers and students had competence in Twi, though some students from rural areas outside of the district spoke languages that no teachers interviewed had competence in.

However, even in classrooms where teachers and students do share Ghanaian languages, teachers do not always view this as a potential pedagogic resource. Some teachers at each of the schools express the belief that the use of local languages interferes with students' English learning. For example, Teacher 8 from School 2 reflected that the language policy was in her view a barrier to teaching effectively. However, she also reported that she uses the local language rarely in order to encourage students to develop their proficiency in English:

> Well, I don't use it that much because I want to try them... I want to help them to have interest in the English language. ...
>
> (Teacher 8, School 2)

The head teacher at School 3 explained that the policy not to use local languages is a means of creating an immersion-like environment, which she believed helps the students to develop proficiency in English:

> Yes, with the teachers, we try that those from P4 will always communicate with them in English language. We try to do that just to keep them using the [English] language so that they become fluent in it.
>
> (Head teacher, School 3)

One teacher noted that she strictly forbids her students from speaking local languages, even pretending that she does not understand them, so that they are forced to develop proficiency in English:

> ... if you don't speak English, you keep quiet. ... I tell them, '... you shut up ...' [chuckling] '... because teacher doesn't understand the Twi. ... I am doing that to encourage them to – just – pick it [up]. ... So that if even they speak the wrong one, they can be corrected.
>
> (Teacher 7, School 2)

These interview excerpts demonstrate that in using English as the only language of the classroom, teachers believe they are acting in their students' best interests, so that students can develop their proficiency in English, then gain access to content, and eventually succeed in the school exams and beyond.

Observations of teaching: limited pedagogic repertoires and absence of student talk

All teachers used English as the main language of their teaching, and the observations revealed that they also primarily held their lessons in lecture format, doing most of the talking and directing students to read aloud, write in their books or respond to the teacher's questions. The teachers talked 60% of the time in all of the lessons observed (n = 15). In 12 of the

Table 4.2 Estimated teachers' talking time

Teacher talking time	*No of lessons*	*Percent (%)*
60–64	3	20
80–84	5	33
90–94	6	40
95+	1	7
Total	15	100

lessons, teachers talked for more than 80% of the time, and in one of these 12 lessons, the teacher talked for over 95% of the time (see Table 4.2). Only one teacher encouraged questioning and discussion. Feedback was primarily limited to correcting students' English pronunciation, which was done in six of the lessons.

Given the narrow range of pedagogic repertoires, in particular the near absence of teachers asking open-ended questions, it is perhaps no surprise that the observations revealed very little student talk in the lessons. Based on the observations, teachers were found to be talking 60–64% of the time, while students were talking 35–40% of the time during the lesson. In as many as 14 of the lessons (93.3%), students spent (effectively) all their limited talking time responding to the teacher in English. There were no observable instances of students talking in pairs or groups. While some students were observed speaking local languages fleetingly and informally to each other, they used them only rarely with the teacher, as in Excerpt 4.1 below where locally relevant (but English-based) terms were used.

With regard to inclusive and supportive communications, these were observed in seven of the lessons (47%). Teachers were observed to be creating an inclusive environment by using their students' names, calling on all of them, chatting one-on-one with them, joking and tolerating some noise and calling-out. In terms of personalizing the teaching content, six of the teachers related the teaching material to the students' backgrounds and experiences, and two used resources other than the textbook.

The observation which revealed one of the fullest uses of instructional time, integrating reading, writing, listening and some speaking for students was a Grade 4 Science lesson taught by Teacher 13 at School 4 (see Excerpt 4.1 below). The teacher started by getting the students to activate their background knowledge by thinking of metals in their environment. She brought in real objects like a hammer, a pair of scissors, a metal cup and a spoon, and briefly allowed some students to handle them. She also involved students in a range of activities throughout the lesson, asking a series of open questions and building on students' responses, and recasting their responses to include adjectives (a metal cup) and collocations (a pair of scissors), as can be seen in the following excerpt:

Excerpt 4.1 Integrated science lesson: metals in your environment

Teacher	*For some time now, we have been talking about … Metals and …?*
A few students	Non-metals.
Teacher	… Non-metals. I would like you to look around the classroom and tell me some of the metals you can find in the classroom. Yes?
Student 1	Cupboard
Teacher	Metal. So, you tell me, if you mention the cupboard … Can you find a metal on the cupboard? And which part has the metal? … Yes?
Student 2	Roofing sheet.
Teacher	Roofing sheet. Thank you. […]
Teacher	Oh! Are you sure there is nothing you can see again?
Student 3	Madam, metal chair.
Teacher	Metal chair. … Okay, so I can see that the desk, part of it, has some metal there. *[Points at another pupil.]* Yes, what were you going to say?
Student 4	Zinc
Teacher	Where is the Zinc? *[Pointing at the roofing sheet above]* It's called roofing sheet. … Yes? … And I said it's called …? Somebody just said what …?
Several students	Burglar Proof …
Teacher	Burglar Proof. Or you can say it's what …? [*With a chorus of pupils* …] Metal Gates!

This dialogue is one instance where it could be argued that the student who responded 'zinc' uses a local language and local knowledge to support learning. The boy used the word 'zinc' as a local term for roofing sheets, based on the commonly used brand name for aluminium sheets with zinc coating, AluZinc, which also relates to the Dangme word 'zingiri'. This response is followed by a student's use of another locally relevant term, 'Burglar Proof', which refers to metal grille doors and windows.

Following this excerpt, the teacher continued to ask students questions and recast their answers, encouraging students to produce their own English. She accepted all their suggestions and responses, which were, however, brief and limited to a few words or phrases. While this teacher exhibited a range of teaching strategies, there were no opportunities for students to undertake extended talk, such as a discussion using provided words or phrases to scaffolded dialogue, or to develop and pose their own questions. A fuller command of language supportive pedagogic strategies may have allowed the teacher to extend students' responses and discussion, thus further enhancing their use of English and their understanding of the scientific content.

Factors influencing the absence of student talk

Teachers' limited repertoires may stem, of course, from being less familiar with interactive, student-centred pedagogies. However, the occurrence of inclusive and supportive communications in almost half of the lessons observed indicates that many teachers have at least been made familiar with student-centred, interactive pedagogies through pre- and in-service teacher education. The interview data point to two additional factors that might be influencing the absence of student talk in the classrooms observed. The first is that teachers perceive that their students are not able to produce the language of instruction. The second is that teachers have either limited awareness of or ability to apply specific multilingual pedagogies that support the development of content-related student talk, and/or that they feel that the language-in-education policy which prescribes English as the main language of instruction provides them with no 'implementational space' to draw on such pedagogies.

As mentioned above, evidence from the classroom observations and the teacher interviews concurred that students' level of proficiency in English was not sufficient to access the curriculum. Some teachers noted in particular students' difficulties in producing English:

> They find it difficult to express themselves. Yes. Though they'll read the thing ... but, to explain it, it's always – sometimes – difficult for them.
>
> (Teacher 11, School 3)

Students' low levels of proficiency in speaking were linked both to lack of exposure to English and to lack of opportunity to use the language, both in and outside of the classroom:

> It's because they're not encouraged in the oral aspect. Yes. The oral aspect is not strong. Yes. They don't speak. They don't speak the [English language] ...
>
> (Teacher 11, School 3)

The interview data seem to illustrate a vicious circle: students are not encouraged to speak in the classroom because teachers are aware of their low levels of English proficiency. However, without classroom opportunities to speak, the students have limited opportunities to develop their English and their knowledge of curriculum content in English. While many teachers mentioned that students' spoken language skills in English were low, there was very little evidence that teachers supported English language development through subject teaching in the classroom. The main strategy mentioned in interviews by all teachers for supporting speaking was correction. Observable examples of features that teachers corrected were vocabulary, tenses and pronunciation. However, these strategies for correcting are not particularly focused or supportive of talking meaningfully about subject content in English. In fact, in classroom situations where students were observed to speak very little or not at all, such correction strategies may work to dissuade students from experimenting with new language.

The interviews revealed that teachers were very aware of the additional obstacles students face when having to think in English. One teacher, for example, remarked that students were only able to undertake 'mechanical' tasks using English, but that 'to creatively think and write, and the command of the language in their writing, that's the problem' (Teacher 3, School 1). Similarly, a head teacher reported that 'their thinking ability in the English language is lacking' (Head teacher, School 3). Despite the awareness of these challenges, students were not allowed or encouraged to use the local languages to develop their knowledge of subject content. The interviews suggest that this occurs in part because teachers feel that the language-in-education policy requires them to use English rather than draw on all of students' languages.

Discussion and implications

This study set out to explore whether, in upper primary classrooms in Ghana where students have emergent proficiency in English, we could find evidence of 'productive classroom talk'. The classroom observations undertaken primarily captured examples of classroom talk which was in English only, strongly lecture- and blackboard-based and often focusing on the reproduction of memorized factual knowledge. Teachers, talk dominated lessons, and teachers relied on a limited range of teaching methods, seldom involving students in activities where students would have to speak at length. The low occurrence of interactive pedagogies in this study seems to suggest what has been asserted elsewhere, that language-in-education policies promoting the use of English increase the likelihood of a reliance on teacher-centred, traditional teaching methods. What was observed could be labelled 'safe talk' – participation which maintains an appearance of 'doing the lesson' without risk of loss of face for the teacher or the students, while little productive talk (and probably also little learning) is actually taking place (Chick, 1996; Williams, 2014). Students were not encouraged to speak much beyond one-word, often drilled, responses. The near absence of classroom activities where students talk with each other, discuss or present information means that students have few opportunities to develop their abilities to think and talk in any language, which then works as an obstacle to their understanding and mastery of curriculum content. That teachers are trying to protect students from losing face by not actively engaging them in dialogue in English was confirmed in the interviews, where many teachers expressed the belief that students were not able to actively take part in more complex thinking and talking about content.

With regard to enacting multilingual pedagogies that support the development of content-related student talk, research in other contexts has illustrated the effectiveness of having students draw on their entire linguistic repertoire to engage in meaningful student talk (García & Wei, 2013; Weber, 2014). The findings of our research in Ghana suggest that, despite the fact that the importance of proficiency in English for accessing the curriculum is increasingly recognized, there is both a relative absence of language supportive pedagogy in content classes and content-oriented language teaching in the English classes (cf. Clegg & Afitska, 2011). Moreover, following the official policy, there was only a minimal use of students' local languages in the classroom in the classes observed. A lack of use of local languages was found even in situations where other studies undertaken in SSA have found that local language use and code-switching can be used for cognitive and affective purposes (cf. Ferguson, 2003; Macaro, 2005). Research investigating the role of translanguaging in Ghanaian classrooms is only starting to emerge, and evidence of an awareness of its benefits at the lower primary level has been documented (Owu-Ewie & Eshun, 2019; Yevudey & Agbozo, 2019). However, in our study of upper primary classrooms in Ghana, there was virtually no evidence of translanguaging, suggesting that the value of using local languages to support content learning at the upper primary level and beyond has yet to be embraced in policy or practice.

While teachers in this study primarily relied on traditional lecture pedagogies, the classroom observations did capture evidence of inclusive and supportive communications. The teachers observed were professional and dedicated, and most were lively and engaging. We observed that students were for the most part clearly listening and responding to their teachers' narratives, even if only providing brief responses. In these classrooms, the students did not seem to be anxious or unwilling to participate, as has been found elsewhere (Opoku-Amankwa, 2009). Students were particularly active in the few lessons which allowed them to connect the content teaching with local knowledge (as in the science lesson about local uses of metals). These findings show that there is good practice that can be built upon, and spaces where teachers' repertoires might be extended to create opportunities for multilingual communications that build bridges to content learning.

Teachers' repertoires that support student talk in order to access content learning can be extended through pre- and in-service teacher education initiatives which support 'language supportive pedagogies' (Clegg, 2010). Further support is required in terms of giving students opportunities to think and talk in the local language before speaking aloud in class.[5] Guidance is also needed for prompting students to talk and for providing them with feedback that encourages them to use the language in which they can best speak independently. Teachers need exemplification of strategies to promote spoken language skills, e.g. setting up pair and group work, student presentations and role plays, scaffolded dialogue using written prompts or phrases, and giving support and praise. They also need an understanding of when and how to use local languages to ensure students understand and make progress. Teachers being able to use local languages and English interchangeably as needed would arguably enhance their teaching skills and make teaching more enjoyable (cf. Ankohmah et al., 2012), allowing space for explaining, checking understanding and enabling students to present what they know. Awareness needs to be raised that all teachers (not just language teachers) are responsible for supporting students' language development, and the teaching of English and Ghanaian languages needs to support the learning of curriculum subjects.

There is also a need for more nuanced policy-to-practice guidance, communicating to teachers that using local languages alongside the language of instruction can enhance, not undermine, teaching and learning. As the policy for use of English from Grade 4 is currently very strictly interpreted, teachers need a mandate to continue using local languages beyond lower primary. Students' English is still emergent at this point, and research has consistently shown that learners generally need at least five to seven years to learn a language well enough to be able to use it for accessing content knowledge (Cummins, 2010). Flexible language-in-education policies (cf. Weber, 2014) should create 'implementational space' (Hornberger & Johnson, 2007) where teachers can use local languages when needed to structure this transition and support the development of English for accessing content.

Conclusion

In the Ghanaian upper primary classrooms of this research, we observed teachers who were enthusiastic about their profession and committed to student learning. Classrooms were purposeful and supportive of children as learners. Relationships between teachers and students were positive. But we also saw how teachers and students operate in a highly restricted linguistic and pedagogical space. The Ghanaian students and teachers who were participants in this study have vast, under-utilized multilingual resources that could be mobilized for learning and productive classroom talk that supports the development of cognitive and linguistic development. Virtually every teacher in Ghana is multilingual (Yevudey & Agbozo, 2019), though they may not necessarily share their students' languages. Being able to communicate and teach using their entire linguistic repertoire would arguably enhance their pedagogical skills and capacities, thereby improving the quality of education and students' learning. Allowing students to use their entire linguistic repertoire would also make it more likely that they would be able to engage in 'productive classroom talk', thinking and reasoning together to develop their language abilities and their mastery of content knowledge. Further research into the implementation and outcome of approaches for supporting multilingual productive classroom talk would increase our understanding of how this can be achieved.

Acknowledgements

We are grateful to the British Council, Education Development Trust and the Open University for funding the research that this study is based on. We would also like to acknowledge Lina Adinolfi and Kristina Hultgren at the Open University for the integral roles they played in carrying out the wider research project, and Sarah Jane Mukherjee and Subhi Ashour for their roles in coding the interview data. We would like to offer special thanks to the school leaders, teachers and students who allowed us insights into their daily lives and language practices at school, and we hope very much to have represented these practices with respect and accuracy.

Notes

1 As in García and Kleifgen (2018), we primarily rely on the term 'emergent' to refer to these multilingual students' developing proficiency in English.
2 These documents are available on the OU's Research website: www.open.ac.uk/research/research-school/resources/policy-information-governance.php.
3 www.baal.org.uk/about_goodpractice_full.pdf.
4 Dangme (or Dangbe) is one of the 11 government-sponsored languages prescribed for use at school. It is spoken in Greater Accra, in south-east Ghana and Togo.
5 Such activities can be undertaken even when the teacher does not speak all of the students' languages (García & Wei, 2013; Trudell & Young, 2016).

References

Alexander, R 2008, *Towards Dialogic Teaching: Rethinking Classroom Talk*, Dialogos, York.

Alexander, R 2015, 'Teaching and learning for all? The quality imperative revisited', *International Journal of Educational Development*, vol. 40, pp. 250–258.

Amfo, NAA & Anderson, J 2019, 'Multilingualism and language policies in the African context: Lessons from Ghana', *Current Issues in Language Planning*, vol. 20(4), pp. 333–337. DOI: https://doi.org/10.1080/14664208.2019.1582945.

Ankohmah, Y, Afitska, O, Clegg, J, Kiliku, P, Mtana, N, Osei-Amankwah, L, Rubagumya, C & Tarimo, E 2012, *EdQual: Language and Literacy Project Overview Report*, www.edqual.org/publications/rpcstrategiesandreports/browse%3Ftheme=language literacy.html.

Brock-Utne, B 2001, Education for all – In whose language? *Oxford Review of Education*, vol. 27, pp. 115–134. DOI: https://doi.org/10.1080/03054980125577.

Bunyi, G 2005, 'Languages in Kenya Classroom', in AMY Lin & PW Martin (eds), *Decolonisation, Globalisation: Language-in-Education Policy and Practice. New Perspectives on Language and Education*, Multilingual Matters, Clevedon, pp. 131–152.

Chick, JK 1996, 'Safe-talk: Collusion in apartheid education', in H Coleman (ed), *Society and the Language Classroom*, Cambridge University Press, Cambridge, pp. 21–39.

Clegg, J 2010, 'The lure of English-medium education' in P Powel-Davies (ed), *Access English EBE Symposium: A Collection of Papers*, British Council East Asia, Kuala Lumpur, pp. 46–62.

Clegg, J & Afitska, O 2011, 'Teaching and learning in two languages in African classrooms', *Comparative Education*, vol. 47(1), pp. 61–77. DOI: https://doi.org/10.1080/03050068.2011.541677.

Cummins, J 2010, 'Instructional conditions for trilingual development', *International Journal of Bilingual Education and Bilingualism*, vol. 4(1) pp. 61–75. DOI: https://doi.org/10.1080/13670050108667719.

Darvas, P & Balwanz, D 2013, Basic Education beyond the Millennium Development Goals in Ghana. How Equity in Service Delivery Affects Educational and Learning Outcomes.

Erling, EJ, Adinolfi, L & Hultgren, AK 2017, Multilingual Classrooms: Opportunities and Challenges for English Medium Instruction in Low and Middle Income Countries, Education Development Trust, Reading www.educationdevelopmenttrust.com/en-GB/our-research/our-research-library/2017/r-multilingual-classrooms.

Erling, EJ, Adinolfi, L, Hultgren, AK, Buckler, A & Mukorera, M 2016, 'Medium of instruction policies in Ghanaian and Indian primary schools: An overview of key issues and recommendations', *Comparative Education*, vol. 52(3), pp. 294–310. DOI: https://doi.org/10.1080/03050068.2016.1185254.

Ferguson, G 2003, 'Classroom code-switching in post-colonial contexts: Functions, attitudes and policies', *AILA Review*, vol. 16(1), pp. 38–51. DOI: https://doi.org/10.1075/aila.16.05fer.

García, O & Kleifgen, JA 2018, *Educating Emergent Bilinguals: Policies, Programs, and Practices for English Learners*, Teachers College Press, New York.

García, O & Wei, L 2013, 'Translanguaging: Language, bilingualism and education', in O García & O Wei (eds), *Translanguaging: Language, Bilingualism and Education*, Palgrave, London, pp. 1–165. DOI: https://doi.org/10.1057/9781137385765

Hattie, JAC 2009, *Visible Learning: A Synthesis of Over 800 Meta-Analyses Relating to Achievement*, Routledge, London.

Hornberger, N & Johnson, DC 2007, 'Slicing the onion ethnographically: Layers and spaces in multilingual language education policy and practice', *TESOL Quarterly*, vol. 41(3), pp. 509–532. DOI: https://doi.org/10.1002/j.1545-7249.2007.tb00083.x.

Hultgren, AK, Erling, EJ & Chowdhury, QH 2016, *Ethics in Language and Identity Research. The Routledge Handbook of Language and Identity*. Routledge, London, DOI: https://doi.org/10.4324/9781315669816

Kerswill, P 2017, *The Contested Role of English in West Africa: Ghana*, Paper delivered at Sheffield Hallam University, Humanities Research Centre, 22 March, viewed 24 April 2020 www.academia.edu/32042749/The_contested_role_of_English_in_West_Africa_Ghana._Given_at_Sheffield_Hallam_University_22_March_2017_?auto=download.

Littleton, K & Mercer, N 2013, *Interthinking: Putting Talk to Work*, Routledge, London.

Macaro, E 2005, 'Codeswitching in the L2 classroom: A communication and learning strategy', in E Llurda (ed), *Non-Native Language Teachers: Perceptions, Challenges and Contributions to the Profession*, Springer, Amsterdam, pp. 63–84.

Ministry of Education Ghana (MoE) 2016, Ghana 2016 National Education Assessment Report of Findings. Education Service, Ministry of Education, Accra, viewed 23 March 2020, http://pdf.usaid.gov/pdf_docs/PA00MHMR.pdf.

Opoku-Amankwa, K 2009, '"Teacher only calls her pets": Teacher's selective attention and the invisible life of a diverse classroom in Ghana', *Language and Education*, vol. 23(3), pp. 249–262. DOI: https://doi.org/10.1080/09500780802582539.

Opoku-Amankwa, K, Edu-Buandoh, DF & Brew-Hammond, A 2015, Publishing for mother tongue-based bilingual education in Ghana: Politics and consequences. *Language and Education*, *29*(1), 1–14. https://doi.org/10.1080/09500782.2014.921194

Owu-Ewie, C & Eshun, ES 2019, 'Language representation in the Ghanaian lower primary classroom and its implications: The case of selected schools in the Central and Western Regions of Ghana', *Current Issues in Language Planning*, vol. 20(4), pp. 365–388. DOI: https://doi.org/10.1080/14664208.2019.1585159.

Pinnock, H & Vijayakumar, G 2009, Language and Education: The Missing Link. How the Language Used in School Threatens the Achievement of Education for All, viewed 2 March 2020, UNESCO, Paris, www.unesco.org/education/EFAWG2009/LanguageEducation.pdf.

Probyn, M 2015, 'Pedagogical translanguaging: Bridging discourses in South African science classrooms', *Language and Education*, vol. 29(3), pp. 218–234. DOI: https://doi.org/10.1080/09500782.2014.994525.

Rosekrans, K, Sherris, A & Chatry-Komarek, M 2012, 'Education reform for the expansion of mother-tongue education in Ghana', *International Review of Education*, vol. 58(5), pp. 593–618. DOI: https://doi.org/10.1007/s11159-012-9312-6.

Rubagumya, CM (ed) 1994, *Teaching and Researching Language in African Classrooms*, Multilnigual Matters, Clevedon.

Trudell, B 2016, The Impact of Language Policy and Practice on Children's Learning: Evidence from Eastern and Southern Africa, UNICEF, New York, www.unicef.org/esaro/UNICEF(2016)LanguageandLearning-FullReport(SingleView).pdf.

Trudell, B & Young, C (eds) 2016, Good Answers to Tough Questions in Mother Tongue-Based Multilingual Education, SIL International, Dallas, viewed 3 April 2020, www.sil.org/literacy-education/good-answers-tough-questions-mother-tongue-based-multilingual-education.

UNESCO 2014, Teaching and Learning Achieving: Quality for All. Education for All Global Monitoring Report 2013-2014, UNESCO, Paris, viewed 5 April 2020, http://unesdoc.unesco.org/images/0022/002256/225660e.pdf.

UNESCO 2016, If You don't Understand, How Can You Learn? Global Education Monitoring Report. Policy Paper 24, UNESCO, Paris, viewed 29 April 2020, https://en.unesco.org/gem-report/if-you-don't-understand-how-can-you-learn.

UNESCO 2019, *UIS Stats: Data to Transform Lives*, UNESCO, Paris http://uis.unesco.org/.

Veen, C, Wilt, V, Kruistum, C, Oers, B, & Michaels, S 2017, MODEL2TALK: An intervention to promote productive classroom talk. *The Reading Teacher*, vol. 70(6), pp. 689–700. https://doi.org/10.1002/trtr.1573

Vygotsky, L 1978, *Mind in Society: The Development of Higher Psychological Processes*, Harvard University Press, Cambridge, MA.

Weber, J-J 2014, *Flexible Multilingual Education: Putting Children's Needs First*, Multilingual Matters, Bristol.

Westbrook, J, Durrani, N, Brown, R, Orr, D, Pryor, J, Boddy, J & Salvi, F 2013, Ped*agogy, Curriculum, Teaching Practices and Teacher Education in Developing Countries*, Department for International Development, London, pp. 1–151. DOI: https://doi.org/10.1080/19452829.2014.991706.

Williams, E 2014, 'English in African politics of education: capital or capital illusion?', *International Journal of the Sociology of Language*, vol. 225, pp. 131–145.

Yevudey, E & Agbozo, GE 2019, 'Teacher trainee sociolinguistic backgrounds and attitudes to language-in-education policy in Ghana: A preliminary survey', *Current Issues in Language Planning*, vol. 20, pp. 338–364. DOI: https://doi.org/10.1080/14664208.2019.1585158.

Part 2

Multilingual learning in pre-primary, primary and secondary schools: lessons learned

5 Apprenticeships in meaning

Transforming opportunities for oral and written language learning in the early years

Carole Bloch and Sive Mbolekwa

Introduction

Proverbs are the palm-oil with which words are eaten

(Chinua Achebe)

When children learn language, they are not simply engaging in one kind of learning among many; rather, they are learning the foundation of learning itself

(Michael Halliday, 1993, p. 93)

In this chapter we focus on the early childhood years and consider the significance of stimulating children's hunger for words in leading them to establish powerful foundations for oral and written language development and use. The ongoing, systemic failure to get young children reading and writing in multilingual South Africa (SA) makes this an urgent and complex task. Attention by prominent researchers has turned most recently to the crucial role that reading for meaning has in the reading process, in addition to word recognition or 'decoding' (Spaull et al., 2020). Further attention is also being paid to the differences between teaching reading in African languages and English, or other European languages. In this chapter, our intention is to problematise the way these literacy issues are being addressed and to share our view of some viable alternative theoretical perspectives and practices in early childhood. In doing so, we hope to widen thinking and discussion about the reading process. This will be useful because the views we hold substantially influence the relative weight of different teaching components in designing and implementing early literacy programmes. Our experience is that the choice of pedagogical approach can either open up or close down the teaching opportunities which motivate and inspire teachers and in turn, children.

Irrespective of languages used, in SA and in wider Sub-Saharan Africa (SSA), a transmission style of teaching with rote learning of decontextualised skills continues to characterise early childhood teaching practice for most children (Biersteker et al., 2008, p. 228), despite policies and curriculum frameworks

DOI: 10.4324/9781003028383-7

which propose otherwise (e.g. Department of Education, 2011). In addition, education systems in SSA are still influenced by the colonial past where local knowledges and languages were not valued. Among many others, McKinney (2017, p. 3) makes the point that SA "ignores the resources that Black and non-middle-class children bring with them to formal schooling". She quotes Makoe (2007, p. 60), who reports the view of a deputy principal in an urban English-medium primary school in Johannesburg that African-speaking children 'have basically no language'. Against this background, teaching and learning in SA needs to take place within a broad framework of the decolonisation and transformation of education, which implies that all cultures, languages and ways of being human are the bedrock on which schooling is constructed. In this chapter, we explore how this aim can begin to be realised in early childhood by ensuring holistic, participatory pedagogical approaches for teaching literacy. Many children in multilingual settings of the Global South and North who use languages to communicate successfully at home and in their communities struggle at school to learn new languages and to read and write:

> A growing number of children and youth live in multilingual environments and develop complex language repertoires – although often not exactly the ones that are expected by the respective education systems. In many of the systems, monolingual language development is considered as the 'normal' prerequisite for learning and can thus be the general basis for teaching. Research shows, however, that multilingualism is not only influential on language acquisition and development, but also on learning in general and should thus be taken into consideration in the organization, contents and methods of teaching.
>
> (Gogolin, 2018, p. 34)

Our chapter is informed by the view that schooling should ascertain, value and develop children's multilingual repertoires and make them the basis on which learning is constructed. This encourages opening up and supporting indigenous African approaches to learning, as outlined here by Nsamenang (2006, p. 296):

> In principle, children are rarely instructed or prodded into what they learn, but discover it during participation. This depicts cognitive development as the unfolding of the abilities to generate the knowledge and skills with which to responsibly and increasingly engage with the world. Accordingly, the onus to understand the social cognition and intelligent behaviour of Africans lies in capturing shared routines and participatory learning, rather than in completing school-based instruments.

We highlight the role of social and experiential learning and propose a holistic early literacy teaching approach which deliberately entwines languages and pedagogy through story and symbolic play (Vygotsky, 1978), discovery (Nsamenang, 2006) and children's first-hand experiences (Louis, 2009; Bruce, 2015; Bloch,

2019). This, we will explain, gives rise to the kind of meaningful emotional and intellectual connections which can stimulate literacy and other learning.

PRAESA's Storyplay approach

The Project for the Study of Alternative Education in South Africa (PRAESA) is an NGO with a history of involvement across various aspects of multilingual education. PRAESA's current work includes training trainers and practitioners to offer holistic language and literacy opportunities for children from birth onwards, and particularly for three to six year olds before formal education begins.[1] We began developing Storyplay for young children in 2015 when we led the Nal'ibali National Reading for Enjoyment Campaign (Bloch, 2015). Our aim with Nal'ibali was to enhance personally meaningful reading and writing cultural practices by growing a love of reading between adults and children, thereby enhancing story-focused literate practices (Bloch, 2018).[2]

In 2016, Nal'ibali became a separate campaign and PRAESA turned its attention to the nuts and bolts of early literacy pedagogy to help influence emerging interpretations of and solutions to the 'literacy crisis' from a teaching perspective. Fleisch (2008, p. 139) summarises this crisis as "a comprehensive and consistent story of educational failure in literacy and mathematics achievement in South Africa". One of the programmes PRAESA currently offers is a nine-week Storyplay programme to practitioners in early childhood settings which involves an apprenticeship process between a mentor and practitioners. The apprenticeship has a range of elements, all of which hinge on building relationships of mutual trust. We draw on the notion of *apprenticeship*, as developed by Rogoff (1990, 2016), which provides a model of activity, involving individuals who are experienced in a practice ('mentors'), participating with 'newcomers' to the practice in an organised, deliberate process. Part of its purpose is to demonstrate and role model the desirable practice to the newcomers who, are motivated to join in – at first on the periphery, but gradually taking ownership and in so doing, exerting influence on how things are done. Also using Rogoff's concept of 'Learning by Observing and Pitching In' (Rogoff, 2016), we aim to develop communities of Storyplay practice.

One morning a week for nine weeks, in the teachers' classroom and working with the children, the mentors ensure cycles of demonstrating and guiding, planning activities, implementing with children, reflecting and revising. The intention is for mentors to shift between initiating and supportive roles, with practitioners (the newcomers) gradually taking over planning and facilitating as they find their own way into the approach. In the materials for the programme, we prioritise the use of suitable stories available in African languages in SA.[3] The chapter is illustrated with examples of classroom work which were recorded in three schools in the areas of Vrygrond, Khayelitsha and Philippi in Cape Town as part of a Storyplay in Action project carried out by PRAESA from 2017 (Bloch 2018, 2019). In two of the settings, where most children and teachers share isiXhosa, this is the language of teaching. In the other, English is mainly used in a setting where most teachers know English or Afrikaans, but do not know isiXhosa, while the children speak a mixture of isiXhosa, Afrikaans, other African languages, French and English. The project aimed to explore ways of ensuring affordable, high quality early literacy provision and practices in under-served communities.

In what follows, we first raise key issues which in our view challenge the development and transformation of literacy learning in SA. We then discuss how we have tried to address these issues and share practical examples of this from the Storyplay in Action project.[4] We end the chapter with an analysis of and suggestions for progress and implementation in other Sub-Saharan contexts.

Key issues challenging literacy learning in SA

The young bird does not crow until it hears the old ones

(Tswana proverb)

Below, we describe four key issues which challenge successful literacy learning opportunities for children in SA as well as the theories and practices that we have embraced in the Storyplay approach to help us address these challenges. We developed Storyplay during a time in SA of much research, policy and training around what teachers need to have, know and do to ensure that children learn to read (Taylor et al., 2017). A good deal of debate has been aroused, at the heart of which are four main interrelated issues: firstly, the importance of addressing the factors which hinder meaning-based, culturally responsive learning; secondly, making space for holistic views of teaching early literacy and the role of multilingualism therein; thirdly, taking into account children's multilingual repertoires; and fourthly focusing on how babies and young children learn. These four aspects will be discussed in more detail below.

Understanding meaning-based, culturally responsive learning

With regard to meaning-based learning, we note the ongoing tendency in preschool, for classroom practice to favour rote-learning, repetition and transmission teaching and to side-line meaning and children's need to communicate and understand to learn. In so doing, children and their family funds of knowledge (Moll et al., 1992) are largely undervalued and often viewed as irrelevant to literacy learning. Recognition of the significance of the very early years (Young & Mustard, 2008) has most recently led in SA to movements towards teaching birth to four year olds (Ebrahim, 2014).[5] Curriculum frameworks for these youngest of learners promoting 'learner centred' informal, play-based teaching using transforming, culturally responsive pedagogies (DOE, 2015; PIECCE, 2019). However, there is much work to be done to change practice as teachers feel under pressure to 'prepare' children for Grade R and Grade 1 using decontextualised skills teaching procedures. Classroom practice often reduces the importance of personal meaning-making and limits learner responses to recall and repetition.

This tends to be the case in English-medium classrooms where the emergent ability of many children to use English makes it hard for them to produce much more than single word items. Themes, which inevitably include shapes, colours, numbers, weather, months and days of the week, are taught, often through oral drill, worksheets and workbooks.

An example of this practice can be seen in the excerpt below, observed in Vrygrond, Cape Town, at the beginning of the Storyplay in Action project. Teacher C is teaching 'triangles' to 25 three- and four-year-old children, who speak a range of languages at home and learn through English at preschool.[6] She holds a small triangle in one hand and a big triangle in the other and asks the children:

> *"What shape are these?"*
> *"Tri ... angle ..."* chorus the children.
> *"And how many sides have they got?"*
> *"Three! "*chorus the children.
> *"Give yourselves a clap"*, says the teacher, smiling.
> She holds up the small triangle, *"Remember, a triangle can be small", then holds up the big triangle, "Or ...?"*
> A few children call out *"Big"*.
> *"Well done!"* says the teacher.

The children's reward is to please their teacher; they have done this before and know the expected answers. All they have to do is recognise, recall and repeat. Such initial decontextualised transmission of discrete skills defines for many teachers what counts as significant learning, its indicators and outcomes.

Turning to literacy teaching in indigenous African languages, we find that the same decontexualised drilling tends to dominate classroom practice. Applying the logic that Grade R prepares children for Grade 1, according to Nel et al. (2016, p. 50), the curriculum requires that:

> When they enter Grade R, these children are expected, amongst other things, to already be able to identify words, recognise words made up of sounds, segment oral sentences into individual words, recognise initial sounds, read high frequency words, answer question based on a story read, form letters using finger painting and copy words and letters.
>
> (DoE, 2011)

Teachers often find the children cannot do these tasks (ibid.). One reason is that practitioners use the same low-meaning, high repetition drilling with learners working in indigenous languages as that used for our English-medium triangles example above. Many teachers have little, if any, training; moreover, trained teachers and teacher educators from higher grades can 'descend' to work with young children without necessarily having relevant training or experience with this age group (Atmore, 2013). Storyplay has been designed with these challenges in mind.

Views of teaching early literacy

Deciding what is appropriate teaching for effective early literacy learning is informed by understandings and models of reading and writing processes. The focus in SA has been largely on a formal process of 'early grade reading' in primary schooling, starting with preparing five and six-year-old children in Grade R for Grade 1 (Richter & Samuels, 2017; Spaull, 2019).[7] We contrast this with a well-established view which we hold, which sees early literacy learning as an integral part of a complex continuum which begins well before school (Bua-lit, 2018; Whitmore et al., 2004).

While there are many variations and versions of learning to read across the world, a fairly simplistic hierarchical, skills-based view underpins most literacy teaching, particularly its beginning stages. Comprehending and 'reading to learn' are described as the outcome of a 'learning to read' process (Pearson et al., 2020; Spaull, 2016). This view, also held widely in SA, is based on the claim that it is an evolutionary fact that oral language learning, i.e. listening and speaking, represents the only 'natural language', acquired in social contexts without teaching (Shaywitz, 2003). Written language, i.e. writing and reading, is understood to be a cultural and artificial invention needing specifically ordered teaching with components initially simplified and taught separately (Spaull & Pretorius 2019: p. 5; Wolf, 2008).

Cognitive neuroscience, in what we see as a reductionist view, offers supporting evidence (Dehaene, 2009; Seidenberg, 2017). They propose that graphophonic language 'cues' (decoding) must be taught through a systematic process whereby 'natural' language is articulated as sounds, when a voice speaks. For reading, these sounds are then mapped onto the particular symbols on the page which combine to become words. They also claim to provide evidence for the need to stress automatic and fluent decoding. The view is that short-term memory will be overloaded without this initial drill for automaticity and fluency. Comprehension is understood to arise from this, although it is not guaranteed (Abadzi, 2006, 2017; Spaull & Pretorius, 2019). The emphasis for teachers is on ensuring that children are taught and learn specific skills so that they can ultimately come to read and write meaningfully. The implication for multilingual teaching with this model is that for each additional language a child learns to read, its sound system should be taught deliberately and separately (Spaull et al., 2020). The diagram in Figure 5.1 depicts an interpretation of this reductionist model by one of us (CB).

This model has been the subject of much critique by scholars who view language and literacy development more holistically (e.g. Altwerger et al, 2007; Edelsky, 1991; Hruby & Goswami, 2011; Strauss, 2004; Strauss et al., 2009). Like them, we view literacy development as multi-directional, integrating complex

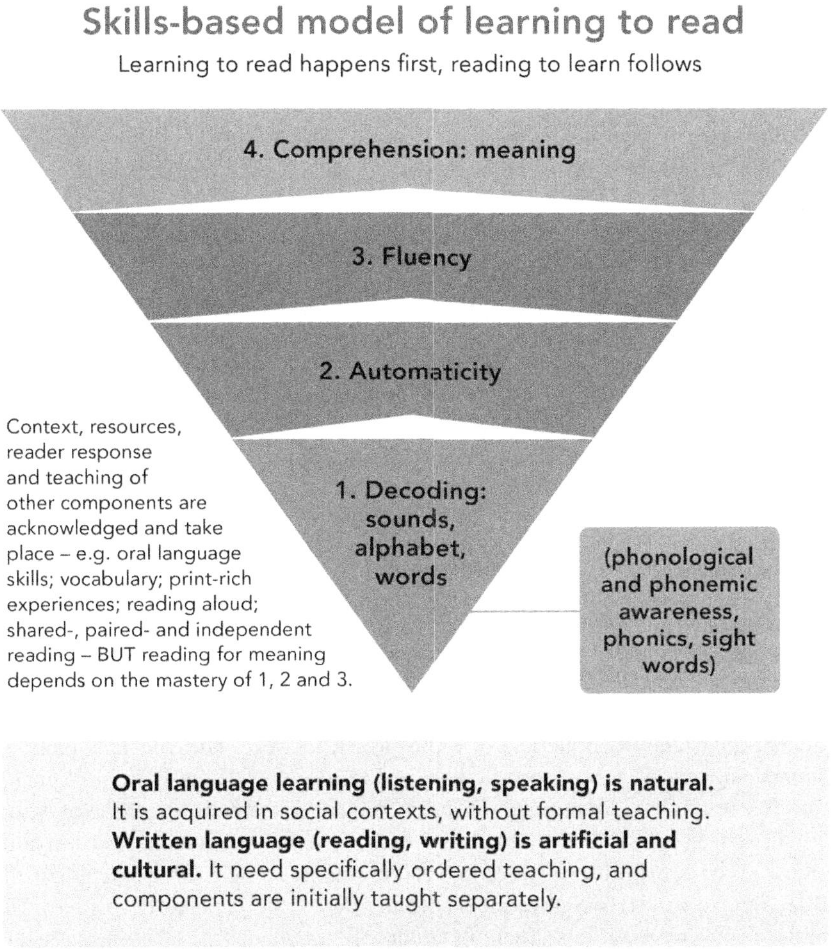
Skills-based model of learning to read
Learning to read happens first, reading to learn follows
4. Comprehension: meaning
3. Fluency
2. Automaticity
1. Decoding: sounds, alphabet, words
(phonological and phonemic awareness, phonics, sight words)
Context, resources, reader response and teaching of other components are acknowledged and take place – e.g. oral language skills; vocabulary; print-rich experiences; reading aloud; shared-, paired- and independent reading – BUT reading for meaning depends on the mastery of 1, 2 and 3.
Oral language learning (listening, speaking) is natural. It is acquired in social contexts, without formal teaching. Written language (reading, writing) is artificial and cultural. It need specifically ordered teaching, and components are initially taught separately.

Figure 5.1 Skills-based model of learning to read.

systems and processes. A growing body of more holistically oriented, integrative neuroscience research reveals evolutionary endowed functions which all human brains share. These operate at great speed without our conscious awareness (Damasio, 2006; Ellis & Solms, 2018; Hawkins & Blakeslee, 2007; Panksepp, 1998). In this view, meaning-making and comprehending *drive* learning. Young children learn to simultaneously use a suite of semantic (meaning), syntactic (grammatical) and graphophonic cues for making meaning in one or more languages (Goodman et al., 2016). The brain naturally 'chunks' experience, including reading and writing, into meaningful units, and these are what is stored in short- and long-term memory, rather than just their components (Bermudez, 2014; Miller, 1956). Such a holistic model views both oral and written language as social practice learned in socio-cultural contexts, through both informal and formal teaching. Although oral language is much older, they both evolved as symbolic systems to communicate meaning (Tomasello, 2003).

Neuroscientific evidence (discussed further below) supports our view of literacy and language development, essentially relating to prediction (Hawkins, 2004; Clark, 2013), pattern recognition (Gray, 2011) and a set of evolutionarily 'hardwired' primary emotional systems (Panksepp, 1998). Children apply their prior knowledge and knowledge of oral and written language to communicate purposefully and express themselves from the start, learning to write and read together, as with speech, in an apprenticeship relationship, with knowledgeable and interactive role models. These role models teach skills and draw children's attention to the purposes and features of print as part of an ongoing process of reading and writing interesting and useful texts. Figure 5.2 shows an interpretation of the holistic, meaning-based model of early literacy by one of us (CB).

Taking into account children's multilingual repertoires

This model also integrates the multilingual repertoires of most children into considerations for literacy teaching. A language-in-education policy has been in effect in SA since 1997 which promotes multilingual education (DBE, 1997), but it has not been systemically implemented. So although 'mother tongue' is understood widely as preferable for the preschool years and the first years of primary education, a magnetic pull to the early use of English persists: many schools use English as language of instruction in the preschool and early years (Du Plessis & Louw, 2008). Inadequate conditions for teaching and learning English often contribute to low school achievement (Fleisch, 2008; Heugh et al., 2007, Ramadiro 2016; Smith, 2011; Smits et al., 2008) and to the widespread culture of low expectations of young children.

When exposed multilingually, children also translanguage (Bua-Lit, 2018; García, 2009; Makalela, 2019) by drawing on their emerging language capacities, both oral and written, to comprehend and compose. Ubuntu[8] translanguaging, which gives South African expression to translanguaging (García, 2009), promotes a "… focus is on what speakers do with the languages rather than what the languages look like" (Makalela, 2019, p. 246) and enriches translanguaging with the ubuntu-related concepts of compassion and community. Referring to García's metaphor of translanguaging as being an all-terrain vehicle (García, 2009, p. 45), Makalela writes:

> It is instructive in showing that while it may seem bumpy and non-linear in its movement, there is a logic that enables it to accomplish its task. Like the logic of a moving all-terrain vehicle, multilingual speakers who use more

Learning how to write+read happens while print is used for personally meaningful reasons

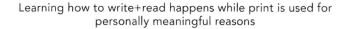

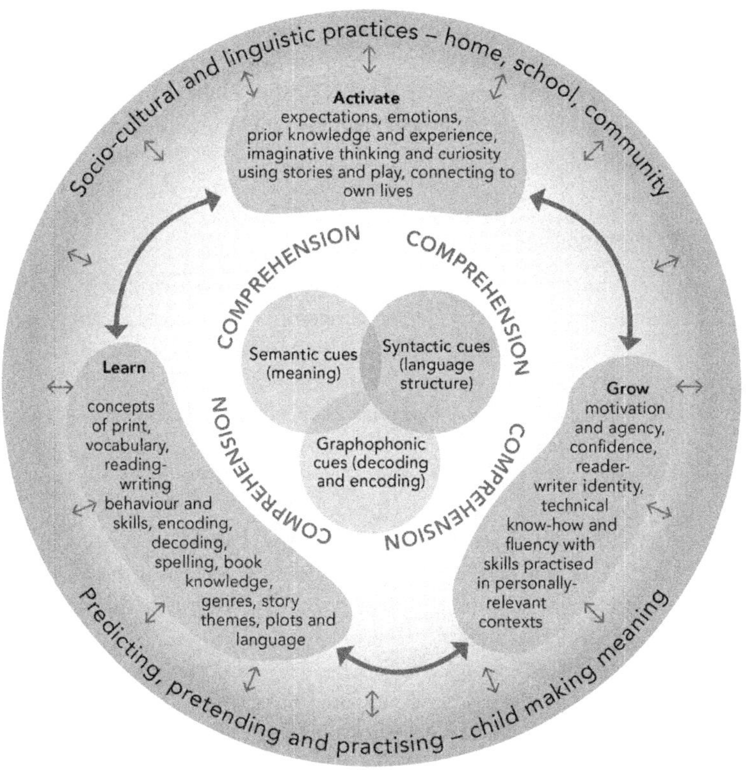

Oral and written language are learned in social contexts with both informal and formal teaching. Although oral language is much older, they both evolved as symbolic systems to communicate meaning.

Children apply their knowledge of oral and written language to communicate purposefully from the start. They learn to write+read from knowledgable and interactive role models who teach skills as these are needed to carry out desirable print related activities.

Figure 5.2 Meaning-based model of learning to read + write.

than one language in the same utterance or in their input/output are able to make sense of the world and of who they are. From the speaker's point of view, the languages are not differentiated as boundaries are overcome by the desire to make meaning.

(2019, p. 240)

This view of language enables us to move beyond arguments for either African languages or English medium which have seemed to paralyse educational progress. It implies a need to better take into account children's multilingual communicative repertoires (Gumperz, 1971; Hymes, 1980) and use them concurrently as resources for literacy learning. Encouraging children to use their repertoires in full and authentic ways intersects seamlessly with holistic early childhood principles and literacy approaches. This can release teachers and children from the burden of overly technical first steps to literacy as we will discuss in the final section of the chapter.

How babies and young children learn

Finally, literacy teaching methods often follow models from formal school without attending to established holistic understandings of the nature of learning in early childhood, as well as the limiting effect on early years education of frequently appalling physical and educational conditions for practitioners, babies and young children (Biersteker et al., 2008; Van der Berg et al., 2013). Storyplay, however, arises from the premise that early literacy learning ought to continue the meaning-making process begun autonomously at birth. By the time they reach preschool, all young children are deep into an apprenticeship of understanding how to join into the particular range of social and cultural ways of being and doing, experienced as 'natural' in their families and communities. Our work builds from the following empirically grounded neuroscientific premises which apply to all human babies at birth.

First, our brains are highly plastic and easily shaped by environmental factors and experience (Ellis & Solms, 2018). The neuronal links which form connections in our brains change all the time in response to the physical, ecological and social environment; this allows learning. Baby brains start off with vast numbers of connections. As they have experiences, some connections are repeatedly used. These thicken and strengthen and create new connections. Connections which are not used get pruned, gradually thinning out (Shore, 1997). This process continues through life, but is most pronounced up to age ten, as our brains shape our development. New learning is always possible, but it happens easily in early childhood.

Thus (culturally and linguistically appropriate) enriched environments and opportunities are key for all children, irrespective of background – including learning how to use written language.

Second, brains use experience to compare things and situations (Ellis & Solms, 2018). Everything new is examined in the light of previous experience and previously learned rules of behaviour. These experiences create expectations which are then either met or not. Learning which builds on what children know already is easier (Bruce, 2012). Thus children who love stories but realise their language is not in picture books can internalise a sense that their language is limited, and experience little desire to learn to read. Children who only experience reading as trying to sound out a text with an inauthentic story line will not expect reading to interest them, while children who have enjoyed treasuries of stories in languages they understand bring both this story language and the anticipation of pleasure to learning how to use written language.

Third, our brains seek and recognise patterns and make predictions (Gray, 2011; Clark, 2013). Our brains continuously filter information, selecting what they need and throwing away masses of data that is irrelevant in the moment. We fill in the information with only partial knowledge because so much happens all the time that it is not possible to use all of the information. Thus, brains have evolved to efficiently predict what is likely to happen, searching for, recognising and classifying patterns. Patterns bring smaller parts together to make meaningful wholes.

Thus, the word 'multilingualism' is easier to recognise and remember than a string of letters, such as 'msiltpbordiluft'. A song or rhyme is easy to memorise and so is a story. We use the pattern of story to organise and make meaning of our lives. All perception proceeds in the same contextual 'holistic' way (seeing, hearing, reading), being based in the same cognitive mechanism, applied in different domains (Ellis and Bloch 2021). Moreover, when we read in any language our brains use prediction:

> Regardless of the orthography, readers, like listeners, are preoccupied with comprehension. They predict meaning, syntactic structures and the written language forms which expresses the language. These aspects of reading are universal and create the parameters in which the features of each writing system and language are used.
>
> (Goodman et al., 1984, p. 24)

Readers, including beginners, make predictions using information from a text (including titles, headings, pictures and diagrams) and their prior knowledge and experiences.

Fourth, we are born with a set of several primary emotional systems developed over time through evolutionary activity (Ellis & Solms, 2018; Damasio, 1994, 1999; Panksepp, 1998), which strongly influence how we behave. They change activity in our brains, are remembered in our bodies and guide neurological development. Thinking cannot happen without this emotional guidance; an emotional tag attaches to every memory, influencing and shaping our reactions. We have an "emotional predisposition that motivates us to learn a language in order to communicate our needs and desires ..." (Ellis & Solms, 2018, p. 156).

Three of the emotional systems appear to be fundamental for learning. First, there is a need to belong, secondly, the need to seek and make meaning, and thirdly, the need to play. Considering the need to belong, babies bond with their mothers or primary caregivers, and then with others seeking security and social connection; confidence arises from and connects into this. This bonding initiates communication and language learning with emotional intention and personal use at the centre (Greenspan & Shanker, 2009). By implication, rejection or a sense of alienation hinders or damages confidence and the will to learn. Second, babies need to seek and make meaning; they are motivated from birth to find out about their world. The reward is intrinsically rooted in the 'doing'. Learning continues in this way if the activities children are involved in are authentic and not exercises stripped of context. Third, babies need to play; they play with sounds, imitating significant adults, soothing and comforting themselves (Weir, 1962). They move to pretend play, as story in action (Paley, 1991) with real and imagined scenarios, rehearsing and consolidating experiences and solving problems. Symbolic play is a precursor to theory of mind and to written language (Vygotsky, 1978). Pretending to be the doctor or patient nudges young minds towards others. Pretending that a box represents a car is only a few steps from appreciating how the letters 'Mama' represent a precious mother. Human emotional contexts are thus integral to effective learning, including learning how to use written language.

Having explored the key issues that the Storyplay approach aims to address, in the following section we offer reasons for, and descriptions of, the approach in practice and consider how it can lead to powerful literacy teaching and learning.

Transformation in and through Storyplay

Story is the taproot of African education. It is also central to human experience, as the shared vehicle for communicating and making meaning (Gottschall, 2012). Story involving reciprocal relationships and experiences, holism, apprenticeships and communal interdependence gave meaning and substance to educational practice in Africa before it was side-lined by colonialism and apartheid (Makalela, 2014; Mbiti, 1989; Owusu-Ansah & Mji, 2013). Drawing on oral literature traditions exposes children to the value and use of creative performance, rhythm, musicality, metaphor and improvisation (Finnegan, 2012). Simultaneously teachers can guide children in the authentic process of bringing written language into their expanding communicative repertoires. The substance of curriculum delivery can thus develop organically from history, existing social realities and from the current knowledge, practices and language strengths of teachers and children and their families. This beautifully complements what we consider relevant: meaning-based perspectives on early literacy learning embedded in a holistic interdisciplinary early childhood pedagogy framed by Froebelian theories that humans are essentially productive and creative (Bruce et al., 2018). Crucially this involves play (Bruce, 2015; Vygotsky, 1978) storytelling and story-acting (Cremin et al., 2017; Paley, 1991) and imaginative thinking (Stanley, 2012). Young children are apprenticed into the "ways with words" (Brice Heath, 1983) of their families by 'Learning by Observing and Pitching In' (Rogoff, 2016). Technical aspects like letters, their sound combinations and spellings should be taught as part of and in the service of communication, while learners transfer the shared concepts they know about print between languages (Saiegh-Haddad & Geva, 2010). We now describe the principles guiding Storyplay, captured in Figure 5.3, and share practical examples from the project in action.

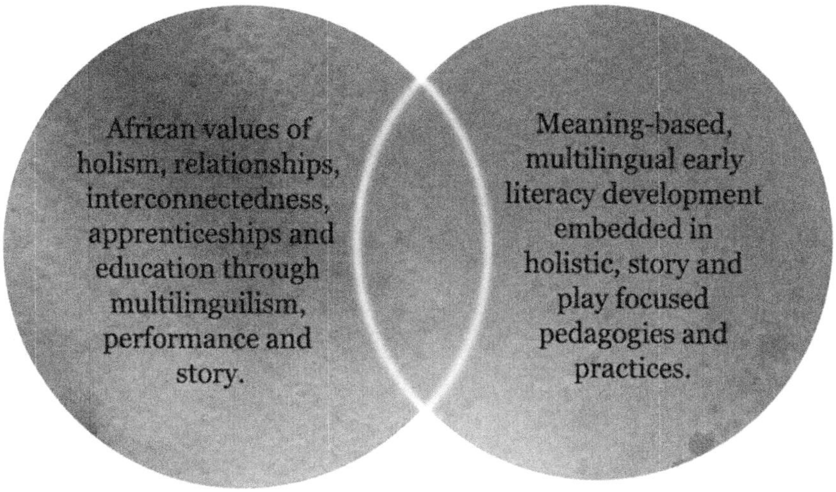

Figure 5.3 Meeting points for power: transformation through holistic African and early childhood wisdoms.

A story fuelled literacy learning cycle

A story-fuelled cycle is a term coined by one of the co-authors of this chapter, Carole Bloch (CB), to make the point that literacy learning in early childhood gathers momentum and power when driven by stories and the narrative form. It implies that stories are living forms of language which grow and flourish with ongoing and regular use. In our work, we have noticed how children hold back their potential for creative expression in classrooms where adults neglect to value meaningful and imaginative uses of language. We have also been relieved to witness the way imagination and motivation spark into life when adults pay central attention to nurturing story and symbolic play among children (Bloch, 2018).[9]

For us, language learning progress is fuelled by children and adults with agency who generate as well as 'consume' personally meaningful print in ongoing culturally and socially relevant ways.[10] Children appropriate and hybridize the stories we share with them (real life and fictional) for their own emotional and intellectual ends. In Storyplay, children also dictate their own stories, which adults write down for them (see Figure 5.4). These stories are later enacted on the 'magic carpet', our version of the storytelling and acting process encapsulated by the work of Vivian Gussin Paley.

Story and its opportunities for symbolic play are ideally integrated in settings which support young children exploring through first-hand experiences. This makes for affordable, high quality and context-relevant learning with regular opportunities for the following: pretend play, block play, drawing, writing,

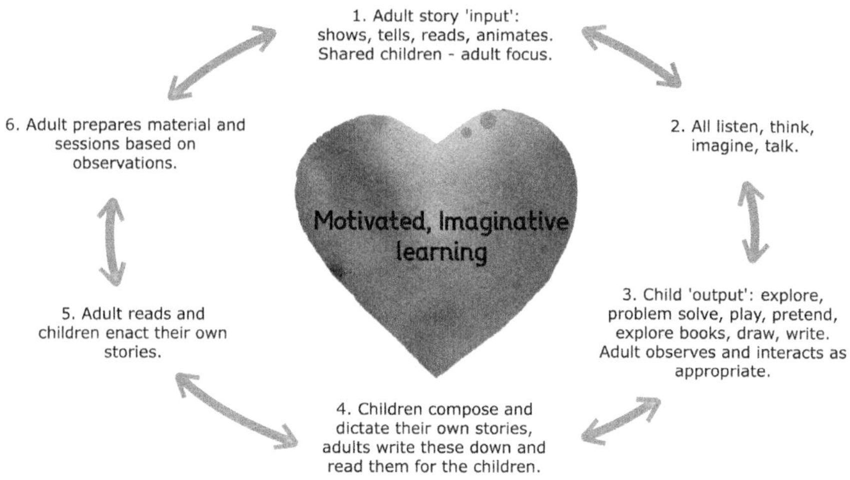

Figure 5.4 The story-fuelled cycle: igniting powerful language use.

book- and/or story-sharing, exploring sand, water and clay or mud, and the use of collected natural and recycled materials and other inexpensive or free topical and interesting materials.

Storyplay needs a good selection of stories; the process encourages teachers to build collections and memory banks of storybooks, personal stories, rhymes and songs to stimulate children's desire to listen, think imaginatively problem-solve, discuss and play. We prioritise suitable stories available in African languages in SA so that teachers get to know which stories 'speak to' them and their emerging readers and writers. The following examples give insight into how this approach works in action.

Stories in action

In the example below, Teacher L begins the story-fuelled cycle (point 1 in Figure 5.4) by reading *Ummangaliso kaHanda* (Xhosa translation of *Handa's Surprise*, Browne, 2016), to 16 three and four-year-old isiXhosa-speaking children. The class is working in isiXhosa. In the book, Handa carries a basket on her head with seven fruits, which she is taking to her friend. As she walks along, she does not notice that one by one, animals are plucking the fruit from her basket. A discussion, which is translated into English by Storyplay mentor Nolubabalo Mbotshwa (NM), ensues (point 2 in Figure 5.4). One child points and says, *'The animals are taking Handa's fruit!'* Another says, *'No, they not taking the fruit, they are stealing because they didn't ask Handa'*. NM asks, *'If you take something from your friend without asking her is that stealing?'*

Several comments follow:

> "Yes, because you must first ask!" .... "No, because that's your friend ... "My brother always takes my things and doesn't ask, so I tell him that he is going to go to jail, because he is stealing .... "I will take my stick and smack the animals, because animals mustn't steal ..." "You won't go to jail, but you will get a hiding from your mom, then you must go sleep".

Facilitating such dialogues by inviting the children to express their views, and thus moving to talking and away from transmission-orientated procedures, is one of the ways in which teachers begin to notice children's language repertoires and learning potential. They see how motivated, animated and focused children become when they connect to, express and discuss their own experiences. It also addresses supporting children's growing vocabularies, because "[t]alk may be cheap, but it is priceless for young developing minds" (Neuman & Dwyer, 2009, p. 384).

The teacher prepares activities to go with the story. Once the teacher has read and talked about it, the children choose an activity which allows them to weave whatever resonates with them from the story into their own play. Children find characters and themes from stories which interest them and make them their own. We illustrate this process (point 3 of Figure 5.4) in extracts from a reflection by one of the co-authors of this chapter, Sive Mbolekwa (SM), after he and a teacher used a story to generate writing by the children.[11] *UMnumzana Mvundla udibana noMnumzana Mandela* (Xhosa version of *Mr Hare Meets Mr Mandela*) (Van Wyk, 2016) is a story which many children enjoy. Mr Hare finds a R200 note with a picture of Mr Mandela on one side. On the other side is Mr Leopard. Mr Hare decides to take it back to the great man himself. The other animals tell him he shouldn't go to the city because he cannot read. But intrepid Mr Hare sets off and has an adventure which involves the note changing hands several times, and it changes colour too! Not noticing how the R200 note is swapped for R100 and then R50, Mr Hare is amazed how this note keeps changing colour and has a new animal on it each time. Luckily, the picture of Mr Mandela remains, and so his journey is not in vain.

SM first describes one of the challenges to enable adults and children becoming generators of meaningful print in African languages. This hinges around teachers observing and recognising young children's learning intentions and agency so that they create opportunities for children to explore and grow as composers at their own pace without enforcing a 'correct' blueprint on them. SM explains how he and the teacher planned together, having discussed the need to offer a series of motivating and meaningful activities for the children to choose from (point 6 of Figure 5.4),

> The teacher and I planned together to put recycled material in the fantasy area for the children to set up shop and sell goods, paper to cut and to make pretend money to buy with at the shop, clay for them to bake the edibles Mr

> Hare saw at the bakery, scrap fabric to cut and sell as clothes, chart paper to draw a map to help Mr Hare find Mr Mandela's house, a recycled cardboard letterbox to post a letter to Mr Hare. We also put out paper for drawing or writing whatever they wanted to and picture books to browse through in the reading area.

How adults shape the learning environment and the nature of the activities they offer to children reflects their teaching views and priorities. This is highly significant: not only does it affect the kind and quality of possible engagements, but also young children's understanding of what their teachers value and what is expected of them. On this occasion, when SM arrived, he noticed that the teacher had interpreted two of the activities differently to what he had envisaged. She had already cut out paper in the shape of money and provided a map of Africa for the children to colour in. SM had wanted the children to be free to make money, and draw maps, in their own way, from scratch. This indicated to SM that further discussion was needed about what qualitatively rich learning involves and how to achieve a balance between providing activities and allowing learners to generate their own:

> Teachers often feel the need to do too much for the learners; they are reluctant to allow the children the agency to do things for themselves at their level of skill, wondering whether the children will learn enough if they are left to their own devices.

The teacher had read the story the day before with the children (point 1 of Figure 5.4). In Figure 5.5, we see a letter from Mr Hare which she 'found' and read out loud to the children as a way to begin the session.

Notes and letters can expand the boundaries of stories to include the children. They can happen at any part in the story-fuelling cycle to create the kind of atmosphere of 'pretend' young children are readily drawn to. In Figure 5.6, we see an example of point 3 of Figure 5.4 as the children reply to Mr Hare's letter. This was done in a shared writing activity where the teacher facilitated a dialogue and then wrote down what the children dictated to her.

In their response, the children shift from addressing Mr Hare to addressing the teacher about what Mr Hare must do. In the moment, this is far less important than the fact that they are expressing their views and seeing this expression manifested as a social, collaboration in print. When children have the desire and confidence to express themselves – and – when they see their words written down, and hear them read aloud, they begin to incorporate in their identity a sense of being a composer–writer *and* belonging to a literate community. This is highly motivating: as often happens when teachers scribe regularly for children, independent writing attempts emerge, like the following one by P. SM explains:

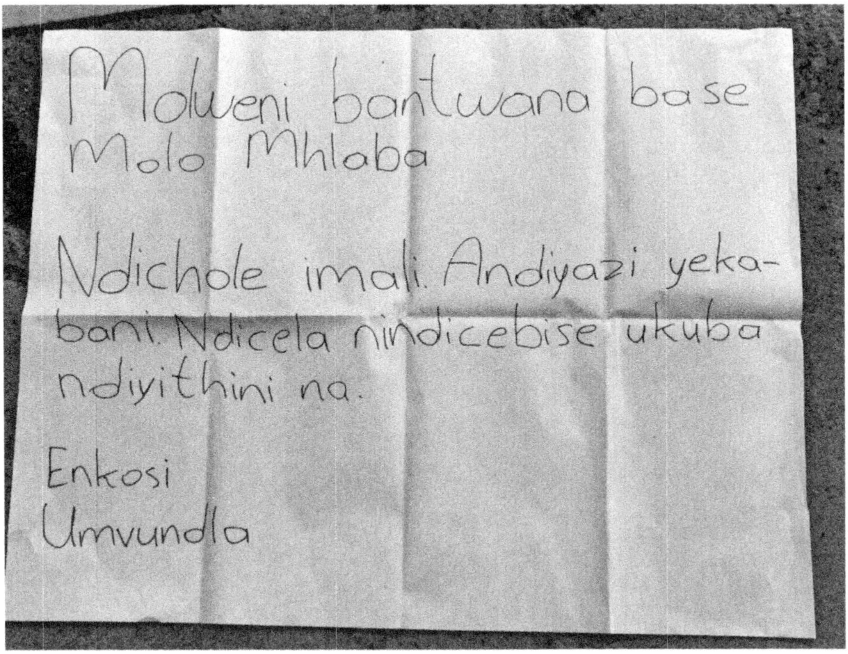

Molweni bantwana base
Molo Mhlaba

Ndichole imali. Andiyazi yeka-
bani. Ndicela nindicebise ukuba
ndiyithini na.

Enkosi
Umvundla

Figure 5.5 Mr Hare's letter to the children.

Translation:
Dear Molo Mhlaba Children, I found money. I do not know to whom it belongs. Please advise me, what do you think I should do with it? Thank you, Hare.

> We noticed how focused [P] was on her writing – she was writing a letter to Mr Hare. We wondered what she was writing. As we did not want to disturb her, we waited until she was finished and was about to put her letter in the post box. We then asked if she could read it for us. Translated from isiXhosa, it reads, "Mr Hare, Mr Mandela died. From P" (Figure 5.7). We then asked her if we could write it for her in such a way that other people could read it.

Without teachers having access to information and knowledge about invented spelling (Ouellette & Sénéchal, 2017) and the processes which move young children's writing from emergent to conventional forms, such a writing attempt can seem unconnected to literacy teaching and progress in learning. Part of the role Storyplay mentors undertake is to support teachers in noticing such progress. SM adds:

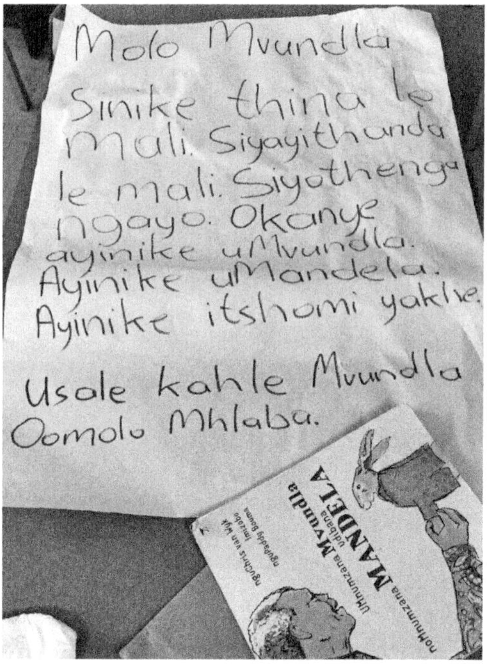

Figure 5.6 The children respond to Mr Hare.

Translation:
Dear Mr Hare,
Give us this money. We love this money. We will buy stuff with it. Or he can give it to Hare.
He must give it to Mandela. He must give it to his friend.
Kind Regards.
Children of Molo Mhlaba.

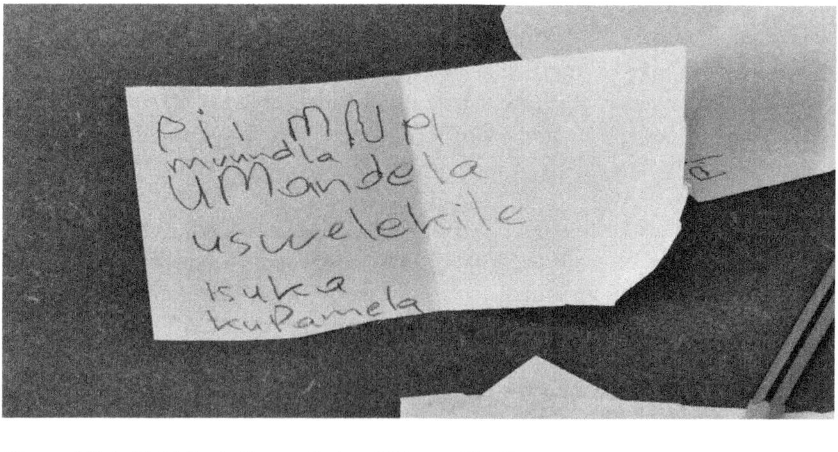

Figure 5.7 A Child Feels Compelled to Write to Mr Hare.

Translation: “Mr Hare, Mr Mandela died. From Pamela”

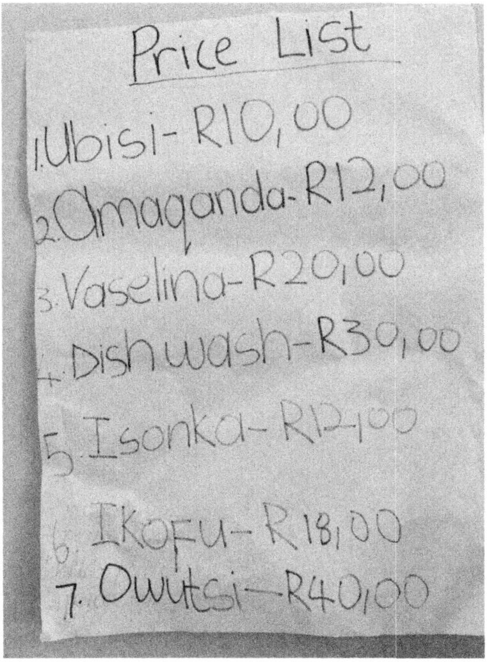

Figure 5.8 The children translanguage, adapting the money theme to their life experiences.
Translation:
1. Milk – R10,00 2. Eggs – R12.00 3. Vaseline – R20,00 4. Dishwashing liquid – R30,00 5. Bread – R12,00 6. Coffee – R18,00 7. Oats – R40,00.

> I talked with the teacher about how P has come to know the genre and format of letter writing and shows an understanding that we write from left to right. It appears that this is what she has seen numerous times in the various, regular writing that adults are doing with the children. She is at the stage where she knows she needs to put together letters to send a message (alphabetic principle) and she has learned to form some. She is still developing phonemic awareness and phonic knowledge required to spell the words she uses as she makes an attempt at writing in an imaginative endeavour in the context of story and play.

During the same session, more writing happens. In Figure 5.8, still linking to money and its power to buy, some children help the teacher write a shopping list. They translanguage in English and isiXhosa as they apply their minds to decide on and price their desired 'essentials'. The teacher is an informal writing role model for the children as she writes the list and they make their contributions in a seamless integration of numeracy, literacy and everyday life, inspired by a story and realised through play.

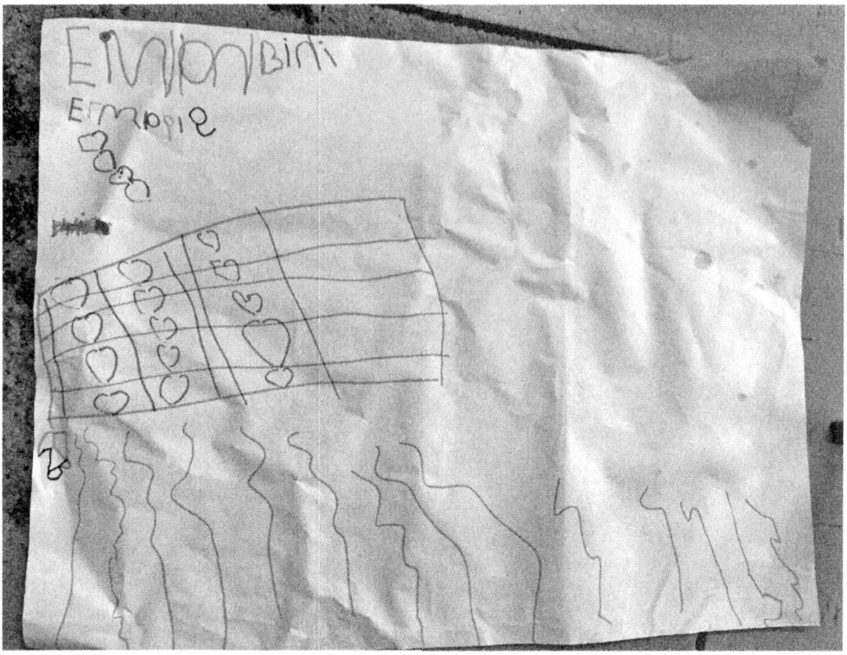

Figure 5.9 An attempt at writing personally significant words, 'emanzini' (in water) 'elwandle' (in the sea).

The final example of writing from this session illustrates how earlier collaborative and imaginative efforts, like the one SM describes below, stimulates independent endeavour:

> One child was copying from a large sheet of paper which was used earlier on in the session, when the teacher and children were thinking of themselves and their travels in relation to Mr Hare, who had travelled to town. The teacher had written down the places as the children told her where they had travelled. This child has attempted to write 'emanzini' which means 'in water' and 'elwandle' which means 'in the sea'.

Self-driven practice in how to write particular words imbued with imagery and meaning for this young girl arose from a prior event which had encouraged enthusiasm and interest among the classroom community.

It should be apparent that in order to normalise writing in African languages, we need to be providing constant, meaning-embedded writing demonstrations. The children use these to inform their emerging physical and mental command of the writing process. In turn, teachers begin to recognise indicators of technical and conceptual understanding. The examples we have shared demonstrate that

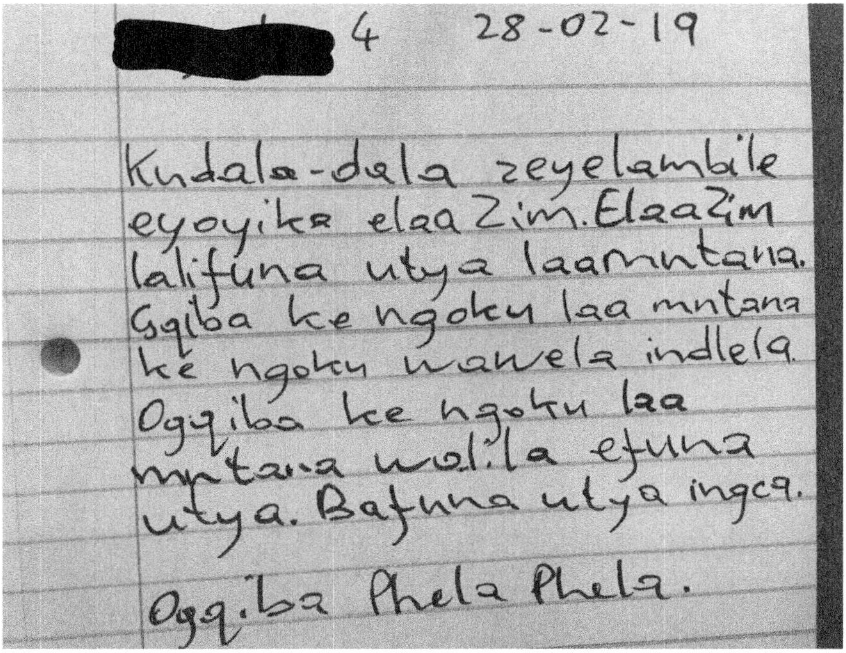

Figure 5.10a Dictating and scribing a child's story in an intimate moment of trust and shared attention.

Translation:
Long time ago, the child was hungry and scared of the monster because it wanted to eat him. He (the child) then crossed the road, crying because he wanted some food. They wanted to eat grass.
The end.

while stories give rise to talk, listening, viewing, reading and writing, children are simultaneously absorbing how written language works and how to make it work for them.

The magic of stories

We now move to describing the magic carpet process which we use to structure and enrich children's language use and learning (points 4 and 5 of Figure 5.4 above). Based on storytelling and story-acting (Bloch, 2018; Cooper, 2005; Lee, 2016; Paley, 1992), it involves dictating, scribing and enacting stories in an interplay which reveals the intimate and immediate relationship between play and story and between writing and reading. The examples which follow occurred in two preschools in Philippi and Kayelitsha, Cape Town, as part of PRAESA's nine-week training and mentoring programme which we offer to practitioners.

Figure 5.10b This young child's composing voice emerges as she dictates her story.

These two children's stories dictated and scribed in isiXhosa were part of a Storyplay session using *OoBhokhwana Abathathu BakwaGruff*, the isiXhosa version of the South African retelling of *The Three Billy Goats Gruff* (Bloch, 2011). They show how children incorporate aspects of stories they hear and think about with their own life motifs, often featuring significant emotional and physical themes. The story is dictated by a four-year-old child in isiXhosa (see the story in Figure 5.10a and the dictating in 5.10b). She creates a human character and focuses on the tragically common themes of fear and hunger; the story serves to make visible and legitimate what she wants to express.

Often children gather round to watch and listen as they wait for their turn. They follow how the teacher writes from left to right and top to bottom; they see that the adult writes slower than the storytelling child can speak; they hear the teacher sound out words and watch her form letters as she transforms the child's own ideas into conventional writing using the alphabet of the particular language. In any context, this is a powerful practice which illuminates how writing can link directly to children's concerns and interests and what purposes writing can be put to; in under-resourced, multilingual settings it has particular value: all we need is pen and paper and children and adults decide which language or language combinations they want to use, crucial in settings where African languages are undermined and neglected in print form.

With sufficient, regular application, this practice can contribute to important attitudinal and relational shifts between teachers and children. Teachers internalise the educational legitimacy of being curious and interested in the child's world and of engaging in authentic writing. They see how to facilitate the children's agency, guiding their composing to give it meaning and they begin to free themselves from the often burdensome position (and though perhaps unintentional, also disrespectful stance) where the teacher is expected to know, simplify, order and transmit everything worth learning to children.

Magic carpet can be done by most adults once they have appreciated and learned the fundamentals of the process. However, a skilled early childhood literacy teacher, trained in a holistic approach, will also recognise the profound teaching moments and learning opportunities which are nested in this 'close-up with print' exercise and how to extend and assess these. They will work deliberately to interest each child in noticing how letters are formed and combined to spell the words which they are verbalising. Teachers learn to do this while keeping overall attention on what the child is saying they want to have written down. They read back what has been written and ask questions to clarify meaning. The story is the child's creation but as a novice writer and reader, she relies on the teacher to illuminate the 'how to' aspect. The teacher draws the child in, sometimes spelling, sometimes sounding out, sometimes noting what letter a word begins or ends in, what an exclamation mark does for expression, etc. This leads to a process of increasing attention to print features and spelling and over time, story structure and style.

Stories are later played out on the 'magic carpet', an area drawn on the floor by tape or chalk (point 5 of Figure 5.4). In Figure 5.11, we see a story in action with a group of isiXhosa speaking four- and five-year-old children. They sit around the magic carpet and listen as the teacher reads out the story. The teacher guides the children to take turns to 'be' in the story, one after another, whoever the character may be. She does not choose who plays particular story roles, thereby promoting fairness (Paley, 1992), and challenging stereotypes. Nor does she

Figure 5.11 Life enacted as a story on the magic carpet.

Figure 5.12a Four-year-old dictates her story to her teacher.

instruct children to perform in a theatrical manner. Occupying the story is more important than the accuracy of performance.

The issue of language pops up frequently; observation allows adults to notice how fluent the children are at dealing with it. In this session, after the teacher had read the children a Pondo fable in isiXhosa, *UmBali Nengonyama* (Mbali and Lion) (Nevin, 1996), a four-year-old girl dictates the following story, adding some English words, to capture first-hand experiences, like 'ibutternut' and the hand sanitiser (which is seen in photograph in Figure 5.12a) they were using instead of water during the drought (see Figure 5.12b).

The aim is not to produce a coherent story the adult would like; it is to encourage this initial creative act, as an essential early step. Developing more conventionally formed stories comes gradually as part of a process which motivates children to identify themselves as writers. As they gain confidence, they act on the knowledge that we all have stories to share and that stories can be composed, written down and then read.

Magic Carpet can also arise from oral storytelling, as in the example below with SM's own story *Inyosi Yobomi (The Bee of Life)* about a forest which was full of animals and beautiful plant life living harmoniously (see Figure 5.13). A monster arrived and destroyed everything till it was 'dead flat on the ground'. Then a little bee came along, looking for Mama and Papa Bee, and wept to discover what

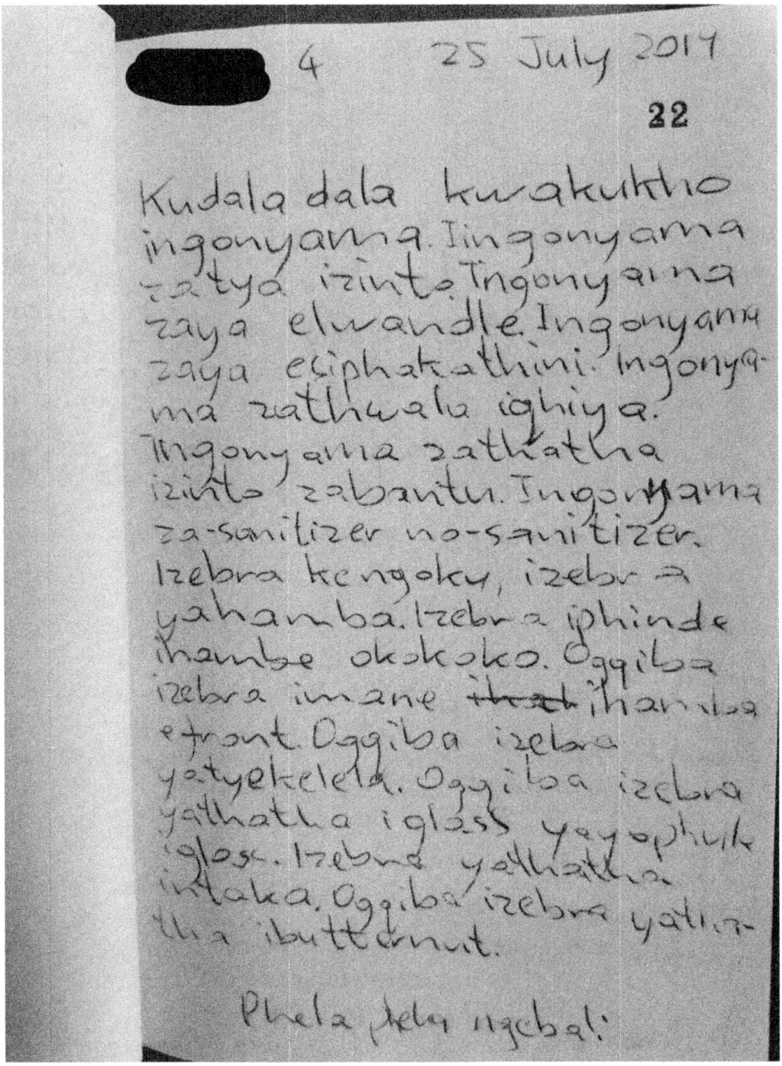

[redacted] 4 25 July 2017

22

Kudala dala kwakukho ingonyama. Iingonyama zatya izinto. Ingonyama zaya elwandle. Ingonyama zaya esiphakathini. Ingonyama zathwala iqhiya. Ingonyama zathatha izinto zabantu. Ingonyama za-sanitizer no-sanitizer. Izebra kengoku, izebra yahamba. Izebra iphinde ihambe okokoko. Oggiba izebra imane ~~ithoah~~ ihamba efront. Oggiba izebra yatyekelela. Oggiba izebra yathatha iglass yayophuk iglass. Izebra yathatha intaka. Oggiba izebra yathatha ibutternut.

Phela phela ngebali!

Figure 5.12b The dictated story.

Translation:

Long, long ago there was Lion. Lions ate things. Lions went to the sea. Lions went to the middle. Lions put on a headscarf. Lions took people's things. Lions even used the sanitiser. The zebra then, the zebra went away. The zebra again went and went. And then it sometimes went in front. And then zebra went in front of others. And then zebra took a glass and broke the glass. Zebra took a bird. And then zebra took the butternut.

The end.

Figure 5.13 Sive reading his story with the children.

the terrible monster had done. We join the isiXhosa story (in English translation) as it draws to an immensely satisfying close:

> *"'Hey! I remember you! You stepped on the trees and squashed them to the ground! You stepped on the animals and laid them flat on the ground! And squashed all the insects! Squashed the bees too, flat on the ground!", she said, anger building up inside her.*
>
> *"Hahaha!", laughed the monster. "What can you do about it? You little bee? Hahaha!"*
>
> *"Hey you! Don't make me angry! You hear...?" warned the little bee. "... What can you do about it? Nothing! Hahaha!" said the monster, laughing off the little bee's warning. The monster walked off lazily, still laughing. ... The little bee got up, flew up high and went straight for the monster. She stung him right on the bum. "Ouch! Ouch!" cried the monster. The little bee stung again. "Ouch! Ouch!" The monster cried. He ran and jumped into the sea. He drowned and was never seen again'".*

The children join enthusiastically, laughing and empathising in utter satisfaction with the little bee as it gets the better of the monster. They then play the story on the magic carpet. SM notes,

> ...We had T leading as the monster, while others chose to be snakes, tigers, lions and a giraffe ... showing that they were listening to my voice, as the storyteller. They were loud when they pretended to fear the monster and were snoring while playing the sleeping animals. But they were quiet when they wanted to hear what was coming next and when the animals were in the meeting to vote for the bee to be their president.

SM is reflecting on voice modulation partly because it is a common challenge to listen and hear due to noise. Even in settings which do not have large numbers of children (e.g. as many as 30), we have observed that many teachers use a very loud voice, and children follow suit. This makes it difficult to listen and be heard in precisely the phase of life where children are intuitively committed language learners. Working on the magic carpet, everyone begins to exert self-discipline in a collective commitment to imagine and pretend – and this helps bring about concentration and turn-taking.

It is clear that rich as the process we describe above is, we have only shared a very partial and indeed early part of the literacy learning trajectory. One of our intentions is to carry out research work with cohorts of children using a holistic approach from age three through eight to provide evidence of their entire journey to becoming conventional readers and writers (Bloch, 1997). This needs to be supported as a priority to properly address the extreme and extremely unjust differences in literacy teaching and expectations of children from affluent, middle class English-oriented homes, and those educated in the (still) systemically often print scarce African language-oriented settings we refer to in this chapter.

Ways forward: the zigzag path of progress in literacy education in SA

> *Language is not a domain of human knowledge (except in the special context of linguistics, where it becomes an object of scientific study); language is the essential condition of knowing, the process by which experience becomes knowledge.*
>
> (Halliday, 1993, p. 94)

Because of current interpretations of how to meet curriculum requirements, there is not yet an easy way to demonstrate the continuum of holistic, culturally relevant literacy learning by children. Skills-based methods are now (globally) being situated within a 'balanced' approach to literacy teaching (Spaull & Pretorius, 2019; Castles et al., 2018), by which is meant that a balance is supposed to be reached between teaching children all of the relevant components. Increasing awareness and acknowledgement that reading is part of people's social and cultural practices has led to growing appreciation that the print-related experiences within which learning to read takes place do matter, and are likely to be different for African language speakers and speakers of English. At the same time, as the Bua-lit collective point out, "it is a myth that a balanced approach can give equal weight to the different methods as each methodology proceeds from a different understanding of what literacy is" (Bua-lit, 2018, p. 4). Furthermore, despite the talk of balance, the message which still reaches many teachers is that reading comprehension is "... the end point of the learning-to-read journey" (Spaull & Pretorius, 2019, p. 11). Teachers exposed consistently to this view (which may also repeat their own experience of learning to read in school) tend to see their priority as being to entrench the 'steps to' decoding before worrying about comprehension. Yet this message holds no certainty, even for those who promote this view, i.e. "Without decoding, there can be no text comprehension; but skill in decoding does not automatically guarantee text comprehension" (ibid., p. 12). Generations of young children have experienced literacy first as predominantly phonics exercises and tests, yet South African children fared the worst out of 50 countries in comprehension testing (Howie et al., 2017) and 60% of children in Grade 6 cannot read with comprehension in any language (Van der Berg et al., 2016).

Unless we are careful, this tendency could unfortunately be reinforced by the increased support for recent research studies "at the interface of linguistic, orthographic, and cognitive processes involved in learning to read in African languages" (Ramadiro, 2019). These studies correctly counter the use of English phonics as a basis for phonics in African languages, paying attention to the different linguistic and structural features between African languages and English. They rightly note the differences between agglutinating languages with transparent spelling systems like African languages and English with its opaque orthography and deeply irregular spelling. However, it is problematic that, due to the consistent spelling of words in African languages and because words can be very long, it is now being claimed that, to benefit young children's literacy learning, 'correctly' and systematically taught phonics (as opposed to phonics being derived from English) is necessary for literacy teaching in African languages. A related point is also made that teaching African languages differs from teaching English because of structural differences, thus 'Western' methods are being claimed as inappropriate for African languages. These points lead to two arguments against the value of a holistic approach such as the one set out in this chapter, both of which we refute. One is that "this method does not readily work for agglutinating languages, especially those with a conjunctive orthography resulting in long words" (Spaull & Pretorius, 2019, p. 5). This statement is a non-sequitur: there are universal principles of learning and reading that apply across all languages, because they are based on the nature of the brain (Ellis & Solms, 2018). Another argument is that "it is unlikely to work outside of an extremely print-rich environment and intensive individual attention both of which are in scarce supply in high poverty contexts with large classes and limited resources, as in South Africa" (ibid.). This argument has its roots in Abadzi (2006, 2017), who argues for mother tongue education and at the same time for a single-track, decoding pedagogy, because she says that

> Though appealing and inherently sensible, the whole language approach puts low-income children at risk for failure. Poor children may well be able to recognize complex visual patterns of script ..., but limitations in vocabulary, phonological awareness, and working memory may prevent them from creating the necessary analogies between language and reading.
>
> (Abadzi, 2006, p. 46)

She claims that "Only when reading becomes fluent can the child concentrate on the meaning of the message". Abadzi also states, "To teach the poor efficiently, we must make learning easiest on their brains" (Abadzi, 2017, p. 11).

This approach to literacy is a restatement of the skills-based teaching method proposed and outlined in Figure 5.1 above, applied particularly and patronisingly to learners from poor backgrounds. We counter it by asking: Do we not make learning easy on the brains of children from affluent families? The brains of children from under-served communities are not essentially any different from the brains of children who have more or all of their education needs met; the issue is that they should have the intellectual and emotional rights to 'the same benefits', interpreted in culturally desirable ways, so they will be in a position to develop the same reading abilities. This kind of argument also of course points to a real problem to do with the supply of resources which will challenge literacy teaching, irrespective of the method or approach used. And with resources there are still unconscionable disparities between African languages and English. Leaving aside considerations about what attention has been given to ensuring written literature exists to tempt children to read in African languages as well as in English,[12] 7% of South African schools (mostly affluent ones) have a functioning school library, few schools have any budget for library materials, library periods or teacher librarians (Mojapelo, 2018, p. 415). The situation is one of severely restricted encouragement and support for elements facilitating authentic role modelling and engagement while abundant attention is given to teaching language structure and components.

We do not think that the opposition which we have described in this chapter between holistic and skills-based views of literacy learning ought to exist; both views acknowledge the ultimate significance of all aspects. The skills-based view, though, supports the cumulative learning of small units of written language separate from meaning; comprehension of texts comes at the end of the process. In doing so, it interrupts young children's orientation to discover and explore. The holistic view, by contrast, claims that paying attention to comprehension is not a separate or delayed activity: we have referred to evidence from neuroscience that supports the process as we show it in Figure 5.2 and the idea that comprehension is at the core of the process all along. To make it separate is to put great hurdles in the way of children reading meaningfully, whichever the language, because it goes against human biology and the way children learn. Remembering is in fact made difficult when small units (without apparent meaning) fill up short-term memory slots and is easier when they are filled with larger meaningful chunks. For any language, "things are easy to remember when we have meaningful frames to put them in. Isolated words are hard to remember but the same words are easy to remember when they are in a meaningful context" (Goodman et al., 2016, p. 125). This evidence also supports the wisdom of indigenous African strategies for memorising important oral texts and underlines the validity of appreciating how learning oral and written language constitute 'learning to mean' (Halliday, 1975).

We want to emphasise here that we are *not* arguing against the relevance of understanding the orthographic and other differences in languages, or between oral and written forms. Nor are we suggesting that conducting research on all aspects of African languages should not be done or that children should not learn to decode. But as Figure 5.2 shows, decoding should be *one* of the suite of cueing strategies which young children are taught simultaneously and encouraged to use. Moreover, teachers need the chance to appreciate how these cueing strategies are all as important for learning to read in African languages as in English.

Regrettably in SA and in SSA as a whole, we experience the same tsunami of systematic and synthetic phonics in education as the one which has hit education systems across the globe to shape teaching reading in English, based on the same skills-based model. The problem we are ultimately highlighting is that the drive to search for meaning can be minimised, deflected or even hidden from view when the teaching of automaticity and fluency takes precedence over comprehension, not only in Africa, but in the UK and USA (Clark, 2017, 2018). A consequence is demotivated learners and 'reading' that fails to concentrate on understanding (Altwerger et al., 2007).

Conclusion

Broad agreement exists that reading concerns meaning-making, and that the outcome of teaching should be "learners who are independent readers, that is, they can read fluently, with comprehension, on their own" (Spaull & Pretorius, 2019, p. 6). We will assume that the same agreement will soon apply to writing. Our position is that people learn through apprenticeships into meaning, and that the living heart of this is observing and joining in to what is considered desirable, valued social and cultural practice, often in an informal teaching process. With a hierarchical model of teaching reading, which places unambiguous prior value on the technical sub-components, apprenticeships are initially into 'instructional nonsense' (Edelsky, 1991), which do not transform magically into apprenticeships into meaning-making.

Continuing to describe comprehension as the hoped for outcome of teaching reading with initial emphasis on decoding, automaticity and fluency leads far too many children (and their teachers) into a culturally, intellectually and above all emotionally demoralising *cul-de sac*; whereas following a holistic model supports a focus on teaching and using skills in the service of meaning, enjoyment, cultural enrichment, real communication and personal emotional involvement. This enables children to learn to write and read with much more motivation and, crucially, much more effectiveness. Such a model is appropriate for literacy teaching in all societies; and utterly essential in countries still dealing with the inequalities wrought by colonialism and apartheid. Systemic delegitimisation of African philosophies, cultural practices and languages finds expression today in the ongoing challenges to radically increase African language book creation and provision, libraries, and writing and reading cultural role models. For this reason, above all else, we prioritise trying to ensure the most satisfying, joyful and motivating experiences with print imaginable, for adults and children alike – expressed through languages dear to them.

A Chinese proverb goes, "Hearing about something a hundred times is not as good as seeing it once". Our urgent task across SSA is to create the kind of opportunities which we have illustrated for pre-service and in-service teachers to see in action so that they can engage directly with the substance of a curriculum interpreted and taught as a continuum through the early childhood years. This will reveal the immense learning potential of young children and will assist us in ridding ourselves of the deficit view which has bedevilled so much education since the imposition of colonialism. As SA begins educating its youngest and most creative citizens, the birth to four year olds, it is more crucial than ever before for this happen.

Acknowledgements

This chapter acknowledges the children and teachers we work with, and the insights and collective experience of PRAESA colleagues, who inspire and support one another to inspire and support others through Storyplay: Lungiswa Dyosiba, Arabella Koopman, Nadia Lubowski, Thandazani Mbagani and Nolubabalo Mbotshwa. We also acknowledge our mentoring colleagues, Tina Bruce, Stella Louis and Sara Stanley.

Notes

1 see PRAESA www.praesa.org.za/papers-articles/.
2 Nal'ibali grew from and was underpinned by PRAESA's years of experience in multilingual education and early childhood literacy (Bloch, 1999; Bloch & Alexander, 2003; Alexander & Bloch, 2010; Bloch et al., 2011). Nal'ibali means 'Here's the story' in isiXhosa and the tagline we chose, 'It starts with a story', reflected the focus of PRAESA's Early Literacy Unit on story, meaning-making and Free Voluntary Reading (Bloch, 2015; Krashen, 1993) as crucial for successful literacy learning. Offering regular bilingual combinations of stories in African languages and English was one pillar; another was supporting adults to set up and run community-based reading clubs.
3 We are using 'story' broadly to include personal, historical, factual or fictional oral and written texts.
4 Permission has been granted from project participants to include the examples and photos featured throughout.
5 The term Early Childhood Development (ECD) refers to the age birth to nine in South Africa. However, up to very recently, early childhood education before school was largely left by government in the hands of the non-formal sector. One preschool year, Grade R was introduced in 2001. Negotiations have recently taken place to move the locus of responsibility for educating young children from birth onwards, from the Department of Social Development to the Department of Basic Education. Grade R is now officially the first year of the Foundation Phase of Primary Schooling. A compulsory Grade 'RR' year is being planned, and Early Childhood Care and Education (ECCE) university level training programmes for teachers of birth to four year olds are underway.
6 We use 'preschool' to include both community and school-based provision up to and including Grade R.
7 When apartheid ended, an unfortunate consequence of putting early childhood development (prior to school) towards the end of the government's attention queue has

been that pre-existing deficit perspectives of the learning needs of young children from under-served communities have been further entrenched. Despite dedicated interventions by many early childhood NGOs, without enough systemic attention to developing alternative, affordable, enriching practices across the sector, a culture of low-level expectations has become normal.

8 Ubuntu is an African cultural and epistemological conception of being, which propagates a communal orientation and continuum of social, linguistic and cultural resources and denotes the interconnectedness of all human existence (Makalela, 2019).

9 The concept arose from and merged CB's training and early childhood literacy teaching experiences (Bloch, 1997, 2000, 2019) with PRAESA's work to promote societal equity and transformation by supporting multilingualism, and raising the status of African languages for writing.

10 There is room for flexibility in the cycle, in the sense that the 'steps' do not have to be followed rigidly. As teachers become more used to the approach, they are able to 'allow' the children more autonomy in order and choice of activities.

11 Observing, thinking about and writing reflections about our work with teachers have helped us develop in knowledge and understanding about how best to mentor.

12 We distinguish literature from 'readers' as follows: the point of writing literature is to create a worthwhile story to read whereas the point of writing a reader is to teach and practice reading. Though some readers have stories worth reading, the focus is different, with different consequences, and we have far more readers than literature; African language literature for children, either original or in translation is still a tiny fraction of that available in English.

References

Abadzi, H 2006, *Efficient Learning for the Poor: Insights from the Frontier of Cognitive Neuroscience, Directions in Development*, World Bank, Washington, DC.

Abadzi, H 2017, 'Turning a molehill into a mountain? How reading curricula are failing the poor worldwide', *Prospects*, vol. 46, pp. 319–334.

Alexander, N, Bloch, C 2010, 'Creating literate communities – the challenge of early literacy', in M Krüger-Potratz, U, Neumann & H Reich (eds), *Bei Vielfalt Chancengleichheit*, Münster, New York, pp. 197–212.

Altwerger, B, Jordan, N & Shelton, N 2007, *Rereading Fluency: Process, Practice, and Policy*, Heinemann, London.

Atmore, E 2013, 'Early childhood development in South Africa – progress since the end of apartheid', *International Journal of Early Years Education*, vol. 21(2–3), pp. 152–162. https://doi.org/10.1080/09669760.2013.832941

Bermudez, JL 2014, *Cognitive Science, an Introduction*. Cambridge University Press, Cambridge.

Biersteker, L, Ngaruiya, S, Sebatane, E & Gudyanga, S 2008, 'Introducing preprimary classes in Africa: Opportunities and challenges', in M Garcia, A Pence & JL Evans (eds) *Africa's Future, Africa's Challenge. Early Childhood Care and Development in Sub-Saharan Africa*, The World Bank, Washington, DC.

Bloch, C 1997, *Chloe's story: First steps into literacy*, Juta & Co Ltd, Cape Town.

Bloch, C 1999, 'Literacy in the early years: Teaching and learning in multilingual early childhood classrooms', *International Journal of Early Years Education*, vol. 7(1),pp. 39–59.

Bloch, C 2011, OoBhokhwana Abathathu BakwaGruff, *The Three Billy Goats Gruff*, Jacana Media, Johannesburg.

Bloch, C 2015, *Nal'ibali and Libraries: Activating Reading Together*, PRAESA Articles, viewed 3 April 2020, http://library.ifla.org/1282/1/076-bloch-en.pdf.

Bloch, C 2018, 'Story by story: Nurturing multilingual reading and writing in South Africa', in N Daly, L Limbrick & P Dix (eds), *Children's Literature in a Multiliterate World*, UCL Institute of Education Press, London, pp. 161–181.

Bloch, C 2019, 'Working with the 10 principles of early childhood education. Revaluing storied and imagination for children's biliteracy learning in South Africa', in T Bruce, P Elfer & S Powell (eds) *The Routledge International Handbook of Froebel and Early Childhood Practice*, Routledge, New York, pp. 68–78.

Bloch, C & Alexander, N 2003, 'Aluta continua: The relevance of the continua of biliteracy to South African multilingual schools', in N Hornberger (ed), *Continua of Biliteracy: An Ecological Framework for Educational Policy, Research, and Practice in Multilingual Settings*, Multilingual Matters, Clevedon, pp. 91–121.

Bloch, C, Guzula, X & Nkence, N 2011, 'Towards normalising South African classroom life: The ongoing struggle to implement mother tongue-based bilingual education', in K Menken & O Garcia (eds), *Negotiating Language Policies in Schools. Educators as Policy Makers*, Routledge, New York and London, pp. 88–106.

Brice Heath, S 1983, *Ways with Words: Language Life and Work in Communities and Classrooms*, Cambridge University Press, Cambridge.

Browne, E 2016, *Ummangaliso kaHanda (Handa's Surprise)*, Jacana Media.

Bruce, T 2012, *Early Childhood Practice: Froebel Today*, Sage, London.

Bruce, T 2015, *Early Childhood Education*. 5th ed. Hodder Education, London.

Bruce T, Elfer, P, Powell S & Werth, L (eds) 2018, *The Routledge International Handbook of Froebel and Early Childhood Practice: Rearticulating Research and Policy*, Routledge, London and New York.

Bua-lit Language and Literacy Collective 2018, How Are We Failing Our Children? Reconceptualising Language and Literacy education, bua-lit collective, Cape Town, viewed 28 April 2020, https://bua-lit.org.za/wp-content/uploads/2018/11/bua-lit-language-literacy-education.pdf.

Castles, A, Rastle, K & Nation, K 2018, 'Ending the reading wars: Reading acquisition from novice to expert', *Psychological Science in the Public Interest*, pp. 5–51.

Clark, A 2013, 'Whatever next? Predictive brains, situated agents, and the future of cognitive science', *Behavioral and Brain Sciences*, vol. 36(3), pp. 181–204.

Clark, MM (ed) 2017, *Reading the Evidence: Synthetic Phonics and Literacy Learning*, Glendale Education, Birmingham.

Clark, MM (ed) 2018, *The Teaching of Initial Literacy: Policies, Evidence and Ideology*, Glendale Education, Birmingham.

Cooper, P 2005, 'Literacy learning and pedagogical purpose in Vivian Paley's storytelling curriculum', *Journal of Early Childhood Literacy*, vol. 5(3), pp. 229–251.

Cremin, T, Flewitt, R, Mardell, B & Swann, J (eds) 2017, *Storytelling in Early Childhood*, Routledge, New York.

Damasio, AR 1994, *Descartes' Error: Emotion, Reason, and the Human Brain*, Grosset/Putnam, New York.

Damasio, A 1999, *The Feeling of What Happens: Body and Emotion in the Making of Consciousness*, Harcourt College Publishers, Fort Worth, TX.

Damasio, AR 2006, *Descartes' Error*, Penguin Books, London.

Dehaene, S 2009, *Reading in the Brain: The New Science of How We Read*, Penguin Books, London.

Department of Basic Education (DBE) 1997, *Language-in-Education Policy*, Government Press, Pretoria.

Department of Education (DoE) 2015, *The South African National Curriculum Framework for Children from Birth to Four*, Department of Basic Education, Pretoria.

Department of Education (DoE) 2011, *Curriculum and Assessment Policy Statement (CAPS) – Foundation Phase Home Language Grades R-3*, Government Press, Pretoria.

Du Plessis, S & Louw, B 2008, 'Challenges to preschool teachers in learner's acquisition of English as Language of Learning and Teaching', *SA Journal of Education*, vol. 28(1), pp. 53–74.

Ebrahim, HB 2014, 'Foregrounding silences in the South African National Early Learning Standards for birth to four years', *European Early Childhood Education Research Journal*, vol. 22(1), pp. 67–76.

Edelsky, C 1991, *With Literacy and Justice for All: Rethinking the Social in Language and Education*, Falmer Press, London.

Ellis, G & Bloch, C 2021, *Neuroscience and Literacy: An Integrative View*, https://doi.org/10.1080/0035919X.2021.1912848.

Ellis, G & Solms, M 2018, *Beyond Evolutionary Psychology: How and Why Neuropsychological Modules Arise*, Cambridge University Press, Cambridge.

Finnegan, R 2012, *Oral Literature in Africa*, Open Book Publishers, Cambridge.

Fleisch, B 2008, *Primary Education in Crisis: Why South African Schoolchildren Underachieve in Reading and Mathematics*, Juta, Cape Town.

García, O 2009, *Bilingual Education in the 21st Century: A Global Perspective*, Wiley-Blackwell, West Sussex.

Gogolin, I 2018, 'Literacy and language diversity: Challenges for education research and practice in the 21st century', in LD Hill, & FJ Levine (eds), *Global Perspectives on Education Research*, Routledge, New York, pp. 3–25.

Goodman, K, Goodman, Y & Flores, B 1984, *Reading in the Bilingual Classroom: Literacy and Biliteracy*, National Clearinghouse for Bilingual Education, Rosslyn, VA.

Goodman, KS, Fries, P, Strauss, S & Paulson, E 2016, *Reading: The Grand Illusion. How and Why Readers Make Sense of Print*, Routledge, New York.

Gottschall J 2012, *The Storytelling Animal: How Stories Make Us Human*, Houghton Mifflin Harcourt, New York.

Gray, P 2011, *Psychology*, Worth Publishers, New York.

Greenspan, SI & Shanker, S 2009, *The First Idea: How Symbols, Language, and Intelligence Evolved from Our Primate Ancestors to Modern Humans*, De Capo Press, Cambridge, MA.

Gumperz, J 1971, *Language in Social Groups*, Stanford University Press, Stanford.

Halliday, MAK 1975, *Learning How to Mean: Explorations in the Development of Language*, Edward Arnold, London.

Halliday, MAK 1993, 'Towards a language-based learning theory of learning', *Linguistics and Education*, vol. 5, pp. 93–116.

Hawkins, J 2004, *On Intelligence*, Holt Paperbacks, New York.

Hawkins, J & Blakeslee, S 2007, *On Intelligence: How a New Understanding of the Brain Will Lead to the Creation of Truly Intelligent Machines*, Macmillan, New York.

Heugh, K, Benson, C, Bogale, B & Mekonnen, A 2007, *Study on Medium of Instruction in Primary Schools in Ethiopia*, Ministry of Education, Addis Ababa.

Hymes, DH 1980, *Language in Education: Ethnolinguistic Essays*, Center for Applied Linguistics, Washington, DC.

Howie, S, Combrinck, C, Roux, K, Tshele, M, Mokoena, G & Palane, NM 2017, *PIRLS Literacy 2016: Progress in International Reading Literacy Study 2016: South African children's reading literacy achievement*, Centre for Evaluation and Assessment (CEA), Faculty of Education, University of Pretoria, Pretoria.

Hruby, GG & Goswami, U 2011, 'Neuroscience and reading: A review for reading education researchers' *Reading Research Quarterly*, vol. 46(2), pp. 156–172.

Krashen, SD 1993, 'The case for free voluntary reading', *The Canadian Modern Language Review*, vol. 50(1), pp. 72–82.

Lee, T 2016, *Princesses, Dragons and Helicopter Stories: Storytelling and story acting in the early years*, Routledge, London & New York.

Louis, S 2009, *Knowledge and Understanding of the World in the Early Years Foundation Stage*, Routledge, London & New York.

Mojapelo, SM, 2018, 'Challenges in establishing and maintaining functional school libraries: Lessons from Limpopo Province', *South Africa Journal of Librarianship and Information Science* 2018, vol. 50(4) pp. 410–426.

Makalela, L 2014, 'Teaching indigenous African languages to speakers of other African languages: The effects of translanguaging for multilingual development', in L Hibbert & CW Van der Walt (eds), *Multilingual Universities in South Africa: Reflecting Society in Higher Education*, Multilingual Matters, Buffalo, pp. 88–106.

Makalela, L 2019, 'Uncovering the universals of ubuntu translanguaging in classroom discourses', *Classroom Discourse*, vol. 10 (3–4), pp. 237–251.

Makoe, P 2007, 'Language discourses and identity construction in a South African multilingual primary school', *English Academy Review*, vol. 24(2), pp. 55–70.

Mbiti, JS 1989, *African Religions and Philosophy*, Heinemann, London.

McKinney, C 2017, *Language and Power in Post-colonial Schooling*, Routledge, New York.

Miller, GA 1956, 'The magical number seven, plus or minus two: Some limits on our capacity for processing information', *Psychological Review*, vol. 63(2), pp. 81–97.

Moll, L, Amanti, C, Neff, D & González, N 1992, 'Funds of knowledge for teaching: Using a qualitative approach to connect homes and classrooms', *Theory into Practice*, vol. 31(2), pp. 132–141.

Nel, N, Mohangi, K, Krog, S & Stephens, O 2016, 'Contextual challenges in early literacy teaching and learning in grade R rural schools in South Africa', *Per Linguam*, vol. 32(1), pp. 47–65.

Neuman, S & Dwyer, J 2009, 'Missing in action: Vocabulary instruction in pre-K', *The Reading Teacher*, vol. 62, pp. 384–392.

Nevin, TA 1996, *Umbali nengonyama: intsomi yamaMpondo (Mbali and the Lion)*, Garamond, Durbanville.

Nsamenang, AB 2006, 'Human ontogenesis: An indigenous African view on development and intelligence', *International Journal of Psychology*, vol. 41(4), pp. 293–297.

Ouellette, G & Sénéchal, M 2017, 'Invented spelling in kindergarten as a predictor of reading and spelling in Grade 1: A new pathway to literacy, or just the same road, less known?', *Developmental Psychology*, vol. 53(1), pp. 77–88.

Owusu-Ansah, FE & Mji, G 2013, 'African indigenous knowledge and research', *African Journal of Disability*, vol. 2(1), p. 30.

Paley, V 1991, *The Boy Who Would Be a Helicopter*, Harvard University Press, Cambridge MA.

Paley, V 1992, *You Can't Say You Can't Play*, Harvard University Press, Cambridge MA.

Panksepp, J 1998, *Affective Neuroscience: The Foundations of Human and Animal Emotions*, Oxford University Press, London.

Pearson, PD, Palincsar, AS, Biancarosa, G & Berman, AI (eds) 2020, *Reaping the Rewards of the Reading for Understanding Initiative*, National Academy of Education, Washington, DC.

PIECCE, 2019, Birth to Four Programme Framework Pedagogies Chapter 6 Summary, Project for Inclusive Early Childhood Care and Education, Johannesburg, viewed 28 April 2020, https://piecce.co.za/wp-content/uploads/2019/09/pedagogies-summary-20190701.pdf.

Ramadiro, B 2016, Early Literacy Learning and Poverty and Social Inequality in Post-apartheid South Africa, The Institute of Training and Education for Capacity-building (ITEC), East London, viewed 20 March 2020, www.itec.org.za/page/5/?option=com_content&view=article&id=85&Itemid=151.

Ramadiro, B 2019, *Futures of Literacy in African Languages*, Litasa 2019 keynote address (unpublished), University of Cape Town.

Richter, L & Samuels, M-L 2017, 'The South African universal preschool year: A case study of policy development and implementation', *Child: Care, Health and Development*, vol. 44(1), pp. 12–18.

Rogoff, B 1990, *Apprenticeship in Thinking: Cognitive Development in Social Context*, Oxford University Press, Oxford.

Rogoff, B 2016, 'Culture and participation: A paradigm shift', *Current Opinion in Psychology*, vol. 8, pp. 182–189.

Saiegh-Haddad, E & Geva, E 2010, 'Acquiring reading in two languages: An introduction to the special issue', *Reading and Writing*, vol. 23, pp. 263–267.

Seidenberg, M 2017, *Language at the Speed of Sight: How We Read, Why so Many Cannot, and What Can Be Done about It*, Basic Books, New York.

Shaywitz, S 2003, *Overcoming Dyslexia: A New and Complete Science-based Program for Reading Problems at Any Level*, A.A. Knopf, New York.

Shore, R 1997, 'What have we learned?', in R Shore (ed), *Rethinking the Brain'*, Families and Work Institute, New York, pp. 15–27.

Smith, M 2011, 'Which in- and out-of-school factors explain variations in learning across different socio-economic groups? Findings from South Africa', *Comparative Education*, vol. 47(1), pp. 79–102.

Smits, J, Huisman, J & Kruijff, K 2008, *Home Language and Education in the Developing World*, paper commissioned for EFA Global Monitoring Report 2009, UNESCO, Paris.

Spaull, N 2016, *Learning to Read and Reading to Learn*, RECEP Policy Brief, Department of Economics, Stellenbosch University.

Spaull, N 2019, Priorities for Education Reform in South Africa, Input Document for Treasury's Economic Colloquium 19 January 2019, viewed 20 March 2020, https://nicspaull.files.wordpress.com/2019/01/v2-spaull-priorities-for-educ-reform-treasury-19-jan-2019.pdf.

Spaull, N & Pretorius, E, 2019, 'Still Falling at the First Hurdle: Examining Early grade Reading in South Africa', in N Spaull & J Jansen (eds), *South African Schooling: The Enigma of Inequality*, Springer Nature, Cham, Switzerland.

Spaull, N, Pretorius, E & Mohohlwane, N, 2020, 'Investigating the comprehension iceberg: Developing empirical benchmarks for early-grade reading in agglutinating African languages', *South African Journal of Childhood Education*, vol. 10(1), pp. 1–14. https://doi.org/10.4102/sajce.v10i1.773

Stanley, S 2012, *Why Think? Philosophical Play from 3-11*, Continuum, London.

Strauss, SL 2004, *The Linguistics, Neurology, and Politics of Phonics: Silent "E" Speaks Out*, Routledge, Abingdon.

Strauss, SL, Goodman, KS & Paulson, EJ 2009, 'Brain research and reading: How emerging concepts in neuroscience support a meaning construction view of the reading process', *Educational Research and Review*, vol. 4(2), pp. 21–33.

Taylor, S, Cilliers, J, Fleisch, BJ, Prinsloo, C & Reddy, V 2017, The Early Grade Reading Study: Impact Evaluation After Two Years of Interventions, Technical Report, www.jet.org.za/clearinghouse/projects/primted/resources/language-and-literacy-resources-repository/egrs-technical-report-13-oct-2017.pdf.

Tomasello, M 2003, *Constructing a Language: A Usage-based Theory of Language Acquisition*, Harvard University Press, Cambridges, MA.

Wolf, M 2008, *Proust and the Squid: The Story and Science of the Reading Brain*, Harper Perennial, New York.

Van der Berg, S, Girdwood, E, Sheperd, D, Van Wyk, C, Kruger, J, Viljoen, J, Ezeobi, O & Ntaka, P 2013, *The Impact of the Introduction of Grade R on Learning Outcomes.* Final Report (Policy Summary, Executive Summary & Evaluation Report) for the Department of Basic Education and the Department of Performance Monitoring and Evaluation in the Presidency, Stellenbosch University Department of Economics, Stellenbosch.

Van der Berg S, Spaull N, Wills G, Gustafsson M & Kotzé J 2016, *Identifying Binding Constraints in Education*, Stellenbosch University Department of Economics, Stellenbosch.

Van Wyk, C 2016, UMnumzana Mvundla udibana noMnumzana Mandela (Mr Hare Meets Mr Mandela), Jacana Media, Johannesburg.

Vygotsky, LS 1978, *Mind in Society: The Development of Higher Psychological Processes*, Harvard University Press, Cambridge, MA.

Weir, RH 1962, *Language in the crib.* Mouton, The Hague.

Whitmore, KF, Martens, P, Goodman, YM, & Owocki, G 2004, 'Critical lessons from the transactional perspective on early literacy research', *Journal of Early Childhood Literacy*, vol. 4(3) pp. 291–325. doi:10.1177/1468798404047291

Young, ME & Mustard, F 2008, 'Brain development and ECD: A case for investment', in M Garcia, A Pence & J L Evans (eds), *Africa's Future, Africa's Challenge. Early Childhood Care and Development in Sub-Saharan Africa*, The World Bank, Washington, DC, pp. 71–92 https://openknowledge.worldbank.org/handle/10986/6365

6 Vignette

Our experiences of enhancing the quality of early childhood education in rural Cameroon and Kenya by drawing on local languages

Annukka Kinnaird and Angela Becker

Introducing a 'soft landing' for school students in Cameroon

Thanks to many initiatives, pre-school enrolment in Africa rose 84% between 1999 and 2015. However, over 80% of children in SSA still have no access to pre-school programmes (Zafeirakou, 2015). In Cameroon, only around 27% of children nationwide have access to pre-school, the figure being even smaller in rural areas. The existing programmes are mostly located in urban areas and are too expensive for many families (UNICEF, 2017). Thus, for many Cameroonian children, starting school is a new experience that they have not been prepared for. Many students have had only minimal exposure to books or written documents at home and there is a gap between the languages students use at home and those that they encounter at school. Many of these students' parents have had little to no experience of formal education or literacy, which means they do not always know how to support their children's transition to primary school. Some parents may also be unconvinced of the value of attending school and of the relevance of what is learned there. One initiative that we developed aimed to 'soften' children's entrance into primary school and to develop their confidence and abilities, which in turn works to convince parents of the value of school education and the development of literacy in African languages.

In this approach, the first month of Grade 1 is dedicated to helping students build their confidence and give them an 'I-can-learn' experience in a secure environment. Students are introduced to school life and rules in their home languages (in this case two minority languages spoken in Northern Cameroon). Drawing on pre-school materials from the Guera development project in Chad (McKone & Abdel-Kerim, 2002; Tyler & Sakine 2014), pre-reading skills and the numbers one to five are introduced by using games and pictures, but no actual letters are taught at this point. Lessons in maths and social sciences are closely linked with students' everyday life both at home and at school. Learning is enhanced by carefully prepared problem-solving questions which demand creative thinking and raise curiosity. Skills learnt during the first month are similar to those learnt at nursery school (*école maternelle*).

DOI: 10.4324/9781003028383-8

Integrating this soft-landing period proved not only important for shaping students' emergent literacy, but also for gaining parents' respect and support for home literacy development and for school in general. After the soft-landing period, one of the Grade 1 teachers told the rest of the team about the father of one student who saw how his only child attending school had, after only one month, learned the numbers one to five so well that he was able to do calculations with confidence. This encouraged the father to send his other children to school (Kinnaird, 2019). Our experience thus suggests that, with the help of the soft-landing period, children feel more confident and ready to start the actual Grade 1 programme, teachers learn to be more creative in their teaching, and parents understand better the utility of what their children learn at school.

Facilitating literacy development in local languages by adapting the Finnish KÄTS approach

In SSA, one of the many ways in which literacy approaches are restricted is that the methods used to teach literacy in indigenous African languages at school may sometimes be overly influenced by methods used for learning to read English or French, the languages dominant in the school systems, as literacy development techniques have been borrowed from English and French-speaking countries. These languages, however, do not have a close letter-sound correspondence whereas many indigenous African languages, like Lulunga and Swahili, do. More similar to many African languages are Finnish and Spanish, which have a much closer letter-sound correlation with easily identifiable syllable breaks (Schroeder, 2013; Kinnaird, 2019). These languages are often better taught with the emphasis being more on syntactic or mixed analytic/syntactic approach than on learning through sight words. Moreover, in most Finnish readers the teaching of plosive sounds is held off until later, even when they might be commonly found in the language. This is because they have been found to be some of the hardest sounds to teach when using a synthetic teaching method which is not based on learning to read 'sight words' but starts with letters and sounds.

We have been successful in drawing on some of these principles in some of the early reading programmes we have been involved in. We have drawn in particular on the Finnish mixed analytic/synthetic KÄTS literacy method (the acronym coming from Finnish words meaning letter, sound, syllable and word), which was first developed in the 1970s by a special-education-needs teacher Sakari Karppi to help children with difficulties in learning to read and write. These methods are now used in primary schools throughout Finland (Lerkkanen, 2017). The first step in this method is that learners listen and learn to recognize and read the new letter; they analyse its place of articulation and write it and then proceed to syllable and word levels. In order to make learning as easy as possible at the beginning, the first letters in a literacy reader are carefully chosen, not only by their frequency count but also because they are easy to hear in isolation (e.g. most voiced sounds including all the vowels) and can be lengthened (Lerkkanen, 2006, 2017). This has led to the practice that most early readers avoid some sounds in the beginning, including the more 'quiet' sounds (e.g. /v/, /h/ and /j/, which are less common in the language anyway) and the fairly common plosives (/t/, /k/ and /p/, where the airflow cuts off, which means they cannot be lengthened). Although the letter /t/ is the third most common letter in Finnish (Pääkkönen, 1991), and even though it marks noun plurals and certain verb inflections, it does not appear in most reading books until the 10th or even 13th letter. The KÄTS idea of teaching the 'easiest' sounds first (and thus avoiding the plosives in the beginning) has stood the test of time, as it is still applied in Finnish reading books.

In Cameroon, a great number of languages are written phonemically. Working with two such languages in the North, we have found it useful to draw on the KÄTS method in literacy development programmes with both primary school students (Grades 1 and 2) and adult learners. Letters are introduced not only based on their frequency but also by applying the principle of 'teachability' where the easiest letters/sounds are taught first, and the more difficult sounds later. It is often possible to create lessons with meaningful sentences at the very beginning even without plosives, which are difficult to pronounce in isolation. The number of meaningful texts that can be fairly easily written without plosives is language-dependent: the more, the better. Vowels (short or long) are good first letters to teach, as they are easy to hear and learn as separate sounds and they can be learned reasonably quickly. With consonants, it is best to start with those that are easy to pronounce in isolation, and which can be lengthened, such as /s/, /r/, /m/ /n/ and /l/. We find it best not to introduce plosives (/t/, /p/, /k/, /d/, /b/, /g/, /ɓ/ and /ɗ/) until at least ten other easier letters have been learnt. We encourage learning to read by analysing sounds and by 'gliding' from one sound to another. We have found that being able to do this as a beginning reader without the confusing exceptions that the plosives cause brings about an element of 'security' and helps learners get a better understanding of what reading is about. They learn the basics of decoding before having to tackle the more difficult sounds, which is crucial for confidence-building. It also facilitates the learning of writing and is, in the long run, much more effective than memorization, particularly with languages where the average word length is longer than in English. When learners learn to 'analyse' sounds in this way, they also develop reading skills which later can be usefully applied to learning to read in English and/or French.

In our experience, this approach can be successful also because it is fairly easy for teachers to learn, especially those with little or no formal education, and it boosts their motivation. In one school 73% of the students learned to read by the end of Grade 1 with a teacher who had no formal training (Kinnaird, 2019). The local community could thus feel that school had a purpose, and they were increasingly supportive of it. Confidence in the local language education programme was also boosted when, years later, the same students sat the end of primary school exams, and the best student of all the schools within the area came from the school that had embraced this approach to teaching reading and writing. While the successful development of literacy depends on the implementation of a holistic approach (see Bloch and Mbolekwa, this volume), an adaptation of the Finnish model can contribute to the empowerment of learners, teachers and communities through written language.

Using TPR to support mother tongue and English literacy development in Kenya

In Kenya, the official language of instruction (LoI) in primary education is based on the primary local language of the school's geographical area (Mose, 2017, p. 217). However, this language policy is not properly or fully implemented, especially in rural areas where the local language should be used (Trudell, 2016). In these areas, the LoI is English, Kiswahili, or most commonly a combination of both (Mose, 2017; Trudell & Piper, 2014). Therefore, our aim in one pre-school programme in Kenya was to bridge the learning gap between the local language and the LoI by using the total physical response (TPR) approach.

TPR uses movement, the coordination of speech and action, alongside the 'I-do, we-do, you-do' methodology to teach oral English as a second language (Fahrurrozi, 2017). First, the teacher gives directions in the local language, then says a word or phrase in English, such as 'jump' while demonstrating the action (I-do). Second, the teacher repeats while having the students follow along (we-do), and finally, the students say and act on their own (you-do). This method is appropriate for use in pre-school since the local language is used to develop vocabulary in English through a kinaesthetic approach (Khorasgani & Khanehgir, 2017), thus supporting the development of the home language *and* the LoI (Noormohamadi, 2008).

This pre-school initiative has proven beneficial for the students and the teachers and had far-reaching impact into the community. First, the students in the pre-school classrooms developed their understanding and use of English and the local language (whether Maasai, Kikuyu or Kamba) throughout the course of the programme, as seen in the pre- and post-assessments documenting expressive and receptive vocabulary competences. Since the TPR approach aims to include local languages, students were encouraged to use them more freely in and out of the classroom, which also boosted their self-confidence. The teachers also experienced first-hand the benefits of using local languages for instruction, which led them to shift their mindsets about their use in education. As teachers in the programme were local residents, the parents could communicate with them freely. Parents were invited to school meetings that informed them about the approach and could experience first-hand their children's learning. The positive effect of using this approach on students' learning meant that the community was more convinced of the value of pre-school education: enrolment increased and absenteeism decreased (Trudell et al., 2019). Moreover, through this approach a shared sense of the value of education was developed in the community, as all participants clearly valued effective learning that is relevant to their community.

Conclusion

These three initiatives show some of the approaches which have proved valuable for using the children's home languages to enhance literacy in early childhood and the quality of education. The effectiveness of these programmes implemented in the rural communities shows that many young children were positively influenced, teachers were motivated to teach in local languages and use new methods creatively, and the parents were involved in ways that brought about greater participation (Kinnaird, 2019; Trudell et al., 2019).

References

Fahrurrozi 2017, 'Improving students' vocabulary mastery by using total physical response', *English Language Teaching*, vol. 10(3), pp. 118–127. https://files.eric.ed.gov/fulltext/EJ1132014.pdf

Khorasgani, A & Khanehgir, M 2017, 'Teaching new vocabulary to young learners: Using two methods total physical response and keyword method', *International Journal of Evaluation and Research in Education*, vol. 6(2), pp. 150–156.

Kinnaird, A 2019, 'A sustainable community-based MTB-MLE model for rural francophone areas', in Kody and Um (eds), *Teaching National Languages and Cultures in Cameroon. Theoretical, Pragmatic and Didactic Approaches*, CERDOTOLA, Yaoundé, pp. 42–56.

Lerkkanen, M-K 2006, '*Lukemaan oppiminen ja opettaminen esi- ja alkuopetuksessa*', WSOY, Helsinki, p. 97.

Lerkkanen, M-K 2017, 'Aapinen ja lukutaidon opetus', in P Hiidenmaa, M Löytönen & H Ruuska (eds), *Oppikirja Suomea rakentamassa*, Suomen tietokirjailijat, Helsinki, pp. 17–38.

McKone, L & Abdel-Kerim, A 2002, *Préparons-nous! Livre de pré- alphabétisation*, Manuel du maître, Association SIL, N'Djamena.

Mose, P 2017, 'Language-in-education policy in Kenya: Intention, interpretation, implementation, *Nordic Journal of African Studies*, vol. 26(3), pp. 215–230.

Noormohamadi, R 2008, 'Mother tongue, a necessary step to intellectual development', *Journal of Pan-Pacific Association of Applied Linguistics*, vol. 12(2), pp. 25–36.

Pääkkönen, M 1991, 'A:sta Ö:hön. Suomen yleiskielen kirjaintilastoja', *Kielikello*, vol. 1, p. 3. https://jkorpela.fi/kielikello/kirjtil.html

Schroeder, L 2013, 'Teaching and assessing independent reading skills in multilingual African Countries: Not as simple as ABC', in C Benson & K Kosonen (eds), *Language Issues in Comparative Education*, Sense Publishers, Rotterdam, p. 247.

Trudell, B 2016, *The Impact of Language Policy and Practice on Children's Learning: Evidence from Eastern and Southern Africa*, UNICEF, Nairobi.

Trudell, B & Piper, B 2014, 'Whatever the law says: Language policy implementation and early-grade literacy achievement in Kenya', *Current Issues in Language Planning*, vol. 15(1), pp. 4–21. DOI: 10.1080/14664208.2013.856985.

Trudell, B, Trudell, J, Gerger, E, Cowman, G & Becker, A 2019, 'Literacy, language and foundational skills in Africa: Learning in unexpected places', *SIL International*, vol. 3, pp. 1–23, viewed 15 August 2019, www.sil.org/resources/archives/79530.

Tyler, C & Sakine, R 2014, *Classes préscolaires au Guera. Guide d'enseignant*, FAPLG, Guera, Chad.

UNICEF (2017). Cameroon Country Programme 2018-2020 Strategy Note Basic Education Programme 2018-2020, UNICEF, Paris, viewed 3 April 2020, http://files.unicef.org/transparency/documents/Cameroon_Strategy%20Note%20-%20Education%20-%20final%20sd.pdf.

Zafeirakou, A 2015, 'Can pre-primary education help solve the learning crisis in Africa?', Education for All Blog. Global Partnership for Education, 3 September, www.globalpartnership.org/blog/can-pre-primary-education-help-solve-learning-crisis-africa.

7 Multilingual learning in Anglophone Sub-Saharan Africa

How to help children use all their languages to learn

John Clegg

Introduction

In Sub-Saharan Africa (SSA), as in some other parts of the world, much of school education is conducted in a language in which most learners are not fluent. For perhaps the majority of learners this joins with other socio-economic factors in removing the chance of getting an acceptable education. Like learners everywhere, they are of course fluent in the language – or languages – of their homes and communities. But in contrast to many monolingual learners, they are rarely permitted to use these fluent languages for learning during the majority of their time in school. A policy which defies good pedagogy and denies children's language rights is maintained across the continent with damaging consequences for individuals, schools and economies.

This chapter argues for all learners to be able to use all their languages in school, within an appropriately supportive pedagogical environment. Although the chapter illustrates Anglophone countries in SSA, a similar state of affairs exists in countries which use other post-colonial languages as the language of instruction (LoI) (Schroeder et al., this volume). The chapter suggests not only that learners often do not possess sufficient ability in the official LoI to get an adequate education, but also that textbooks and curricula make language demands on them which they cannot meet. It therefore proposes that learners should learn through a language in which they are fluent for a much longer period of time than is at present normally the case.

Although learners in SSA may speak several African languages, this chapter adopts a shorthand, referring to a home or community African language as L1 and to the official LoI – in this chapter English – as L2. The chapter will generalise about contexts in Anglophone SSA, looking at commonalities, despite the fact that circumstances differ within and between countries. Throughout the chapter, many learners will be described as having low or emergent ability in the LoI. This is not a deficiency. It is the normal state of L2 learners anywhere who are required to learn in L2 after only three years of language learning at three hours per week and minimal exposure to the language beyond school.

DOI: 10.4324/9781003028383-9

Education in L2 in SSA

In most of SSA, former colonial languages – mainly English, French and Portuguese – are used as LoI. Learners often start to use these languages officially as LoI from Grade 4 onwards, after early years education in an African language. In some countries the switch occurs later than Grade 4; in Tanzania, for example, it occurs at the end of Grade 7. In some schools in other countries, L2s are used as LoI from the first day of schooling, often in defiance of government policy stipulating early L1-medium education (Trudell, 2016).

Many children in SSA, when they start to learn curricular content in L2, are not fluent in it at all. A rich African literature on language in education shows that levels of language ability in the LoI are often far lower at the switch of medium, than the level which would be necessary for them to use it for learning subjects (Criper & Dodd, 1984; Macdonald, 1993; Alidou & Brock-Utne, 2006; Williams & Cooke, 2002; Dutcher, 2004; Probyn, 2005; Brock-Utne, 2012; Prinsloo et al., 2018).

All L2 language abilities – listening, speaking, writing and reading – are limited. Research data on learner listening and speaking ability (e.g. Erling et al., 2016; this volume) shows that in many contexts, learners at the end of Grade 3 may find it difficult to compose short sentences orally without support. They respond to teachers with infrequent, short responses (Hardman, 2008), if at all, and cannot easily engage in L2 talk in groups or pairs without support (Erling et al., 2016; this volume), probably until well into the secondary phase. Many cannot talk in L2 about complex subject contents without support by the end of secondary schooling. Because L1 use is often proscribed, low ability to talk in L2 can make many classrooms fairly quiet (Arthur, 1996; McKinney, 2017). The type of learning talk usually assumed to be at the heart of the acquisition of curricular knowledge (Alexander, 2017; Mercer, 1995) is rarely possible. Teachers, confounded by the difficulty of teaching in a language which many learners cannot speak well – and in which they themselves may not be confident – often have recourse to 'safetalk' (Chick, 1996), a form of classroom discourse which makes low cognitive and linguistic demands on learners.

With regard to writing, at the switch of medium learners may find it similarly hard to write short sentences about complex contents in L2 accurately without support; and limitations on writing ability may persist until matriculation, endangering learners' capacity to demonstrate subject knowledge in L2-medium examinations (SPINE, 2009).

In terms of reading, many learners at the switch of medium will find it hard to read the simplest text in L2. Uwezo (2012) data, for example, shows that 47% of Tanzanian learners at the end of year 7 (English-medium (EM) schooling starts in secondary form 1, year 8) could not read a year 2 text in English. Although levels of ability in English LoI vary between countries, similar data exist for other contexts in SSA (Williams, 2011; UNESCO, 2016). This level of L2 ability normally excludes the possibility that most learners can read conventional subject textbooks in English at the switch of medium and for some time thereafter. This is one – though not the only – reason why classroom reading events are rare (Taylor & Vinjevold, 1999; Probyn, 2005, 2006; Fleisch, 2008). Others include the fact that textbooks – where available – are often written for English-fluent learners (see below). This barrier to effective reading in English about complex contents is likely to remain in place for many years and for some learners throughout schooling; after matriculation it can continue to restrict learner ability to study in EM higher education (Brock-Utne & Holmarsdottir, 2003; Galabawa & Senkoro, 2010; Dukhan et al., 2016).

A large 'language gap' exists between the English language ability which learners bring to the start of EM education at the switch of medium and the language demands of the EM curriculum at this point, which are much higher and may expand faster than learner language ability, making learning a constant struggle to comprehend and express curricular contents. This gap has been partially measured, in particular by Macdonald (1993). Erling et al. (this volume) show that only about a third of Ghanaian students achieve minimum competency in English when they switch to English LoI in Grade 4. Williams (2011) reported that in 2004, 0.77% of Rwandan students in primary Grade 6 could read adequately for the purposes of English-medium education. The language gap remains visible in curricula and learning materials in SSA, as will be discussed further below.

Some learners in SSA succeed in learning in school through L2. They may be helped in doing this by high socio-economic status (SES), higher literacy levels amongst parents and some use of L2 in the home. Many learners, however, come from families with low or very limited print literacy, low SES, no home use of the L2 LoI and little exposure to it in the community. Learners who do not use the LoI in the home may have higher dropout and repetition rates and lower levels of attainment (Smits et al., 2008); this is especially the case with rural children, poorer children and girls (Smits et al., op. cit.). Long school journeys, inadequate nutrition, poor school resourcing and ineffective teacher education can exacerbate the problem (Smith, 2011).

What the messages which commentators convey about language-in-education skills in SSA is worrying. The World Bank (2008, p. 25) claims that 'in SSA countries, the majority of students struggle to learn academic content because of the foreign medium' and that 'the issue of proficiency in the instructional language at the secondary education is a major obstacle to learning for most students in SSA'. Probyn (2006) and Heugh (2006) suggest that learners in South Africa (SA) do not have enough L2 ability to benefit from L2-medium learning. Of SA in particular, Holmarsdottir (2005, p. 377) claims: 'students' competence in English is so limited that no "real" learning is taking place'; Heugh et al. (2007, p. 58) note in a study of Grade 8 learners in SA the 'high incidence of learners who appear to have either no or marginal literacy skills'.

The situation in which learners find themselves in schools across SSA, struggling to learn in a language which they do not speak well enough to do so, represents an educational emergency. It is acknowledged as such in a wide range of publications on language in education in SSA (e.g. Dutcher, 2004; Clegg,

2019) and is explicitly highlighted by UNESCO (2016). Low levels of ability in the LoI are partly – perhaps largely – responsible for high dropout (UNESCO, op. cit.) and low personal and institutional school achievement (Galabawa & Senkoro, 2010; Pinnock, 2009), poor links between school, community and home and lack of social justice (McKinney, 2017) and must surely contribute to national skills shortages and, in the final analysis, reduced national economic performance (Williams, 2014).

Most informed commentators on this emergency propose solutions which involve system changes: this often means learners learning for longer in their L1. Heugh (2006) and others suggest six years in a well-resourced context and eight years in a poorly-resourced one. This is doubtless necessary and is considered further below, but it is probably a long-term solution: states in SSA are notoriously reluctant to acknowledge the necessity for extended L1-medium schooling. Some measures could be effected in the shorter term. The next section focuses on one of these: multilingual learning.

Multilingual learning

Multilingual learning refers to a classroom in which teachers teach and learners learn subjects using their L1 and at least one other language. When it is proposed in this chapter that schools in SSA teach multilingually, it means that, whenever learners start to use an L2 as LoI, they should be using not only the L2 but all the languages at their disposal. They should do this before the introduction of L2 as a medium, in preparation for it, during the transitional period in which they become more fluent in L2, and thereafter, in varying degrees, until the end of schooling. In SSA, multilingual learning is used successfully, for example in South Africa (Bloch et al., 2010), but only to a limited extent – as it is in the world at large – and indeed the use of L1 in the classroom is often officially proscribed (McKinney, 2017).

Curricula in SSA – as is the convention in most parts of the world – separate language abilities according to individual language codes: an African L1 and an originally European language as L2. Multilingual education, by contrast, combines language abilities together into one picture of overarching language ability; this meta-ability is expressible in different modes (oral and written), in different varieties (social and academic), with different levels of fluency and in multiple languages. This concept is sometimes referred to as a 'translanguaging view' of learning and is represented by García et al. (2017) as a holistic language ability, enacted in one or more languages.

Figure 7.1 shows how García and her colleagues visualise the holistic language ability of a minority language user (Mandarin), a recent arrival, in a Los Angeles school, described as 'one of the top students'. The visual uses a five-point scale (not shown completely) adopted by some US states for measuring learner language performance: *entering*, *emerging*, *developing*, *bridging* and *commanding* (García et al., op. cit.). The child has *commanding* oral fluency and literacy in Mandarin and *developing* oral ability and *emergent* literacy in English. The

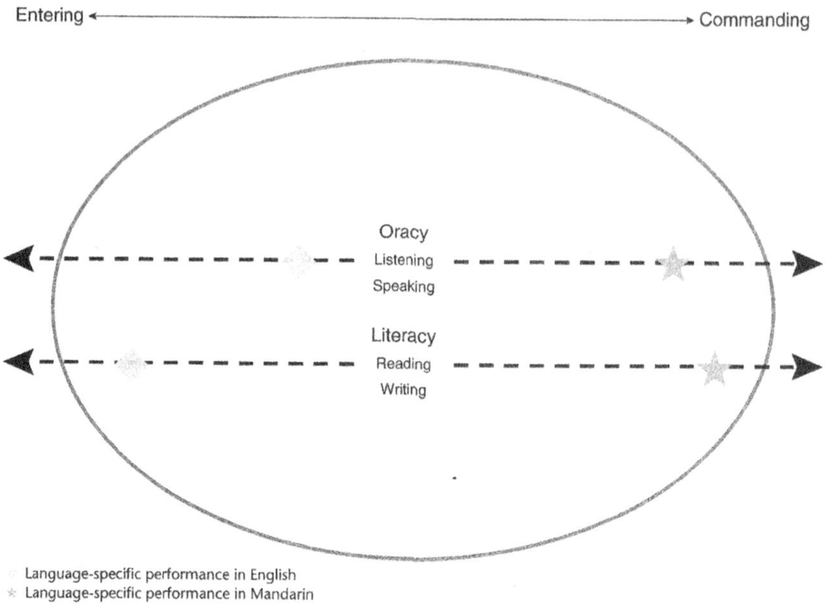

Figure 7.1 Language ability as a holistic capacity.

child thus has high language ability overall. If her language ability were to be assessed conventionally – i.e. in the LoI only – she would be ranked as *emergent* to *developing*, especially as regards literacy, and it would be hard to perceive that she is a 'top student', because her subject knowledge would mainly be perceptible in Mandarin.

This is therefore a good example of the benefits of evaluating language ability by reference to the user's whole and multilingual language resource, as opposed to their ability to use the LoI only. Describing a learner's multilingualism in this holistic way, as García et al. (2017) do, is crucial to understanding and installing multilingual education. The focus of the next section will be to describe the multilingualism of learners in SSA in this way.

A translanguaging view of the school language abilities of learners in SSA

It is often unwise to generalise about the language abilities of learners across SSA: there are significant differences between and within countries. Nevertheless, research in many different contexts shows a picture which is similar in respect of the extent of children's multilingualism. In this section we will take the example of a typical Grade 4 child in Ghana, but the resulting picture of multilingualism is recognisable in other contexts.

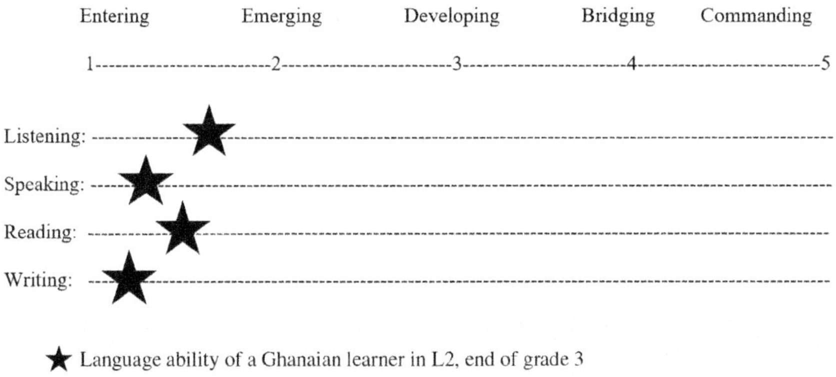

Figure 7.2 Language ability of a Ghanaian learner in L2, end of Grade 3.

Erling et al. (this volume) discuss a cohort of learners in the Greater Accra Region in Ghana. In this area, Twi is the dominant community language, but Ga is the local language designated for use as LoI at the lower primary level, as the area is indigenously Ga-speaking. Learners must therefore develop some competence in Ga upon starting school. In addition, in Grades 1–3, English is used increasingly and taught formally as a subject; from Grade 4 onwards it is used as LoI. At this point learners' ability in English is 'emergent' and 'not sufficient to access the curriculum' (Erling et al., op. cit.). If we apply to a typical Ghanaian child in this cohort at the beginning of Grade 4, the device which García et al. (op. cit.) use, representing her ability to learn in school using English L2, it would look something like Figure 7.2, approximate and unscientific as it is.

The child has *entering* L2 skills. When listening to the teacher presenting curricular concepts, she will understand something, but will often fail to understand fully. Her speaking ability will lag behind listening: she can make some short and grammatically and lexically very simple sentences on familiar topics but may find it hard to compose a short sentence orally about a new curricular concept; the same will apply to her writing. She can read very simple short texts about familiar concepts but will find it hard to read about new concepts in a subject textbook; indeed, she will often find it impossible, given the unreadability of many L2-medium textbooks in SSA – an issue to which we will return below (see also Clegg & Milligan, this volume). To ask a learner to learn complex subjects with this level of L2 ability is not a serious proposition.

The danger argued in this chapter is that we take a monolingual view of these data. If we do, we end up describing the child's language and learning ability in terms of what she cannot do. We conclude that the learner is a very limited L2 language user, whose low skills in this language will severely damage her educational chances. If we teach this learner only in L2, that is likely. But if we take a translanguaging view, we will conclude, by contrast, that she is a skilled multilingual user of African languages with developing literacy skills in at least one of those languages, and in addition, has early oral and literacy skills in English. Many – perhaps most – learners in SSA at the switch of language medium, possess similar multilingual abilities (Makalela, 2018; McKinney, 2017). Given a multilingual classroom environment with good enough teaching, they should thrive. By contrast, they have low chances of learning effectively in L2 alone. Under these circumstances, they must be permitted to use all their language resources, in both L1 and L2, if they are to have access to the curriculum.

In support of this proposition, let us investigate further the multilingual language skills which this average Ghanaian child possesses. If she is a Twi-speaker, she can at the very least, speak it with oral social fluency. She has also spent three years in school developing literacy and learning subjects in Ga, the lingua franca in her region. She will probably speak it at the *bridging* level and has initial literacy in it an *emerging* level. This is a picture of fairly normal grade-appropriate language-in-education ability in the local language of learning for many learners in SSA. For this learner – with strengthened literacy in Ga, which may not be adequate – these abilities alone are a basis for her to learn subjects.

In addition to her multilingual abilities in African languages, the Ghanaian child has the early L2 (English) abilities shown in Figure 7.2. If we represent her whole multilingual language resource in this way, it might look something like Figure 7.3. This is a 'translanguaging view'. It shows that she has more language skills than the average monolingual learner. She is probably socially fluent in more than one L1 and has early literacy skills in one of these; she also has initial social and literacy capacities in L2. If we see these L1 and L2 skills in combination, as a holistic capacity, and used in a multilingual classroom, this child has language

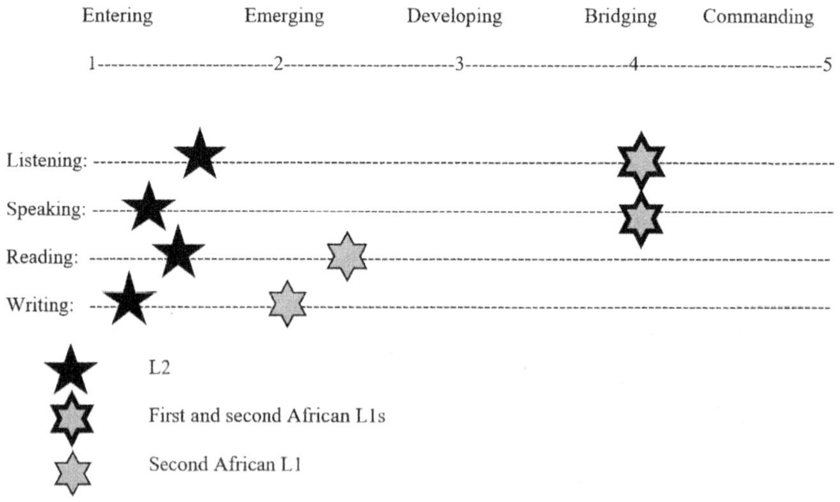

Figure 7.3 Language ability of a Ghanaian learner in L1 and L2, end of Grade 3.

abilities which would be considered remarkable in those parts of the Global North where amongst majority language users monolingualism is the norm.

The translanguaging advantage

It is important to add, however, that the language abilities shown in Figure 7.3 do not yet give a full picture of what multilingual learners in SSA can do linguistically. This is because in a translanguaging classroom a learner can exceed with her holistic language ability what she can achieve in languages viewed and taught separately (García et al., 2017). She has, in other words, what may be called a 'translanguaging advantage'. The translanguaging view of language in education, in which learners make use of all their languages for learning, has a variety of cognitive, linguistic, (August & Shanahan, 2006), social, cultural, emotional and equity-related advantages (Baker & Wright, 2017; García et al., 2017; Benson, 2002). Here we will focus on the advantage in terms of the learner's ability to learn content and language. In this view, a combined use of languages is more than the sum of its parts.

To illustrate this, let us take two examples from multilingual classroom practice, not real recorded events, but nevertheless familiar to teachers who work with bi- and multilingual learners. Imagine a learner at the beginning of Grade 4 who is an *entering* reader in English, working in an English-medium science lesson. The learner has no experience of reading a science text, with its low-frequency lexis, unfamiliar concepts and formal academic grammar and discourse. This is exemplified by the extract from Grade 4 science in SA (Barnard et al., 2015) shown in Figure 7.4. Many South African learners in the average Grade 4 classroom will find it difficult to read. If, however, learners talk in groups in L1 about the topic and visuals of the text before reading it, they will be able to discuss what they already know about the topic; when they then read the text in English, they will find it easier. A bilingual glossary and guided reading tasks would make it even easier. If, after reading the text, they talk about it again in L1, referring bilingually to L2 terms as they do so, they will comprehend it even better. Their L2 reading capacity is thus higher – perhaps *emerging* – for having talked about it in L1, than their individual measured L2 level (García et al., 2017); and their understanding of the subject content is thus higher.

To take a second example: learners who are asked to discuss the contents of the Figure 7.4 text in English will not be able to do so. Their oral ability at the beginning of Grade 4 is slightly less than *emerging* and nowhere near sufficient to enable them to talk about a complex text in L2. However, if they discuss it in their L1 and are then asked to prepare in their groups, using L1, to give a brief report in very simple sentences in English to the whole class on the contents of their discussion, they may be able to compose some fairly accurate simple L2 sentences. Similarly, many learners at the switch of medium to English will not be able to compose a short written text about the topic in English. Their L2 writing ability is *entering+*. However, if they work in groups in L1, to discuss the contents of their L2 paragraph, use L1 to plan its structure and sequence and compose

Visible differences between animals

You have already seen some differences between animal tails and limbs. Animals have different sizes, shapes, body coverings and sense organs.

Size and shape

Some animals are big and others are small. Look at the whales and elephant in Figure 5. Compare these sizes to a mouse and a flea. Animals come in different shapes, too.

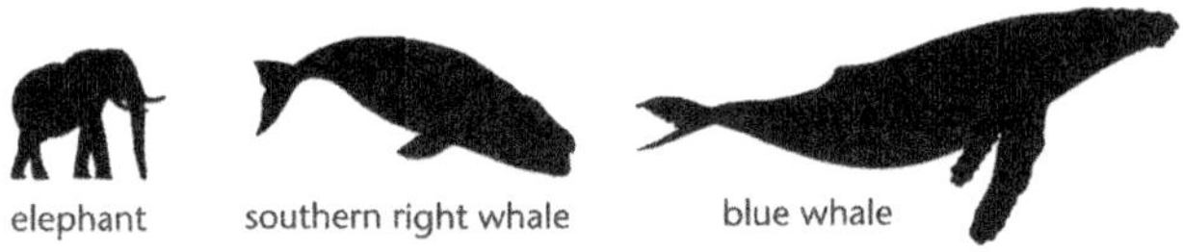

Figure 5 Big, bigger, biggest

Look at Figure 6. A giraffe's long legs and neck make it very tall. But a zebra has short legs and a short neck. A starfish is shaped like a star and has five limbs. An earthworm is like a long, thin tube and has no limbs at all!

giraffe zebra starfish earthworm

Figure 6 Tall and short; star- and tube-shaped

Body covering

All animals have a body covering. Some, like you, have more than one kind. Your body is covered with skin. On top of your head is a cap of hair. Different types of body coverings can be seen in Figure 7.

wild cat fur bird feathers snake scales

Figure 7 Different types of body covering.

Figure 7.4 Extract from a science and technology textbook, Grade 4 South Africa.

Scales are hard or bony plates that you find on fish, reptiles and other animals. They often overlap like tiles on a roof.

New word

scales – hard or bony plates that protect the skin of some animals

Sense organs

The sense organs are usually found on the head of an animal. Look at the pictures of the caracal, ostrich and spider in Figure 8 below.

caracal ostrich spider

Figure 8 Sense organs of animals

Did you know?

The ostrich is a bird but it cannot fly. It is too heavy for its wingspan. But it can run up to 70 km an hour – as fast as a very fast horse!

The most noticeable thing about the caracal is its big ears with black tufts of fur on the ends.

If you look at the picture of the ostrich close up in Figure 9, you will see that it has nostrils on the side of its beak. So like all other birds, it also has a nose. It also has two large eyes and two small ears. The ears are on both sides of the head, but are hidden under feathers.

And what about a spider's sense organs? Many spiders have eight eyes on the top of their head. The spider uses the hairs on its body for feeling and sensing.

Figure 9 An ostrich close up

Activity 2 **Describe the visible differences between animals**

Pair work

Look closely at the pictures of the three different animals in Figure 8 above and answer the following questions.

1 State which animal you think has the best sense of hearing. Give a reason for your answer.
2 Order the animals from smallest to biggest.
3 Write one sentence for each animal to describe the differences in:
   - type and number of limbs
   - body covering
   - sense organs.

Figure 7.4 Cont.

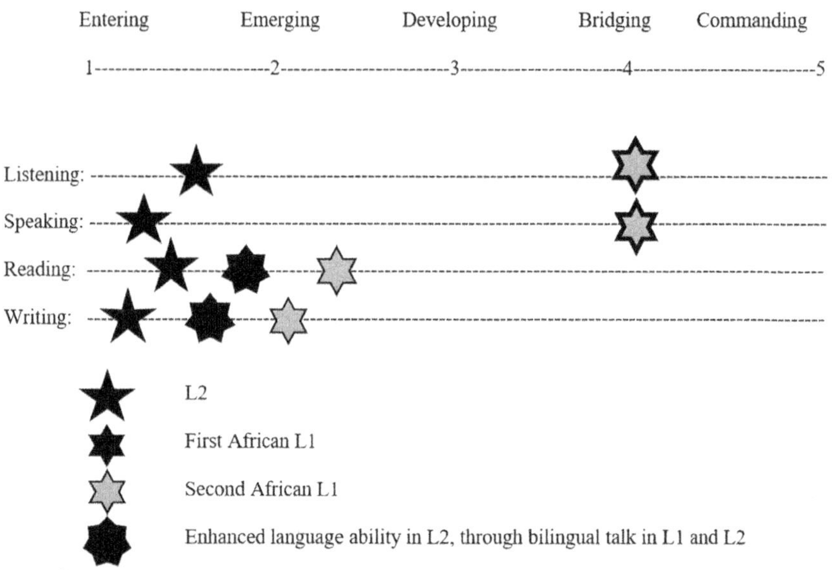

Figure 7.5 Enhanced language ability of a Ghanaian learner in L1 and L2, end of Grade 3.

their sentences in L2, they may be able to generate a short simple text in English. Again, working collaboratively in L1 enables a student to be able to say or write in L2 what she could not have said or written working solo in L2. In addition, L1 talk allows the learners to grasp the subject better. Translanguaging is above all a collaborative enterprise: learners work in more than one language, but they also work together.

These examples of the translanguaging advantage enable the picture of separate language abilities shown in Figure 7.3 to be changed. The learner, communicating in two languages can now be shown, in Figure 7.5, to have better capacity to talk, read and write in English L2 than would appear if these L2 abilities were measured alone. The visual – again making no attempt to be exact or scientific – shows bilingually enhanced L2 language ability.

However, in most educational contexts in SSA, the learner cannot use her bi-/multilingual abilities. Learners in other parts of the world who can use their L1 as LoI can proceed to use their L1 language abilities to learn subjects throughout schooling; as they do so they will hopefully develop in the LoI the variety of academic language – cognitive academic language proficiency (CALP) – which this requires. The child in SSA at Grade 4, however, must abruptly stop using her fairly well-developed L1 abilities for learning. Although she is a developing bilingual, she must abandon the languages in which she is most skilled (her L1s) and restrict herself to learning in the language in which she has least ability (her L2). Depriving a learner of major learning resources – linguistic, cultural, community-related – is a common feature of monolingual education in L2: learners who speak the LoI as L2 must often abandon their L1-related resources (Espinet et al., this volume). This makes it very difficult to learn both curricular contents and CALP. In addition, in assessment and when she comes to public examinations, the learner in SSA will be assessed in reference to the subject knowledge which she can express in her least fluent language (L2), as opposed to any knowledge which she may possess but can only express in her most fluent languages (L1s). Assessment in a language in which the candidate is not proficient risks giving a faulty and unfair account of the knowledge they possess (SPINE, 2009). Much classroom and public assessment in SSA runs this risk. By any stretch of the imagination, this is a linguistically skilled child who is deprived of her language rights. What she needs is the opportunity to use all her languages to learn.

On the face of it, this is an extraordinary state of affairs. On the one hand children are openly denied their linguistic human rights (Stroud, 2010; Skuttnab-Kangas, 2000); on the other, a patently ineffective form of schooling is maintained, with undoubted long-term damage to national economies across SSA (Djité, 2008; Williams, 2014). It amounts to a predisposition to conceal a large portion of a child's language abilities – normally those in which she is most fluent – and to validate for learning a small portion – those in which she is least fluent. Double standards operate openly here. In the Global North, refusal to recognise a child's fluent languages in education would not be countenanced for majority language users and would face legal challenge. It is, however, permissible and common for minority language users. International advisers would not accept disadvantaging majority language speakers in the Global North but do so in the Global South; and in this there is no doubt a hangover of institutionalised racism dating back to colonial times. In SSA the situation is by and large not openly questioned by ministries or international advisers (Heugh, 2006), to the extent that it took a UNESCO paper (2016) to ask rather obviously: 'If you don't understand, how can you learn?' What causes governments to maintain a clearly damaging system of education is a complex of varying factors related to popular attitudes to language, historical language use, resourcing constraints, and lack of political leadership. The topic is large and widely debated (Dutcher, 2004; Clegg, 2019) but not further pursued here.

What this chapter does attempt to do is to promote feasible alternatives. A government in SSA, instead of placing a language barrier in a child's way, can consider other options. The child could, in the period following an early switch of medium, learn in two (or more) languages: L2 and at least one L1. It is perfectly possible – though not widely practised in SSA or anywhere else – to preserve an early switch to L2 as an official LoI, but to recognise the difficulty of learning in L2 by giving status to L1s as alternate, though subordinate LoIs. This does not obviate the unequal struggle to learn subjects in a language which the child does not speak well enough to do so; but it makes learning easier. An example of this is shown in Clegg and Milligan (this volume), which illustrates bilingual science materials for use in Grade 4 Rwanda. Here, oral work is bilingual, but literacy is monolingual: learners talk and listen in two languages but read and write in English. This is a respectable use of multilingual learning, but it is limited: it preserves English as the LoI and with that the inevitable barrier to learning. It serves as a bridging strategy to help learners and teachers cope with that emergency; but however much it increases the scope for learning, that learning cannot be said to be in any way as effective as learning in a language in which the learner is fluent. In the long run, if schools in SSA wish learners to learn effectively at some point in L2, education in L1 and effective L2 teaching will have to be extended until learners possess L2 – or multilingual – skills which are good enough for them to learn subjects satisfactorily.

Early-exit programmes

L1-medium learning in SSA is normally limited to a short (mainly three-year) period of early years L1-medium learning, called an 'early-exit' programme. Not only is this a very short period for language-learning – as will be discussed below – but low SES, low exposure to the LoI and low resourcing often make learning in L2 after this period slow, laboured and ineffective (Ball et al. 2015; Baker & Wright, 2017). Learners can learn effectively in L2 – as for example in immersion education in North America or Content and Language Integrated Learning (CLIL) in Europe – but the circumstances which favour this often include high SES, high exposure and high resourcing. Given the socio-economically less favourable context of SSA, a much longer period of L1-medium learning recommends itself. Numerous international reports and agreements have supported L1-medium education over several decades (e.g. UNESCO, 1953, 2003). Many commentators on language in education in SSA (e.g. Schroeder et al., this volume) suggest that learners should learn in their L1 for a minimum of six years.

The next sections look at the idea of extended L1-medium education and address two specific reasons why it is essential: firstly the 'language gap', that is, the gap between learners' L2 abilities and the L2 demands of the curriculum which a short period of L1-medium education creates; and secondly the CALP skills which learners need to develop in L2 and which only a lengthy period of L1-medium education can deliver.

Extended L1-medium education: the language gap

The language gap describes the difference between what learners working in L2 can do with language, and the academic demands which the curriculum makes. The gap can be large – as is often observed in the education of language minority learners, for example in the USA (Cloud et al., 2009). In SSA some research has highlighted the gap: Macdonald (1993), for instance, measured the lexical gap in the South African curriculum, showing that in South Africa the vocabulary which the EM subject curriculum in Grade 4 demands is about 5000 words but that the English curriculum up to that point delivered 800. Using the examples of Tanzania and South Africa, this section will look at the gap:

- between what learners in SSA can do in English L2 at the end of L1-medium learning and the L2 skills which are required of them by subject textbooks at the beginning of L2-medium learning; and
- between the level of English L2 which the English syllabus provides for by the end of L1-medium learning and the L2 skills which are required by ministry subject curriculum documents at the beginning of L2-medium learning.

The language gap in textbooks in Tanzania

The gap between the demands of English-medium textbooks at the switch of medium and the English language ability of learners can be very large. Uwezo (2012, p. 9) research, already mentioned, showed that 47% of learners in Tanzania Grade 7 primary could not read the following Grade 2 text in English.

> *Asha lives in Moshi town. She lives near a market. Every day she buys fruits. She likes oranges.*

Compare this text with a science text for Tanzanian learners in Grade 8 (secondary Grade 1), shown in Figure 7.6 (Magasi, 2008). This text is intended for learners in their first year of EM education, immediately after the year in which 47% of learners could not read the year 2 text shown above. The language gap is huge. A glance at the difference between these texts suggests that most Tanzanian learners at the beginning of Grade 8 would not be able to read it. Data, generated partly using the digital vocabulary profiler Lextutor (2019), confirm that: it is long (368 words); the sentences are fairly long (average sentence length 11.2 words). They are also grammatically fairly complicated (8 subordinate clauses, 5 passives). The text is full of unfamiliar vocabulary: (4.35% of academic words per text; 16.03% of subject-specific words) – high scores in readability terms even for native-speakers. Visuals are not used to illustrate concepts in the text. There is no bilingual glossary and no reading support task. The book has however, been certified by the Tanzanian Institute of Education for use in Grade 8 (secondary form 1). Its measured readability – as measured by the digital readability tool Readable (https://readable.com) – is 8.8: i.e. it can be read by *native speaker/English-fluent* users of English only towards the end of Grade 8 in an English-speaking country. Tanzanian Grade 8 learners, with levels of reading ability indicated above, need a text with a native-speaker readability measure of about 2–3, preferably with built-in language support and tasks of a multilingual character. It is clear that in certifying this textbook as appropriate for Grade 8, no consideration has been given to level of learner L2 ability. No criticism is made here of the book as a biology textbook; the science contents may or may not be accurate and age-appropriate. But to learn science from the book, learners must be able to read it; most will not.

This 'readability gap' – as well as the matter of inaccessible textbooks as a whole – is found in Tanzania both in textbooks published by local publishers exemplified in Figure 7.6 and by major international publishers such as Pearson

Cytoplasm
Inside the cell membrane, there is a transparent jelly-like fluid called cytoplasm. It fills most portions of the cell. It may contain particles such as chloroplasts or starch grains.
In some cells, it is able to flow about. In the cytoplasm, the processes essential to the cell are carried out. It is also a place where food is stored. In plants food is stored as starch while in animals it is stored as glycogen.

Nucleus
The nucleus consists of nucleoplasm bounded by a nuclear membrane. It is always embedded in the cytoplasm. It is frequently void of shape and lighter in colour than the cytoplasm. The nuclear envelops the nucleus separating its contents from the cytoplasm. It also consists of chromatin material and nucleolus. The nucleus performs these functions:

- It controls the life processes of a cell such as growth, respiration and cell division.
- It controls hereditary characteristics of an organism.

Chloroplasts
A chloroplast is a specialized member of a family of closely related plant organelles called plastids. Chloroplasts contain the green pigment, chlorophyll, along with enzymes and other molecules that function in the photosynthetic production of sugar. Chloroplasts convert sun energy to chemical energy stored in sugar molecules. These are the sites of photosynthesis; found in plants, algae, euglena and green bacteria.

Cell vacuoles
Vacuoles and vesicles are both membrane bound sacs within the cell, but vacuoles are larger than vesicles. Vacuoles have various functions. Mature plant cells contain a large central vacuole enclosed by a membrane called tonoplast. The tonoplast is selective in transporting solutes; therefore, the solution inside the vacuole, called cell sap differs in composition from cytoplasm. The central vacuole has got these roles:

- It reserves important organic compounds such as proteins.
- It is the plant cell's main respiratory of inorganic ions such as potassium and chloride.
- Many plant cells use their vacuoles as disposal sites for metabolic by-products that would endanger the cell if they accumulated in the cytoplasm.
- Some vacuoles contain pigments that colour the cells such as red and blue pigments of petals that help in attracting pollinating insects to flowers/ fruits.
- Vacuoles may also protect the plant against predators by containing compounds that are unpalatable to animals.

Figure 7.6 Excerpt from a science textbook for Tanzanian learners year 8 (secondary form 1).

(see for example Bayliss (2006), a biology textbook which is equally unreadable by Grade 8 learners). It is also found in many other countries in SSA (Chimombo, 1989; Murila, 2004), as a glance at many textbooks for Grade 4 in current use will show: a similar example of unreadable text from Grade 4 Rwanda is shown in Clegg and Milligan (this volume).

Some textbook authors in SSA make an effort to render texts accessible. Consider the extract from a SA textbook for Grade 4 science (Barnard et al., 2015) in Figure 7.4. Unfamiliar vocabulary is dense: subject-specific, low-frequency vocabulary includes parts of an animal, for example: *body covering*, *tube*, *scale*, *tuft*, *nostril*, *wingspan*. General academic vocabulary includes: *visible*, *compare*, *overlap*, *noticeable*, *hidden*. None of these words will – quite understandably – be taught by the L2 syllabus up to Grade 4 which will focus on general-purpose high-frequency words. Nevertheless, although this makes reading hard, an effort has been made to keep sentences short, style familiar and terms illustrated by visuals.

Linguistically demanding oral and written activities are also common in subject study generally in SSA. Take, for example, the learners, half of whom in Grade 7 Tanzania could not read the Grade 2 text shown above. Magasi (2008, pp. 108, 130) contains questions for these learners such as:

> *Distinguish between prokaryotic cells and eukaryotic cells*
> *What are the advantages of bacteria?*

Learners would find it hard to answer these questions in their L1; most cannot do it in L2. Indeed, these activities would be hard for English-fluent adults (readers may like to try them for themselves!).

The language gap in the curriculum in South Africa

We now turn to curriculum documents, to explore whether a similar gap exists between the language demands made by subject syllabuses at the beginning of the first year of L2-medium education and English language syllabus specifications at the end of the previous year. With this in mind, we look at curriculum documents for South Africa and ask: does the South African English syllabus up to the end of Grade 3 provide learners with the English language skills they need to study subjects in English from Grade 4?

Table 7.1 shows a selection of the academic skills required of learners studying one subject (natural sciences and technology) in SA in Grade 4 term 1 alone (Department of Basic Education, 2011b). These skills are normal components of a science syllabus; but they are linguistically demanding activities. They require learners to express complex thinking processes (e.g. *sort*, *describe*, *record*, *design*, *evaluate*, etc). To express any one of these functions, the learner needs to deploy key phrases which are linguistically marked as belonging to a scientific genre and which are not contained in the basic general-purpose English L2 syllabus

Table 7.1 Academic literacy skills required in Grade 4 term 1 natural sciences and technology, South Africa

- Sort a selection of living and non-living things
- Identify and describe the parts of a plant
- Identify and describe the parts of an animal
- Grow plants from seeds and measure and record their growth
- Describe different habitats
- Design, draw and evaluate an animal shelter

for Grades 1 to 3 (Department of Basic Education, 2011a). Sorting alone, for example, requires learners to be able to use classifying phrases such as:

> *There are 3 types of…*
> *…fall into 3 categories.*
> *We/you/one can classify … according to …criteria.*

Sorting also requires learners to read and write about classifying things, as is exemplified in Figure 7.4.

In addition, the syllabus requires learners to use a large number of subject-specific words. In only one sub-section of the science syllabus Grade 4 term 1 learners need to learn words for 'the basic structure of plants: roots, stems, leaves, flowers, fruits, seeds; and visible differences between plants: such as size, shape and colour of roots, stems, leaves, flowers, fruits and seeds' (Department of Basic Education, 2011b, p. 17). Thus, in only one topic of only one subject (science) in term 1 of Grade 4 in SA, we see that the normal curriculum makes exacting academic language demands on the learner who has newly switched to learning subjects in English. If we were to investigate in the SA documents all the skills in Grade 4 term 1 in all subjects, (and further, in all the Grade 4 textbooks in term 1) we would arrive at a daunting list of academic language skills and vocabulary items, covering one term only.

There is, of course, nothing unexpected about these language demands. Content study anywhere at Grade 4 in L1 requires language skills at roughly this level. The question is: can learners in SSA learn enough English L2 in Grades 1 to 3 at 3–4 lessons per week to prepare them for it? Normal practice in foreign language teaching at this rate of weekly exposure would not achieve it; but it is useful to look at the degree to which the L2 (English) language syllabus – in SA referred to as the English First Additional Language (FAL) syllabus – in Grades 1 to 3 enables learners to meet these very high, and particularly academic, language demands at Grade 4 (Department of Basic Education, 2011a).

Selected statements from the English FAL syllabus at the end of Grade 3 (i.e. just before learners start learning subjects in L2) – indicative of the coverage of the syllabus – are set out in Table 7.2. The statements, and the English FAL syllabus as a whole, show that learners should be able to listen to simple teacher talk and to oral stories and non-fiction texts. They should be able to make short

Table 7.2 Selected objectives from the English FAL syllabus, end of Grade 3, South Africa

Listening
Follows instructions; understands simple questions; responds to simple requests; identifies an object from a simple oral description; listens to a simple oral recount; listens to short stories, personal recounts or non-fiction texts and answers comprehension questions on them
Speaking
Gives instructions; makes simple requests; talks about objects in a picture or photograph; gives a simple oral recount; participates in a short conversation on a familiar topic; retells a story; with the teacher's help, gives a simple summary of a non-fiction text; performs simple action rhymes; plays language games
Reading
Reads a short written text (a Big Book or other enlarged text) with the teacher; answers literal questions about the story; reads aloud from own book in a guided reading group with the teacher
Writing
Writes increasingly complex lists with headings; writes a paragraph of 6–8 sentences on a familiar topic; organises information in a chart, table or bar graph; writes a simple personal recount; together with the teacher, writes a simple story; uses the writing process (drafting, writing, editing and publishing)

sentences (instructions, requests, simple descriptions) and string sentences together in texts to provide simple oral recounts and information texts. They should be able to participate in short oral conversations. They are still at an early stage in reading (guided reading and Big Book reading). They should be able to write short texts (6–8 sentences), including recounts and give a simple summary of a non-fiction text.

Subject-orientated topics and related vocabulary are not mentioned in these statements; instead, topics are restricted to the familiar. Learners' vocabulary would have to be radically extended to handle the subject-specific vocabulary used, for example, in Figure 7.4. Thinking skills such as those specified in the natural sciences and technology syllabus (see Table 7.1) are also not covered. In terms of reading, the English syllabus assumes that learners are still at an early, semi-dependent stage reading Big Books; many would therefore find it hard to read the kind of text shown in Figure 7.4.

Furthermore, this English FAL syllabus may be ambitious for learners whose English ability is emergent (see above): there are skills shown in the extract which it is doubtful that many learners at the end of Grade 3 can actually use. For example, any activity requiring learners to speak or write an extended text will be hard, e.g. *gives a simple oral recount; participates in a short conversation on a familiar topic; retells a story; gives a simple summary of a non-fiction text.*

Despite these examples of potential over-estimation of learners' abilities, the English FAL syllabus in SA does a reasonably good job of describing what L2 learners in SA can be expected to learn in the first three years of schooling. This is, however, unlikely to enable them to read the kind of text they will encounter at the beginning of Grade 4 and to talk and write in the way the subject requires. It does not teach academic or subject-specific vocabulary. There is, in this end-of-Grade 3 English syllabus, no obvious lexical connection with the subject curriculum which the learner will need to learn in English at the beginning of Grade 4. In vocabulary terms, the lexical gap measured by Macdonald (1993) is likely to be maintained.

In summary, the English FAL syllabus is therefore very probably like many English syllabuses before the switch of medium in SSA (Clegg, 2017), and indeed like most L2 syllabuses elsewhere in the world in that they teach social, not academic English (McKinney, 2017) and thus do not prepare learners to use the L2 as LoI (Qorro, 2010). Not only does the syllabus fail to teach academic language skills, it seems to register no need to do so. It may also overestimate learners' real English L2 abilities at the end of Grade 3; and finally, it is largely unrelated to language demands made in subject syllabuses within the same curriculum.

The South African curriculum is not an exception. Curricula elsewhere in SSA also make almost impossible language demands. In the Rwandan social studies curriculum for Grade 4 (Clegg, 2015), on day 1, learners with very limited English language skills indeed are asked to:

- analyze different economic activities carried out in his/her district in comparison with her/his neighboring districts
- state how socio-economic activities contribute to the development of the district
- explain the importance of socio-economic activities in the development of the district.

These tasks are so far in excess of what Rwandan learners are both cognitively and linguistically capable of either in L1 or L2 at this point that hardly any learners will be able to do them.

This brief discussion of textbooks and curricula in two countries exemplifies two issues which are widespread both in language and content learning as a whole and in SSA in particular:

a. Content learning materials often assume native-like L2 fluency, whereas at the beginning of EM learning, learner L2 ability is often only emergent.
b. The L2 language syllabus makes little attempt to teach the academic language skills which the content curriculum demands.

In addition, however, the language gap is a consequence of time available for language learning. The argument for extended L1-medium schooling would claim that a period of a good six years of effective language teaching is needed in order to teach learners enough L2 – and especially English CALP – for them to use it effectively as LoI. Three years, at about 3–4 lessons per week, up to a switch of medium at Grade 4, is far too short. Indeed, few learners, in low- or high-income countries, can be expected to achieve even social fluency after such short early language learning experience. In particular, they cannot do this without broader community exposure (McKinney, 2017). Many learners in SSA may not experience much L2 outside the classroom and in the community. For these children, English in the English lesson is the main basis for L2 language ability up to Grade 4. Furthermore, academic language use requires a higher standard of L2 ability than social fluency (Pflepsen, 2015). In any context, a short, low-exposure programme cannot provide this. A short period of L2 learning creates the language gap between what a learner can do with L2 at the beginning of Grade 4 and the language demands which the curriculum makes from then on. If this gap is large, learners will not be able to use L2 for learning subjects. A longer period of L2 learning (and especially CALP) development could reduce it.

Furthermore, L2 teaching in preparation for L2-medium education may not be effective enough. One reason, already mentioned, is that it is unlikely, anywhere in SSA, to orientate itself to academic language (Clegg, 2005) and will focus largely on social language. Another is that teachers themselves may feel unconfident in both their L2 ability and their language teaching skills (Evans & Cleghorn, 2012; Read, 2015; British Council, 2015). A more effective L2 syllabus, pedagogy and teacher-education may be necessary.

In drawing attention to the language gap, we should avoid giving the impression that failing to teach the English language skills, which English-medium subject learning requires, is a problem unique to SSA. This critical 'language-blindness' is an observable feature of most school systems in which learners are required to learn subject content in L2. It is a regular complaint in the education of language minorities in, for example, the USA or the UK, where minority learners with as yet low ability in the LoI are immersed in mainstream classrooms, struggling to understand subject concepts (Cloud et al., 2009). Recent projects in system-wide English-medium subject learning – such as that in Malaysia (Gill, 2014) have failed at least partly because learners did not have the academic language skills in English to learn subjects. A recent report (UNICEF, 2019, p. 86) on language in education in South and South East Asia states that, 'children face a huge burden of incomprehension in the early years when they study through the medium of an unfamiliar language'.

The fact that learners do not have enough L2 skills at the switch of medium to learn subjects is only one reason why this change of LoI cannot take place early. A second reason is the fact that they cannot yet use the academic variety of L2, and it is to this that we now turn.

Extended L1-medium education: the CALP-focussed curriculum

A crucial objection raised to early-exit programmes relates to the transfer of CALP skills from L1-medium to L2-medium education. It is assumed that the academic language skills to do with, for example, reading and writing academic texts, which learners use in L2-medium subject learning after the switch of medium, should be first developed in L1 (Cummins, 2009). Many of these academic L1 skills are then thought to be available to transfer to the learning of subjects in the L2.

By and large, there is academic consensus that this transfer takes place best once CALP skills are fairly effectively acquired in L1 (Cummins, 2000); as mentioned above, a period of between six and eight years is considered necessary to achieve this, both in SSA and elsewhere (World Bank, 2008). Many commentators agree that three-year early-exit programmes cannot provide strong L1-medium CALP skills: there is not enough time to establish them (Heugh, 2006); CALP development takes longer (Cummins, 2000). Because these programmes cut off L1-medium learning too early, start L2-medium learning too early and thus fail to provide learners with established L1 CALP skills which transfer easily to L2, they are thought to carry a lot of responsibility for low school achievement in SSA (Heugh, 2009; McKinney, 2017).

There is also a question of the intensity and structural detail of a high-CALP early years curriculum. In order for the transfer of academic language skills from L1 to L2 to take place, they must be more explicitly taught than would be required of learners who learn through L1 throughout schooling (Cummins, 2009; Cloud et al., 2009). For maximum effect this should occur at four points in the curriculum: the L1 syllabus, the broader L1-medium subject curriculum before the switch of medium, the L2 syllabus before and after the switch of medium and the L2-medium subject curriculum after the switch of medium, forming an explicit 'CALP bridge' between the two media of instruction in the teaching of subjects and in subject materials (Pflepsen, 2015). Thus, the teaching of early CALP skills should be coordinated across the teaching of both languages and subjects in L1 and L2. This would ideally require a high-CALP early years literacy programme and a strong role for CALP in early years L1-medium subject teaching and in L2 teaching both before and after the switch of medium. In addition, since low SES correlates strongly in SSA with low home familiarity with the L2 and thus low ability of the learner to use L2 for learning (Smits et al., 2008; Smith, 2011), poverty and its educational concomitants of low family education and low print literacy would have to be addressed through home-school links and home literacy support programmes. All this is demanding, but not impossible. Crucially, however, it is not possible within the straitjacket of a three-year early-exit programme (Cummins, 2000, 2009). The effect of such a programme is therefore to maintain the language gap.

Language supportive pedagogy

Multilingual learning, in an extended L1-medium programme – especially one which leads to a bilingual programme – is a natural and necessary means of making it possible for learners to add a new LoI while minimising loss of access to the curriculum. It is, however, not enough. Even a late transition to L2-medium education within a framework of multilingual learning involves a potential loss of vital language and learning capacity. For this reason, teachers in L2-medium classrooms in SSA need, in addition, to deploy a pedagogy which is appropriate to learners learning subjects with emergent ability in the L2. Pedagogies exist whose purpose is to support learners working in L2 with L2 abilities which are still developing. They are used in the education of language minorities (Cloud et al., 2009; Gibbons, 2015) and in CLIL (Ball et al., 2015). These language supportive pedagogies (LSP) (Clegg & Simpson, 2016) are not widely used elsewhere and are rare in SSA (but see Rubagumya, this volume; Barrett et al., this volume). The main feature of LSP is that it uses a range of strategies to amplify meanings (Gibbons, op. cit.) beyond what is normal in the conventional classroom, supports learners in the face of high language demands and allows them to deploy cognitive resources towards new curricular concepts. This means, for example, that teacher talk involves much more 'redundancy' than is normal: e.g. teachers exemplify, paraphrase, use visuals and L1. They also use a range of language supportive task types unfamiliar in conventional classrooms to help learners listen, read, talk and write bilingually and in L2 despite low and emergent L2 ability levels. LSP is not further developed in this chapter, but the chapter by Clegg and Milligan (this volume) describes it in more detail and contains examples of materials of this kind developed for Rwanda.

Conclusion

Learners in schools across SSA tend to have rich multilingual language resources but are required to learn using the languages in which they have least ability and to which they have least exposure. This depresses their capacity to achieve acceptable levels of education and inflicts significant harm to national school performance, to personal, community, cultural and economic development and to access to social justice.

This chapter has proposed ways of avoiding this damage to personal and national development. Multilingual education offers the possibility of increased levels of school attainment and language ability, as well as personal confidence, cultural strengthening, community cohesion and home-school links (Benson, 2002). The World Bank (2008, p. 22) agrees: 'the bilingual way out of the language problem in SSA acknowledges both the cultural as well as the cognitive aspect of mother tongue instruction'. Extended L1-medium education will enable learners to claim what is considered across the world to be a right and will contribute to higher levels of attainment.

To implement multilingual learning and extended L1-medium education requires considerable – but wholly feasible – changes to the structure of education, especially in educational publishing and teacher-education. Publishers will need to adopt new principles for textbook design and teachers who work in a multilingual classroom will have to use a well-defined pedagogy which is different from conventional monolingual teaching. Both ways of working are available in the wider world. This chapter does not enlarge on these issues, but the topics are pursued in detail in Clegg and Milligan (this volume).

Most importantly, however, change will need to be attitudinal and political. Breakthroughs would not be hard to achieve. There are small-scale initiatives in SSA pursuing such models and reported in the chapters of this book. If any country in SSA were to develop any one of these projects at scale, it would excite interest from all over the world. With informed policy-making with regard to language in education, and targeted expenditure in schools and teacher education institutions, SSA could become a seed bed for radical and effective ideas in multilingual learning which would be in the vanguard of practice everywhere.

References

Alexander, R 2017, *Towards Dialogic Teaching: Rethinking Classroom Talk*, Dialogos, York.

Alidou, H & Brock-Utne, B 2006, "Experience I - teaching practices – teaching in a familiar language", in H Alidou et al. (eds), *Optimizing Learning and Education in Africa – the Language Factor: A Stock-taking Research on Mother Tongue and Bilingual Education in Sub-Saharan Africa*, ADEA, Paris, pp. 85–100.

Arthur, J 1996, "Code-switching and Collusion: Classroom Interaction in Botswana primary schools", *Linguistics and Education*, vol. 8, pp. 17–33.

August, D & Shanahan, T 2006, *Developing Reading and Writing in Second Language Learners: Report of the National Literacy Panel on Language Minority Children and Youth*, Lawrence Erlbaum Associates, Mahwah, NJ.

Baker, C & Wright, WE 2017, *Foundations of Bilingual Education and Bilingualism*, Multilingual Matters, Bristol.

Ball, P, Kelly, K & Clegg, J 2015, *Putting CLIL into Practice*, Oxford University Press, Oxford.

Barnard, T, Bevan, W, Collett, H, McKay, R & Turley, C 2015, *Natural Sciences and Technology, Learner's Book 4*, Oxford University Press, Cape Town.

Bayliss, D 2006, *Biology Forms 1 & 2 Students' Book*, Pearson, Harlow.

Benson, C 2002, "Real and potential benefits of bilingual programs in developing countries", *International Journal of Bilingual Education and Bilingualism*, vol. 5, pp. 303–317.

Bloch, C, Guzala, X & Nkence, N 2010, "Towards normalizing South African classroom life: The ongoing struggle to implement mother-tongue based bilingual education", in K Menken & O García (eds), *Negotiating Language Policies in Schools*, Routledge, Abingdon, pp. 88–106.

British Council 2015, *British Council Endline Assessment of English Language Proficiency of School Teachers in Rwanda*, British Council, Kigali.

Brock-Utne, B 2012, "Language and inequality: Global challenges to education", *Compare: A Journal of Comparative and International Education*, vol. 42(5), pp. 773–793..

Brock-Utne, B & Holmarsdottir, H 2003, "Language policies and practices – some preliminary results from a research project in Tanzania and South Africa", in B Brock-Utne, Z Desai & M Qorro (eds), *Language of Instruction in Tanzania and South Africa (LOITASA)*, E and D, Dar-Es-Salaam, pp. 80–101.

Chick, K 1996, "Safe-talk: Collusion in apartheid education", in H Coleman (ed), *Society and the Language Classroom*, Cambridge University Press, Cambridge.

Chimombo, M 1989, "Readability of subject texts: Implications for ESL teaching in Africa", *English for Specific Purposes*, vol. 8, pp. 255–64.

Clegg, J 2005, "Recognising and countering linguistic disadvantage in English-medium education in Africa", in H Coleman, J Gulyamova & A Thomas (eds), *National*

Development, Education and Language in Central Asia and Beyond, British Council Uzbekistan, Tashkent, pp. 255–264.

Clegg, J 2015, *The Role of English in the Revised Curricula for Mathematics, Science and Social Studies in Rwanda 2014*, unpublished report for the British Council Rwanda, Kigali, Rwanda.

Clegg, J 2017, *The English-medium Curriculum in African Education Systems: Do Have Enough English to Cope with It?*, unpublished presentation, Africa TESOL, Kigali.

Clegg, J 2019, "How English depresses school achievement in Africa", *ELT Journal*, vol. 73, pp. 89–91.

Clegg, J & Simpson, J 2016, "Improving the effectiveness of English as a medium of instruction in sub-Saharan Africa", *Comparative Education*, vol. 52, pp. 359–374.

Cloud, N, Genesee, F & Hamayan, E 2009, *Literacy Instruction for English Language Learners*, Heinemann, Portsmouth, NH.

Criper, C & Dodd, WA 1984, *Report on the Teaching of the English Language and its Use as a Medium in Education in Tanzania*, The British Council, Dar es Salaam.

Cummins, J 2000, *Language, Power and Pedagogy: Bilingual Children in the Crossfire*, Multilingual Matters, Clevedon.

Cummins, J 2009, "Fundamental psycholinguistic, sociolinguistic and sociological principles underlying educational success for linguistic minority students", in T Skuttnab-Kangas, R Phillipson, AK Mohanty & M Panda (eds), *Social Justice through Multilingual Education*, Multilingual Matters, Bristol.

Department of Basic Education 2011a, *Curriculum and Assessment Policy Statement; Grades 1-3; English First Additional Language*, Department of Basic Education, Pretoria.

Department of Basic Education 2011b, *Curriculum and Assessment Policy Statement; Grades 4-6; Natural Sciences and Technology*, Department of Basic Education, Pretoria.

Djité, P 2008, *The Sociolinguistics of Development in Africa*, Multilingual Matters, Clevedon.

Dukhan, S, Cameron, A & Brenner, E 2016, "Impact of mother tongue on construction of notes and first-year academic performance", *South African Journal of Science*, vol. 112, pp. 1–6.

Dutcher, N 2004, *Expanding Educational Opportunities in Linguistically Diverse Societies*, Centre for Applied Linguistics, Washington D.C.

Erling, E, Adinolfi, L, Hultgren, A, Buckler, A & Mukorera, M 2016, "Medium of instruction policies in Ghanaian and Indian primary schools: An overview of key issues and recommendations", *Comparative Education*, vol. 52, pp. 294–310.

Evans, R & Cleghorn, A 2012, *Complex Classroom Encounters: A South African Perspective*, Sense, Rotterdam.

Fleisch, B 2008, *Primary Education in Crisis: Why South African Children Underachieve*, Juta, Cape Town.

Galabawa, J & Senkoro, F 2010, "Implications of changing the language of instruction in secondary and tertiary education in Tanzania", in B Brock-Utne, Z Desai, MAS Qorro & A Pitman (eds), *Language of Instruction in Tanzania and South Africa – Highlights from a Project*, Sense, Rotterdam, pp. 145–156.

García, O, Johnson, SI & Seltzer, K 2017, *The Translanguaging Classroom: Leveraging Student Bilingualism for Learning*, Caslon, Philadelphia.

Gibbons, P 2015, *Scaffolding Language, Scaffolding Learning*, Heinemann, Portsmouth, NH.

Gill, S 2014, *Language Policy Challenges in Multi-Ethnic Malaysia. Multilingual Education*, Springer, Dordrecht.

Hardman, F 2008, "Teachers' use of feedback in whole-class and group-based talk", in N Mercer & S Hodgkinson (eds), *Exploring Talk in School*, Sage, London, pp. 131–150.

Heugh, K 2006, "Theory and practice – language education models in Africa: Research, design, decision making, and outcomes", in H Alidou, A Boly, B Brock-Utne, Y Satina Diallo, K Heugh & H Ekkehard Wolff. (eds), *Optimizing Learning and Education in Africa – the Language Factor: A Stock-taking Research on Mother Tongue and Bilingual Education in Sub-Saharan Africa*, ADEA, Paris, pp. 101–125.

Heugh, K 2009, "Literacy and bi/multilingual education in Africa: recovering collective memory and expertise", in T Skuttnab-Kangas, R Phillipson, AK Mohanty & M Panda (eds), *Social Justice through Multilingual Education*, Multilingual Matters, Clevedon, pp. 103–124.

Heugh, K, Diedericks, M, Prinsloo, CH, Herbst, DL & L Winnaar, 2007, *Assessment of the Language and Mathematics Skills of Grade 8 Learners in the Western Cape in 2006*, Human Sciences Research Council, Pretoria.

Holmarsdottir, H 2005, *From Policy to Practice: A Study of the Implementation of the Language-in-Education Policy (LiEP) in Three South African Primary Schools*, University of Oslo, Oslo.

Lextutor, viewed 12 December 2019, < www.lextutor.ca/>.

Macdonald, C 1993, *Towards a New Primary Curriculum in South Africa*, Human Sciences Research Council, Pretoria.

Magasi, SC 2008, *New Essentials of Biology for Secondary Schools*, Nyambari Nyangwine Publishers, Dar Es Salaam.

Makalela, L 2018, *Shifting Lenses: Multilanguaging, Decolonisation and Education in the Global South*, CASAS, Cape Town.

McKinney, C 2017, *Language and Power in Post-Colonial Schooling*, Routledge, Abingdon.

Mercer, N 1995, *The Guided Construction of Knowledge*, Multilingual Matters, Clevedon.

Murila, B 2004, "Using science textbooks in Kenyan schools", in A Peacock & A Cleghorn (eds), *Missing the Meaning: The Development and Use of Print and Nonprint Text Materials in Diverse School Settings*, Palgrave Macmillan, New York, pp. 121–132.

Pflepsen, A 2015, *Planning for Language Use in Education: Best Practices and Practical Steps to Improve Learning Outcomes*, *RTI/*USAID Bureau for Africa.

Pinnock, H 2009, *Language and Education: The Missing Link How the Language Used in Schools Threatens the Achievement of Education For All*, CfBT and Save The Children Alliance.

Prinsloo, CH, Rogers, SC & Harvey, JC 2018, "The impact of language factors on learner achievement in Science", *South African Journal of Education*, vol. 38, pp. 1–14.

Probyn, M 2005, "Language and the struggle to learn: The intersection of classroom realities, language policy and neo-colonial and globalisation discourses in South African schools", in A Lin & P Martin (eds), *Decolonisation, Globalisation: Language-in-Education Policy and Practice*, Multilingual Matters, Clevedon, pp. 153–172.

Probyn, M 2006, "Language and learning science in South Africa", *Language and Education*, vol. 20, pp. 391–414.

Qorro, M 2010, "Testing students' ability to learn through English during the transition from primary to secondary schooling", in B Brock-Utne, Z Desai, M Qorro & A Pitman (eds), *Language of Instruction in Tanzania and South Africa – Highlights from a Project*, Sense, Rotterdam, pp. 157–188.

Read, T 2015, *Where Have All the Textbooks Gone? Toward Sustainable Provision of Teaching and Learning Materials in Sub-Saharan Africa*, World Bank, Washington D.C.

Skuttnab-Kangas, T 2000, *Linguistic Genocide in Education – or Worldwide Diversity and Human Rights?* Routledge, New York.

Smith, M 2011, "Which in- and out-of-school factors explain variations in learning across different socio-economic groups? Findings from South Africa", *Comparative Education*, vol. 47, pp. 79–102.

Smits, J, Huisman, J & Kruijff, K 2008, *Home Language and Education in the Developing World*, paper commissioned for EFA Global Monitoring Report 2009, UNESCO, Paris.

SPINE 2009, "Investigating the Language Factor in School Examinations: Exploratory Studies", report for Study 5.1 of SPINE research programme, University of Bristol, Bristol, viewed 12 December 2019, <www.bristol.ac.uk/spine/publication%20and%20 reports/study5.1report>.

Stroud, C 2010, "African mother-tongue programmes and the politics of language: Linguistic citizenship versus linguistic human rights", *Journal of Multilingual and Multicultural Development*, vol. 22, pp. 339–355.

Taylor, N & Vinjevold, P 1999, *Getting Learning Right*, Pearson Education, Cape Town.

Trudell, B 2016, "Language choice and education quality in Eastern and Southern Africa: A review", *Comparative Education*, vol. 52, pp. 281–293.

UNESCO 1953, *The Use of the Vernacular Languages in Education*, Monographs on Foundations of Education, No. 8, UNESCO, Paris.

UNESCO 2003, *Education in a Multilingual World*, UNESCO, Paris.

UNESCO 2016, *If You Don't Understand, How Can You Learn?*, Global Education Monitoring Report Policy Paper, UNESCO, Paris.

UNICEF 2019, *Early Literacy and Multilingual Education in South Asia*, UNICEF, Kathmandu.

Uwezo 2012, *Are Our Children Learning? Annual Learning Assessment Report 2012*, Uwezo Tanzania, viewed 12 December 2019, < www.uwezo.net/wp-content/uploads/2012/08/TZ_Uwezo2012ALAReport.pdf>.

Williams, E 2011, "Language policy, politics and development in Africa", in H Coleman (ed), *Dreams and Realities: Developing Countries and the English Language*, The British Council, London, pp. 36–56.

Williams, E 2014, "English in African politics of education: Capital or capital illusion?", *International Journal of the Sociology of Language*, vol. 225, pp. 131–145.

Williams, E & Cooke, M 2002, "Pathways and labyrinths: Language and education in development", *TESOL Quarterly*, vol. 36, pp. 297–322.

World Bank 2008, *Curricula, Examinations, and Assessment in Secondary Education in Sub-Saharan Africa*, World Bank, Washington, DC.

8 Vignette

Implementing language supportive pedagogy to support content learning in Tanzania

Casmir M. Rubagumya, Eliakimu Sane and Jesse Julius Ndabakurane

Introduction

Tanzania, like many countries in SSA, boasts a wealth of indigenous languages (approximately 150), but it is different in that Kiswahili is spoken as a second language – and used as a lingua franca – by around 90% of the population (Schmied, 1991). The official language policy stipulates that the language of instruction at the primary level is Kiswahili, with English as a compulsory subject. At the secondary level, English becomes the language of instruction while Kiswahili is taught as a compulsory subject. However, there are no adequate preparations for students to learn through English and not enough resources dedicated to supporting students to learn the language. Moreover, due to poverty, many parents do not have the resources required to give their children access to the English language, books and materials used in schools are beyond the reach of many students, and so teachers act as the sole providers of English language input, with many of them having only emergent competence in the language themselves. While official policy documents from 2014 mention the possibility of using Kiswahili as a language of instruction in secondary education, no clear guidelines for this have been issued and the status quo for English language instruction has mostly been upheld. There is an ongoing academic debate over whether the switch to Kiswahili in Tanzanian secondary schools would be beneficial, with some supporting the continued use of English (Kadeghe, 2010) and others arguing for the switch to Kiswahili as the language of instruction beyond primary school (Qorro, 2004; Rubagumya, 2009; Brock-Utne & Skattum, 2009, to mention just a few). However, neither side provides a solution to help students learn through the policy as it is interpreted and implemented today. As there are many people in Tanzania who are eager to learn and use English, and there is no sign of changing the language policy in the near future, we cannot anymore wait for the conclusion of the continuing debate. Given this situation, this vignette describes how the language supportive pedagogy (LSP) approach was developed and implemented at the secondary school level in Tanzania, after the switch from

DOI: 10.4324/9781003028383-10

education through the medium of Kiswahili to English. It first provides a definition of LSP and the principles underlying it and then provides examples of how the approach works in practice.

The LSP approach

The LSP approach described in full in Clegg and Milligan (this volume), was developed through The Language Supportive Teaching and Textbooks Project (henceforth LSTT), introduced in Tanzania in 2013. This project mainly aims to facilitate content learning among students whose English proficiency is relatively low by developing their subject specific language. It thus sought to promote teaching and learning activities which help students to improve their understanding of subject content and develop subject specific language. It did this through designing, developing and trialling textbook materials in selected secondary schools in Dodoma, Morogoro and Lindi Region in Tanzania. LSP is an extension of LSTT and it has been collaboratively undertaken by the University of Dodoma, St. John's University of Tanzania and Bristol University (see further Barrett et al., this volume).

LSP demonstrates how the learning of a second language can be facilitated through strategic multilingual instruction using the students' first and/or most familiar languages. It is both a theory and a practice. As a theory, it is influenced by interactionist theory (Vygotsky, 1978) which emphasizes that learning occurs through interaction. Students need to interact among themselves, with teachers and with the teaching and learning materials. This interaction is possible only when students are enabled to use a language that they are more familiar with (in this case Kiswahili). As a practice, LSP facilitates the teaching and learning of English through subject instruction to improve the implementation of the Tanzanian language policy as it is now being interpreted and implemented (Barrett, 2017). LSP has been introduced into subject methodology (pedagogy) courses at the University of Dodoma and St. John's University of Tanzania and in three teachers' colleges: Butimba, Morogoro and Mpwapwa. LSP is guided by the following principles:

- Students learn more effectively and efficiently when they start with the known and move to the unknown.
- A student's mother tongue (or familiar language) is a resource and not a problem in learning a second language and learning through a second language.
- If used strategically, the mother tongue (or familiar language) can help students learn a second language and through a second language.
- Textbooks in a second language should be made accessible to students in terms of vocabulary, length and complexity of sentences.
- Students should be encouraged to participate in classroom activities that develop language skills: listening, reading, speaking and writing.

LSP makes strategic use of students' first languages to help them learn both the subject and language of instruction. The term "strategic" is used here to mean using the students' first or familiar language only when necessary; for example, to translate important concepts or ask students to discuss some issues in the language and then the teacher guides them to express the same issues in the target language. In the LSP approach, CLIL subject teachers are asked to embed language objectives when preparing the lessons and engage students in activity-rich lessons, all of which enhance the development of language skills along with learning subject content. In planning and teaching language through subjects, teachers are asked to consider three language aspects: subject specific vocabulary, general language and subject genres. The language objectives require subject teachers to equip themselves with some language aspects such as correct spelling, semantic variations and pronunciation of jargon and key terms in the discipline. The teacher is responsible for helping students to learn the subject content as well as to develop the subject-specific language. The subject-specific language can mainly be developed through the help of the relevant subject teacher. Many teachers, particularly science teachers, claim that language issues should be entrusted to English language teachers. However, it is difficult for most English language teachers to help the students to develop the vocabulary, structures, and symbols for learning subjects such as Biology, Mathematics, Chemistry, Geography or History. The LSP project advocates that every teacher should be a language teacher. This does not imply that non-language subject teachers should be equipped with the same expertise in language that language teachers have, but they should be in a position to assist students to develop subject specific language and other aspects such as pronunciation and grammar.

LSP in action

During the teaching and learning process, the subject teacher assists students to sharpen their language skills for both academic and informal purposes. The teacher's language assistance involves offering model pronunciation, spelling, word meanings and construction of sentences. In addition, teachers are asked to design and develop activities that reinforce both the subject knowledge and acquisition of language skills, i.e. speaking, listening, reading and writing. Such classroom practices are doable and helpful to students. LSP has proved helpful to students with limited English proficiency and, in particular, those who went through public primary schools where Kiswahili was the sole language of instruction. The evidence and insights are highlighted in recent research on the teaching and learning of Chemistry and English that was conducted in five regions of Tanzania in secondary school education (when students are approximately 13 to 16 years old). In these regions, student teachers who were exposed to LSP were involved in developing shorter passages or texts to support the students to improve their language skills. A set of teaching and learning activities was used to improve students' understanding of subject content and the acquisition of subject specific language. Such activities, which were widely done in groups, facilitated the students' readiness to communicate in both English and Kiswahili, the home language of the students in this region. While interacting with the subject matter in their groups, the students were also given the freedom to choose the language that they would use to make the interaction even easier. The teachers were oriented to the strategic use of Kiswahili during the teaching and learning process, for example when English could not easily help students to understand what was being taught. In the instances where students could not conceptualize English concepts, they were encouraged to switch to Kiswahili in order to clarify the intended idea or message and then the teacher guided them to express it in English. The integration of Kiswahili into the teaching and learning process does not suggest the replacement of English as the sole language of instruction. Instead, it is made to operate as a co-language of instruction in the instances when the need arises. Where a translation of a concept may not be helpful, teachers are asked to make an interpretation using the target language.

In activities, students are expected to develop relevant knowledge, skills and competencies required of them in the subject and improve their academic English use. While doing the tasks, students are allowed to discuss content topics in Kiswahili and prepare their presentations to the whole class in English. This strategy helps students to make a link between the knowledge that students learnt during Kiswahili-medium education and the knowledge that they are currently developing in English. To help students prepare presentations, guidance is provided on how to structure their work in English. Students are supported with relevant English vocabulary and structures for presenting their work. The principles of LSP recommend that subject teachers should:

- guide students to do activities by giving them clear instructions. The teacher can use their home languages as necessary
- encourage students to discuss activities using the languages that they are familiar with to clearly conceptualize the content and connect it with what they learnt before
- make sure that all students fully participate in class activities;
- help students prepare their presentations in English
- make sure that all students get equal opportunities to prepare and present responses to the class
- encourage more girls to participate actively because in many rural schools, boys get more opportunities to participate compared to girls, and
- clarify all unclear points to encourage students to read further.

Conclusion

In this vignette, we have attempted to show that challenges of language in education in multilingual and low-resourced contexts are not insurmountable. Giving the example of an innovation being trialled since 2013 in Tanzania, we argue that a language that students are more familiar with can be used strategically to help them learn a second language and learn through a second language. For this, subject teachers need to develop skills to be able teach subject-relevant English and provide support to students as they teach the subjects. This innovation seems to be working and is supported by teachers and students in the schools where it has been trialled. However, the innovation has not yet been approved by the Tanzanian Ministry of Education. Time will tell whether the innovation can be scaled up and made sustainable beyond the life of the current project.

References

Barrett, A 2017, *Implementing language supportive in teacher education: An ongoing CIRE research project*, viewed 24 June 2019, <https://cire-bristol.com/2017/11/07/implementing-language-supportive-pedagogy-in-teacher-education-an-ongoing-cire-research-project/>.

Brock-Utne, B & Skattum, I (eds) 2009, *Languages and Education in Africa*, Symposium Books, Oxford.

Kadeghe, M 2010, 'In defense of continued use of English as the language of instruction in secondary and tertiary education in Tanzania', 'in B Brock-Utne, Z Desai, M Qorro & A Pittman (eds), *Language of Instruction in Tanzania and South Africa – Highlights from a Project*, Sense, Rotterdam.

Qorro, M 2004, 'Popularising Kiswahili as a language of instruction through the media in Tanzania', in B Brock-Utne, Z Desai & M Qorro (eds), *Researching the Language of Instruction in Tanzania and South Africa*, African Minds, Cape Town.

Rubagumya, CM 2009, 'Language in education in Africa: can monolingual policies work in multilingual societies?', in JA Kleigfen & JC Bond (eds), *The Languages of Africa and the Diaspora,* Multilingual Matters, Bristol.

Schmied, J 1991, *English in Africa: An Introduction,* Longman, London.

Vygotsky, L.S 1978, *Mind and Society: The Development of Higher Psychological Processes,* Harvard University Press, Cambridge, MA.

9 Creating translanguaging inquiry spaces in bilingual classrooms

Ivana Espinet, Maite T. Sánchez and Gladys Y. Aponte

Introduction

> I think [our students] ... appreciate how our classroom is very diverse, and that they're able to learn from each other (...) With our unit about community, it's all ... about embracing the differences of the children in our classroom, but also the diversity in the community.
>
> (Teacher 1, 23 March 2019)

While the potential of translanguaging is widely recognized as a means of supporting equitable quality in education, given the multilingual nature of the majority of schools in Sub-Saharan Africa (SSA) (Bunyi, & Schroeder, 2016; Guzula et al., 2016; Heugh, 2015; Makalela, 2015; Probyn, 2015), there are few accounts of how translanguaging spaces can be created in schools. While we understand that translanguaging spaces need to be created with an understanding of the local context of each community, this chapter provides examples of how educators fostered translanguaging spaces within the educational context of New York City (NYC) that we believe can be adapted to other contexts.

In the United States, federal government policies have become more rigid, emphasizing English-only instruction and leaving aside students' home language practices (García & Kleifgen, 2018). However, even in this national context, bilingual education programs in New York State are growing. CUNY-NYSIEB (City University of New York-New York State Initiative on Emergent Bilinguals) stems from Ofelia García's work on translanguaging pedagogy. The goal of CUNY-NYSIEB is to collaborate with educators and administrators in schools to develop ecologies of bilingualism/multilingualism and to build on students' home language practices (García & Kleyn, 2016). This chapter provides insight into how researchers and educators partnered to create "translanguaging transformational spaces" (Sánchez et al., 2018) in one school in NYC. It focuses on the design and implementation of an inquiry project with a group of Grade 1 teachers from an English-Spanish dual language bilingual public elementary school in NYC.

We begin the chapter by providing a background of the neighborhood and the school. Next, we give an overview of the inquiry project and describe three of the activities in which the children and teachers engaged. During and after

DOI: 10.4324/9781003028383-11

the project, researchers from CUNY-NYSIEB planned and observed classroom activities, collected student work and debriefed with the teachers about their reflections and observations during the class activities. Throughout the chapter, we share some of the ideas, impressions and evolving understandings that the teachers shared, as well as examples of student work. We also show how, through this collaboration, the educators in the school developed and valued practices that leveraged the rich repertoire of cultural and linguistic resources of their students, their families and communities, as illustrated by the quote from one of the teachers at the beginning of the chapter.

Rethinking the cultural and linguistic resources of underprivileged and marginalized communities

Schooling in the United States has historically been set up with the goal of assimilation. In order for students to "achieve in school" in the ways that are sanctioned by public education, families and students are asked to lose or deny their languages, literacies, cultures and histories (Paris & Alim, 2017). Latinx cultural and linguistic practices in the United States have been traditionally marginalized, misheard and devalued (Rosa & Flores, 2017, Suárez-Orozco et al., 2008; Valenzuela, 1999). Public schools in the United States have often been guided by the goal of mainstreaming students into dominant society by "subtracting" their community experiences and connections, their language and their culture (Valenzuela, 1999). Around the world, minoritized groups' linguistic and cultural practices have also been marginalized and marked as having low status within national and local contexts. For example, in the context of some SSA countries, the languages of former colonizers were initially chosen as the languages of education when many new African countries emerged from colonialism. Even though later on many countries devised national language policies that supported the use of African languages in education, many of the language attitudes of teachers and some community members continue to devalue the use of indigenous language practices in schools (Bunyi & Schroeder, 2016; Henriksen, 2014; Nyati-Ramahobo, 2006). For example, Henriksen (2014, p. 300) describes how, despite Mozambique's linguistic and cultural diversity, one key challenge of implementing bilingual education in urban areas in Mozambique is "the need to change the negative attitudes toward the use of the Mozambican languages in education, particularly among the urban groups." It is important to note that, while in the United States, English is socially, culturally and institutionally positioned as the dominant language, in SSA, many students may only encounter English in the context of schooling.

While research has pointed to the power of culturally sustaining pedagogies (Paris & Alim, 2017), in many US settings, families' and communities' sources of knowledges are still not part of what is considered school knowledge and their linguistic practices are often stigmatized. Furthermore, the multimodal ways of knowing and learning that families, communities and children enact outside of school are often excluded from the classroom space, including in bilingual/multilingual classroom settings.

Although public schools in New York State have offered bilingual education as an option since the 1970s, in the last two decades, there has been an increase in dual language bilingual education (DLBE) programs in which instruction is carried out in two languages and the aim is for students to become bilingual, biliterate and bicultural. This is due to regulation that if there are 20 or more grade-level students that speak the same home/primary language, the school districts are mandated to start a bilingual program in which students are taught all content areas in both languages. Most of DLBE programs provide half of their instruction in English and the other half in a language other than English (LOTE). These programs are thus referred to in this chapter as bilingual, even though many of the students in such programs may be multilingual—having access to more than two officially recognized languages. Despite this, many DLBE programs are set up with a monoglossic belief that minoritized bilingual students ought to be two monolingual speakers in one (Grosjean, 1982), adopting language allocation policies that prescribe an exclusive space for English and another exclusive one for the language other than English (Sánchez et al., 2018). There is also the expectation that students will use socially-constructed "standard" language practices that "belong in school." This implicitly and explicitly devalues the dynamic non-dominant language practices of bilingual/multilingual students and families, perpetuating hierarchies of languages (Flores & Rosa, 2015).

As an alternative, translanguaging pedagogy aims to ensure that all bilingual students are instructed and assessed in ways that value their home language practices and provide equal educational opportunities (García et al., 2017). García and Wei (2014, p. 137) use the term translanguaging to describe "the way in which bilinguals use their complex semiotic repertoire to act, to know, and to be." Multilinguals draw strategically on a varied repertoire of social and linguistic multimodal practices to think, learn and communicate effectively. In order to make space for student's multilingualism, it is essential that we leverage and build on those home and community practices. A translanguaging stance is the philosophical belief that multilingual students' language practices work together and that the classroom space must promote collaboration across content, languages and students' homes and communities (García et al., 2017). The practices that we describe in this chapter were conceived from a translanguaging stance.

During the 2018–2019 school year, Hudson Elementary School collaborated with CUNY-NYSIEB to design translanguaging transformational spaces (Sánchez et al., 2018). In order to create these spaces, it was important to set up structures for purposeful planning and reflection. All the school staff participated in an initial professional development session in which Ofelia García and the three authors of this chapter explored translanguaging in the context of dual language bilingual programs. After this initial session, all grades (kindergarten–5th) worked in grade teams during two school-wide afterschool planning sessions and then continued to meet in grade teams with CUNY-NYSIEB researchers to finish planning and then debrief as the projects in each grade were implemented.

Each grade team implemented a project during different times in the year. They all documented their experiences and shared their work as well as their reflections with the rest of the school. At the end of the year, all grade teams gathered in one final professional development session in which they reflected on the process, the challenges and the implications for continuing their work in the classroom.

Although the authors worked with all of the teachers in the school, the focus of this chapter is on the work with the Grade 1 teachers. Designing activities in which the Grade 1 students worked as bilingual/multilingual language ethnographers was an attempt to create a translanguaging space to foster students' awareness and criticality of language itself and in which students could draw on all of their linguistic multimodal resources, challenging prevailing linguistic hierarchies in school and society overall.

The neighborhood and school community

The Manhattan neighborhood in which the school is located, Washington Heights, is made up predominately of people from Dominican and Latinx[1] descent, although the demographics are changing as it gentrifies.[2] Currently, 48% of the population are born outside of the United States.[3] While the neighborhood has people born outside of the United States from more than 55 different countries, two thirds come from the Dominican Republic, along with a strong presence of people of Puerto Rican, Mexican and Ecuadorian descent. In addition, 72% of the population self-identifies as Latinx (New York State Office of the State Comptroller, & DiNapoli, 2015).

Hudson Elementary School[4] is a public school in the Washington Heights area with a school-wide English-Spanish dual language bilingual program that serves students from kindergarten to fifth grade. According to the New York City Department of Education, 68% of the students in the school are classified as economically disadvantaged.[5] In the year in which this inquiry project took place, the school had approximately 400 students. Of the total population of the school, almost 30% of the students were officially classified as multilingual language learners[6] (School Register, NY DOE, 2019a). However, approximately 75% of the students used languages other than English at home; mostly Spanish, but also French, German, Hebrew, Italian, Mixteco, Russian, Swedish, Tagalog and Turkish (NYC DOE, 2019b). One of the school's main goals is to develop students' bilingualism and biliteracy. The administration and the teachers emphasize the value of establishing positive and trusting relationships with families and the community.

Designing a transformative inquiry: overview and rationale

As educators, we are always in the process of developing our stance. Our understandings and beliefs are not static; instead, they are constantly evolving, based on our experiences with our students and in the world outside of schools.

The process of designing and implementing this project provided a chance for the teachers to examine their ideological stances about students' home and community language practices and to build on them. The authors of this chapter worked with the teachers, designing curricula intended to open up translanguaging spaces in which the children could use their full multimodal repertoires to co-create knowledge. In addition to fostering students' awareness and criticality of language itself, this project intended that students take a lead in this process by asking questions and gathering data to answer them.

The Grade 1 teachers began by identifying an essential question: How do community members use language? In order to design curricula from a translanguaging stance that reflects culturally sustaining values, it was essential that the planning started from a systematic examination of the resources that the students, families and community had, so that they could be leveraged. At the beginning of the process, the teachers answered the following questions:

- What do you think your students already know about this topic?
- What are some resources that your students or their families have that can contribute to the inquiry?
- What resources are available in the community?
- What are some multimodal ways of inquiry that you imagine your students doing?

After they answered these questions as a group, they used the information that they had collected to design classroom activities to take advantage of those resources. An essential component in the design process was that teachers had a chance to spend time discussing the question: What are some multimodal ways of inquiry that you imagine your students doing? This guided the teachers in expanding how children conducted research in their classrooms. Classroom inquiry provides a content-rich environment that fosters opportunities for children to think and write about what they are learning as well as to make connections to their inquiry question(s) through literature. While traditionally, literacy teaching has focused on reading and writing, scholars have theorized about the need to expand our traditional notions of literacy. In 1996, the New London Group introduced the concept of *multi-literacies*, theorizing changing the " 'what' of literacy pedagogy" to include six design elements in the meaning-making process: linguistic, visual, audio, gestural and spatial meaning as well as multimodal interplay. Since then, the theoretical and practical exploration of multimodal literacies has expanded toward multiple perspectives. However, classroom literacy instruction is still mostly focused on print literacy (Lotherington & Jenson, 2011). The Grade 1 teachers planned activities that expanded on the traditional notion of literacy to include other modes of gathering and analyzing information, such as the use of images.

While in previous years, the teachers had done community inquiry projects in which they had, for example, focused on community workers or looked at the physical environment of their community, this was the first time that they explored the question: How do community members use language? Another essential shift that the teachers made during the planning stage was the decision that, as bilingual/multilingual ethnographers, the children should use language fluidly throughout the process, rather than following a strict separation of languages. The teachers introduced the concept of translanguaging and explained that while schooltime is generally separated between "English time" and "Spanish time," they would use language flexibly during the inquiry. The teachers described what ethnographers do and explained that the students would approach the study of language in their community as bilingual/multilingual ethnographers. Although it was important to have an initial plan, inquiry is a messy, fluid process. In the next sections, we share three activities that the Grade 1 students engaged in as bilingual ethnographers: a community walk, creating linguistic family maps and recreating scenes using images and dialogue.

A walk around the community as bilingual ethnographers

One of the first activities was an investigatory walk around the school's neighborhood. In order to analyze the richness of knowledge in their community, particularly the linguistic resources, the Grade 1 teachers took their students out of the school to gather data about how people in their neighborhood use language. Prior to embarking on this exploration, the children listed a variety of local places that they wanted to visit, including the corner bodega (grocery store), restaurants, a bank, outdoor vendors and a clinic. The students also generated a list of specific questions that they wanted to explore: Who lives in our community? What are the resources in our community? How do people in our community use language?

The children travelled around several city blocks, observing and discussing what they saw as multilingual ethnographers. They heard and saw a variety of languages; Mixteco conversations took place at a fruit stand, Chinese was written at the school entrance and at a nearby restaurant, the halal food truck vendor spoke French and Arabic, signs in Hebrew were displayed at the historic Jewish university nearby, and most business awning signs were in Spanish and English. Mixteco is a widely spoken indigenous language in Mexico and is the home language for many Mexicans living in NYC, but it is often not recognized in the context of schooling. Having the children hear it at the fruit stand and recognize it as a language in their community made it visible and brought it to their discussions in the classroom.

As the neighborhood exploration continued, the children entered several businesses to ask questions that they had brainstormed in Spanish and English: What work do you do in our community? How do you use language? How do you communicate with customers who don't speak the same languages as you? Why is it important for you to speak more than one language in this community?

The first stop the students made was the corner bodega across the street from the school. Many of the students knew the clerk, but they had not previously inquired about his use of language. He shared that he grew up speaking Arabic and English, but he also learned Spanish from customers and people in the neighborhood. He explained that speaking Spanish has helped him make more friends and maintain his clientele. Similarly, at the local bank, the teller explained that the employees in the bank speak many languages because many of their customers speak Korean, Japanese or Spanish in addition to English.

At the local clinic, an emergency medical technician highlighted that being bilingual allowed him to assist more people during emergencies. The nurse explained that even though her Spanish fluency is still emergent, most of the clinic's staff speaks Spanish and the clinic provides interpretation services for clients who speak other languages. A doctor who uses English and Spanish with her patients reminded students that language is not always verbal; she explained that she reads body language and facial expressions to understand people's emotions and ailments.

During the walk, teachers made a deliberate effort to model curiosity and interest in learning from community members. For example, when students stopped to speak to a vendor selling traditional Dominican desserts like *habichuela con dulce* (sweet beans) and *maíz caquiao* (corn pudding) from a small cart at the corner, one of the teachers asked what the Dominican word *caquiao* meant and the food vendor explained that it meant "cracked corn." The teacher told the students she was excited to learn a new word. As the students continued to stroll around the neighborhood, they asked questions in English and Spanish and they heard people translanguaging in the street as they communicated with each other.

The last stop was Empanada Monumental, a local restaurant that sells a variety of Dominican style empanadas (turnovers, or patties) and other Latin American dishes. There, the teachers allowed each student to select an empanada to take back to the classroom. After placing the order, the teacher asked students to analyze the language she used to order their empanadas, and then she pointed to the overhead screen that displayed the selection of food sold there. Since some students in the class are emergent readers, the teacher read some of the foods listed on the menu aloud and then asked students to discuss their observations with one another as they waited for the empanadas to be prepared. At first, students pointed out that the menu was bilingual, but then they noticed that most of the words were not in both languages. The class decided that words like *coffee*, *dessert*, *alitas* and *smoothie* had images next to them to help customers understand their meaning. Later, during their debrief in the classroom, they also concluded that some of the food names, like *tostones*, *salchipapa*, *pasteles en hoja* and *yaroa* cannot be translated since they are culturally-tied to Colombia, Venezuela, the Dominican Republic and Puerto Rico. Before heading back to the school to enjoy their empanadas and reflect on their trip around the neighborhood, the classroom teacher assistant pointed out the numerous photos of the Dominican Republic that decorated the restaurant wall. As a Dominican New Yorker who travels to the country often, she was able to answer questions students had about the images. The photos included images of Dominican baseball players and historical figures as well as images that portrayed rural lifestyles in the Dominican Republic; cooking over a wood fire, a farmer with his goat and a woman selling food outdoors helped students see how many of their neighborhood's wealth of resources are tied to the cultural practices that immigrants share.

Soon after the walk, the teachers reflected on the value of leveraging the community as a resource for learning:

> Talking about and observing translanguaging in the community helped the students to think flexibly and creatively about their own language use. Many students expressed excitement and pride in their multilingualism.
>
> (Teachers joint written reflection, 3 June 2019)

Afterwards, when the first graders were back in at their school, they reorganized their classrooms to create play centers that reflected the community. They incorporated some of the things that the class saw during their walk into the play centers. The children processed and recreated their observations as they pretended to cook *pastelitos*, worked in the medical clinic and played *peluquería* (hair salon) using a variety of linguistic, gestural and other meaning-making resources. Play is essential in providing the foundation for children's lifelong learning (Cohen et al., 1997; Souto-Manning, 2017). It also creates an opportunity for educators to observe and build on students' semiotic practices. During play, children use their entire multimodal repertoire to express familiar themes and explore new ideas (Edwards et al., 2017). By setting up the classroom space in a way that encourages students to use all of their communicative resources in the play centers, the teachers encouraged her students to bring their multilingual imaginations and diverse communicative practices into their play.

In reflecting on the project and on her work in the classroom, one of the Grade 1 teachers shared:

> [The children] have been able to take what they've learned from their research and apply it. Or maybe it's their way of synthesizing it and processing it through play, so we'll definitely continue to use inquiry and play in their translanguaging space.
>
> (Teacher 1, personal communication, 23 May 2019)

One of the essential insights that the teachers came away with is that, in creating opportunities for children to recreate their observations through play, they also used play to process what they had learned. One of the crucial elements of the inquiry process is that children have a chance to analyze what they observed, make inferences and come up with new ideas. Traditionally, we think of the analysis process as one that is done as a discussion or in writing. However, in these Grade 1 classrooms, the students used the play centers to make new meaning through play.

Family linguistic identity maps

A few days after the community walk, the Grade 1 students continued their inquiry project, discussing how they use language in their families. In class, students brainstormed with their peers and shared the languages that they use with different people in their lives, and wrote and drew their responses. The teacher displayed the students' work on a bulletin board (see Figure 9.1). Among the students' responses were that they use Spanish (and/or English) with one or both of their parents, with siblings, with friends and in other social situations (going to the store or at the beach). Several wrote that they use Spanish to speak with one of their grandparents.

Twice a month, the school hosts Family Fridays in which families are welcomed into their children's classrooms for about an hour. During this time, they participate with the children in activities related to something in which they are engaged at school. During one Family Friday two of the Grade 1 classrooms had the first graders and their family members answer question: "How do community members use language?" but that time, they focused on their own families. As in the inquiry process with the students, for that Family Friday, instead of doing it in Spanish as usual, they used language more flexibly. Students and their families started asking each other about the languages they use with different members in their families.

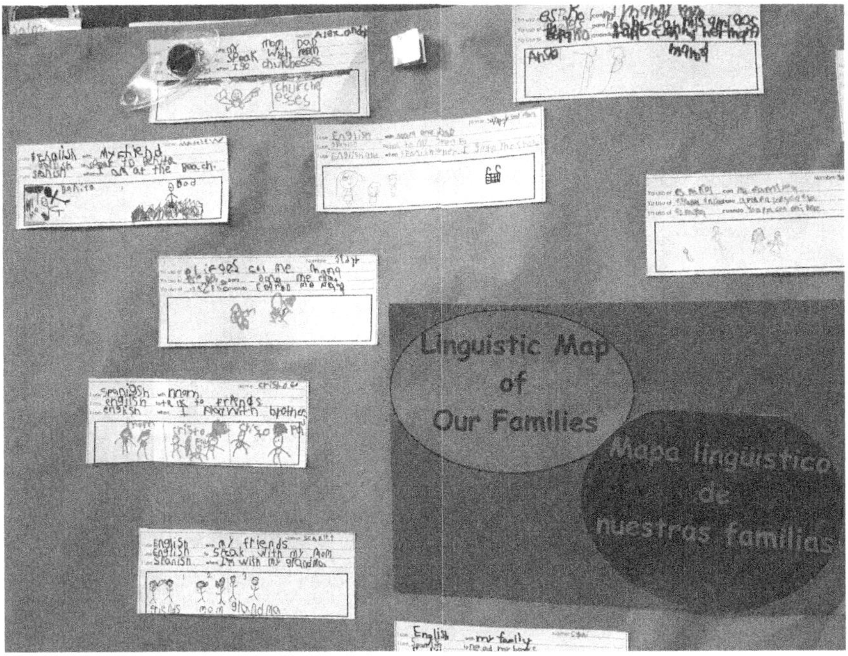

Figure 9.1 Display of students' reflections on the use of different languages in their life.

The culminating activity for that Family Friday was for each child to create a linguistic map that identifies each of the languages that the student speaks, along with the situations in which and the people with whom they speak. Family members not only worked with their own child but they also asked other children about the languages that they use and helped them create their own linguistic maps. Figure 9.2 is an example of a language map by a student who uses English and Spanish to communicate with different people in his life and in different contexts. For English, the student noted that he uses it with his *familia* (family), *en el parque* (in the park), in *el programa* (the school's bilingual program) and with Mr. Angel. For Spanish, he also noted *familia*, *leer español* (reading in Spanish), *en casa* (at home) and with his *tía* (aunt).

In one of the Grade 1 classrooms at the end of the Family Friday's meeting, all attendees sat in a circle and were asked to pick one family member to share in which language they communicate. One of the teachers noted that she learned that parents speak a variety of languages and that students in the classroom had the opportunity to learn that classmates also used Russian, German or Hebrew in addition to English and/or Spanish. One mother shared that they spoke Mixteco at home in addition to Spanish and how important it was for her that her children learn Mixteco. While Mixteco is a widely spoken indigenous language in Mexico,

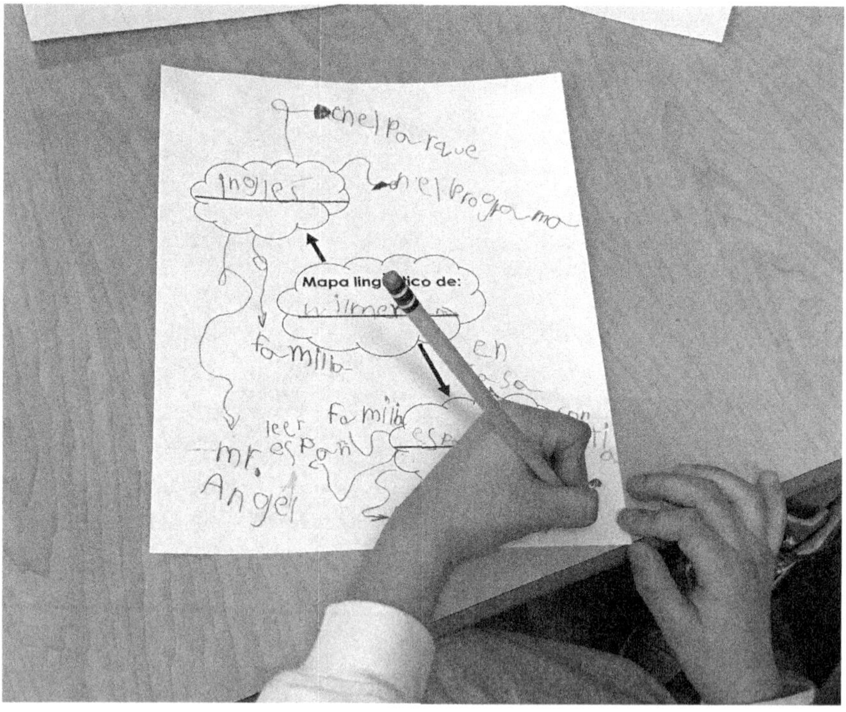

Figure 9.2 Language map of a bilingual student.

in the context of schooling it is often rendered invisible as educators often assume that Spanish is the home language for Mexican children (Perez et al., 2016; Velasco, 2014). In addition, Mixteco speakers have often experienced racism and discrimination within Mexican society, in which Spanish is linked to higher status and social mobility (Perez et al., 2016; Velasco, 2014).

The teacher stated that hearing the parent sharing that they spoke Mixteco at home "was a big learning moment for the class because a lot of the kids didn't know that that child was trilingual" (personal communication, 23 May 2019) The teacher shared later that this conversation prompted another child to later include Mixteco in his linguistic map. Velasco (2014, p. 18) points out that "like their parents, Mixteco children seldom acknowledge their background." Opening up a space for parents to talk about their language practices provided a chance for children to also examine and share their families' practices in a context in which they were valued.

The family linguistic identity maps provided a platform for multiple conversations about language. During the Family Friday's meeting, but also in subsequent encounters, parents, teachers and students discussed the different ways in which the children and their families use language even when they are speaking Spanish or English. They talked about words that Dominicans use versus those used by Colombians or Mexicans. They challenged the idea that there is one "correct" way of speaking Spanish, considering how they have observed people in their community using a variety of registers to communicate with each other.

Creating the linguistic identity maps prompted students, family members and teachers to examine how languages other than Spanish and English are present in the lives of their families and communities and to think about how they use their languages with different people and for different purposes. They also provided an opportunity to bring to light and value linguistic practices, such as Mixteco, that have been marginalized or rendered invisible in the context of schooling. This activity created an awareness of power dynamics between languages. The students also had a chance to talk about their differences and similarities, providing a space for emergent bilinguals' experiences to be valued and to build an understanding that their differences make them unique.

The activities described above that happened in a school in a diverse neighborhood in NYC, could be particularly relevant in the contexts of SSA where families' translanguaging practices involve a multiplicity of languages. For example, Hibbert (2016, p. 138) explains how terms such as "mother tongue," "first language" and "home language" are inadequate in South Africa because students cannot be allocated to uncomplicated categories: "a young person in South Africa can very easily have a Xhosa speaking mother but consider English her home language because it was the main language spoken in the home, and Afrikaans to be first language because she studied it at 'first language' level at school." Asking students and families to map their language use with a variety of people and contexts can bring to light the value of their multilingual lives and prompt discussions about how different language practices are valued in each community.

Multimodal ways of analyzing and sharing

While the teachers had envisioned using multimodal ways of learning in their initial inquiry planning, when they were immersed in the process, new ideas emerged and they modified their plans based on what the children and adults learned along the way. One example of this was an activity that they designed, using photos the teachers had taken during the community walks and the Family Fridays. Aida Walqui (2006) describes how students appropriate new language by engaging in activities that recreate text by transformating linguistic constructions that they find modelled in one genre into forms in another genre. This activity provided the stage for children to use images and text as a platform to analyze and share what they had learned from first hand observations.

Different communicative modes have different affordances—potentials and constraints for making meaning (Bezemer & Kress, 2008). Using images prompted the students to do semiotic work that combined their recollection of oral exchanges, images documented by the teachers, and their written recreations of dialogues. As bilingual/multilingual language ethnographers, the children analyzed how different members of their community used multiple semiotic modes. Following that, the children created a new multimodal text to process their findings and share their complex metalinguistic analysis.

For this activity, the teachers shared printed photos with the children, some taken during the community walk, some during the Family Friday where students created their linguistic maps and some from the internet that recreated scenes that they experienced during the walk and the Family Friday. The children, working in pairs, selected two images that they wanted to use, then added speech bubbles to recreate dialogues that they had heard or that they imagined people having. In Figures 9.3 and 9.4 below, we present two examples, one with an image from the community walk and the other from Family Fridays.

Figure 9.3 shows an image taken during the community walk at a neighborhood restaurant specializing in food from different Latin American countries. that students encountered during their community walk. In the background, there are signs in English and Spanish: "fresh food," "homemade pasteles." The students added these to their dialogues. One person says "Hay muchos niños aquí Matthew" [There are many children here, Matthew]. The other one answers: "We have to make más pastelitos Jairo." In recreating this dialogue, the children who authored the piece not only embedded translanguaging in the dialogue, something that they witnessed constantly as they strolled around the neighborhood, but also included themselves ("muchos niños") as referenced in the dialogue that they report people having.

Figure 9.4 is another image with students' recreation of dialogues heard during the community walks. It shows a mom talking to two children (although one child is partially hidden by the dialogue bubble) during the Family Friday activity (described in the section above). The students who worked on this image added the dialogue: The mom speaks in English to one of them, "I speak Spanish to my baby," and to the other child, she explains her language practices

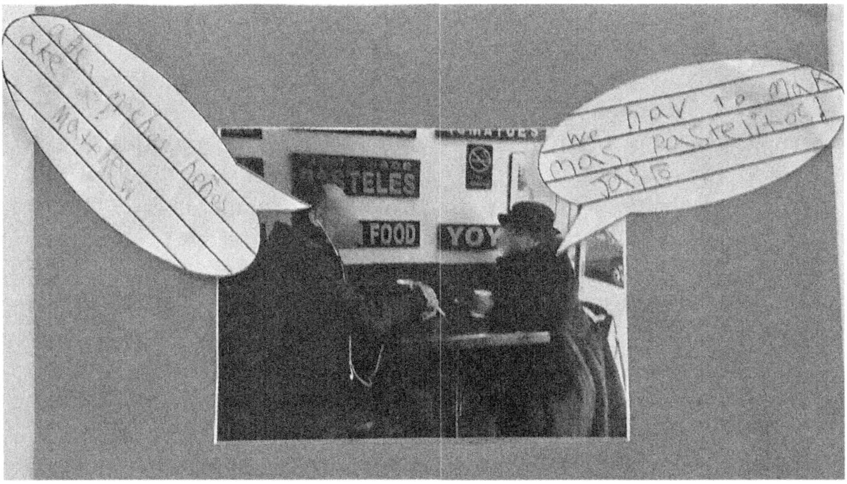

Figure 9.3 Students' recreation of a dialogue using an image from the community walk.

Figure 9.4 Students' recreation of a dialogue during the Family Friday.

in Spanish, "Yo ablo español y entiendo Mixteco" (sic) [I speak Spanish and understand Mixteco]. In recreating this scene using images and dialogues, the children share their understanding that speakers choose features of their linguistic repertoires to address different audiences at different times. The mom in the picture is deconstructing her language practices—including Spanish, English and Mixteco—to explain them to the speakers, but she is also translanguaging as she makes choices based on her audience. The children purposely chose to use both Spanish and English in their dialogue to stress the fluid language practices that the mom in the image used during her classroom visit.

The children performed a very sophisticated metalinguistic analysis—that is they were able to think and talk about languages and how they are leveraged to express meaning to different audiences—by using the images to recreate dialogues. Positioning the students as bilingual/multilingual ethnographers meant that their analysis was in constant motion, listening, observing, talking, reading, writing and making meaning, creating new knowledge that they shared with their peers and families.

At the end of the activity in which the students recreated dialogues, one of the teachers reflected on the process and her own preconceptions of how the children might use the images and dialogues. She thought that the children might choose, for example, to portray speakers based on race and to therefore reproduce stereotypes. However, she found that was not the case in the children's work. She realized that instead, the children based their dialogues on their observations and the conversations that they had in the classroom throughout the unit.

In designing a platform for the process of analysis in which children used multiple modalities to make sense of their observations, the teachers created a space to also draw out the affordances of each medium. Images have multiple layers of meaning; there is no single correct reading of an image. Instead, there are multiple interpretations (Rose, 2007). While the children did not create the images, in this activity, they chose them and added dialogue to represent themselves and others, using their work to speak back to dominant notions of language use.

In the context of the multilingual SSA settings, an activity like this one can prompt students to observe their community, using photographs (as it was done in this case) or drawings (as an adaptation) and recreate the dialogues and non-linguistic forms of communication. Creating this work and sharing with their peers could open up critical discussions about the value of translanguaging and the richness of communicative resources that are available to them in their communities outside of school.

Conclusion and implications for educators

In this chapter, we described the process of designing activities that engaged students in exploring the question: How do community members use language? We focused on three activities during the inquiry that the Grade 1 teachers designed for students to engage multimodally in studying the language practices of their community. The children analyzed and made sense of their findings through play-based learning and by recreating their observations with images and dialogues. These activities, in which the children were able to explore the ways in which people in a multilingual community use language, fostered students' awareness and criticality of language itself. While the context for this work was NYC, we believe that many of these activities can inspire educators working in multilingual settings in SSA to adapt them to their contexts in order to create spaces in which children critically focus on how their community members use language. The planning methodology that we shared can serve as a blueprint for how educators can plan an inquiry project that focuses on dynamic language use in school settings.

In order for educators to adapt this work to the context of SSA, it is essential to start by setting up school structures that provide space for purposeful planning and reflection, including time and space to collaborate with each other. However, individual teachers may also do this work in their own classroom, even if the larger school structures do not encourage this work. In order for educators to plan and implement such inquiry project, they need to:

- begin the process by examining what they know about students' home and community language practices and what they need to learn
- canvas the resources that students or their families have that can contribute to the inquiry
- brainstorm what are multimodal ways of inquiry that they imagine their students doing.

In providing an account of the activities that the Grade 1 children did during the inquiry, we found that as these children observed authentic and fluid language use in their neighborhood walk and reflected on their families' translanguaging practices and their own, they opened up opportunities for classroom discussions that brought to the forefront their families' and communities' sources of knowledge and highlighted the value of linguistic practices that might previously have been rendered invisible. In designing classroom activities from a translanguaging stance, the teachers privileged the multimodal ways of knowing that students brought to the classroom. This opened up a space for teachers to imagine their students' learning experiences as driven by the affordances of the complex semiotic resources that are available to them and their communities. In their design, the teachers created a space in which the children could question and investigate.

In this chapter, we also shared the teachers' own reflections as they observed their first graders working as language ethnographers and making sense of their learning. From their point of view, these activities provided a platform to make connections between the community and the school and to create awareness of the wealth of resources that the neighborhood and families had to offer. While Washington Heights has often been perceived as having low resources and Latinx families in particular have been stigmatized by their language use, focusing the inquiry on how community members used language and using translanguaging throughout the process provided a platform for children and teachers, as collaborators, to examine language practices and to view their community as a rich resource for learning.

We believe that educators in multilingual settings could use this model as a platform to foster students' linguistic awareness and pride. When we came back to the school the following school year, the teachers in the school continued to implement the inquiry projects. They reflected that the second time they implemented the inquiry unit, they started with more knowledge about the language practices of the students in the school and they were better prepared to foster discussions with the children. In implementing these kinds of projects in SSA context, while individual teachers may do these types of inquiry project by themselves, it will have a larger impact if administrators make sure that there is time allocated for teachers to reflect and share what they have learned in their individual classrooms with each other and to think critically about languaging in their communities. The teachers in Hudson Elementary School were able to grow their practices as they continued to guide the students in inquiry projects because they had had a chance to reflect and share with each other. This is an essential component that is the core of the work that we have shared in this chapter.

Notes

1 We use the gender-neutral alternative to Latino/a. Traditionally, Spanish grammar has a gender binary (masculine or feminine) and uses the masculinized version of words as universal. This tradition tends to make women invisible as well as people with non-conforming or fluid gender identities. By using an inclusive language, we join the cause that tries to combat discrimination and invisibility through language use.
2 Gentrification is a process of neighborhood change through the influx of more affluent residents. While gentrification often increases the economic value of a neighborhood, it can also force out low-income residents due to the increased cost of rent and goods.
3 We use the term immigrants to refer to people who were born outside of the United States.
4 The name of the school has been modified to maintain confidentiality.
5 According to New York State Department of Education "economically disadvantaged" students are those who participate in, or whose family participates in, economic assistance programs, such as the free or reduced-price lunch programs.
6 This is the official designation that the New York State Department of Education adopted in 2014 for students who are not proficient in English, according to New York State's standardized assessment. The NYC Department of Education began to use the term "Multilingual Learners" in 2017; previously, they had used the term "English Language Learners."

References

Bezemer, J & Kress, G 2008, 'Writing in multimodal texts: A social semiotic account of designs for learning', *Written Communication*, vol. 25(2), pp.166–195. https://doi.org/10.1177/0741088307313177

Bunyi, G & Schroeder, L 2016, 'Bilingual education in Sub-Saharan Africa: Policies and practice', in O Garcia, A Lin & S May (eds), *Bilingual and multilingual education*, Springer, Cham, pp. 1–18.

Cohen, DH, Stern, V & Balaban, N 1997, *Observing and recording the behavior of young children*, (5th ed), Teachers College Press, New York.

Edwards, S, Cutter-Mackenzie, A, Moore, D & Boyd, W 2017, 'Finding the balance: A play framework for play-based learning and intentional teaching in early childhood education', *Every Child*, vol. 23, pp. 14–15.

Flores, N & Rosa, J 2015, 'Undoing appropriateness: Raciolinguistic ideologies and language diversity in education', *Harvard Educational Review*, vol. 85(2) pp. 149–171.

García, O, Johnson, SI and Seltzer, K 2017, *The translanguaging classroom: Leveraging student bilingualism for learning*, Caslon, Philadelphia.

García, O, & Kleifgen, JA 2018, *Educating emergent bilinguals: Policies, programs, and practices for English learners*, Teachers College Press, New York.

García, O, & Wei, L 2014, *Translanguaging: Language, bilingualism and education*, Palgrave Macmillan, London.

Grosjean, F 1982, *Life with two languages: An introduction to bilingualism*, Harvard University Press, Boston.

Guzula, X, McKinney, C & Tyler, R 2016, 'Languaging-for-learning: Legitimising translanguaging and enabling multimodal practices in third spaces', *Southern African Linguistics and Applied Language Studies*, vol. 34, pp. 211–226.

Henriksen, S 2014, 'Identity and Pluralism in Africa: The Case of Mozambique', *Acta Semiótica e Lingvistica*, vol. 19(2), ISSN 0102-4264

Heugh, K 2015, 'Theory and practice-language education models in Africa: Research, design, decision-making and outcomes', in A Ouane & C Glanz (eds), *Optimising learning, education and publishing in Africa: The language factor: a review and analysis of theory and practice in mother-tongue and bilingual education in sub-Saharan Africa*, UNESCO, Hamburg, pp. 105–156.

Hibbert, L 2016, *The linguistic landscape of post-apartheid South Africa: Politics and discourse*. Multilingual Matters, Bristol.

Lotherington, H, & Jenson, J 2011, 'Teaching multimodal and digital literacy in L2 settings: New literacies, new basics, new pedagogies', *Annual review of applied linguistics*, vol. 31, pp. 226–246.

Makalela, L 2015, Moving out of linguistic boxes: the effects of translanguaging strategies for multilingual classrooms, *Language and Education*, vol. 29(3), pp. 200–217. https://doi.org/10.1080/09500782.2014.994524

New York City Department of Education 2019a, *School Register*. viewed 16 July 2019, <www.nycenet.edu/PublicApps/register.aspx?s=M103>.

New York City Department of Education 2019b, *Comprehensive Educational Plan 2018-19*, viewed 9 April 2019, < www.nycenet.edu/Documents/oaosi/cep/2018-19/CEP_M103.pdf>.

New York State Office of the State Comptroller & DiNapoli, TP 2015, *An economic snapshot of Washington Heights and Inwood*. Office of the State Comptroller, New York City Public Information Office.

Nyati-Ramahobo, L 2006, Language policy, cultural rights and the law in Botswana, in M Putz, J Fishman & J Neff-van Aertselaer (eds), *Along the Routes of Power: Explorations of Empowerment through Language*, De Gruyter, Berlin, pp. 285–303.

Paris, D & Alim, S (eds.) 2017, *Culturally sustaining pedagogies: Teaching and learning for justice in a changing world*, Teachers College Press, New York.

Perez, W, Vasquez, R, & Buriel, R 2016, 'Zapotec, mixtec, and purepecha youth: Multilingualism and the marginalization of indigenous immigrants in the United States' in S Alim, J Rickford & A Ball (eds) *Raciolinguistics: How language shapes our ideas about race*. Oxford University Press, New York, pp. 255–272.

Probyn, M 2015, Pedagogical translanguaging: Bridging discourses in South African science classrooms, *Language and Education*, vol. 29(3), pp. 218–234.

Rosa, J, & Flores, N 2017, 'Do you hear what I hear? Raciolinguistic ideologies and culturally sustaining pedagogies', in D Paris & S Alim (eds), *Culturally sustaining pedagogies: Teaching and learning for justice in a changing world*, Teachers College Press, New York, pp. 175–190.

Rose, G 2007, *Visual methodologies: An introduction to the interpretation of visual materials*, Sage, London.

Sánchez, MT, García, O & Solorza, C 2018, 'Reframing language allocation policy in dual language bilingual education', *Bilingual Research Journal*, vol. 41(1), pp. 1–15.

Souto-Manning, M 2017, 'Is play a privilege or a right? And what's our responsibility? On the role of play for equity in early childhood education', *Early Child Development and Care*, vol. 187(5–6), pp.785–787. DOI: 10.1080/03004430.2016.1266588.

Suárez-Orozco, C, Suárez-Orozco, M & Todorova, I 2008, *Learning a new land: Immigrant students in American society*, The Belknap Press of Harvard University, Cambridge.

Valenzuela, A 1999, '*Subtractive schooling: U.S.-Mexican youth and the politics of caring*, State University of New York Press, Albany.

Velasco, P 2014, 'The Language and Educational Ideologies of Mixteco-Mexican Mothers', *Journal of Latinos and Education*, vol. 13(2), pp. 85–106.

Walqui, A 2006, 'Scaffolding instruction for English language learners: A conceptual framework', *International Journal of Bilingual Education and Bilingualism*, vol. 9(2), pp. 159–180.

10 Vignette

Using the community to foster English–Kiswahili bilingualism in Kenya

Kepha Obiri and Alexandra Holland

Introduction

The Aga Khan Academy Mombasa is an International Baccalaureate (IB) continuum school situated in Mombasa, Kenya. The school has a predominantly Kenyan student body and aims to develop young people as ethical and pluralistic leaders who can use their learning to make positive change in their communities. While the school is private and sits outside the national education system, it does not cater to the elite: Entrance is based on merit and financial aid is available for students, to ensure access regardless of their financial circumstances. In educating students to take on leadership roles in their local context, it is essential that students have an excellent mastery of local languages. Although most students in the Junior School are from the local Mombasa community, many arrive with English as their dominant language, showing an imbalance in their exposure to local and international languages, even by the age of six. Students are able to access the curriculum in English, but need continuing exposure to academic Kiswahili. The Academy has implemented a bilingual IB Primary Years Programme (PYP) in Kiswahili and English to address this imbalance, developing both languages in parallel with one another.[1] Drawing on the work developed at CUNY-NYSIEB (e.g., García & Kleifgen, 2018), the Academy has developed a programme which allows students to access the curriculum through English and Kiswahili and a translanguaging approach is used to build cognitive academic language ability (CALP) in both languages. In this vignette we describe the development of a unit focusing on local history, and how, in addition to planning for multilingualism in the curriculum, the engagement of the local community through field trips and guest speakers has allowed us to develop students' understandings and skills through both languages.

Planning for language outcomes in the curriculum

The Academy delivers the curriculum through English and Kiswahili, using a Content and Language Integrated Learning (CLIL) approach that intends to highlight students' focus on the functions of language (cf. Ball, Kelly, & Clegg,

DOI: 10.4324/9781003028383-12

2015). In planning our materials, we always keep in mind the question "What do we want students to be able to *do*?" In every unit, students focus on particular language functions, and relevant vocabulary and grammatical structures to perform these functions are also explicitly taught. In the unit on *Local History*, for example, the language functions are *explanation* and *description*. In the unit, students learn about the city of Mombasa in the past and in the present, describing how Mombasa would have looked then and how it looks now. A key focus is the development of the Old Town around Fort Jesus, a fort built by the Portuguese in the 1590s to protect the Old Port. Students' explanations of why Mombasa changed are done mainly in the past tense, as this is a history unit, and so the development of students' ability to use the past tense confidently and accurately is a key language focus. Another language focus of the unit is learning vocabulary related to the unit's subject-specific content, using key terminology from geography and history in both languages. Finally, questioning is an essential skill as the students use people in the community to help them learn more about Mombasa's history. We prepare students to inquire into the history of the city through lessons on how to form questions, which cover both the Kiswahili and English language needed, and better questioning techniques.

Inviting guest speakers

Field trips have proved to be a useful way of providing input in Kiswahili, but they do not always provide a conducive environment for introducing students to new vocabulary. Experience has taught us that the excitement stemming from being out of the classroom and speaking with someone new can mean that students can find it difficult to try out new words and phrases. For this reason, we have sometimes invited a guest speaker to class a few days before a trip in order to introduce some of the anticipated language. For the unit on history, for example, we invite the school bus driver, a longstanding member of the local Swahili community with a wealth of knowledge about how the historic centre of Mombasa, that contains Fort Jesus, changed over time. This provides valuable support to teachers who are not originally from Mombasa and may not have the same depth of knowledge of the city's history and culture, and also gives students a role model from the local community who values Kiswahili and uses the language at a high level.

Through his talk, and the questions that follow, students are introduced to new knowledge and new language and are able to practice asking powerful questions. When inviting guest speakers, we brief them in advance about the language goals for the session, so that we can be sure that the important words and constructions are used during the talk, e.g. the use of the past tense, subject specific terminology and a range of descriptive adjectives. During the talk, students are able to practice asking questions about the topic and see the use of descriptive and explanatory language modelled by an expert speaker of Kiswahili. This proves to be a very effective means of pre-learning the relevant language before field trips, and helps to consolidate the bringing together of the language and content.

After this session, the students work in groups to design the questions for the guides they will meet on their field trip to Fort Jesus. They can use any language to discuss their ideas but have to prepare their questions for the field trip in Kiswahili. This processing phase allows students to consolidate the new knowledge and language that they have learned and to think about the next steps for their investigation, fostering their curiosity and ability to inquire.

Using the local environment as a means of input

One of the greatest challenges in the development of the bilingual programme at the Academy has been the lack of suitable curriculum resources in Kiswahili, as the national curriculum for this age group is taught in English. This can make it challenging to balance the language of input in a unit of inquiry. To address this, in many units we look to the local community to become a resource for students' learning. In the unit on history, students went on a field trip to Fort Jesus, a fort constructed by the Portuguese in the 1590s to guard the Old Port in Mombasa. Fort Jesus provided opportunities for students to use descriptive language to think about what the fort looks like now, and how it might have looked in the past. In thinking about the changes of ownership – from the Portuguese, to the Omani Arabs, to the British – students are able to use the language of explanation to show why each group wanted to rule Mombasa. Students have also used the local community and environment to connect to Kiswahili in other units. In a unit about *Ecosystems*, for example, students visited a local National Reserve to investigate the interconnectedness of the animals living there and in an *Expression* unit, students connected with traditional dance groups in the local community to find out more about how their dances reflected their cultures.

While community input for Kiswahili is necessary for authentic language learning, it is not always straightforward. Whilst local guides can provide extensive input in terms of knowledge, understanding and skills, it can be a challenge to prepare them for communicating this input to students. Often the guides are expert Kiswahili speakers but they are more accustomed to presenting their tours in English. They can sometimes find it difficult to talk about the topic in Kiswahili, and may need time to think about ways to describe the relevant concepts or events in precise, accessible Kiswahili, suitable for primary school children. We have therefore learned to carefully brief the guides about their use of language during tours so that they are clear about the content and language goals for the trip and conscious of their role in providing input for students in Kiswahili. We have also learned that the interactions between students and local guides are improved if students prepare their questions in advance so that we can share these with the guides beforehand. The guides then have time to plan their responses and think through how to present them in Kiswahili that is accessible for students of this age group.

Assessment

Assessment in each of the units is carefully designed to ensure that the students use the language skills they have developed throughout the unit of inquiry in authentic ways. The assessment in this unit is prepared at the unit planning stage and focuses on descriptive and explanatory language structures, the use of the past tense, and the use of key terminology, all in Kiswahili and English.

With regard to the unit on *Local History*, students work in groups to recap what they have learned during the tour of Fort Jesus and decide whether their questions about the fort have been answered. They can choose to discuss their learning in English or Kiswahili, with most groups opting for English. The process of taking the information they have learned from the guide in Kiswahili and discussing it in English helps to further embed the knowledge and understandings and prepares the students to show their learning in both languages.

One means of assessment is the production of bilingual brochures, designed to allow the students to transfer information between languages in different ways. When introducing Mombasa in Kiswahili, the students use their knowledge of descriptive writing to create an evocative picture of their home town. In demonstrating their understanding of Mombasa's history and describing the changes that have taken place, students show their ability to use the present and past tense accurately in both English and Kiswahili. When explaining Mombasa's repeated invasions and occupations in the past, students use a range of subject-specific terminology including the names of countries and nationalities. This is also the case when they are describing and explaining the changes witnessed in Mombasa over time.

When setting assessment tasks, students' relative strength in both languages have to be considered. We have found it important to balance choice and prescription. If we allow students completely free choice, many will use their weaker language for only the simpler parts of the assignment. We therefore specify the language to be used for at least some of the assessment. These tasks encourage students to make connections between the content they have learned and the language that has been developed in context.

Conclusion

The model of bilingual pedagogy developed in this school can support the development of the national language in tandem with English, ensuring that students maintain contact with their local context and culture. We believe that the model of having students learn from their local community could also be a powerful addition to the national curriculum, as students can then better relate their learning to the world around them. These techniques would work in any educational context, for any age group, and can be linked to any area of the curriculum. Even in low resource contexts, students can visit sites within walking distance of their school, perhaps local businesses or public facilities that have real-life links to their curriculum. Moreover, if getting out of school is a challenge, it is possible to bring in a wide range of guest speakers. Members of staff at the school can be drawn on for their expertise – in our context, students came to see their bus driver in a different capacity, as an "expert" in the history of the local community. Parents, community members and alumni can all be called upon to share their knowledge with students, and to be models of the language being learned for authentic purposes. While supporting the development of English and Kiswahili requires creative planning, the rewards for students are great. Students develop expertise in both languages and a profound understanding and respect for their local community, culture, and history. These are essential elements in developing students who will be the future leaders of their communities.

Note

1 This is a bilingual programme in the two national languages of Kenya, Kiswahili and English. Students speak may speak other languages as well - there are 40 indigenous languages in Kenya, as well as migration languages such as Gujarati or Kutchi. It offers sessions with parents about the importance of home languages, and gives ideas about how these can be supported. It also has a small collection of books in other languages in the library, as well as wordless picture books that parents can use with younger students in any language. In practice, however, these languages are maintained for social, rather than academic functions.

References

Ball, P, Kelly, K & Clegg, J 2015, *Putting CLIL into Practice*, Oxford University Press, Oxford.

García, O & Kleifgen, JA 2018, *Educating Emergent Bilinguals: Policies, Programs, and Practices for English Learners*, Teachers College Press, New York.

Part 3

Multilingual resource development and teacher education

11 Multilingual learning and language-supportive teaching in Rwandan learning materials

John Clegg and Lizzi O. Milligan

Introduction

This chapter concerns learning materials which are appropriate for learners in multilingual schools in Sub-Saharan Africa (SSA). These learners often possess language abilities in their first and community languages (L1) which would allow them to learn effectively in school, but are required by the education system to abandon those languages at an early stage (often Grade 4) and learn through an additional language (L2)[1] in which they are not proficient (e.g. Macdonald, 1990; Uwezo, 2017; Probyn, 2005; Hollmarsdottir, 2005; Ouane & Glanz, 2011; Heugh et al., 2007; Prinsloo & Heugh, 2013; Brock-Utne, 2013). At this point – and often for several years thereafter – many do not possess the level of language ability which would allow them to use the L2 effectively as a language of instruction (LoI) for learning subjects. Lack of ability in the LoI restricts many learners, in SSA and elsewhere, to a level of school achievement which is much lower than they are capable of (UNESCO, 2016b; Clegg & Simpson, 2016).

The chapter argues for an approach to pedagogy in schools in SSA which meets these learners' needs, in that it is (a) multilingual and (b) 'language supportive'. Both these terms describe distinct and non-conventional approaches to teaching and learning and are explained in more detail below. Suffice it to say here that a multilingual pedagogy encourages the use of all a learner's linguistic resources – whether L1s or L2s – in the classroom; and a language supportive pedagogy (LSP) compensates for learners' low and emergent L2 skills and amplifies their cognitive ability.

Textbooks are not widely available in schools across SSA (Read, 2015); UNESCO calls this lack of availability a key impediment to improving teaching and learning in these contexts (UNESCO, 2016a). Of the English-medium textbooks in current use, many are difficult – if not impossible – for learners to read: the chapter provides evidence of this. They are normally written in English only and make no reference to multilingual learning; many also do not provide the requisite language support which emergent L2 learners need. For this and other reasons, it is likely that many English-medium textbooks in current circulation are not put to good use – in many cases not used at all – in classrooms.

DOI: 10.4324/9781003028383-14

Multilingual and language supportive textbooks can provide readable materials for L2-medium learners. The chapter exemplifies these pedagogical features by reference to materials produced for Grade 4 science in Rwanda by the LaST (Improving Learning Outcomes through Language Supportive Textbooks and Pedagogy) project, which was run by Bristol University and the British Council and funded by the UK Department for International Development, and which is outlined below. We argue that unless these features are designed into learning materials in SSA, many learners will continue to be unable to use them.

The case for multilingual learning in SSA

Multilingual education is variously defined. A simple definition is that it refers to education which uses two or more languages as LoI.

For some, multilingual education can refer to using more than one LoI, but in separate lessons. Bilingual education, for example, often separates LoIs in the school timetable. Similarly, the terms bi- and multilingual education are sometimes used to describe the serial use of LoIs (Weber, 2014): children start learning in one language and add another LoI later. In some school systems, in what is sometimes described as 'transitional' or 'subtractive' multilingual education, the early LoI is discarded. This LoI is often the strongest language the child has – the language of home or community; the later LoI may be one which the child speaks much less well. This is normally the case in SSA where – at least according to policy – learners begin their school careers using the L1 as LoI and then change (often at Grade 4) to use another (usually a post-colonial language), leaving the L1 behind. Educational data from Tanzania, for example, shows the English L2[2] ability level which can result from this policy: whereas nearly 9 out of 10 (89%) of Standard 7 students were able to read a story at Standard 2 level in Kiswahili, fewer than half (48%) could do so in English (the L2) (Uwezo, 2017). Since English-medium schooling in Tanzania starts in Grade 8, this level of English ability radically reduces learners' chances of reading subject textbooks. There are cases in SSA where learners start learning with extremely low or zero ability in the L2 LoI. In Cameroon, for example, children learn in English or French from the first day of primary schooling (Kuchah et al., 2020).

It is stretching a point to refer to these systems in SSA as multilingual education. Indeed, much education of this kind divorces languages within school and operates monolingually. After the onset of education in the L2, many ministries, schools and teachers officially forbid the use of the L1 in the classroom (see below). The effect of this on learners is to block their ability to use for learning the languages in which they are most fluent, not to mention negative effects on confidence and cultural identity which are associated with the suppression of the L1 (García & Wei, 2014) .

For these reasons 'early-exit' education through the L1, as the above form of schooling is called, is not seen as a 'strong form' of multilingual education. Strong forms do not discard languages of instruction but develop them all with a view to achieving good levels of multiliteracy and multilingualism (Baker &

Wright, 2017). Strong forms also prioritise the L1 and develop it throughout schooling along with other LoIs (Heugh & Skuttnab-Kangas, 2012). Such models are sometimes referred to as mother-tongue-based multilingual education (Weber, 2014).

Other reasons are adduced in language in education debate in SSA (Clegg, this volume) to show that three years of L1-medium education is not sufficient. Firstly, three years at roughly three lessons per week are not long enough for a learner to learn the L2 well enough to use it as the LoI. Secondly, L2 teachers in SSA in Grades 1–3 may be unconfident in their own L2 ability and their ability to support learners in learning subjects in the L2 as LoI (Read, 2015; British Council, 2015). Thirdly, English syllabuses in Grades 1–3 in SSA are in most cases orientated to social uses of English and are unlikely to contain much of what is known as cognitive academic language proficiency (CALP) which learners need in order to learn curricular contents after Grade 3. Fourthly, it is argued that learners who develop CALP in their L1 can then transfer parts of those academic language skills to L2 (Cummins, 2000); but developing L1 CALP to the extent which allows this transfer to take place takes much longer than three years. Finally, the 'language gap' (Clegg, this volume) between what a learner can do with English at the end of Grade 3 and the language demands which the curriculum makes starting from Grade 4 is very large. A longer period of L1-medium learning and L2 language (and especially CALP) development could reduce it.

An effective education in SSA would provide at least six years of L1-medium education; Heugh (2006) properly suggests eight years in a poorly-resourced context. Learners could then transition to L2-medium schooling, bilingual education or formal multilingual education. Multilingual learning could thus have a role in the transition from L1- to L2-medium or to bilingual schooling or as a pedagogy in its own right for subject teaching after extended L1-medium primary education (e.g. Campaign for Education, 2013; Heugh & Skuttnab-Kangas, 2012; Ouane & Glanz, 2011). It could also have a role as an interim pedagogy within early-exit programmes from Grade 4 onwards, as a way of increasing achievement in the face of the struggle to learn subjects with inadequate L2 skills. This is the function of the multilingual materials presented in this chapter.

Views of multilingual education which differ from the serial early-exit form described above refer to the use of two or more languages in the same classroom and see mixing of languages in the act of learning as the essence of the practice (García et al., 2017). The concept of 'translanguaging' is often linked with this view of multilingual education. Translanguaging in school refers to the use of all a learner's language and cultural resources for educational meaning-making in the lesson. Whereas curricula conventionally separate language abilities according to individual language codes, translanguaging pedagogy combines language abilities together into an overarching language meta-ability expressible in different languages, modes, varieties and levels of fluency (Clegg, this volume; Espinet et al., this volume).

It is useful to distinguish between formal and informal translanguaging. In informal translanguaging, the restriction of understanding arising when most in the classroom do not speak the LoI well enough influences both learners and teachers to use all the languages of the classroom in a spontaneous attempt to increase comprehension and expression. In the form of code-switching, learners and teachers working in the L2 – in SSA and elsewhere – often mix languages in this way to overcome linguistic barriers to learning (Heugh, 2009; Clegg & Afitska, 2011; Probyn, 2015). Translanguaging is also, however, a formal, planned pedagogy with a specific socio-educational philosophy (Espinet et al., this volume; Shank Lauwo, this volume; García et al., 2017), albeit still not widespread, and involving specified teacher and learner roles.

In the wider world, bi- and multilingual education for L2-medium learners achieves good results in terms both of subject knowledge and ability in the dominant LoI. In the education of language minorities in the USA some schools offer bilingual education for minority learners because solid research (Thomas & Collier, 2002; Baker & Wright, 2017) shows that it pays off in terms of subject achievement and English language ability. This is in contrast to unsupported immersion in the LoI – the system common in SSA – which the same research shows to be the least effective policy. Similarly, translanguaging claims to offer benefits in terms both of learning subjects and of developing ability in the L2 LoI (August & Shanahan, 2006) and is currently a concept at the cutting edge of multilingual education, especially in language minority education in the USA (Espinet et al., this volume; García et al., 2017). Much academic opinion in SSA agrees that using L1 benefits learners cognitively, academically, socially and culturally (e.g. Trudell, 2016). A change of language policy in the direction of multilingual education in SSA is thus one major lever which ministries have, to mitigate the damage to educational standards which low learner L2 ability inflicts.

There are successful initiatives and instructive debate in planned multilingual education and classroom translanguaging in SSA (e.g. Kerfoot & Simon-Vandenbergen, 2015; Makalela, 2015, Obiri & Holland, this volume). Multilingual education is notably practised through the work of PRAESA, University of Cape Town (Bloch & Mbolekwa, this volume). English/Afrikaans bilingual education has been familiar in South Africa (SA) for a long time (Heugh, 2009).

Multilingual education makes sense for learners in SSA. They are often skilled language users. By the time they reach Grade 4, they can be orally and socially fluent in two or three languages and have an initial degree of skill in the L2 LoI, having learned it for three years. They therefore speak more languages than majority (as distinct from minority) language learners in many high-income countries, who often have only one. However, whereas many of these latter learners can use their entire language resource for school learning, learners in SSA have to discard the majority of their language resource – their L1s – and use only that small portion of it in which they are least skilled – their L2 (Clegg, this volume). The effect of this, as outlined above, is to reduce school achievement. This is not a sustainable form of education. As is the case in any L2-medium learning context in which learners do not have the L2 language ability to learn subjects effectively, a formal multilingual pedagogy is needed.

The role of language supportive education in SSA

In addition to the multilingual classroom, a language supportive pedagogy is also appropriate in SSA. After an early-exit programme, but even after an extended L1-medium programme, the level of L2 ability of most learners in SSA not likely to be wholly adequate for L2-medium learning. Reading subject textbooks and speaking and writing about subjects in L2 would still be difficult. Language supportive education is a form of learning adapted for education in a developing L2. What follows is an outline of its features.

Learning in any language requires the learner to use the language variety specific to education, referred to above as cognitive academic language proficiency or CALP. CALP skills are cognitively and linguistically demanding. They include, for example, understanding a teacher talking about concepts, reading about them in a textbook, talking about them with a teacher or with peers, writing about them, taking notes, making oral presentations, using complex visuals (diagrams, charts, graphs, etc.), doing internet searches, etc. These academic language uses are different from the social language we use in our daily lives. Academic language requires low-frequency, high-specificity vocabulary. It displays long, fairly complex sentence structure with complex discourse patterns. Learners do not normally simply pick it up; they have to learn it explicitly (Cummins, 2000).

Learners also need to use informal language – or what Cummins (1984) called Basic Interpersonal Communications Skills (BICS) – in the classroom, mainly in talk and listening. In L1-medium learning, informal talk is interwoven with formal talk in classroom discourse; it is often used in early concept development and in any given lesson gives way gradually to more formal talk and finally to formal writing as a concept takes on sharper definition in the mind of the learner (Gibbons, 2015).

Many learners in SSA, especially at Grade 4, have only the very beginnings of L2 ability: they have neither BICS nor CALP in the LoI. They are thus different from learners working in a fluent L1. The latter can engage in BICS talk, which can then lead to CALP in talk, writing and reading. Learners with only initial L2 skills, however, may not speak the L2 fluently enough to use it for informal talk, let alone talk about complex subjects. That can reduce their classroom responses to the teacher to short and infrequent utterances (Erling et al., this volume; Hardman, 2008). It also makes it impossible to talk with peers about a concept with anything approaching the requisite detail, or the capacity to use even grammatically simple common thinking functions such as description (*It has slimy green skin*) or hypothesis (*Maybe it's a frog*).

The effect of this is manifold: learners may not be able to talk about new concepts effectively in L2 for several years after Grade 4. Indeed, observers of classrooms in SSA report lessons in which for this reason learner-talk hardly features (Arthur, 1994; Erling et al., this volume). They will acquire formal reading slowly. In addition to the inbuilt inaccessibility of textbooks (see below), this will considerably constrain their ability to read about subjects. Learner writing will also be highly limited for several years, making it very hard to write about content with the degree of fluency and detail which content learning requires. Many will encounter the difficulty which is common to contexts in which learners learn new concepts in a poorly developed L2: the cognitive burden of learning both new concepts and new language is too high and makes learning slow and ineffective. Achievement within the subject is severely reduced.

LSP is a distinct pedagogy designed to help learners learn content when their command of the LoI, both social and academic, is in its earlier stages. It offers learners strong linguistic scaffolding, which reduces the language demands made on them by a high density of new language forms, thus enabling them to focus away from new language and deploy attention to new conceptual contents. The pedagogy thus has a compensatory effect: it compensates for high L2 demands and thus increases the ability to deal with high cognitive demands. It is a non-conventional pedagogy, used in minority education in, for example, North America, Europe and Australasia (Cloud et al., 2009; Gibbons, 2015), as well as in Content and Language Integrated Learning (CLIL) in Europe (Ball et al., 2015). It is normally taught to trainees in in-service teacher education (INSET) rather than in Initial Teacher Education (ITE). In SSA, it is rarely used in classrooms or taught in either INSET or ITE (Afitska et al., 2013; Alidou, 2009; Clegg, 2017; Probyn, 2006); however, Rubagumya et al. (this volume) and Barrett et al. (this volume) illustrate its use in Tanzania. This chapter illustrates its development for use in Rwandan classrooms.

Key features of LSP are summarised in Figure 11.1. They refer to the teaching of speaking, reading and writing within subjects (listening overlaps with reading), as well as the use of visuals and the learners' L1s. With regard to teacher-talk, for example, teachers may use a highly 'redundant' form of talk; i.e. they increase the amount of definition, exemplification, repetition and paraphrase which would

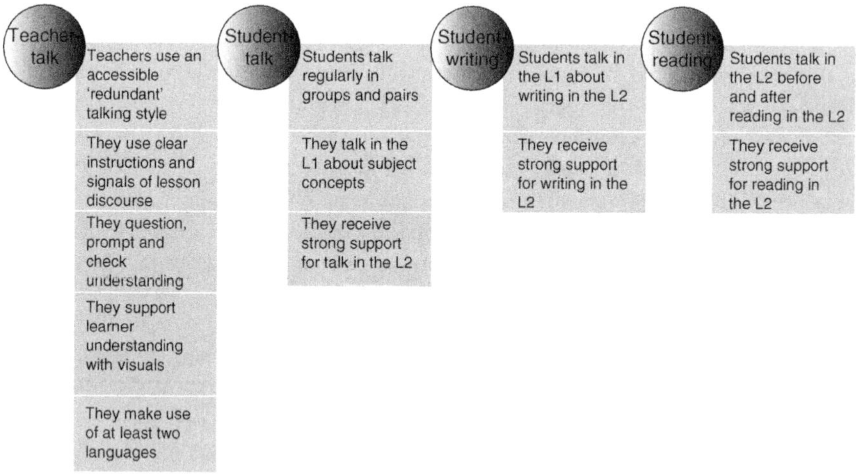

Figure 11.1 Features of language supportive pedagogy.

be the norm in conventional teacher-talk. They will also amplify meanings by using visuals. They will help learners to respond to teacher-questions by using short-answer questions and prompts, and will repeat, paraphrase and expand on responses. They will make exaggerated use of discourse structure in teacher-talk, by inserting explicit signals of organisation (*Let's start with*, *for example*, *another way of saying this is*, *let's sum up*, etc.). They will also, where appropriate, use the learners' L1s – if possible, within a formal version of translanguaging.

With regard to reading, textbooks specifically designed for these learners use a variety of ways of amplifying comprehension. Text length, average sentence length and the density of unfamiliar vocabulary are limited. The meanings of new terms are conveyed by textual context or, where appropriate, through visuals and bilingual glossaries. Learners are invited to use L1 to pre-discuss the potential contents of a text in L2 and to compare understandings in L1 after reading. Reading is also facilitated by a wide range of reading support tasks which are unfamiliar in conventional LoI-fluent reading pedagogy. These features are also illustrated in the materials examples below.

In the plenary classroom, learners are helped to talk in the L2 by teacher-support for learner responses as outlined above. When learners talk with peers, the L1 will often be for some years the only language in which they can talk about complex curricular topics. However, a range of tasks to support learners in their L1/2 talk in groups and pairs can also be used, which again are unfamiliar in conventional classrooms. L1 group talk can also help learners talk in the L2: for example, group talk in the L1 about a new concept makes it easier to report on it orally, however briefly, in the L2. This is an example of the so-called 'translanguaging advantage': learners working in more than one language find that this increases their fluency in the L2 (Clegg, this volume).

Language supportive teachers also use a range of support tasks for generating simple writing in the L2. In addition, L1 use will help L2 writing: again, the translanguaging advantage applies in that learners will find it often easier to discuss concepts first in the L1 and then write in the L2; and to talk collaboratively in the L1 about ongoing group writing in the L2. Examples of some of the practices outlined above, as they are reflected in the LaST project materials for Rwanda and in materials for Language Supportive Teaching and Textbooks (LSTT), a Tanzanian project (Rubagumya et al., this volume; Barrett et al., this volume), are presented below.

Multilingual and LSP in school publishing in SSA

Multilingual textbooks are rare in any context (Campaign for Education, 2013), though in SSA, some L1-medium subject textbooks exist (Mahalela-Thusi & Heugh, 2004). In many contexts, multilingual stories are fairly common (e.g. *Nal'ibali*, *African Storybook*, *Mantralingua*), but subject textbooks seldom give space to both the L1 and L2. This is the norm both in subject learning for L2 users of the LoI, such as in minority education or CLIL, and in materials for bi- and multilingual teaching of subjects. Although in both kinds of teaching the classroom may present a multilingual site, the textbook often gives primacy to the L2.

There are several reasons why materials privilege one language. Firstly, in L2-medium subject teaching the L1 is often seen as having secondary status. It is considered to be used in the service of L2 development and subject knowledge. Secondly, in SSA, attitudes to the status of L1 in education play a role. Ingrained attitudes in government and in the population in SSA still express the illusion that colonial languages such as English and French are proper carriers of knowledge, while African languages cannot serve this function (Djité, 2008). Irrational resistance in the educational establishment to the L1 in textbooks and multilingual teaching is strong (Djité, op. cit.; Mchombo, 2014; Kamwangamalu, 2016). Thus, many education authorities will not countenance the multilingual classroom (Bloch et al., 2010; Erling et al., 2016; McKinney, 2017; Probyn, 2015). By way of example, the English/Kinyarwanda bilingual materials reported on in this chapter met with scepticism from the Rwandan ministry at the time. By contrast, the Tanzanian materials (see below) received wider official support because Tanzania has formally welcomed Kiswahili as a permissible LoI in secondary schools.

Thirdly, the number of L1s represented in a multilingual classroom may militate against multilingual materials. Where learners in one classroom speak several L1s, there is, practically speaking, no space for all of them on the page. In addition, the textbook may need to be used by learners with different L1s in different parts of a region: including reading passages in one L1 may deter learners who use another. The market for multilingual subject textbooks also needs to be wide, commercially speaking, and open to users of different L1s (Weber, 2014). It is of course much easier to introduce L1s into the textbook in an education authority in which all or most learners speak one language, as is the case with Kinyarwanda speakers in Rwanda.

Fourthly, in SSA but also elsewhere, multilingual materials are scarce simply because multilingual education itself is only just establishing itself (Herzog-Punzenberger et al., 2017). This is partly because it is relatively new as an officially sanctioned school practice; and in SSA it is partly because of reluctance on the part of education authorities to recognise the multilingual classroom (Djité, 2008; Chimbutane, 2018).

It should, however, be noted that it is not difficult to overcome these publishing restrictions on the multilingual textbook if a narrower interpretation of the multilingual classroom is used (see also Trudell & Young, 2016). In balanced multilingual education, two or more languages should have equal status in oral and written forms. If, however, the use of L1s is mainly effected through talk, it does not take up much space on the page beyond an instruction to use L1s orally. This is exemplified in the LaST materials shown below. It does not amount to balanced multilingualism, but it does, at some cost to language equality, help to alleviate the problems of bi- and multilingual publishing discussed above.

Conventional subject textbooks in SSA

In addition to the problem of the absence of L1s, textbooks in SSA – as indeed elsewhere – rarely reflect LSP. Textbooks are often written as if they were designed for native speakers or L2-fluent users (Clegg, 2015). Passages in these textbooks for low-L2 ability learners in SSA are often harder to read than passages for native-speakers or English-fluent users in, for example, the UK (Clegg & Simpson, 2016). Many learners in SSA therefore do not have the L2 language ability to read them (Glewwe et al., 2009).

Let us look at a typical textbook from Rwanda. School language policy in Rwanda requires learners to learn in an African language until Grade 4, when they switch to using English as LoI. Figure 11.2 shows a reading passage from a recently used Rwandan science textbook (Serugo & Mpummude, 2010) published by Longhorn publishers for Grade 4 learners at the beginning of English-medium education, which is fairly typical in its design of textbooks in Rwanda and elsewhere in SSA. At Grade 4, Rwandan learners have very little English language ability. According to Williams (2011), in 2004 only 0.77% of Rwandan students in Primary Grade 6 could read adequately for the purposes of English-medium education; an Early Grade Reading Assessment (EGRA) study (2012) of Rwandan learners concluded that students' (Primary Grade 6) reading comprehension in English was 'extremely poor'. The passage demonstrates none of the features of LSP – of accessible texts or of reading support pedagogy, which would help those learners. It is not designed with L2-users in mind, but resembles a text written for English-fluent users. It is indeed no easier to read (see Table 11.1) than a text for English-fluent learners in the UK (see Appendix). All but a small minority of well-educated urban learners in Rwanda will fail to read it.

Table 11.1 uses manual and computer (using *Lextutor*)[3] analyses to give what is no more than an indication of differences between reading passages in very roughly comparable textbooks: the conventional text (published by Longhorn) for Rwandan Grade 4 learners in Figure 11.2, the Rwandan Grade 4 LaST materials discussed in this chapter and illustrated below (Figure 11.3) and the text (see Appendix) for UK primary learners (Johnson, 2007). The two Rwandan texts are comparable in that they are designed for the same age range in Rwanda; the UK text is taken at random from a UK science textbook for Primary Grades 4–6 and is thus only relatively comparable. In terms of grammatical complexity, the conventional Rwandan (Longhorn) text is the hardest to read, the LaST text the easiest. In vocabulary terms, the Rwandan (Longhorn) text contains the most subject-specific words, although the LaST text contains the most general academic words. In respect of sentence length, the Rwandan (Longhorn) and UK texts contain the longest sentences, the LaST text the shortest. Bearing in mind that the UK text is designed for English-fluent users and the other two for learners with minimal English in Grade 4 Rwanda, the readability data confirm what an unscientific glance will show: many Grade 4 learners with minimal English will find the Rwandan (Longhorn) text almost impossible to read.

The tongue

The tongue rolls food. It helps roll the chewed food into a round ball making it easy to swallow. The tongue pushes the ball of food down the oesophagus during swallowing.

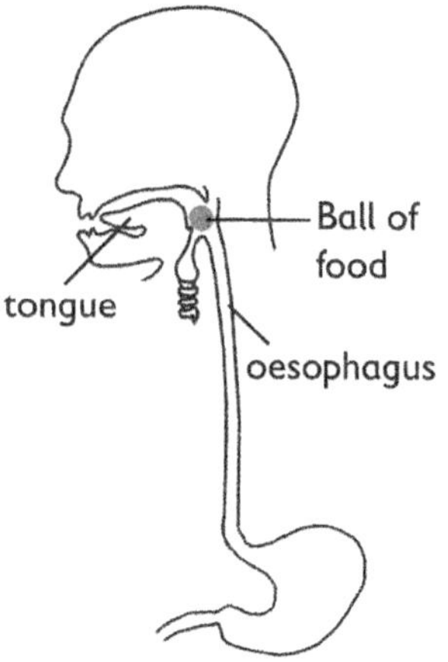

The salivary glands

The salivary glands produce saliva which makes the food soft. It also makes the mouth and gullet smooth so that food moves easily.
Saliva contains a substance which breaks down starch to make it simple for the body to take in and use.

The Pharynx

This is the soft area at the top of the throat where the passage to the nose and mouth connects with the throat. It has a soft piece of flesh called the epiglottis. The epiglottis closes the air passage to prevent food from going into the lungs.

The oesophagus

The esophagus is also called the **gullet.** This is a tube through which food from the mouth enters the stomach.

The stomach

The stomach is like a bag made of muscles. It stores the food we eat for about 3-4 hours. It produces a substance which digests proteins.

Figure 11.2 Extract from a science textbook for Grade 4 learners in Rwanda.

We have argued that conventional textbooks may be unreadable for many learners and that textbooks in SSA often fail to reflect either the multilingualism of learners or the language support which they need in order to learn subjects in L2. The next two sections present classroom materials which aim to show that both are essential to successful learning in schools in SSA and in particular to the design of textbooks which low-L2 ability learners can read.

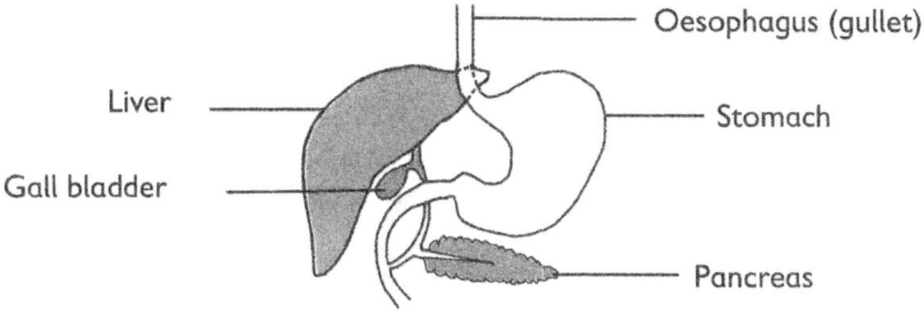

The small intestines

- This is a long coiled organ of the digestive system.
- It is where digestion of food ends.
- The digested food enters blood from the small intestines. This process is called absorption.
- Blood transports the digested food to all parts of the body.
- The small intestine is also called the ileum.

Large intestines

- Any food that is not absorbed or taken into the blood in the small intestines passes into the large intestines.
- Here water is absorbed from the undigested food back into the body. This leaves unwanted material called **faeces.**

Rectum

The faeces move from the large intestines to the rectum where they are stored for some time. When the person is ready to remove them they pass to the anus.

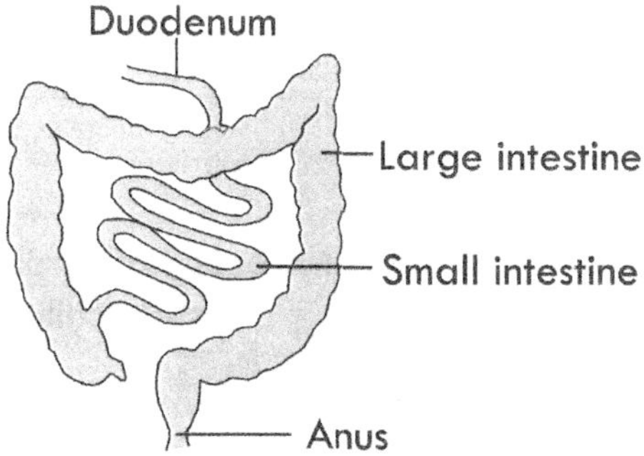

Figure 11.2 Cont.

Table 11.1 Comparing the readability of textbooks

Text	*Readership*	*Grammatical complexity*		*Words per sentence*	*Vocabulary*	
		Passives (% of text)	*Subordinate clauses (% of text)*		*General academic words*	*Subject-specific words*
Longhorn Rwanda text	Minimal English	4 1%	9 2.9%	12.8	1.32%	7.95%
LaST Rwanda text	Minimal English	0	1 0.25%	8.5	1.58%	1.84%
UK text	Fluent English	2 1.9%	1 1%	12.9	0.97%	5.8%

LaST project research methods and outcomes

The LaST project ran in Rwanda between 2014 and 2016 (Milligan et al., 2016). The project aimed to explore the effectiveness of language supportive textbooks and associated pedagogy training for Primary Grade 4 (P4) teachers. Rwandan and East African authors, illustrators and publishers were trained in language supportive techniques. They then designed textbooks that were given to 550 P4 learners in eight primary schools, purposively sampled across four regions of the country to include town, rural and remote schools. Thirty-three P4 maths, social science and science teachers were trained in LSP by project trainers. The training consisted of one full day of practical work with teachers in each school. Teachers studied the features of LSP and practised the activities which characterised the textbooks. The teachers then used the textbooks for a four-month period,[4] during which their teaching practice was observed three times by project team members who had led the LSP training and gave feedback following each observation.

The project utilised a mixed-methods quasi-experimental design to assess textbook use and language supportive pedagogic practice both quantitatively and qualitatively in the classroom and their impact on learner participation and outcomes. To assess the impact on learning outcomes, P4 learners at the eight project schools and eight comparator schools were given two different vocabulary and comprehension tests based on the science, maths and social science syllabi covered prior to the intervention and for the relevant four-month period. Independent t-tests were used to see if there was a statistically significant difference in scores between those who had been involved in the intervention and those who had not. To see whether the difference between test scores in the two groups could be explained by the project/comparator school grouping, the ANOVA test of variance was used. To analyse the effectiveness of LSP, 71 classroom observations were undertaken, combining quantitative measures (e.g. how many learners were present, number of questions asked by the teacher) and qualitative assessment by the researcher of how the lesson went. Classroom observation data were mainly analysed quantitatively for the three main measures of language supportiveness – more consistent use of textbooks as teaching and learning materials, more learner-talk and more learner-centred learning. Observation and test data were supplemented by eight learner focus groups and interviews with teachers and headteachers. This qualitative data was analysed thematically, both within and across the participant groups.

The headline finding from the research was that we witnessed an improvement in learning outcomes for those learners who participated in the intervention. In the pre-test, learner vocabulary and comprehension were low with a total percentage mean for all students of just 36.53% (N = 1075). The differences across the sixteen schools were small. By comparison, in the post-tests, across the three tests, the mean scores for learners at the project schools was 63.09% (N = 550) compared with 47.00% for those at the comparator schools (N = 525); a difference of 16.09%. While we have advised caution concerning the interpretation of these findings, given the intensive nature of the support to teachers and the short time period of the intervention, this does provide a clear evidence base for the potential for LSP and language supportive as well as multilingual materials to have an important impact on children's learning. It is also important to note that the improvements can be seen across the different school types and children of differing levels of achievement.

When analysing the classroom and interview data, it becomes clear that classroom use of Kinyarwanda is a key contributor in explaining the improved learning outcomes. Headteachers, teachers and learners reflected on how using Kinyarwanda impacted on their engagement and participation. For learners, this was the most commonly cited benefit of the using the materials in the classroom. Their responses focused, in particular, on the use of glossaries and spoken activities in L1 to support initial introduction to a new topic:

> In these books, activities are better because we are given opportunity to discuss in groups to explain to each other. But in the other books the teacher copies the exercises on the board and we start doing them. These books encourage discovery because of group discussion.
>
> (Learner, Nyagatare Rural)

This was also supported by headteachers and teachers who spoke about how it had impacted on learner engagement and participation:

> Learners also appreciated the textbooks saying that they have words that help them understand. They are really motivated to read these books. Sometimes I enter the classroom and find students reading on their own because they can get the meaning without the teacher's intervention. Since they easily

> interact with the books all the time they are free, the teachers get surprised to find that children have some knowledge on the new topics and this makes them active in the lesson.
>
> (HT, Nyagatare Rural)

> Where the teacher was using Language Supportive Pedagogy, learners were motivated and participating but where it was not being used the learners were passive.
>
> (HT, Kamonyi Town)

What is important to note here is that the use of Kinyarwanda did not limit learners' English use. In fact, classroom observations showed that a wider range of children were responding to teacher questions in English, often with longer than single word answers. The potential for speaking activities in the L1 to support access to the curriculum in the L2 is clearly demonstrated. This is particularly significant given that the commonly adduced reason for explicitly forbidding the use of L1 in LoI policies is that it is (inaccurately) assumed that it negatively impacts on the development of the L2.

Multilingual learning and LSP in the LaST project

In this section we exemplify uses of multilingual learning and LSP as evidenced in the Rwandan LaST materials and the Tanzanian LSTT materials. Because multilingual pedagogy is neither widely available in materials nor in academic debate, we look at it in considerable detail in this section.

Multilingual learning

In the LaST materials, both teachers and learners use L1 and L2. Teacher uses of L1 are normally only referred to in teachers' notes. They are expected to:

- switch into L1 to aid understanding, e.g. L1 definitions of new terms
- engage in L1-medium exchanges where these seem pedagogically necessary
- provide occasional L1 prompts where teacher questions in L2 are not understood
- facilitate occasional learner L1 responses where learners cannot express them in L2
- use occasional short pauses after L2 questions to enable brief L1-medium discussion by learners of L2-medium answers
- use L1 for occasional personal exchanges with learners.

Learner uses of L1 are often recognised on the textbook page. Learners are encouraged to:

- use L1 orally with peers to discuss a curricular topic
- use L1 orally with peers to prepare for reporting to the whole class in L2
- use L1 orally with peers to discuss the topic of an L2-medium reading/listening passage before reading or listening to it
- use L1 orally with peers to compare understandings of an L2-medium reading/listening passage after reading or listening to it
- refer to a bilingual glossary before, while and after reading
- use L1 orally with peers to discuss the ongoing composition of an L2-medium writing passage.

Other uses of teacher and learner L1 in multilingual classrooms can be seen in the literature on multilingual learning, e.g. Celic and Seltzer (2013). Examples of multilingual learning as outlined above can be seen in the extracts from LaST materials (LaST, 2014) shown in Figure 11.3.

The purposes of L1 talk are varied. In activity 22, learners talk in L1 to prepare to read a text in English: they remind themselves what they know about the topic and predict what may occur in the text (activity 23). In activity 23 the learners read in English and refer where necessary to the bilingual glossary. Activity 24 is a post-reading L1 talking activity: learners check whether they have understood the same things and make L1 references to L2 words in the text. Activity 25 is also a L1 post-reading activity: learners read in English and check with each other in L1 if they have understood text and labels. In activity 26 learners observe and talk in L1 about what they see; they also read the L2 items in the chart and talk in L1 about how to fill it in (in L2).

Activity 27 is crucial for the learners' understanding of the key scientific concepts in the experiment. The discussion is conducted in L1: they cannot do it in L2. The teacher will also need to guide groups' discussions in L1. Having understood in L1 the conclusions which may be drawn from the experiment, learners can now write in L2. In this example of the translanguaging advantage, they would not have been able to do this had they not previously talked in L1. They cannot, however, write without support. Activity 28 therefore provides a writing framework: learners fill gaps. They will discuss in L1 how to complete the activity in L2. Finally, activity 29 enables them to express the key learning point in this lesson, in English, by providing an L2 sentence starter. To complete it, however, they will need to talk about their L2 sentence in L1.

The learning sequence illustrates translanguaging: learners learn through a guided mix of two languages. As already mentioned, almost all the talk is in L1. There are several reasons for this. Firstly, at the beginning of Grade 4 the learners can say little in L2, but a lot in L1. Secondly, talk plays a vital role in the development of new concepts (Wells, 1987; Mercer, 1995) and to virtually eliminate it from the classroom by a restriction to L2-talk deprives lessons of a key driver of concept development. Thirdly, learning talk oils the wheels of other learning activities such as reading and writing. Learners can do them better in L2 if they talk about them in L1. This also illustrates the translanguaging

Germination

Activity 22: Talking in Kinyarwanda about germination

Work in groups. Look at the diagram on page 23. Talk in Kinyarwanda about how seeds grow into plants. Say what conditions you think they need.

Activity 23: Reading about germination

Read the text. Find out what seeds need for germination.

A plant grows from a seed. When we plant seeds, they germinate. That means they grow into seedlings. To germinate, seeds need three conditions:
• water
• air
• warmth

New words	
Kinyarwanda	**English**
intete	seed
ingemwe	seedling
umwuka	air
ubushyuhe	warmth
ibisabwa	conditions
kumera	germinate

Figure 11.3 Extract from the LaST science materials: Grade 4 Rwanda.

advantage: learners read and write better in English if they talk in L1 about texts and about the ongoing construction of writing.

LSP

The LaST materials embody a range of language supportive activities. These have been discussed in general terms above, are summarised in Figure 11.1 and illustrated in Figures 11.3 and 11.4.

Support for listening to the teacher is not visible on the textbook page. It appears in the ways in which the teacher adjusts her classroom talk to make

Activity 24: Doing an experiment

Work in groups. Read the text. Talk in Kinyarwanda and find the things you need.

An experiment to find the conditions for germination

Things you need:

- bean seeds
- 4 empty water bottles of the same size
- cotton wool
- water

New words	
Kinyarwanda	**English**
ibishyimbo	bean seeds
agacupa ka parasitike	plastic water bottle
kirimo ubusa	empty
bingana	same size
ipamba	cotton wool
amazi	water

Activity 25: Reading instructions

Work in groups. Read the instructions and look at the pictures below. Talk in Kinyarwanda and follow the instructions.

What to do:

Cut the top off the bottles and use the base as a cup as shown in the picture. Arrange the water bottles and seeds as shown in the pictures on page 22.

New words	
Kinyarwanda	**English**
hatuje	safe
firigo	fridge

Figure 11.3 Cont.

In water bottle A put dry cotton wool and the seeds.
In water bottle B put cotton wool, the seeds and water.
In water bottle C put cotton wool, the seeds and water.
In water bottle D put wet cotton wool, the seeds and oil on top of the water.
Put the water bottles in a safe place. Put water bottle B in a cold place, e.g. a fridge.
Look at the water bottles after four days.

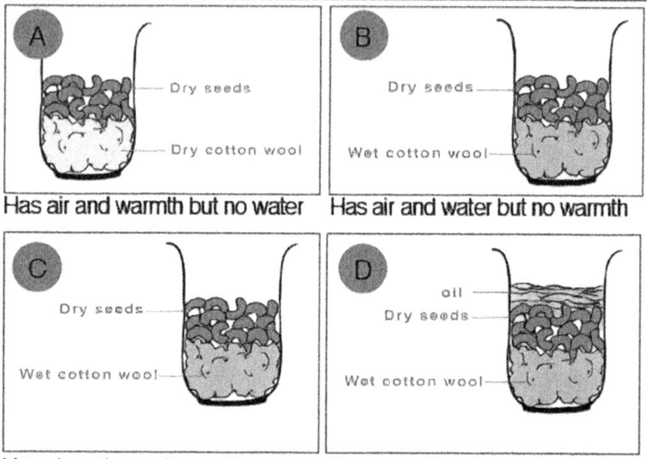

Has air and warmth but no water — Has air and water but no warmth

Has air, water and warmth — Has warmth and water but no air

KINYA RWANDA

Activity 26: Talking In Kinyarwanda about germination

Work in groups. After 4 days look at the 4 water bottles and talk in Kinyarwanda about what you can see in each bottle. Fill in the table below.

Tin	Conditions	Have the seeds germinated? (yes/no)
A	Air Warmth	
B	Air Water	
C	Air Water Warmth	
D	Water Warmth	

Figure 11.3 Cont.

Activity 27: Talking in Kinyarwanda about germination

Work in groups. Talk in Kinyarwanda about the results of the experiment. Say why the seeds germinated in one bottle and not in the others. Say what the experiment shows: what conditions do seeds need to germinate?

Activity 28: Writing about germination

Draw the 4 bottles in your exercise books: look at the pictures on pages 22.

Write about the experiment like this:

In bottle ... there are seedlings. The seeds have germinated. There is air, water and warmth.

In bottle ... there are no seedlings. The seeds have not germinated. There is ... but no...

Activity 29: Writing about germination

Work in groups. Talk in Kinyarwanda and write a conclusion for your experiment, like this:

To germinate, seeds need...

Figure 11.3 Cont.

it accessible to the learner. The main strategies which she will employ (see Figure 11.1) are to:

- use redundancy in her talk, e.g. defining, exemplifying, repeating and paraphrasing
- use a range of visuals
- use short-answer questions and prompts, and to repeat, paraphrase and expand on responses
- insert explicit signals of organisation into her talk.

With regard to support for learner-talk and writing, the teacher uses a range of tasks such as: sentence starters, substitution tables, writing frames and gap-filling.

ENGLISH **Activity 28: Talking in English about uses of soil.**

Work in groups. Talk about soils using the table.

We use	loam clay sand	soil	for	building. growing crops. making pots.

Figure 11.4 Extract from the LaST science materials.

In Figure 11.3, supported writing activities are shown in activities 28 and 29. In activity 28 learners describe their observations in L2. It leads on from activity 27 in which they discuss these observations in L1. Activity 28 also shows the translanguaging advantage: it would be harder to write in L2 if discussion had not first taken place in L1. Activities 28 and 29 are guided writing tasks in L2 requiring the learner to insert items of 1+ words in length. Without writing support of this kind, most learners at the beginning of L2-medium education cannot write these sentences in L2. In Figure 11.3, no guided talk activities in L2 are shown. Figure 11.4 shows a guided talk activity (activity 28 in a different sequence) from another part of the same materials, dealing with soils. In this task, learners who could not produce these oral sentences unsupported, are enabled to talk about soils.

With regard to support for reading, accessibility can be provided by paying attention to specific features of a reading passage (see Table 11.2). It should contain some of the following features:

- Limited text length
- Limited average sentence length
- Limited density of unfamiliar vocabulary
- Conveying of the meanings of new terms by textual context (e.g. definition, exemplification)
- Repetition of key words
- Clear structure in sentence and discourse.

Activity 25 in Figure 11.3 shows a short text (70 words) and reasonably short average sentence length (10 words per sentence). There is a fairly high density of unfamiliar words (*tin, cotton wool, seeds, wet, dry, oil, safe, fridge, on top of*), which is to be expected in a text about new subject-specific concepts. The meanings of these items are conveyed by the visuals and the bilingual glossary. The text gains clarity in its discourse structure by repetition of the phrase *In tin A/B etc* and of the lexical items *tin, cotton wool, seeds, water* etc.

Support for reading can also be provided by:

- a range of tasks to support reading, such as pre-, while- and post-reading questions, sequencing sentences, text/picture matching, read and fill in a chart, read and label a diagram
- a range of visuals, such as: diagrams, line drawings, photographs, charts, graphs
- bilingual glossaries.

In Figure 11.3, activity 22 shows a pre-reading task in L1 which enables learners to read in L2 more easily. Post-reading tasks in L1 are shown in activities 24 and 25: these enable learners to check each other's understanding of the text. Activity 23 gives a reading purpose which helps learners, while reading, to look only for what is necessary. Activity 25 is a sentence/picture matching task; activity 26 is a chart-filling task. Bilingual glossaries appear in activities 23, 24 and 25. Without these aspects of reading support, the texts would be too hard for the learners to read.

In addition to the Rwandan LaST project materials, we also include in Figure 11.5 an excerpt from bilingual materials produced by the LSTT project in Tanzania (Barrett et al., this volume; Rubabgumya et al., this volume). Some features of these materials are similar to those described above in relation to the Rwandan materials. For example, learners talk in Kiswahili before they read in English (activity 5.1) and before they write in English (activity 5.3). They also talk in Kiswahili about key concepts (activity 5.2) so that they can ensure good understanding of them. They also refer to a bilingual glossary. In contrast to the Rwandan materials, however, the materials are more balanced in their representation of English and Kiswahili: the learners read a text and study a concept web in Kiswahili. They may also make their own word web in Kiswahili or English (activity 5.2).

The key features of language supportive textbooks, as they have been discussed and illustrated above, are summarised in Table 11.2.

The characteristic features of a language supportive and multilingual approach to materials as illustrated in the examples above are essential if learners with low and developing ability in the LoI are to understand the content of lessons. However, LSP hardly ever appears in textbooks in SSA to this extent. Some textbook authors and editors make an effort to increase accessibility of reading passages; many do not, producing passages which are often harder to read than passages used in books for L2-fluent readerships such as the UK. Hardly any textbooks in SSA support talk and writing as in the examples above. Textbooks which use more accessible texts but do not support talk and writing may be read with a degree of understanding by learners, but they will still not be able to talk or write about concepts. This severely limits their value.

Conclusion

This chapter has attempted to show that many learners in SSA cannot read their English-medium textbooks, partly because the learners have not been taught

Key ideas

Physical, mental and emotional fitness

Freedom from disease or pain

Mwongozo

Mtandao wa maneno (word web) ni orodha ya maneno yanayohusiana. Andika neno "health" au "afya" katikati ya kipande cha karatasi. Zungushia duara neno hilo kisha fikiria neno lingine linaloelekea au kufanana na neno afya. Mfano: neno "hosipitali". Chora mshale kutoka kwenye neno afya halafu andika neno hosipitali mbele ya mshale. Ongeza mishale mingine kutoka kwenye neno afya na uandike maneno mengine yanayohusiana na neno afya. Angalia mfano ufuatao

Glossary

admitted **kulazwa hospitali**
body **mwili**
mind **akili**
several **nyingi/mbalimbali**
physically **kimwili**
mentally **kwa akili**
Socially **kijamii**

UNIT 5.1 Health

Activity 5.1: Being in the hospital

Have you ever been **admitted** in the hospital? Do you know anyone who has been admitted to hospital? Discuss the following questions with your neighbour in kiswahili.

1. What happened before you were admitted?
2. How did you feel before you were admitted?
3. What happened after the treatment by the doctor?

Meaning of Health

Every time we meet a friend, we ask "how are you" or "habari yako" in Kiswahili. We do this to know how our friend feels and about his or her health. Health is the general condition of **body** and **mind**. But what does it mean when someone says he or she is feeling well or healthy?

Activity 5.2

1. Discuss with your neighbour in Kiswahili what it means to be healthy.
2. Make a word web with your neighbour. You can make your word web in Kiswahili or English. A word web helps you to understand the word 'healthy' and all the words related to the word healthy. For help, look at the HELP box (mwongozo).

What does 'healthy' mean? If you are healthy, you are well. You are not sick. You are well in **several** ways. Firstly you are **physically** well: your body is working properly. Secondly, you are **mentally** well: you are well in your mind. Thirdly you are **socially** well: you have friendships and good relationships with your family.

Activity 5.3

Discuss with a partner in Kiswahili:

1. Describe the meaning of the following words:
   (i) physical
   (ii) mental
   (iii) social
2. Think about people you know who are physically, mentally, and socially healthy. How do you know that these people are healthy?
3. Write the characteristics of people who are physically,

Figure 11.5 Extract from the LSTT biology materials: Grade 8 Tanzania.

enough L2 skills to enable them to do so and partly because publishers do not take their L2-medium readers into account. Learners are clearly disadvantaged by this, most obviously because it reduces their access to a major source of curricular knowledge, but also because it cuts them off from their main source of CALP in

Table 11.2 Key features of language supportive textbooks

- **Multilingualism is promoted:**
  - Much learner-talk is in L1s or is bilingual, e.g.:
    - before and after reading in the L2
    - before whole-class reporting in the L2
    - before and while writing in the L2
  - Teachers are expected to make use of L1 in their talk with learners
- **Texts are readable, i.e.:**
  - They are short
  - Sentences are short
  - They have clear discourse structure
  - They are supported by visuals
  - Unfamiliar vocabulary is limited
  - Key terms are repeated
  - L1 glossaries are used
- **Visuals are used to support learning:**
  - They represent a varied range, e.g. drawings, photos, diagrams, charts
  - They perform specific functions, e.g. support for reading, writing, talk, vocabulary
- **The full repertoire of language supportive tasks is used to support learners using L2 when they:**
  - speak
  - read
  - write

L2 and makes it more difficult to demonstrate knowledge in assessment. It also makes it hard for them to share school knowledge via the textbook with their parents. Of the many disadvantages that arise from learner failure to understand in L2-medium schooling, the loss of access to textbooks is therefore perhaps the most severe.

A different pedagogy, both multilingual and language supportive, would help learners learn more effectively. Whereas many textbooks are currently unreadable and thus unused, this pedagogy would allow learners to use them. This approach to teaching and learning, when adopted by ministries, will require of them a major change in pedagogical principle and practice, which they will need to convey to publishers when commissioning textbooks. Authors and editors will in turn need to develop the requisite expertise. At present, given the widespread publication of textbooks which learners cannot read, it seems that in SSA many publishing houses do not possess it. It is, however, at hand. Successful multilingual and language supportive projects operate in SSA. In addition, international publishers (for example Oxford University Press) operating in Rwanda and SSA in general without using this expertise, nevertheless apply it successfully in other parts of the world, for example in CLIL publishing in Spain. Consultancy expertise for publishers is also available.

Children learn partly from textbooks. In SSA it needs spelling out that to do so they should be able to read them. The fact that in SSA many cannot is something which should concern stakeholders, not least from the viewpoint of the money spent on them. Nevertheless, it is not widely discussed in ministries, the aid community, the publishing industry and even in the otherwise rich academic discourse about language and education in SSA. It has significance for the achievement of the individual child, for the overall effect of schooling, for education budgets and ultimately for national economies. Readable textbooks, especially when they support teachers who may not be pedagogically confident enough, can change school practice.

Notes

1 In this chapter, L2 refers to English, despite the fact that for many learners it is a 3rd, 4th or further additional language. This would also apply in contexts where other post-colonial languages (e.g. French, Portuguese) serve as the official language of instruction in schools.
2 In Tanzania, Kiswahili, normally a LoI, is often a second language for many children. Here, as throughout the chapter, L2 nevertheless refers to English.
3 Lextutor (2020) is an open-source, online vocabulary analysis tool that allows users to explore vocabulary, e.g. nuances of form, meaning and collocation of words (see www.lextutor.ca/).
4 We are grateful for data on the training to Jane Czornowol, LaST project manager.

References

Afitska, O, Ankomah, Y, Clegg, J, Kiliku, P, Osei-Amankwah, L & Rubagumya, C 2013, 'Dilemmas of language choice in education in Tanzania and Ghana', in L Tikly & A Barrett (eds), *Education Quality and Social Justice in the Global South: Challenges for Policy, Practice and Research,* Routledge, London, pp. 154–167.

Alidou, H 2009, 'Promoting multilingual and multicultural education in francophone Africa: challenges and perspectives', in B Brock-Utne & I Skattum (eds), *Languages and Education in Africa: A Comparative and Transdisciplinary Analysis,* Symposium Books, Didcot, pp. 105–131.

Arthur, J 1994, 'English in Botswana primary classrooms: functions and constraints', in C Rubagumya (ed), *Teaching and Researching Language in African Classrooms,* Multilingual Matters, Clevedon, pp. 63–78.

August, D & Shanahan, T 2006, *Developing Reading and Writing in Second Language Learners: Report of the National Literacy Panel on Language Minority Children and Youth,* Lawrence Erlbaum Associates, Mahwah, NJ.

Baker, C & Wright, WE 2017, *Foundations of Bilingual Education and Bilingualism,* Multilingual Matters, Clevedon, UK.

Ball, P, Kelly, K & Clegg, J 2015, *Putting CLIL into Practice,* Oxford University Press, Oxford.

Bloch, C, Guzala, X & Nkence, N 2010, 'Towards normalizing South African classroom life: the ongoing struggle to implement mother-tongue based bilingual education', in K Menken & O Garcìa, *Negotiating Language Policies in Schools,* Routledge, Abingdon, pp. 88–106.

British Council 2015, *British Council Endline Assessment of English Language Proficiency of School Teachers in Rwanda,* British Council, Kigali.

Brock-Utne, B 2013, 'Language and liberation', in C Benson & K Kosonen (eds), Language Issues in Comparative Education: Inclusive Teaching and learning in Non-dominant Cultures, Sense, Rotterdam, pp. 77–93.

Campaign for Education 2013, *Mother-Tongue Education: Policy Lessons for Quality and Inclusion*, Campaign for Education, Johannesburg.

Celic, C & Seltzer, K 2013, *Translanguaging: A CUNY-NSYIEB Guide for Educators*, CUNY-NSYIEB, New York.

Chimbutane, F 2018, 'Multilingualism and education in Sub-Saharan Africa: policies, practices and implications' in A Bonnet & P Siemund (eds.), *Foreign Language Education in Multilingual Classrooms*, John Benjamins, Amsterdam, pp. 57–75.

Clegg, J 2015, *Developing Readable English-Medium Textbooks in Rwanda*, unpublished paper presented at the 49th Annual International IATEFL Conference and Exhibition, Manchester, UK.

Clegg, J 2017, 'The English-medium curriculum in African education systems: do learners have enough English to cope with it?', unpublished presentation, Africa TESOL, Kigali.

Clegg, J & Afitska, O 2011, 'Teaching and learning in two languages in African classrooms', *Comparative Education*, vol. 47, pp. 61–77.

Clegg, J, & Simpson, J 2016, 'Improving the effectiveness of English as a medium of instruction in sub-Saharan Africa', *Comparative Education*, vol. 52(3), pp. 359–374.

Cloud, N, Genesee, F & Hamayan, E 2009, *Literacy Instruction for English Language Learners*, Heinemann, Portsmouth, NH.

Cummins, J 1984, *Bilingualism and Special Education: Issues in Assessment and Pedagogy*, Multilingual Matters, Clevedon.

Cummins, J 2000, *Language, Power and Pedagogy: Bilingual Children in the Crossfire*. Multilingual Matters, Clevedon.

Djité, P 2008, *The Sociolinguistics of Development in Africa*. Multilingual Matters, Bristol.

EGRA 2012, *Early Grade Reading and Mathematics in Rwanda; Final report*, RTI/USAID.

Erling, EJ, Adinolfi, L, Hultgren, A, Buckler, A & Mukorera, M 2016, 'Medium of instruction policies in Ghanaian and Indian primary schools: an overview of key issues and recommendations', *Comparative Education*, vol. 52, pp. 294–310.

García, O, Johnson, SI & Seltzer, K 2017, *The Translanguaging Classroom: Leveraging Student Bilingualism for Learning*, Caslon, Philadelphia.

García, O & Wei L 2014, *Translanguaging: Language, Bilingualism and Education*, Palgrave Macmillan, New York.

Gibbons, P 2015, *Scaffolding Language, Scaffolding Learning*, Heinemann, Portsmouth, NH.

Gilmour, I. (2001) *Food Chains*. Winchester: Neate.

Glewwe, P, Kremer, M & Moulin, S 2009, 'Many children left behind? Textbooks and test scores in Kenya', *American Economic Journal: Applied Economics*, vol. 1, pp. 112–135.

Hardman, F 2008, 'Teachers' use of feedback in whole-class and group-based talk', in N Mercer & S Hodgkinson (eds), *Exploring Talk in School*, Sage, London, pp. 131–150.

Herzog-Punzenberger, B, Le Pichon-Vorstman, E & Siarova, H 2017, 'Multilingual Education in the Light of Diversity: Lessons Learned', *NESET II report*, Publications Office of the European Union, Luxembourg.

Heugh, K 2006. 'Theory and practice – language education models in Africa: research, design, decision making, and outcomes,' in H Alidou, A Boly, B Brock-Utne, Y S Diallo & H E Wolff (eds), *Optimizing Learning and Education in Africa – the Language Factor: A Stock-taking Research on Mother Tongue and Bilingual Education in Sub-Saharan Africa*. Paris: ADEA.

Heugh, K 2009, 'Contesting the monolingual practices of a bilingual to monolingual policy', *English Teaching: Practice and Critique*, vol. 8, pp. 96–113.

Heugh, K, Diedericks, M, Prinsloo, CH, Herbst, DL & Winnaar, L 2007, *Assessment of the Language and Mathematics Skills of Grade 8 Learners in the Western Cape in 2006,* Human Sciences Research Council, Pretoria.

Heugh, K & Skuttnab-Kangas, T 2012, 'Peripheries take centre stage: reinterpreted multilingual education works', in T Skuttnab-Kangas & K Heugh (eds), *Multilingual Education and Sustainable Diversity Work: from Periphery to Centre,* Routledge, Abingdon, pp. 263–283.

Hollmarsdottir, H 2005, *From Policy to Practice: A Study of the Implementation of the Language-in-Education Policy (LiEP) in Three South African Primary Schools,* University of Oslo, Oslo.

Johnson, P 2007, *Animals and Plants,* Schofield & Sims, Huddersfield.

Kamwangamalu, N M 2016, *Language Policy and Economics: The Language Question in Africa,* Palgrave Macmillan, London.

Kerfoot, C & Simon-Vandenbergen, A (eds) 2015, 'Language in Epistemic Access: Mobilising Multilingualism and Literacy Development for More Equitable Education in South Africa', *Language in Education,* vol. 29, pp. 177–185.

Kuchah, K, Milligan, LO, Ubanako, VN & Njika, J. (2020). *English Medium Instruction (EMI) in a Multilingual Francophone Context: An Investigation of the Learning Resources and Strategies of Primary School Children in Cameroon,* British Council.

LaST 2014, *P4 Science,* University of Bristol and British Council.

Macdonald, C 1990, *Main Report of the Threshold Project,* The Human Sciences Research Council, Pretoria.

Mahalela-Thusi, B & Heugh, K 2004, 'Terminology and schoolbooks in Southern African languages', in B Brock-Utne, Z Desai & M Qorro (eds), *Researching the Language of Instruction in Tanzania and South Africa,* African Minds, Cape Town, pp. 177–201.

Makalela, L 2015, 'Moving out of linguistic boxes: the effects of translanguaging strategies for multilingual classrooms', *Language in Education,* vol. 29, pp. 200–217.

Mchombo, S 2014, Language, learning and education for all in Africa, in Z Babaci-Wilhite (ed), *Giving Space to African Voices: Rights in Local Languages and Local Curriculum,* Sense, Rotterdam, pp. 21–47.

McKinney, C 2017, *Language and Power in Post-Colonial Schooling,* Routledge, Abingdon.

Mercer, N 1995, *The Guided Construction of Knowledge: Talk amongst Teachers and Learners,* Multilingual Matters, Clevedon.

Milligan, L, Clegg, J & Tikly, L 2016, 'Exploring the potential for language supportive learning in English Medium Instruction: a Rwandan case study', *Comparative Education,* vol. 52, pp. 328–342.

Ouane, A & Glanz, C (eds) 2011, *Optimising Learning, Education and Publishing in Africa: The Language Factor. A Review and Analysis of Theory and Practice in Mother-Tongue and Bilingual Education in sub-Saharan Africa,* UNESCO/ADEA, Hamburg.

Prinsloo, CH & Heugh, K 2013, *The Role of Language and Literacy in Preparing South African Learners for Educational Success: Lessons Learnt from a Classroom Study in Limpopo Province,* HSRC Press, Cape Town.

Probyn, M 2005, 'Language and the struggle to learn: the intersection of classroom realities, language policy and neo-colonial and globalisation discourses in South African schools', in A Lin & P Martin (eds), *Decolonisation, Globalisation: Language-in-Education Policy and Practice,* Multilingual Matters, Clevedon, pp. 153–172.

Probyn, M 2006, 'Language and learning science in South Africa', *Language and Education,* vol. 20, pp. 391–414.

Probyn, M 2015, 'Pedagogical translanguaging: bridging discourses in South African science classrooms', *Language and Education,* vol. 29, pp. 218–234.

Read, T 2015, *Where Have All the Textbooks Gone? Toward Sustainable Provision of Teaching and Learning Materials in Sub-Saharan Africa*, World Bank, Washington D.C.

Serugo, I & Mpummude, W 2010. *Understanding Science and Technology*, Longhorn, Nairobi.

Thomas, W & Collier, V 2002, *A National Study of School Effectiveness for Language Minority Students' Long-term Academic Achievement*, Center for Research on Education, Diversity & Excellence, Santa Cruz, CA & Washington DC.

Trudell, B 2016, *The Impact of Language Policy and Practice on Children's Learning: Evidence from Eastern and Southern Africa*, UNICEF Eastern and Southern Africa.

Trudell, B & Young, C (eds.) 2016, *Good Answers to Tough Questions in Mother Tongue-Based Multilingual Education*. SIL International, Dallas. Retrieved from www.sil.org/literacy-education/good-answers-tough-questions-mother-tongue-based-multilingual-education.

UNESCO 2016a, *Every Child Should Have a Textbook*, Global Education Monitoring Report Polcy Paper, UNESCO, Paris.

UNESCO 2016b, *If You Don't Understand, How Can You Learn?*, Global Education Monitoring Report Policy paper, UNESCO, Paris.

Uwezo 2017, *Are Our Children Learning? Uwezo Tanzania Sixth Learning Assessment Report*, Twaweza East Africa, Dar es Salaam.

Weber, J 2014, *Flexible Multilingual Education: Putting Children's Needs First*, Multilingual Matters, Bristol.

Wells, G 1987, *The Meaning Makers: Children learning Language and Using Language to Learn*, Hodder and Stoughton, Abingdon.

Williams, E 2011, 'Language policy, politics and development in Africa', in H Coleman (ed), Dreams and Realities: Developing Countries and the English Language, The British Council, London, pp. 39–55.

Appendix Extract from a primary science textbook from the UK

More on growing

Most plants grow best if they are kept warm and have plenty of light and air, and enough water. Plants make their own food in their leaves using water, air and light.

Plants also need small amounts of other substances to grow well. Farmers add these **nutrients** to fields in fertilisers. At home, you might sometimes put 'plant food' onto a potted plant to keep it healthy. The nutrients in the fertiliser dissolve in water in the soil, and are taken into the plant through its roots.

Not all plants need the same conditions. Some plants are **adapted** to grow in different places.

Pondweed grows under water.

Cactus plants can grow in very dry conditions.

12 Translanguaging, multimodality and authorship

Cultivating creativity and critical literacies through multilingual education in Tanzania

Monica Shank Lauwo

Introduction

Learners bring rich linguistic and semiotic resources with them to any learning space. In the face of evidence about the dire state of literacy in East Africa and beyond (e.g., Uwezo, 2019), pedagogies that incorporate learners' most familiar languages and modes of meaning-making hold promise for deepening meaningful learning and improving literacy in both familiar and additional languages. Translanguaging and multimodality offer possibilities for embracing learners' full linguistic, semiotic, and cultural resources as the foundations of learning and knowledge production, while also supporting the constant expansion of these resources. By making diverse communicative resources available, translanguaging and multimodality offer opportunities for meaning to be constructed in a plurality of ways, opening space for engagement with creative alternatives, enabling more equitable relations of power, and democratizing opportunities for knowledge production. Amidst neoliberalism's insistence on standardization, individualism, and the exacerbation of inequality, translanguaging and multimodality can increase opportunities for creativity, collaboration, and engagement with alternatives to the status quo.

This chapter explores how pedagogies of translanguaging and multimodality can be supportive of investment in learning and knowledge production, the creativity to think and imagine otherwise and the authoring of texts, meanings, and alternative futures. Specifically, it examines the work of a community learning centre in Northern Tanzania that embraces local languages, knowledges, and semiotic resources alongside school-valued codes and modes. In contrast to mainstream Tanzanian schools, which are either Kiswahili-medium or English-medium and tend to be dominated by monolingual ideologies (e.g., English-only policies), the community learning centre is founded on a belief in the power of familiar languages and semiotic resources in learning and knowledge production. As such, it incorporates Maa (Maasai language, the dominant local language), Kiswahili (the national language), and English simultaneously in all teaching and

DOI: 10.4324/9781003028383-15

learning, while centring multimodality, including orality, singing, drawing, and dramatization. Based on a three-year critical action research study at the community learning centre, this chapter examines the impact of translanguaging and multimodality on learner investment, creativity, and authorship, with an underlying interest in challenging entrenched power relations and constructing more equitable alternatives.

Translanguaging and multimodality

The rapid mushrooming of attention to translanguaging represents the growing realization of the ubiquity of fluid linguistic practices throughout the world, and their utility in educational environments. García and Li understand translanguaging as involving "the ways in which bilinguals use their complex semiotic repertoire to act, know, and to be" (García & Li, 2015, p. 237). McKinney and Tyler (2019, p. 146) focus on translanguaging as "a normative communicative practice among bi/multilinguals; an ideological position which resists the notion of named languages as autonomous, bounded objects; and a descriptive term which incorporates semiotic modes beyond language". This chapter draws particularly from the South African scholar Leketi Makalela's work on Ubuntu translanguaging, which, in alignment with Ubuntu, an African cultural and epistemological conception of being, emphasizes wholeness and the interdependence of all languages (and people) (Makalela, 2015a, 2015b, 2015c). Makalela understands an Ubuntu worldview to be about a "communal orientation and continuum of social, linguistic and cultural resources and denotes the interconnectedness of all human existence" (Makalela, 2015a, p. 214). Ubuntu translanguaging thus reflects an understanding that "one language is incomplete without the other" (Makalela, 2015b, p. 297), and that languages "are not bounded but overlap with one another" (Makalela, 2015a, p. 214).

Translanguaging's orientation to wholeness and interdependence extends to non-linguistic semiotic systems, and is thus inclusive of multimodal meaning-making. According to Li (2018, p. 22), "Translanguaging reconceptualizes language as a multilingual, multisemiotic, multisensory, and multimodal resource for sense- and meaning-making". Multimodality, as understood by South African scholar Pippa Stein, is about "how human beings use different modes of communication, like speech, writing, images, gesture, and sound to represent or make meaning in the world" (Stein, 2008, p. 871). The expansion of concepts of language and literacies to include multimodality enriches opportunities for meaning-making, cognition, and learning, since "modes have different affordances – potentials and constraints for making meaning" (Kress & van Leeuwen, 2001, p. 22). While this chapter understands translanguaging to be inclusive of multimodality, it continues to use the word multimodality alongside translanguaging to emphasize the centrality of multimodality to the dynamics of investment, creativity, and authorship explored in this study. At the same time, it acknowledges that social semiotics perspectives might understand multimodality to be inclusive of translanguaging and not the other way around (e.g., Adami,

2019), and as such includes both terms to emphasize the inclusion of both linguistic and semiotic features.

Translanguaging has been shown to be a transformative pedagogical practice in diverse educational contexts throughout the world (e.g., García & Li, 2014; Makalela, 2015a; McKinney & Tyler, 2019; Shank Lauwo, 2018). Makalela (2015c, p. 130) demonstrates that translanguaging offers a "way to increase epistemic access for multilingual speakers and to valorise the plural sense of who they are". Angel Lin, in a study based in Hong Kong, argues that we

> need to recognize the crucial role of translanguaging and trans-semiotizing in the dynamic flow of co-making of knowing and meaning, without which what is left in the classroom would mainly be parroting without active ownership of learning on the part of the students.
>
> (Lin, 2019, p. 12)

García and Li (2014) observe how translanguaging "embraces both *creativity*; that is, following or flouting norms of language use, as well as *criticality*; that is, using evidence to question, problematize or express views" (García & Li, 2014, p. 24). With its potential to increase epistemic access, valorize plural identities, support the co-construction of knowledge and active ownership of learning, and nurture creativity and criticality, translanguaging offers an invaluable pedagogical and meaning-making resource.

Tanzanian context

Tanzania, like most other African contexts, is a richly multilingual country with more than 130 local languages. Kiswahili is the national language and lingua franca, and has historically been associated with national unity, decolonization, and Tanzanian identity. English, a language unfamiliar to the majority of the population (the highly educated and elite excepted) enjoys a high status through its association with international opportunities, the job market, and social mobility. Kiswahili is the language of instruction in government primary schools, after which point there is an abrupt shift to English-medium at the secondary level. Extensive research since the 1970s has shown English to be a barrier to meaningful learning at both secondary and tertiary levels due to insufficient English proficiency (see Qorro, 2008 for a review). In spite of 50 years of concerted advocacy, two policy drafts legislating a shift to Kiswahili-medium secondary schooling (in 1969 and 1982 – see Brock-Utne, 2005), and an Education Policy of 2014 ostensibly making Kiswahili the language of instruction at all levels of schooling, the language of instruction in post-primary schooling has remained resolutely English.

In this context, language discourses have largely pitted Kiswahili and English against each other in antagonistic opposition (Blommaert, 2014), thereby depressing possibilities for multilingual education. At the same time, the 130+ local languages have been muted in formal schooling. Schools are characterized by monolingual ideologies, whereby students are punished for speaking languages other than Kiswahili at primary schools, and punished for using Kiswahili at secondary schools. In this context, there is urgent need for alternative approaches to language education that validate and embrace learners' full linguistic repertoires, while supporting learners to constantly expand these repertoires.

Cheche Community Library

In response to the need for alternative approaches to education grounded in familiar languages and ways of knowing, Cheche Community Library in Monduli, Northern Tanzania, offers educational programming that takes learners' existing linguistic, semiotic, and cultural resources as the starting point. All of its activities embrace translanguaging, with emphasis on Maa, Kiswahili, and English. As a richly multimodal environment, Cheche activities include singing, storytelling, drawing, games, creative play, dramatization, writing, and reading. There is a strong emphasis on creativity and critical literacies and an interest in the production – not just consumption – of knowledge. While Cheche seeks to supplement children's school learning (including reading and writing, content knowledge, and Kiswahili and English language skills), it also aspires to explore alternative paradigms of education, with a commitment to local relevance, awakening critical consciousness, and catalysing transformation for individuals and society. It pushes back against neoliberalism's emphasis on standardization, individualism, and reproductive thinking, with the cultivation of creativity, collaboration, and the agency to think and imagine otherwise.

Cheche is run predominantly by youth volunteers from the local community, and operates out of a room lent by a community member for this purpose. While it currently receives minor monthly contributions from friends of Cheche to support volunteer stipends and supplies, Cheche was initiated by community members and me with no funding whatsoever, and is sustained predominantly by the time, energy, and passion of community members. It is open to all, six days per week, with no cost to attend. Cheche attracts children from babes in arms (brought by their older siblings) to teenagers and beyond. It is a joyful space, seeking to nurture curiosity and investment in learning. Participants are a combination of Maa-dominant and Kiswahili-dominant speakers, representing a wide range of abilities and schooling backgrounds. In spite of the dominance of Maa in this community, most participants had never engaged with written Maa prior to their involvement at Cheche.

Methodology

This paper draws from a critical action research study conducted at Cheche Community Library over a three-year period, from 2015 to 2018. It examines my own work as a facilitator, in collaboration with other facilitators (youth from the local community), during library sessions (weekday afternoons/evenings, and Saturdays). As action research is iterative and ongoing, involving cycles of observation-reflection-action-evaluation-modification and moving in new directions (McNiff & Whitehead, 2011), this research has addressed diverse and evolving questions over the course of these three years (see Shank Lauwo, 2018, 2019 for other aspects of this work). This paper draws from an array of data sources, including extensive field notes, texts created by library participants, video recordings, photographs, and audio recordings.

Research questions

The questions addressed in this paper relate to the potential role of pedagogies of translanguaging and multimodality with regards to three particular points of interest: investment, creativity, and authorship. Specifically, the three research questions are as follows:

1. How can translanguaging and multimodality contribute to investment in learning and knowledge production?
2. How can translanguaging and multimodality support the development of creativity?
3. In what ways can translanguaging and multimodality increase space for all learners to position themselves as authors of meaning and texts?

Investment, "a sociological complement to the psychological construct of motivation" (Darvin & Norton, 2015, p. 37), is essential for sustained, meaningful learning to take place. Darvin understands investment as "commitment to the goals, practices, and identities that constitute the learning process and that are continually negotiated in diverse relations of power" (Darvin, 2019, p. 19). Indeed, meaningful learning is contingent upon learners' investment in the language and literacy practices of a given context and learners' ability to invest is entangled with relations of power. In their model of investment in applied linguistics, Darvin and Norton (2015) understand investment to occur when the ideological environment affirms and renders audible a learner's identities and forms of capital (Bourdieu, 1991).

Creativity is understood by Li (2011a, p. 374) as "the ability to choose between following and flouting the rules and norms of behaviour, including the use of language, and to push and break boundaries between the old and the new, the conventional and the original". This paper embraces this understanding, while adding that creativity involves the ability to think and act innovatively, and to generate alternatives to the status quo. Creativity is deeply related to critical literacy, both being about engagement with options and "challenging existing norms, practices and relations of power" (Darvin, 2019, p. 1).

Authorship is understood here to be about the production of unique meaning, and occurs in diverse modes and languages. Authorship is centrally about power and voice, and involves the use of literacies to construct and legitimize ideas, worldviews and realities. Investment, creativity, and authorship are all related to the development and employment of literacies, all play important roles in learning and meaning-making, and all hold seeds for transformation and the generation/redistribution of power.

My positionality in this community is that of an insider-outsider, as I have lived here since 2010, but I myself am not from this community, having grown up in Canada. I am also racially distinct from other members of this community (an ever-present emblem of my outsider-ness), and have had different exposures and opportunities from most members of this community. I am fluent in Kiswahili and English, and my proficiency in Maa is still at an emergent stage. As a co-founder of Cheche Community Library, I undertook this action research study in order to critically engage with the implications of Cheche's work, to seek ways to improve our practice and to document affordances and challenges of pedagogies of translanguaging and multimodality in this context.

I now turn to an exploration of what translanguaging and multimodality have meant for issues of investment, creativity, and authorship at Cheche Community Library, with particular attention to the negotiation of power and possibilities for transformation. The following sections examine questions of investment, creativity, and authorship by exploring experiences of multilingual authorship, changing relationships with literacies, and the centring of local knowledges, epistemologies, and community relationships

Multilingual authorship

At Cheche Community Library, there is a strong emphasis on productive literacies, an interest in what we *do* or *produce* with our literacies. Productive literacies are about using our literacies to create or produce something new, to intervene in the world, in contrast to the *reproductive* literacies which tend to be emphasized in exam-based schooling. Productive literacies are related to authorship and knowledge production, which are central to Cheche's core commitment of supporting participants to author alternative futures. As the texts and kinds of knowledge these children encounter at school rarely reflect their own realities, authoring their own texts is a political process that asserts the legitimacy of the ideas, languages, and cultures of the children and their communities, positioning these as valid forms of knowledge and as book-worthy.

While authorship takes multiple forms, including oral storytelling, drawing, singing, and dancing, some of this multilingual knowledge production eventually takes the form of books. Through their involvement in the library, the children of Cheche Community Library are prolific authors and illustrators of multilingual books, written bilingually and trilingually in various combinations of Maa, Kiswahili, and English. Some of the stories featured in these books are retellings of traditional Maasai stories narrated to the books' authors by grandparents or elders, others are re-versionings of stories encountered elsewhere, and others yet are original stories developed by the authors. Cheche publishes these books by printing them into booklets, which then become part of Cheche's collection with copies also distributed to the authors and illustrators and sometimes also to their schools. Thus, this pedagogical process of authorship also results in the development of new learning materials that are reflective of local children's ideas and ways of knowing.

The books authored by Cheche participants frequently represent long processes of becoming, and their significance resonates far beyond the final products of the books themselves. To illustrate the long trajectories these books represent, I will focus on the journey of one particular author, who I will call Rama.

Rama has been a highly engaged participant in Cheche since its inception. A class three pupil of about 12 years of age when he first began attending, he was a fluent reader of Kiswahili, his dominant language and the language of instruction at his school. Rama is ethnically Chagga from Kilimanjaro region, but, unbeknownst to the facilitators, Rama had picked up Maa through his interactions with Maasai communities. His remarkable expertise in the language gradually became known to Cheche facilitators and participants with increasing clarity.

Early on, Rama showed immense interest in Maa books at Cheche, books that had been printed from the African Storybook (www.africanstorybook.org). Collaborating together with Maasai children, he poured over Maa texts, thrilled by the novelty of seeing a familiar oral language featured in books. Rama was an active participant in read alouds of books in all three of Cheche's main languages, and actively made contributions in Maa, as well as Kiswahili, and occasionally in English. During one of the first read alouds of a Maa book, Rama astounded the group with his expertise and leadership, translating Maa into Kiswahili both with and for the other children (some of whom were unfamiliar with Maa). With negligible English proficiency at the beginning of his Cheche participation, Rama gradually, and tentatively, developed the courage to read basic English books – especially those with engaging illustrations. He scaffolded his meaning-making with astute readings of the illustrations and insightful queries and commentaries in Kiswahili.

The first time a trilingual book (Maa, Kiswahili, English) was introduced to Cheche, Rama was enthralled for over an hour with a single 14-page children's book, entitled *Olkínkí Le Oó Imotónyi/Mfalme wa Ndege/King of the Birds*. He painstakingly read all of the Maa aloud, needing to sound most of it out syllable by syllable (in contrast to his near-fluent reading of Kiswahili). When reading with me, he would explain in Kiswahili what he had discovered in Maa, meticulously making connections between the Maa and Kiswahili texts. Upon his discovery that where the Kiswahili version read 'wa kifalme', in Maa it read 'sapuk', he discussed how some concepts do not exist in certain languages and thus meaning changes through translation. As we were negotiating our understandings of the various bird varieties featured in this story, using the Kiswahili and Maa names (which were not familiar to us) and the illustrations, Rama found the English to bring greater clarity, stating, 'Huyu ni eagle, ee?' ('This is an eagle, right?').

As Rama continued reading this book with Maiko, a male facilitator strong in Maa (with a strong contingent of intrigued younger observers), the focus continued to be on making sense of the Maa text, which was done largely through translations into Kiswahili and discussions in Maa. As they continued their detective work, Rama became impassioned in his objection to a certain

Maa/Kiswahili translation. Covering up the Maa and Kiswahili, he requested I translate the English version into Kiswahili, in order to bring a third linguistic perspective into the debate on the passage's meaning. In this way, meaning was dynamically negotiated and multiplied across all three languages, illustrations, and co-readers.

These multilingual texts, amidst a translanguaging space (Li, 2011b) that affirmed and nurtured his identities of expertise, were generative for Rama, as he eventually decided that he too could write a book. He requested paper from the library, and a few days later returned with the tale of *Akilinyingi and the Giants* scrawled in Kiswahili on those now dirty and crumpled sheets of paper. Rama then workshopped his story with other children at Cheche, who applauded his work and asked some questions, all in Kiswahili. He worked with a facilitator to improve his text, largely through the facilitator asking Rama the same kinds of provocative questions children are encouraged to ask of all texts at Cheche. Rama later worked with a facilitator, Janeth, to translate the whole story into Maa, a deeply collaborative process that involved often heated discussion and occasional consultations with the few Maa books available at Cheche. Neither he nor the facilitator had previous experience writing in Maa. Later, an older community member and I joined Rama and Janeth to look at the Maa version, as we debated word choices, syntax, conjugations, and spellings, with Rama making impressively persuasive arguments for certain editorial decisions, offering examples, comparisons, and metalinguistic observations. I supported Rama to then translate the Kiswahili version into English. Rama requested a local shopkeeper, Ali, who had gotten involved in Cheche as a visual artist, to create illustrations to complement his trilingual texts. The result is an exquisite trilingual illustrated storybook, about a young boy who gets lost in a forest, is captured by a giant, and is eventually cleverly rescued by a kindly crow and reunited with his family (see Figure 12.1).

Throughout this whole journey, the multilingual environment, and particularly the presence of Maa, deepened Rama's investment in reading, discussing, and writing. Engaging with Maa, both oral and written, enabled Rama to claim the identity positions of expert and teacher. Reading and writing trilingual texts sparked metalinguistic awareness and discussions, as well as collaborative translingual and multimodal meaning-making. It balanced power relations, as meaning was negotiated between different co-readers (and writers), between different languages and across modes. The ways in which meaning was negotiated and multiplied across different modes and roles offer prime examples of transmediation, "the act of translating meanings from one sign system to another" which "increases students' opportunities to engage in generative and reflective thinking" (Siegel, 1995, p. 455). Rama's meaning-making processes echoed Lemke's (1998, p. 312) observation, that "Meanings in multimedia are not fixed and additive (the word-meaning plus the picture-meaning), but multiplicative (word-meaning modified by image-context, image-meaning modified by textual context), making a whole far greater than the simple sum of its parts". This multiplicative process of meaning-making applies equally to

Ore engolong' nabo nelo engukuu aing'oru endaa. Neing'ua Akilinyingi tiang'. Nelotu orkuruk nejoki Akilinyingi, "Koo, njoki oloito paaliki." Neisho oloito. "Koo, njoki engiring'o paaliki." Neisho engiring'o.

One day, the giant went to look for food. Akilinyingi was left at the giant's home. A crow came and said, "Koo, give me a bone and I'll tell you something important." Akilinyingi gave her a bone. "Koo, give me some meat and I'll tell you something important." Akilinyingi gave the crow some meat.

Siku moja jitu alienda kutafuta chakula, na akamwacha Akilinyingi nyumbani. Kunguru alikuja na akamwambia Akilinyingi, "Koo, nipe mfupa nikuambie." Akilinyingi akampa Kunguru mfupa. Kunguru akasema, "Koo, nipe nyama nikuambie." Akilinyingi akampa nyama.

Figure 12.1 A page from Rama and Ali's trilingual book, *Akilinyingi oo Ingukuuni/Akilinyingi and the Giants/Akilinyingi na Majitu.*

multilingualism/translanguaging and collaboration/multi-person interactions as it does to multimodality.

This process of making meaning across participants, languages, and modes created a sense of interdependence as various participants (myself included) relied on each other's diverse sets of expertise, while simultaneously affirming and expanding each of our multilingual, multimodal repertoires. Rama's Maa-invoked agency emboldened him to suggest 'better' alternatives to the author's use of language, challenging a written text in a way that was unprecedented in his interactions with Kiswahili and English texts. The translanguaging space granted voice to his remarkable linguistic expertise which is silenced in mainstream schooling, and supported him to claim the power to author a book in a deeply creative and collaborative process. The translanguaging space transformed Rama's relationship with literacies and with learning. The diverse ways in which other children's relationships with literacies shifted through engagement with this translanguaging space is the subject of the next section.

Changing relationships with literacies

Through frameworks of translanguaging and multimodality, Cheche Community Library seeks to promote broad notions of literacies. Far more than decoding, reading the word and the world (Freire, 2007) is about engaging with texts and the world holistically, making meaning from all available modes using all available senses, and imagining how these words and worlds could be constructed differently with very different outcomes. Through a discussion of read alouds, picture reading, the generative possibilities of critical interventions, and a book-cum-newscast, this section demonstrates how approaching reading with translanguaging and multimodal orientations can nurture creativity, investment, and ownership of meaning-making, while generating more equitable power relations.

At the heart of nearly all Cheche sessions is at least one read aloud. Regardless of which language/s a book is written in, Cheche read alouds are always fluidly multilingual, with participants being free to make contributions in any language/s. Three or four keywords for each story are selected, translated by participants into Cheche's three main languages, and, after rich oral use in the contexts of stories, children write these words on the trilingual word wall. Participants collaboratively make interventions in texts, which can involve altering one part of the story and exploring how this can alter the whole course of the story, creating 'missing scenes' and developing prequels and/or sequels. Interventions and response activities are highly multimodal, involving oral discussion and narration, drawing, dramatizing, singing, writing, and creative play. While children's most familiar languages are their greatest resources when making creative and critical interventions, they delight in peppering their contributions with newly acquired vocabulary in less familiar languages, creating opportunities for authentic use of emergent language abilities and performing multilingual identities.

Read alouds socialize participants into the joys of books, while developing understandings that meaning is negotiable, interpretations are fluid, and that written texts represent but one perspective which we can challenge, add to, or alter. Meaning-making includes engaging with illustrations, embodied responses (e.g., leaping for joy, taking on a character's gait or facial expressions), and collaborative idea-generation. Texts written in less familiar languages become accessible through translanguaging, and participants experience meaningful, expressive language use untethered by the boundaries of named languages, while expanding their linguistic repertoires. Perhaps most importantly, readers develop dispositions of reading beyond the literal meaning of texts, they exercise the power to challenge the written word, and they imagine how texts can be transformed to represent alternative realities, perspectives, or interests.

When such multilingual, multimodal, interactive approaches to reading are nurtured and valued, it opens up space for creativity, learning, and identities of competence which are often stifled in mainstream schooling environments. One particular eight-year-old boy, Denis, was an especially enthusiastic participant in read alouds, which invited him into interactive relationships with texts. He became a prolific picture reader, narrating stories by reading illustrations, including dramatic dialogues between characters, vivid descriptions, and elegant story lines. While his peers were often fixated on written words, his eyes would scan the entire page, reading minute details of the illustrations and connecting them together to make insightful inferences and creatively author unique meanings. His picture reading granted him access to books in all languages. His narrations were in Kiswahili, his dominant language, with frequent interweavings of newly acquired Maa and English vocabulary. Denis was deeply invested in his literacy practices, claiming the power to take ownership over his own meaning-making.

Denis's creative approaches to reading stood in stark contrast to many other children's performances of their ideas of 'literacy'. Most children who had been to school would focus on the written text, haltingly sounding out words syllable by syllable, or silently moving their fingers across written words, frequently without comprehension or attention to meaning-making. Denis, who had not been to school, had not been subjected to the decontextualized decoding of exam-oriented literacy, leading me to question in my notes, "If [Denis] had been disciplined into institutionalized education, would he be able to do what he does?". Significantly, Denis's picture reading enabled "performance before competence" (Cazden, 1981), allowing him to courageously perform an identity as a competent reader even as his ability to read written words was still emerging. Certainly, Denis, with his exceptionally imaginative multimodal readings of books, was more successful in making meaning and more invested in the process than his written-word-fixated peers – an investment in texts that will propel his development of diverse literacies. Denis's approach to reading, with its excitement and fresh insights, inspired other children to become more attentive picture readers, leading to more empowered, insightful, and creative interactions with texts.

Often the fluid interactions with books and the claiming of power to re-version stories were generative of entirely new creations. In one circumstance, after participating in a read aloud of *Grandfather Twilight* by Barbara Berger, 14-year-old Neema decided that there were some things that the author did not explain properly. She set to work writing her own explanation of how this old man came to live a magical existence in the forest, responsible for putting the pearly moon up into the night sky each evening. What emerged was an emotional tale of a young boy, orphaned by tragedy, who was directed by the protective spirits of his late parents to find a sense of belonging and purpose amongst animal friends in the forest. Neema authored this story in Kiswahili, her dominant language, and later worked with a facilitator to strengthen it. She illustrated the full story, and, with my assistance, translated it into English, the language of instruction for her as a secondary school student and a challenging language for self-expression for her. When the printed version came out, she facilitated a read aloud of her bilingual, illustrated book. The children were active in asking her questions, and were fascinated by the idea that the author had left some things out that Neema needed to explain more fully. Neema's critical intervention would not have been possible in an English-only environment, as her emergent English proficiency without the support of her full linguistic and multimodal repertoire would have limited her comprehension of and critical engagement with the story. Neema's authorship of this *Grandfather Twilight* prequel and her sharing it with other children generated an enthusiasm amongst other children to author their own stories, and helped to demystify the process of authorship as something that they too are capable of doing.

The generative nature of empowered readership takes multimodal forms of authorship far beyond the bilingual writing, illustrating, and oral narrating demonstrated by Neema. One example of this is the collective re-versioning, re-semiotization,[1] and re-genre-ing of *Nyani Mtu*, by R. M. Zahor. *Nyani Mtu* is a Kiswahili book in which a monkey is turned into a human, gets married, and has human children, only to eventually transform back into a monkey and flee to the forest. A group of ten children read this book together, asking questions of the text, and engaging in frequently laughter-filled discussions of potential responses. As many of these children were new to Cheche and had little previous exposure to critical questions, it was important for a facilitator (in this case me) to act as a co-participant, and to engage alongside the children in asking genuine questions that she as reader is itching to explore. With a small amount of modelling, children's questions quickly shifted from asking (and rapidly answering) literal or vocabulary-oriented questions (e.g., the meaning of 'tweta') to more substantive, discussion-generating questions (e.g., 'How did the woman learn to read when she was changed into a human as an adult?'). These kinds of questions shifted the site of knowledge from the text to their own imaginations and critical capacities, bringing attention to ways in which texts are partial, incomplete, the result of decisions by an author to include certain information while leaving other issues unaddressed. Three girls collaboratively authored a sequel, which they read to the group. The group then asked these authors the same kinds of critical questions they had been asking of *Nyani Mtu*, pushing the authors' thinking forward about their own work.

We then discussed what a newscast might look like if such an incident were to take place in Monduli. The children suggested a newscast should begin with a brief history of this human-monkey, followed by interviews with various witnesses, and should be first set in the news studio then go out to the site. They set about assigning their roles, then dove directly into the newscast – with an audience of young children avidly taking in the whole news program with glee. The ensuing newscast demonstrated not only the actors' comprehension and memory of the story, but also a process of creative co-construction and re-semiotization of a new, living story, with dimensions, implications, and characters far beyond the contours of the original text. We heard from a studio reporter, an on-site reporter and interviewer (applying her question asking skills to her new professional role) and the human-monkey's husband, two children, and neighbour. The actors improvised first person accounts of the story, exploring backstory, emotions, and potential future courses of action, demonstrating a deep empathy with the characters. The case of the newscast dramatization illustrates how multimodal collaborative engagement with a text not only collectively empowers participants to creatively extend the meaning of the received text, but to experience stories and contents of books as living, changeable, and incomplete. These reader-authors exercised their own creative power by taking on diverse perspectives and multimodally co-constructing the storyworlds far beyond the scope of the author's and illustrator's original story. The translanguaging space allowed them to choose the linguistic resources which would most readily support their improvised dramatization, which in this case was mostly Kiswahili, in consortium with their gestures, facial expressions, intonation, and movements.

Re-centring the local: community-engaged knowledge production

In her study of Aboriginal perspectives on literacy, Jan Hare documents literacy practices of Anishinaabe elders and explores the challenges and imperatives of simultaneously learning the "whiteman's" teachings focussing on print literacy and traditional Aboriginal literacies (Hare, 2005). Certainly, in the Maasai community of Monduli, there is a sense of alarm that traditional literacies and knowledges, in addition to the Maasai language, are being lost, with many members of older generations pointing to schooling as a prime culprit (Shank Lauwo, 2020). Affirming the importance of traditional literacies and languages *alongside* school learning, Cheche Community Library's approach resonates with Lin's (2019, pp. 12–13) assertion:

> The aim of education is not to replace students' multiple and flexible communicative means (both linguistic and beyond linguistic) with school-valued codes or to construct a semiotic hierarchy privileging the school-recognized codes. Rather, teachers need to recognize that these different semiotics and social languages, although in tension, constitute a continuous holistic repertoire of the learner that is constantly expanding and changing through one's dialogic encounters with "otherness."

In order to embrace the "continuous holistic repertoire", Cheche strives to integrate both "school-valued codes" and local epistemologies and semiotic resources into a single space. Engagement with elders is an essential means of centring local knowledges. This engagement happens in a variety of ways, including through the encouragement of participants to spend time learning from their elders and to bring that learning back to Cheche, and through elders' direct involvement in Cheche activities.

Glory is one child who took up the invitation to interact with her grandmother and document her learnings. During her first few days at Cheche, Glory (a class six pupil) and her cousin "found themselves all the Maa books they could and were very *joyfully* reading together...They said they had never read Maa books before, not even a Bible" (field notes, January 19, 2016). "They had clear reactions of surprise and joy when we sang [in Maa], and joined in the singing" (field notes, January 20, 2016). After just a brief interaction with this translanguaging space, Glory went home with a piece of paper and an invitation to write a story told to her by an elder. The very next day, she returned with two stories that her grandmother told her in Maa and that she had written in Kiswahili, her predominant language of reading and writing. These were exceptionally well-written, particularly one story about a rabbit and a princess. The day after that, she returned with a Maa version of her beautiful rabbit story. She

Binti Mfalme alikuwa na Mjomba Kaka ambaye alitoroka nyumbani. Kila mara Binti Mfalme alijaribu kumkamata Mjomba Kaka lakini akashindwa. Ilikuwa ni vigumu kumkamata Mjomba Kaka.
The Princess had a Giant Lizard who had run away from home. Many times, the Princess had tried to catch the Giant Lizard, but each time she failed. It was impossible to catch the Giant Lizard.
Ore ina Entito Olkarsis neeta Olakwi niisik ninye tiang Olakwi. Ore Olakwi nerway aibung'a.

Figure 12.2 A page from Glory's trilingual book, *Sungura na Binti Mfalme/The Rabbit and the Princess/Enkitejo o Entito Okitok*.

announced that while she had done this collaboratively with her sister-in-law, they had not figured out an adequate translation for one word, 'amri', which she left a spot for in the Maa version. She read her bilingual story confidently and expressively, in response to which more children asked for paper so they too could write multilingual stories. Glory also requested more paper so she could write an English version with the support of her sister-in-law that evening. Over the next few weeks, her attendance was frequent in spite of a busy schedule at home, as we worked together to improve the Kiswahili version (involving fleshing out her written story to include details she narrated orally) and to write an English version, and she drew illustrations and wrote her biography for the back cover (see Figure 12.2).

When this trilingual book was printed and presented to Glory's school, together with another book by another pupil, the two author-illustrators were paraded to every class in the school by their mesmerized teachers. The Maa version generated particular excitement amongst their fellow students, as they had never encountered Maa being endorsed at school before. These books continue to be cherished additions to both the school library and Cheche Community Library, securing Glory's fame in the community as an author and an illustrator.

Excitement for the multilingual books of Glory and others quickly burst through the library's walls and out into the community. One middle-aged Maasai woman, Esta, became energized by her own prospects as an author after reading the children's books, saying, "I can do this too". Over the course of several weeks, she engaged an elderly man to tell her traditional Maasai stories as she tended the family shop. She filled two entire notebooks with these stories, which she wrote in both Maa and Kiswahili after listening to the elder's Maa narrations. Significantly, as a 44-year-old primary school graduate and mother of eight, Esta

Nemwo ilmurran aulo ukuni areshu endiamasi toieremeta. Nelotu endiamasi ore mbebau kutukaji neikene ndung'anak irura. Nejo endiamasi, "Shee?? Jatiakakii ndung'anak ilee. Je metii ilee!"

Vijana watatu walikwenda nje na mikuki kumsubiri mnyama. Mnyama alipofika mlangoni akawahesabu watu waliokuwa wanalala na akashangaa. "Mbona niliambiwa wapo sita?! Mbona ni upungufu wa hao sita?"

Figure 12.3 A page from Esta and Ali's bilingual book, *Oloyote loo Ilmurran wee Endiamasi/ Hadithi ya Vijana na Mnyama*.

had not previously been familiar with traditional Maasai stories, and had certainly never before written in her own language of Maa. Ali, the youth who illustrated Rama's book, created beautiful illustrations for several of these stories, and the books were printed (see Figure 12.3). Proud and composed, Esta shared her book about Endiamasi, a Maasai monster, with the children of Cheche, taking on the role of a teacher and showing great concern with educating these children about Maasai culture. The children, transfixed, eagerly asked questions, and Esta explained how these monsters, half human half metal, still exist in the forests, but have now moved further away due to increasing human settlement.

This process of authorship, involving the elder, Esta, Ali, as well as children as meaning makers, was catalysed by Esta's expanding imagination of her own capabilities as she interacted with Cheche participants' multilingual books. Investment in this process generated opportunities for intergenerational learning, a form of education which Esta's mother bemoans is being displaced by formal schooling (Shank, 2016). Tragically, before the books were printed, the elder passed away, but now his stories live on in the form of books and Esta's memories of his oral narrations. Certainly, this process generated community investment in a range of literacy practices, placing local knowledge at the centre, while supporting intergenerational learning and collaboration and expanding identities of power as authors, teachers, and knowledge producers.

Elders' direct involvement in the library also supports the grounding of literacy practices in local ways of being and knowing. Elders share stories and reflections on the past (and future!) with Cheche participants. This is facilitated by a fluid interweaving of both Maa and Kiswahili, with facilitators assisting with shuttling between languages to ensure that the elders' teachings are accessible to all. Orality is centred in these sessions, which frequently also include singing and lively questions from the children (in both Maa and Kiswahili). The incorporation of elders and local knowledges into the literacy practices of the library asserts possibilities for the coexistence of local knowledges and 'school knowledge'. It also pushes back against the tendency of schooling to privilege book learning and to teach students to look down upon local wisdom and knowledge, tendencies which *Education for Self-Reliance*, a 1967 Tanzanian policy document, sought hard to uproot (Nyerere, 1967/2004). The involvement of elders grants power to the local community, centring elders as knowers, teachers, and knowledge producers, and validates local semiotic and epistemological resources as essential aspects of the "continuous holistic repertoires" (Lin, 2019) that education must expand, not replace.

Conclusion

Through an exploration of multilingual authorship, changing relationships with literacies, and community-engaged literacy practices, this chapter demonstrates ways in which translanguaging and multimodality support participants' investment in learning and knowledge production, foster creativity, and support the authoring of new texts and meanings. The translanguaging space (Li, 2011b) cultivated throughout this study enabled learners whose abilities and identities of competence would be invisibilized in mainstream schooling to claim power as authors, readers, and knowers. By challenging monolingual ideologies and creating an environment embracing participants' full linguistic and semiotic repertoires, the translanguaging space validated participants' diverse identities and pre-existing cultural capital. This enabled participants to invest in the literacy practices of the learning centre, thereby opening themselves up to opportunities to expand their linguistic and semiotic repertoires and to explore expanded identity options. Learners' investment facilitated not only the development of language and literacy practices that are essential for success at school (e.g., English, reading and writing abilities), but also the claiming of agency to creatively author their own multilingual, multimodal productions.

Through fluid engagement with knowledge and stories in dynamic processes of translanguaging and re-semiotization, participants experienced stories as living, changeable, and incomplete. They learned to "recognise texts as selective versions of the world; they are not subjected to them and they can imagine how texts can be transformed to represent a different set of interests" (Janks, 2010, p. 22). Indeed, the process of authoring their own books helped to demystify the written word, highlighting ways in which books are authored by fallible human beings with their own perspectives and interests, and as such can be contested and altered. The process of authoring also served to generate new learning materials that reflect and thereby validate participants' own languages (including Maa, a language with scant educational resources), realities, and worldviews. As these children develop relationships with texts as negotiable and incomplete, they develop the practice of intervening in both texts and the world, being subjected to neither texts nor the status quo and claiming the power to imagine and author alternative futures.

Li (2011b, p. 1223) posits that translanguaging creates "a social space for the multilingual user by bringing together different dimensions of their personal history, experience and environment, their attitude, belief and ideology, their cognitive and physical capacity into one coordinated and meaningful performance". In this study, the translanguaging space supported learners to bring together diverse aspects of their identities and abilities "into one coordinated and meaningful performance", whereby their literacies and identities from various domains of their lives could be explored and expanded as a "continuous holistic repertoire" (Lin, 2019, p. 13). Reflecting the principles of Ubuntu translanguaging, the meaning-making practices explored in this study represent a "continuum of social, linguistic and cultural resources" (Makalela, 2015a, p. 214), through which languages and modes were experienced as interdependent and overlapping, and meaning was multiplied across people, languages and modes. Through validating diverse ways of knowing and of reading the world, these translanguaging practices assert the complementarity of different languages, literacies, and knowledges, and point to possibilities for school-valued codes and modes to coexist with a rich diversity of ways of being and knowing.

Glory's aunt once described the relationship between 'school knowledge' and Maasai language and culture thus: "[My daughter] stays with Swahili people there [at school], so she learns that of Swahili people there, and I teach her what is ours. So she will be combining, she knows traditions from there, and traditions from here" (quoted in Shank, 2016). Glory's aunt's understanding of the 'combining' of diverse traditions is related to what Walter Mignolo describes as "border thinking" (Mignolo, 2000) and the borderlands theory of Chicana scholar Gloria Anzaldúa. These borderland combinations move between various languages, modes, and epistemologies, but also beyond them, to create a space of newness, criticality, and transformation. Li Wei (2018) asserts that a translanguaging space acts as a Third Space, which "does not merely encompass a mixture or hybridity of first and second languages; instead it invigorates languaging with new possibilities from a site of creativity and power" (Li, 2018, p. 24). Indeed, the translanguaging space explored in this study affirmed existing identities and linguistic and semiotic repertoires, enabled the expansion of these identities and repertoires, but also opened possibilities for the generation of something new, something transformative.

The experiences of Cheche Community Library point to opportunities for such creative Third Spaces to flourish, supported by the affordances of translanguaging and multimodality. Operating in a context of low financial resources and sustained predominantly by the commitments of time and energy of community members, Cheche offers pedagogical approaches that have relevance for diverse multilingual contexts across Sub-Saharan Africa and beyond. As a community centre, Cheche has more freedom to innovate pedagogically than the curriculum- and policy-constrained environments of formal schooling. However, the insights derived in this space have important implications for mainstream schooling, pointing to the urgency of embracing learners' full linguistic, semiotic, and cultural resources in teaching and learning. The adoption of pedagogies of translanguaging and multimodality in mainstream schooling, in ways large and small, would offer opportunities to enhance investment, creativity, and authorship, while creating opportunities for increasing integration and cross-pollination between the worlds of school and home.

Glory's aunt, while embracing possibilities for 'combining', also acknowledges that sometimes when children "are taught the languages of other people [at school], they leave behind their language of Maa" (quoted in Shank, 2016). Indeed, the ideological environments of schools, often characterized by monolingual policies and intense pressure to succeed on standardized exams, can sometimes result in "replacing or denigrating [students'] existing ways of speaking" rather than "expanding their repertoire (of ways of speaking/thinking) as a whole" (Lin, 2019, p. 13). An ideological shift is needed in order to frame language and literacy learning as an expansion (rather than replacement) of linguistic and semiotic repertoires, and to position existing communicative practices and epistemological orientations as foundational resources in schooling. Initiatives that effectively implement translanguaging and multimodal pedagogies can be part of such an ideological shift, by expanding imaginations of what such pedagogies might look like and gradually contributing to their normalization. In order for translanguaging and multimodal pedagogies to be broadly taken up in mainstream schooling, the development of assessment practices that are multilingual and multimodal is a crucial next step that will play a critical role in further validating and giving weight to multilingual, multimodal abilities and encouraging translanguaging pedagogies. Regardless of context, learners' rich linguistic, semiotic, and cultural meaning-making repertoires offer foundational resources for knowing, learning, and knowledge production, and represent powerful assets in the service of invested learning, transformation and the creative authoring of more equitable futures.

Note

1 Re-semiotization refers to the movement of ideas across different semiotic modes, communicative practices, and contexts, resulting in the emergence of new meanings (Iedema, 2003).

References

Adami, E 2019, 'Multimodal sign-making in today's diversity: The case of Leeds Kirkgate Market', in A Sherris and E Adami (eds), *Making signs, translanguaging ethnographies: Exploring urban, rural and educational spaces*, Multilingual Matters, Bristol, pp. 36–54.

Blommaert, J 2014, *State ideology and language in Tanzania* (2nd ed.), Edinburgh University Press, Edinburgh.

Bourdieu, P 1991, *Language and symbolic power*, Harvard University Press, Cambridge, MA.

Brock-Utne, B 2005, 'The continued battle over Kiswahili as the language of instruction in Tanzania', in B Brock-Utne & RK Hopson (eds), *Languages of instruction for African emancipation: Focus on postcolonial contexts and considerations*, Mkuki na Nyota, Dar es Salaam, pp. 51–88.

Cazden, C 1981, "Performance before competence: Assistance to child discourse in the zone of proximal development," *Quarterly Newsletter of the Laboratory of Comparative Human Cognition*, vol. 3(1), pp. 5–8.

Darvin, R 2020, 'Creativity and criticality: Reimagining narratives through translanguaging and transmediation', *Applied Linguistics Review*, vol. 11(4), pp. 581–606.

Darvin, R & Norton, B 2015, 'Identity and a model of investment in applied linguistics', *Annual Review of Applied Linguistics*, vol. 35, pp. 36–56.

Freire, P 2007, *Pedagogy of the oppressed* (30th anniversary ed.), Continuum, New York.

García, O, & Li, W 2014, *Translanguaging: Language, bilingualism and education*, Palgrave Macmillan, Hampshire.

García, O & Li, W 2015, 'Translanguaging, bilingualism, and bilingual education', in W Wright, S Boun & O García (eds), *The handbook of bilingual and multilingual education*, John Wiley & Sons, West Sussex, pp. 223–240.

Hare, J 2005, 'To "know papers": Aboriginal perspectives on literacy', in J Anderson, M Kendrick, T Rogers & S Smythe (eds), *Portraits of literacy across families, communities, and schools*, Lawrence Erlbaum, Mahwah, NJ, pp. 243–275.

Iedema, R 2003, 'Multimodality, resemiotization: Extending the analysis of discourse as multisemiotic practice', *Visual Communication*, vol. 2(1), pp. 29–57. https://doi.org/10.1177/1470357203002001751

Janks, H 2010, *Literacy and power*, Routledge, New York.

Kress, G & van Leeuwen, T 2001, *Multimodal discourse*, Bloomsbury, London.

Lemke, J 1998, "Metamedia literacy: Transforming meanings and media", in D Reinking, L Labbo, M McKenna & R Kiefer (eds), *Handbook of Literacy and technology: Transformations in a post-typographic world*. Erlbaum, Hillsdale, NJ, pp. 312–333.

Li, W 2011a, 'Multilinguality, multimodality, and multicompetence: Code- and modeswitching by minority ethnic children in complementary schools', *The Modern Language Journal*, vol. 95(3), pp. 370–383. https://doi.org/10.1111/j.1540-4781.2011.01209.x

Li, W 2011b, 'Moment analysis and translanguaging space: Discursive construction of identities by multilingual Chinese youth in Britain', *Journal of Pragmatics*, vol. 43(5), pp. 1222–1235. https://doi.org/10.1016/j.pragma.2010.07.035

Li, W 2018, 'Translanguaging as a practical theory of language, *Applied Linguistics*, vol. 39, pp. 9–30.

Lin, AM 2019, 'Theories of trans/languaging and trans-semiotizing: Implications for content-based education classrooms', *International Journal of Bilingual Education and Bilingualism*, vol. 22(1), pp. 5–16. https://doi.org/10.1080/13670050.2018.1515175

Makalela, L 2015a, 'Moving out of linguistic boxes: The effects of translanguaging strategies for multilingual classrooms', *Language and Education*, vol. 29(3), pp. 200–217.

Makalela, L 2015b, 'Breaking African language boundaries: Student teachers' reflections on translanguaging practices', *Language Matters*, vol. 46(2), pp. 275–292.

Makalela, L 2015c, 'Translanguaging practices in complex multilingual spaces: A discontinuous continuity in post-independent South Africa', *International Journal for the Sociology of Language*, vol. 234, pp. 115–132.

McKinney, C & Tyler, R 2019, 'Disinventing and reconstituting language for learning in school Science', *Language and Education*, vol. 33(2), pp. 141–158. https://doi.org/10.1080/09500782.2018.1516779

McNiff, J & Whitehead, J 2011, *All you need to know about action research*, Sage, London.

Mignolo, W 2000, *Local histories/global designs: Coloniality, subaltern knowledges, and border thinking*, Princeton University Press, Princeton.

Nyerere, J 2004, 'Education for self reliance', in E Lema, M Mbilinyi & R Rajani (eds), *Nyerere on Education/Nyerere Kuhusu Elimu*, E&D Limited, Dar es Salaam, pp. 67–88.

Qorro, M 2008, 'A review of the literature on the language of instruction research in Tanzania', in M Qorro, Z Desai & B Brock-Utne(eds), *LOITASA: Reflecting on Phase I and entering Phase II*, E&D Vision, Dar es Salaam, pp. 27–59.

Shank Lauwo, M 2018, 'Power, literacy engagement, and polyphonic identities: Translanguaging in a Tanzanian community library', *Southern African Linguistics and Applied Language Studies*, vol. 36, pp. 133–146.

Shank Lauwo, M 2019, 'Ubuntu translanguaging and social justice: Negotiating power and identity through multilingual education in Tanzania', in N Avineri, LR Graham, E Johnson, R Riner & J Rosa (eds), *Language and social justice in practice*, Routledge, New York, pp. 88–96

Shank Lauwo, M 2020, 'Language ideologies in multilingual Tanzania: Parental discourses, school realities, and contested visions of schooling', *Journal of Multilingual and Multicultural Development*. https://doi.org/10.1080/01434632.2020.1760286

Shank, M 2016, 'Language education in Maasai Land, Tanzania: Parental voices and school realities'. Master's thesis, OISE, University of Toronto, Canada.

Siegel, M 1995, 'More than words: The generative power of transmediation for learning', *Canadian Journal of Education*, vol. 20(4), pp. 455–475. https://doi.org/10.2307/1495082

Stein, P 2008, 'Multimodal instructional practices', in J Coiro, M Knobel, C Lankshear, & D Leu (eds), *Handbook of research on new literacies*, Lawrence Erlbaum, New York, pp. 871–898

Uwezo 2019, *Are our children learning? Uwezo Tanzania learning assessment report*, Twaweza East Africa, Dar es Salaam.

13 Vignette

Creating multilingual resources as part of teacher education in Uganda

Cornelius Wambi Gulere and Kevin Kezabu Lubuulwa

Introduction

It is widely recognized that developing strong literacy skills and a love for reading lays the foundation for children's success both in and beyond school. This love is best cultivated in languages that are most familiar to children and through books about topics to which they can relate. These topics can then serve as a bridge to the development of content knowledge. However, in the context of Uganda, as in several other SSA countries, children who enter school need to develop an understanding of curricular concepts in both local languages and English. The language policy requires that early grade learners should be instructed in their mother tongue until Grade 4 in primary school, at which point English is formally introduced as the language of instruction. After this point, local languages continue to be taught as subjects throughout the primary curriculum, and they are often used informally in classrooms for communicating difficult concepts. In reality, though, there is a tendency to favour the use of English throughout schooling, even in the early grades. This is both due to a lack of teachers available to teach in local languages and to limited access to materials in these languages. In particular, teachers lack training in using the languages strategically for the purpose of learning through them.

The reliance on English in education, even at the primary level, makes local publishers reluctant to invest time and money in the creation of local language resources. This is also due to the low purchasing power of readers in SSA, the lack of demand for reading materials in indigenous African languages and the many languages in which resources need to be created. There is thus a need to find alternative means of creating multilingual resources for teaching content and under-published languages. The production of multilingual resources has been made easier by non-profit organizations such as African Storybook (ASb) and Pratham Books, who have created open license digital publishing models that make it possible for people to create, adapt, print and read stories on digital devices. These platforms host a range of open-source reading materials, and offer opportunities for further content creation through writing and translating so that communities who need resources can translate and/or create and then

DOI: 10.4324/9781003028383-16

share, adding to the repository. The majority of stories on ASb have been written by African authors, and mainly contain traditional folktales and contemporary stories as well as some poems and songs. All the stories are illustrated, either by professional illustrators or by the users themselves. Many of the stories have been checked for content and language through a peer review process, so that quality is ensured. ASb also collaborates with organizations doing similar work, such as Pratham Books' StoryWeaver, a digital repository of multilingual stories from India which has been extended to include resources in multiple languages, including indigenous languages that most publishers have no interest in. These storybook initiatives address the shortage of contextually appropriate books for early reading in the languages of Africa, so that increasingly more children can have the opportunity to read and enjoy books in their home languages.

This vignette describes a project which brought together student teachers and staff in teacher education programmes in Uganda to collaboratively create a collection of books in African languages, thus responding to the following challenges within the Ugandan education system:

1. The need to support teachers' language development so that they can deliver the curriculum in local languages, and
2. The need for teachers to develop writing, translation and digital publishing skills, so that they can create teaching materials in local languages.

The vignette provides insight into the challenges of this project, and how they were overcome, by looking into the reflections of the student teachers involved, which they wrote as part of their coursework. The vignette closes with recommendations for others endeavoring to create content for learning in local African languages.

The context of the project

This collaboration, led by one of the authors (Gulere), involved 350 student teachers and staff at the Faculty of Education and Arts at the Uganda Christian University, Mukono (UCU) and 45 student teachers at Bishop Willis Core Primary Teacher Training College of Kyambogo University (KY), Iganga, over a period of nine months between June 2017 and October 2019. The project was embedded as coursework within the teacher education programme for six cohorts of student teachers at these institutions. Student teachers learnt online digital publishing and translation skills to produce reading materials in their local languages as well as in English. These were both original texts and translations from existing as well as original texts. Original texts were mostly poems, songs and short stories. Courses included face-to-face elements like class workshops as well as communication over various social media platforms (email, Skype, Hangouts, WhatsApp and messaging). The student teachers were instructed on how to access and use the online resources to read, write, create and translate children's storybooks. The co-author (Lubuulwa) as an action researcher herself and online facilitator came in at the stage of writing this vignette as she felt strongly that this story needed to be told.

Most of the student teachers had never done any substantial writing in their local languages before. Though many speak these languages well, they were not confident in the orthographies and grammars of the languages. This confidence, however, grew during the course. Some were able to access orthographical support from their peer reviewers. All 26 languages used in the materials have some guidance with regard to orthography, though not all readily accessible at the time book creation was being done. When undertaking translations, student teachers had the freedom to choose which language and level they wanted to work with. At first, most opted for lower-level books that were simple and short. Over time, many of them moved onto more complex books whose subject matter was of personal interest and general appeal to their language community. Some of them also went on to author their own books for the database.

When translating, student teachers first produced a draft, and then they consulted a minimum of three other speakers of the language within the university, village and language community groups to improve the drafts (if translations were into English, only two local expert consultations were required). These peer reviewers provided support on language and style. After responding to the feedback, they published their storybook online. The platform administrators at ASb and StoryWeaver offered support in the publishing process, which afforded us all learning opportunities beyond the classroom.

In order for the books to count as coursework, student teachers had to submit a printed copy along with a reflective text on the process, challenges and lessons learned from the experience of creating the book. In assessing the storybooks, creativity and language were considered as well as feedback from peer reviewers, platform administrators and target readers in the community. Students' active participation in the online space also counted towards their coursework evaluation.

Through this initiative, more than 2000 storybooks have been created: 700 on StoryWeaver and 1500 on ASb. The books have been produced in 26 Ugandan languages (Ateso, Aga-Karimojong, Acholi, Alur, Dhopadhola, Kakwa, Kilundi, Kinyarwanda, Kiswahili, Kumam, Kup-Sabiny, Lubukusu, Lango, Luganda, Lugbarati, Lugwere, Lusoga, Lulamoogi, Lumasaaba, Lukhonzo, Runyoro, Rutooro, Runyankore, Rukiga, Rufumbira, Samia) as well as Yoruba and English. This project has thus substantially contributed to alleviating the book famine in Ugandan languages. Moreover, student teachers have developed their skills in reading, writing and publishing both in local languages and English, not to mention developments in their confidence and creativity.

Project challenges and successes

While the project has been successful in producing a number of resources in Ugandan languages, the project director and the student teachers also faced a number of challenges, detailed below, along with some of the solutions that arose.

One of the key hesitations expressed at the outset of the project was that participants did not have the required competencies in the local languages to be able to write and translate stories in these languages. As one student teacher expressed:

> Starting out to translate in my local language Runyoro, I knew it was going to be a daunting task because I have been exposed to an all English-speaking environment with less training in my own mother tongue, which made writing the local language a bit dreadful.

However, many of the student teachers found that working in the local languages got easier over time, and by working on this project, their competencies and confidence grew, for example:

> I gained the confidence to translate and my peer editors commended me for the great work. This made me happy because Kumam is not my mother tongue but it's one of two.

The student teachers found that their vocabulary in the local languages developed by taking part in the translation of books:

> I learnt new words especially in the books that I translated which had animals for example ... which I did not know some of their names in local language .... Books of level three, four, and five had very many hard and new words which increased my vocabulary ....

When the student teachers had difficulties with certain aspects of language, they learned to draw on the knowledge of others in their communities, for example, fellow students or lecturers at the university, other tribe members in the community or religious leaders who had been involved in translating the Bible into local languages. The reflections on being involved in the project gave the impression that their competence in African languages improved. As one noted, 'I have learnt how to write my language better and also pronounce.'

Not only did the student teachers develop their competence in local languages, but they also developed a stronger sense of the importance of these languages and an awareness of the need to sustain these languages through projects like this. They also came to realize that literacy in these languages, and not just English, was important for children, and that developing this literacy, and resources in local languages, was not as difficult as they had previously thought. As one student teacher noted:

> this experience has taught me to appreciate my mother tongue and make it a resolution that my own seeds must speak and write both the mother tongue of my wife to be and [me].

Overall, a sense of pride could be detected in the reflections about developing competencies in local languages and their role in creating resources in these languages. Some student teachers even noted that they were inspired to continue to write creatively in local languages:

> In this project, I have been inspired to become a writer and also be proud of my mother tongue because it is important for everyone to know how to speak their local language in order to communicate better.

The project helped to change people's attitudes to local languages by giving them more exposure to and practice in them. Through this, the student teachers developed a sense of responsibility for maintaining their languages and also inspiration to write creatively and engage in translation.

While many of the student teachers had positive attitudes towards the project, they also noted considerable challenges. One of the most obvious challenges was technical difficulties. There were only a limited number of computers available to work on, and accessing and using the required programmes was not always easy and required training, trial and error and persistence. Failures in electricity or the wireless network would sometimes cause frustrating setbacks. As one student teacher noted, 'technical aspects slowed down and sometimes discouraged the content creators and readers.' Despite these frustrations, the student teachers were proud when they completed their texts and translations and happy to have made a significant contribution to the growing repository of books.

Another challenge was time. Student teachers noted that translations took longer than was originally expected. As one student teacher noted, 'we were working under pressure since we had a lot of work to do besides translating books.' Some reported a significant commitment to the project, having worked from early morning until late in the evening. They also had to rely on colleagues and other community members to support with the translations, and they noted that this was often difficult because of time constraints.

Frustrations were also felt because, despite the significant time investment needed to work on the local language materials, not all members of staff at the teacher education institutions supported this project. Some argued that it was too time consuming or that it was not suitable for coursework. Other staff also turned down students' requests to act as peer reviewers. One student teacher notes:

> During my end of year appraisal I stated [that working on this project was] my greatest achievement but was advised to drop it and instead concentrate on the traditional teaching methodologies. I agreed, but on that same day, that evening, my lecturer got a letter announcing that our community service project had won the coveted community service grant award for 2017.

The fact that the project was valued by the community went a long way towards validating the student teachers' work on the project, who were pleased that not only did they gain a sense of self-satisfaction, but their work was also recognized publicly.

Recommendations

Our recommendations for others embarking on other similar projects is to keep in mind that, although such projects may depart from the traditional teacher education curriculum and be marked by technical challenges, they result in positive outcomes both for the student teachers involved and the children at school. Teacher education institutions should therefore embrace such projects as a means of fostering local language use and education, as the student teachers involved are also more prepared for using local languages in their teaching. To make such projects sustainable and to ensure that the resulting materials reach early readers at school, it is important to engage with a range of stakeholders, e.g. faith-based organizations, family and village community members, local language boards, local language experts, National Curriculum Development Centers and universities. Such projects for developing local language literacies and producing local language resources can be adapted by other universities and education organizations, not only in teacher education but also disciplines such as creative writing and journalism. Involving student teachers in the production of tangible resources strengthens their abilities and confidences, and also makes their education more authentic and practical. Overall, this project has been able to address to some extent the children's book famine in Ugandan local languages. It has made humble contributions to sparking a love for learning and reading in African languages, alleviating the shortage of reading material in these languages, and stimulating interest and enhancing mastery in these languages. Many student teachers, parents, local leaders and children have commended its results. The intensity of its methodology requires much time and many players working in partnership to lobby and act. There were challenges along the way; however, our experience has shown that these challenges are worth facing, and, when persistent, can be overcome.

Acknowledgements

The authors are grateful to the following supporters of this project: African Storybook Team SA, the Hewlett Foundation, the Neil Butcher Foundation SA, Story Weaver ICT Team IN, the Uganda Christian University Community Service, the Uganda Community Libraries Association, and student teachers and staff in the Faculty of Education and Arts at the Uganda Christian University and at Bishop Willis Core Primary Teacher Training College of Kyambogo University at Iganga UG as well as all of the students who gave their time to writing and translating stories.

Links to some of the stories created on StoryWeaver are given below.

Agnes Kabonesa: https://storyweaver.org.in/users/15391-agnes-kabonesa

Cornelius Gulere: https://storyweaver.org.in/users/44646-cornelius-wambi-gulere

Ekiyakia Ezekiel: https://storyweaver.org.in/users/21773-ekiyakia-etatai

Juliet Zawedde Namutooro: https://storyweaver.org.in/users/21587-juliet-zawedde-n

Maurice Lamony: https://storyweaver.org.in/users/15584-maurice-lamony

Yobu Mwesigwa Magada: https://storyweaver.org.in/users/127509-yobu-mwesigwa-magada

14 Processes of pedagogic change

Integrating subject and language learning through teacher education

Angeline M. Barrett, Zawadi Richard Juma and Francis William

Introduction

There is a substantial and growing body of research arguing for multilingual educational practices in multilingual societies (Wright et al., 2015). These arguments are evidenced by small to medium scale classroom research, involving qualitative observation of classrooms, interviews or larger surveys with teachers and, less frequently, consultation with learners (Cenoz, 2017). The research evidence has been collected from diverse multilingual contexts, ranging from the city states of East Asia (Lin & He, 2017), hyperdiverse cities of Europe (Duarte, 2018), and, pertinently for this edited book, diverse rural and urban landscapes of low- and middle-income countries within sub-Saharan African (Msimanga & Lelliot, 2014; Probyn, 2015; Terra, 2021) and across the Global South (see for example contributions to Shoba & Chimbutane, 2013; Coleman, 2017). Taken individually, the studies are small and context-specific in their conclusions. Cumulatively, they provide a robust evidence base for the potential of bilingual or multilingual educational practices to promote inclusive quality education, as this volume illustrates. It is harder to find evidence on how to take multilingual education (MLE) to scale. Yet, in many formerly colonized countries that use a European language as the language of instruction (LOI) within the state education system, this is precisely the challenge.

Lack of evidence on scale up is not specific to MLE. Samoff et al. (2013) over many years developed a review of scale up of education initiatives in sub-Saharan Africa. They found very few examples of successful innovation going to scale. More often, projects, which were extraordinarily successful at improving the quality of education in a specific place and time, faltered when ministries attempted to scale them. This does not bode well for using the evidence basis from numerous successful but mostly small-scale initiatives to influence national policy in the direction of MLE across an education system. There are, as Samoff et al. (2013) point out, many understandings of 'going to scale.' Most commonly it is understood as replicating a small pilot at the system-level. Here, however, we are interested in the process by which concept and practices of a pedagogic innovation are shared across education institutions. We are concerned in particular with

DOI: 10.4324/9781003028383-17

teacher education institutions, which we argue should be viewed as a "fulcrum for change" (Stuart, 2002). Teacher educators are well-positioned to influence large numbers of student teachers at the start of their careers. They are expected to be pedagogic experts who engage in school-based research, most especially those based in university departments of education. Further, they are networked into schools, not least via their students, whose training includes a few weeks posted to a school for teaching practice placements. Hence teacher educators' own theories of learning and how they communicate and model these for student teachers are central to scale up:

> pedagogical renewal does depend largely on teacher development .... But just as student learning is significantly determined by the quality of teaching (of teachers by extension), teacher development (conceived as teacher learning) is in part determined by the quality of the learning opportunities which teachers (prospective, beginning and experienced) engage in. The quality of such learning opportunities is, in turn, determined in part by the quality of the designers and facilitators, that is, teacher educators and trainers.
>
> (Dembélé & Lefoka, 2007, p. 547)

The Language Supportive Teaching and Textbooks (LSTT) project in Tanzania capitalized on the positional advantages of teacher educators to develop and disseminate a pedagogic approach which draws on bilingual strategies to strengthen science and mathematics teaching and learning at the lower secondary level. It did so by bringing teacher educators together in cross-disciplinary teams of science or mathematics and language specialists to reflect on and revise their own practice through a lesson-study approach to professional inquiry. In this chapter, we set out the background to the project and briefly outline the nature of the pedagogic innovation it developed before explaining the process of collaborative professional inquiry through which it was scaled up from one to five institutions. We finish by highlighting the essential elements of the process of professional learning and draw out implications for the design of scale up of MLE. Critical features of the process point to the importance of collaborative professional learning for endogenous innovation that is directed towards ongoing inquiry and innovation rather than replicating an ideal practice.

Background to LSTT

In Tanzania, state primary education, which enrols a large majority of students and is the only available provision in most rural areas, uses Kiswahili as the LOI, whereas English is used in all secondary schools (Sumra & Rajani, 2006). For most students, the transition in LOI is abrupt and challenging and this has been observed to impede science learning (Mwinsheikhe, 2009; Juma, 2015). Distinctive features, therefore, of LOI transition in Tanzania are that it occurs after seven years of education and, by this point, a large majority of learners are fluent in an African language, in this case the national language Kiswahili.

Whilst language in education researchers have advocated a change in policy for four decades (Tibategeza & du Plessis, 2012), the implemented policy has not altered (Ministry of Education, Science and Technology, 2018). Meanwhile, in the last ten to fifteen years lower secondary education has expanded rapidly and Tanzania now has a policy of universal secondary education. During Phase 1 of LSTT (2013–2016) researchers at the University of Dodoma, including teacher educators, collaborated with the University of Bristol to develop learning materials. This initial research was initiated by a request from the government authority responsible for curriculum development, Tanzania Institute of Education (TIE), which was also a partner in the Phase 1. In 2013, TIE had newly been granted a remit to publish textbooks and so, suggested a project focused on textbooks in science, mathematics and English, which were viewed by government as priority subjects. The project developed, piloted and evaluated learning materials for three subjects, English, biology and mathematics that were accessible to learners with low levels of English fluency and aimed to develop language proficiency as an integral part of subject teaching. An excerpt from these materials is included in Clegg and Milligan (this volume; see also Mtana & O-saki, 2017).

Following this first phase of research, in 2016, the team at the University of Dodoma were keen to see the pedagogic approach of their materials introduced into schools. However, at that time the University of Dodoma was scheduled to deliver a 'Special Diploma' to an anticipated intake of 9000 students, graduates from four years of lower secondary education. This represented an almost tenfold increase in science education students on the numbers the University typically enrolled on the existing B.Ed. programme as well as a qualitative change in the educational level of the students. The demands of this one-off teaching programme limited the capacity of the LSTT team to conduct a large research and professional development project in schools. The 'Special Diploma' did, however, appear to offer an opportunity to introduce language supportive pedagogy (LSP) to a large number of student teachers. The team, therefore, turned their attention to their own teacher education programmes and their own practice as teacher educators. They also invited a neighbouring private university, St. John's University of Tanzania to collaborate in the project. Before the project had started most of the 7000 students initially enrolled on the Special Diploma intake were transferred by the Ministry of Education to three teachers colleges. These three teachers colleges were duly invited to collaborate in Phase 2 of LSTT. The obligatory transfer prompted large numbers of students to leave the programme. In total, across the two universities and three teachers colleges and across the Special Diploma and Bachelors in Science Education programmes, LSTT reached around 5700 mathematics and science student teachers. In 2018, the Ministry of Education reported that there were 6305 students training in science and mathematics in education (Ministry of Education, Science and Technology, 2018, p. 33). During its project lifetime therefore, Phase 2 of LSTT reached an estimated 90% of mathematics and science student teachers in the country.

Both phases of the project were funded through the Partnership for Strengthening Innovation and Practice in Secondary Education (PSIPSE), a funding collaboration of three North American-based trust funds. Each of the authors played a leading role in the project. The chapter is the product of our considered reflection on the programme. This included a review of project documents, including reports compiled by small teams of teacher educators, who collaborated to integrate language supportive theory and practice into their units, reports by teacher educators assessing students' teaching practice during placements in secondary schools and reports on professional development workshops conducted with teachers in schools and other teacher educators towards the end of the project lifetime.

Language supportive pedagogy for secondary school science

Clegg and Milligan (this volume) outline the main features of LSP for schools (see also Barrett et al., 2014; Barrett & Bainton, 2016; Mtana & O-saki, 2017). In their vignette, members of the LSTT team, Rubagumya et al. (in this volume), describe the central features of LSP for teacher education in Tanzania as it was developed in Phase 2. Here, we focus on the process through which this approach was developed and scaled up and only discuss briefly the features of the pedagogic approach. In borrowing techniques from modern foreign language teaching and integrating them into science and mathematics subjects, this approach has features in common with Content-Language Integrated Learning (CLIL) (Coyle, 2007). It has been developed through a collaboration between linguists, including those with language education expertise, and science educators. In some respects, the pedagogic approach is similar to *Baseline*, an English for Subject Learning large-scale project conducted in Tanzania by the British Council. *Baseline* designed and implemented a six-week 'pre-Form one' English language course for primary school graduates preparing for secondary school (Mkonongwa& Komba, 2018). To develop capacity for its delivery within Tanzania, *Baseline* recruited English language teaching experts from outside Tanzania and posted them to teachers colleges, including two of the three teachers colleges that partnered in LSTT Phase 2. There are many other examples in the literature of external language experts conducting professional development with science teachers in schools (see for example contributions to Tang and Danielsson, 2018). However, within Tanzania, the collegial collaboration of science and language experts was, to our knowledge, novel. Within secondary schools, English teachers' role in supporting students' language development is limited to teaching the English syllabus. In tertiary institutions, English for academic purposes is delivered as a separate unit of study, known as Communication Skills, that is compulsory for all students and delivered by language specialists, with no support from subject specialists (Komba & Mohamed, 2017). LSTT was not novel therefore in drawing on language expertise to strengthen science and mathematics education. Rather its novelty rests on the way that it drew on the expertise that already existed on the staff of teacher education institutions and sought to deepen this expertise through a process of collegial collaborative inquiry as an approach to integrating features of MLE in a monoglossic policy context. The University of Bristol, UK, was a partner in the project; its role mainly involved project design and management and not the provision of technical or pedagogic expertise.

Bringing language and science educators together to reflect on and improve their courses and programmes brought their different educational theories into conversation. Language education in Tanzania is influenced by the cognitivist tradition that views additional language learning as a cognitive process of internalising the linguistic system of a language with a target of native-like fluency (Valdés et al., 2015). It focuses on learning the grammatical rules and patterns of the language and hence, there is an emphasis on modelling and correcting grammar, syntax and pronunciation. This approach is grounded in a monoglossic view of languages as fixed, homogeneous independent units. It assumes bilingualism to be a form of parallel monolingualism, whereby the bilingual person is either speaking in one language or the other (Flores & Beardsmore, 2015). A longstanding frustration for secondary school English teachers in Tanzania is that their efforts to model the rules and patterns of English are continuously undermined by colleagues teaching other subjects, who use non-standard English with inaccurate grammar, spelling and pronunciation (Qorro, 2009).

Science teacher educators within the project teams in both the universities and the teachers' colleges were influenced by constructivist theories of learning, which underpinned earlier science education projects in Tanzania (e.g. Ottevanger et al., 2005). Constructivist theories of learning recognize that learners build on preexisting knowledge, making it important for teachers to elicit and challenge students' 'misconceptions' (Cakir, 2008). In other words, articulating prior understanding is part of the process of making sense of and learning to articulate new concepts. Social constructivism, influenced by Vygotsky, emphasizes the role of language and social interaction in mediating the learning process and hence learning science involves learning the formal scientific language of scientists (Scott et al., 2007). From research piloting and evaluating learning materials in secondary schools during Phase 1 (Barrett et al., 2014), as well as team member's experience as teacher educators, regularly visiting schools, we knew that secondary science teachers in Tanzania share a broad-based consensus that good teaching engages learners in dialogue, discussion, observation of the natural world around them, laboratory demonstrations and practical experimentation.

However, science educators in many schools serving disadvantaged areas are just as frustrated as their English teaching colleagues. This is because their students do not respond to attempts to engage them in discussion through the medium of the English (Mwinsheikhe, 2009). Students do, of course, have prior knowledge of school science and the natural world, knowledge that during their primary education they articulated in Kiswahili. They may also be used to discussing their informal observations of the natural world in an ethnic community language. In the terminology of Rubagumya et al. (this volume), familiar knowledge is encoded in a familiar language. To work around this, science teachers commonly improvise bilingual strategies, translating key points and instructions into Kiswahili, or more simply, default to teaching entirely in Kiswahili (Barrett et al., 2014). This can leave teachers with a sense that their practice is illegitimate because it contravenes Tanzania's monoglossic language policy. Whilst these approaches may well build on students' understanding of the science curriculum, it does not develop their ability to talk and write about scientific ideas in English. As research on assessment and language in Zanzibar has shown, secondary school students frequently cannot demonstrate their knowledge of science in national examinations, which are conducted in English (Rea-Dickins et al., 2009).

The 50 teacher educators in the LSTT project were already influenced by a constructivist view of learning and the sociocultural view that learning is not just an individual process but a socially and historically situated one (Farnsworth et al., 2016). It was not difficult for them to appreciate and accept a sociolinguistic description of learning in a second language as an iterative process of shifting back and forth between the informal registers of students' 'thinking language' and the formal, or in Halliday's (1993) terms 'scientific' registers, of the target language (see also Lemke, 1990). Guzula et al. (2016) describe this as a movement between exploratory talk and presentational talk or "written-like language" (p. 214), where the former is associated with building understanding and explaining (McKinney & Tyler, 2019). 'Code switching' between an African and European language is a feature of Tanzanian science and mathematics classrooms, as it is in other African schools (Clegg & Afitska, 2011; Msimanga & Lelliot, 2014; Probyn, 2015). However, as Setati et al. (2002) observed in rural South African schools, the transition from expressing prior knowledge in a familiar language to articulating scientific concepts accurately (both scientifically and linguistically) in formal English is for many learners a broken, incomplete learning journey.

The pedagogic approach developed by LSTT drew on insights from both constructivism and the cognitivist approach. Students were given time to process new scientific concepts in their familiar language and encouraged to relate them to their preexisting knowledge through various strategies that ranged from giving the Kiswahili translation of key subject specific vocabulary (a quick way to orientate students by signalling the relevant previous learning from primary school) through to exploratory practical activities. Allowing time for students to express and discuss their ideas in a familiar language is also key (Probyn, 2015; Barrett & Bainton, 2016). Most commonly the 'familiar language' students chose for discussion was Kiswahili. However, students are free to use a community language or translanguage (García & Wei, 2015). Students are then encouraged and supported to report the conclusion of their discussion in English. Being non-prescriptive about the language students used in small group discussion and tolerant of stumbling English that is "hesitant and incomplete" in classroom dialogue (Barnes, 2008, p. 5, quoted in Moate, 2010, p. 41) increased their confidence to start talking and expressing their ideas in class. At the same time, the approach provided structured support for developing the vocabulary and practising the grammatical rules and patterns associated with secondary school science through using strategies that are commonplace in modern foreign language classrooms such as role-play, fill the blank, sentence starters and vocabulary lists. In this way science teaching reinforces the learning of grammar covered primarily in English lessons, whilst building subject-specific vocabulary and supporting students to gain proficiency in the subject-specific genres of writing used in secondary school science. Explicit attention to pronunciation is also a feature of LSP through consistent correction of mispronunciations. This all requires creating an affirmative classroom climate, where students feel safe to take risks, practise speaking in English without fear of humiliation and share their ideas about science in whichever language they are most comfortable. Teachers need to practise a degree of consistency in correcting linguistic errors, particularly recurring errors, without slipping into pedanticism that distracts from rather than supports science learning.

When running workshops with teachers and teacher educators, we have found that it is commonly assumed that LSP is about allowing teachers to use Kiswahili. The focus, however, is firmly on students' use of language and their learning journey from being primary school-level scientists who talk about science in Kiswahili to being lower secondary school scientists, able to express key concepts in scientific English and apply those concepts within the multilingual world beyond the school gate (Barrett & Bainton, 2016). We hesitate to use the term 'bilingual,' first because this can be perceived as contravening the implemented monolingual LOI policy and second because our approach only aims to develop formal reading and writing skills in one language, English.

Implementing language supportive pedagogy in teacher education

The LSTT project shifted from its first phase of developing learning materials to the second phase of implementation in teacher education for pragmatic and opportunistic reasons explained above. Shifting activity to teacher education posed two challenges. First, only the team at the University of Dodoma had been involved in Phase 1 and so the concept of LSP was new to most other team members. Second, team members were clear from the outset that it was not enough to teach about LSP but that teacher educators should also model the pedagogy through their own teaching with the student teachers. This involved not only adapting the approach to different educational levels but also to a very different type of subject, namely education. The project needed to develop a methodology for scale up that was both a process of professional learning and a process of inquiry and ongoing innovation. Hence, the process of scale up was a process of collaborative professional learning, as Dembélé and Lefoka (2007) have argued it should be. Drawing inspiration from previous research within Tanzania (Eriksson & Osaki, 2018), we adapted the lesson-study methodology for collaborative professional inquiry. Lesson study originated in Japan, where in large schools the same lesson will be delivered several times to different class groups (Doig & Groves, 2011). A team of teachers collaboratively designed a lesson plan for the first lesson and then progressively refined this each time the lesson is taught. Improvements are based on feedback from observers in the team and data collected from a small number, typically around three, case study students, who are observed in class and who may be briefly interviewed after the lesson. Lesson study has since been adapted for various contexts.

Subject-teaching methods courses were the obvious starting point for introducing the theory and practice of LSP. These units of study are taken midway through the undergraduate- and diploma-level teacher education programmes. They focus on subject-specific pedagogy for one subject. For example, the Mathematics Teaching Methods course includes learning theories, lesson planning and assessment design specific to secondary school mathematics. The courses typically end with two sessions of micro-teaching, in which small groups of students take turns to demonstrate to their peers a short lesson they have planned.

In our adaptation, the collaborating teams of teachers consisted of a mix of subject and language specialists. Each included two or three subject specialists responsible for course delivery, one or two language specialists from the same institution and around two visitors from other institutions in the project, who joined the team once or twice in a semester and were involved in delivering a very similar course in their own institution. In this way the constitution of teams allowed for sharing of expertise across disciplines and institutions whist having the necessary flexibility to accommodate team members, who have full teaching timetables in their own institution and may have to travel for a full day to visit another institution. The science or mathematics tutors, who owned the course, led on lesson planning and delivery. However, between three and five sessions out of the fifteen that made up the course, were planned and evaluated collaboratively. Data were collected from five case study students during and immediately after these sessions. Some teams also conducted a short test at the beginning and the end of the course to measure changes in students' views on bilingual education or their ability to express scientific knowledge in English. At the end of the semester, each team collated a report detailing changes to the course, lesson delivery and findings from the five student case studies. Although a single lesson was not immediately repeated, as in the original Japanese model, as different institutions delivered very similar courses at different times in the year, insights that developed out of lesson study of a course in one institution could inform its implementation in another. In this way, the University of Dodoma shared the concepts and some of the teaching strategies they had developed during Phase 1, with four other teacher education institutions. Tutors at the two teachers colleges, which had been involved in the earlier British Council *Baseline* project, shared their repertoire of interactive strategies. At the same time, however, innovation was an ongoing process with new ideas and practices being developed for teacher education.

During the project lifetime, teams completed two lesson-study cycles. The major change reported within cycle one was a shift from mainly using 'lecture method' to more interactive sessions. Teaching sessions incorporated group discussion and presentations on education content (e.g. forms of assessment in biology) from groups of students or micro-teaching. Students were given readings in advance of the session, which were then discussed in class. The lesson would close with feedback from a language specialist on language use, which frequently focused on explicit correction of grammatical errors and mispronunciations that had recurred in the lesson. Explicit attention to pronunciation, grammar and vocabulary became the established and accepted norm throughout lessons with subject teachers paying particular attention to scientific or education vocabulary. In their micro-teaching demonstrations, students also explicitly addressed vocabulary, used demonstrations, initiated class discussion and, in some sessions, provided structured support for reading and writing. In the first year, participating teacher educators reported that collaboration through lesson study was demanding on their time but the cooperative approach to problem-solving and sharing of expertise across subject and language specialists generated an enthusiasm around their teaching that had not existed previously. Both language and subject specialists deepened their understanding of the language demand of their subjects and together developed strategies to support students to practice talking, reading and writing in English. Colleagues were regularly talking with each other about their teaching and in so doing, reflecting on the design and delivery of their courses and trying out curricular and pedagogic changes that would give students greater opportunity to develop as teachers.

The adapted lesson-study approach was dynamic. It transformed our two-dimensional plans for scaling up the implementation of LSP into a multidimensional open-ended process of pedagogic development conducted by an expanding cross-institutional community of practice (Farnsworth et al., 2016). The reports each team produced, showed how they usually started with basic ideas about LSP. These focused on the strategic use of Kiswahili in student discussion combined with attention to language through ensuring understanding of subject specialist vocabulary, modelling use of simple accessible grammatically accurate English and consistent affirmative correction of grammatical errors and mispronunciation (see Rubagumya et al.'s vignette for further detail). From this basis, however, lesson-study teams took their inquiries in different directions. The Chemistry Teaching Methods group at the University of Dodoma in their second cycle, explored the relationship between conceptual learning and language proficiency. The Physics team developed an interest in how practical demonstrations and experiments support conceptual learning and subgenres of writing used in laboratory reports and scientific inquiry. The Biology group, which was contending with large class sizes of 260, experimented with using micro-teaching to deliver nearly all components of the course. This involved them providing coaching to teams of two or three students, who collaboratively prepared a micro-teaching demonstration, and then engaging the rest of the class in critical discussion. Hence, they turned micro-teaching into a strategy to simultaneously develop students' language proficiency for teaching, subject knowledge and pedagogical knowledge and skills.

Team members' understanding of LSP deepened considerably as over two years of repeated lesson-study cycles, they became more engaged with the theory behind LSP and its implementation became increasingly routine. The most detailed lesson-study reports were, inevitably, produced by teams at the University of Dodoma, who had been working with and developing the concept of LSP and its practice the longest. It was here that researchers were more ambitious in changing their practice and most systematic in evidencing the change in student learning. Over two years, their attention shifted from the language skills to the pedagogic skills of the students. Reports from the Teachers Colleges were much less detailed as may be expected as college tutors, who are not expected to conduct independent research as part of their job. More frequent visits and mentoring from team members might well have facilitated the further development of research skills and more detailed engagement with the theory of LSP. However, college tutors were quick to grasp the core principles of LSP. In putting these into practice, they drew on their existing repertoire of interactive teaching and learning strategies.

College or university-based courses are just the first step in student teachers' training. Very quickly tutors became concerned with how to support their students during the crucial period of teaching practice, when they are placed in a school and teach a full timetable for a period of six weeks. The student teachers were scattered to schools around the whole country, where they would attempt to implement in school classrooms the teaching methods they had learned in university and college lecture halls. Two weeks after the students' departure, their tutors were likewise scattered around the country, visiting students in schools for a half day of supervision and observation. The two universities, which have greater autonomy over their curriculum, revised their processes to maximize the potential for mentoring during these brief visits. They took time to discuss and if necessary revise lesson plans with students before a lesson was observed and to discuss their observations with them after the lesson. The observation instrument was also revised to explicitly address language supportive features. In these discussions, student teachers demonstrated consistent attention to their students' use of language. Students provided specific examples of how they supported their secondary school students with learning vocabulary, checked their understanding of key terms and were constantly monitoring their own speech to ensure they were modelling accurate use of language. As one of the University of Dodoma student teachers explained:

> I used LSP [Language Supportive Pedagogy]. Sometimes, I translated in Kiswahili; I allowed them to discuss some issues in Kiswahili. I asked them to define some concepts and asked some students to say what it meant in Kiswahili...I asked them to discuss some concepts in Kiswahili and asked them to say what they found in English, I supported them to say what they failed to say in English.

Student teachers also commented on how their students and fully qualified colleagues at the teaching placement schools responded to their practice:

> One day, I entered class after History class and I found some History notes on the board. Because students know that I help them to understand some language issues as I teach, they asked me to tell them the meaning of a word from the History notes on the board.

However, reactions from staff were not always favourable:

> Teachers here were surprised seeing us teaching English. They considered us wasting time to teach English, they wanted us to quickly chip in making calculations with students.

The logistics of assessing students' teaching practice across a large country meant that teacher educators visited students from across subject disciplines, including non-science students. It was at this point that the University of Dodoma team observed that several humanities students also demonstrated and talked about their use of LSP, despite none of their university courses being included in the LSTT project. The tutors surmised that students from different subject disciplines in the same placement school collaborated on lesson planning and shared ideas. In the second year of Phase 2, teacher educators used the teaching practice visits as an opportunity to explain to school leaders the logic behind the LSP. This was intended to build support within the schools for the students' practice of LSP. In some instances, it led to requests from schools for workshops for their permanent staff.

The lesson-study collaborative approach made every participant in the project a leader of the initiative in their own lecture hall or classroom, as was evidenced in the lesson-study reports. With leadership came a sense of ownership and a commitment to promote and disseminate the approach. In total around 50 teacher educators from the five participating institutions were involved in lesson-study teams. However, the reach of the project went further as those participants shared their new-found expertise with colleagues within their institution, insisting that all teacher educators should be exposed to LSP. Members of the core team of 50 also conducted workshops with secondary school teachers in collaboration with four separate secondary education quality improvement projects in Tanzania. The universities had a high degree of autonomy over their course design and curriculum compared to the teachers colleges. Hence, they were able to implement more wide-ranging changes, including changes to assessment to include examination questions related to LSP. The teachers colleges, however, emphasized the need for institutional change and demanded workshops to introduce LSP to all members of teaching staff. They were also keen to share the approach with their partner schools and involved their students in this activity, for example by inviting students to conduct lesson demonstrations in partner schools. The teacher educators participating in the language supportive project had become champions for LSP spreading the theory and classroom strategies through their existing networks.

The authors of this chapter have in common a background in science education. None of us claimed expertise in language education before engaging in the project and so we count ourselves amongst the participants, who have come to fuller understanding of how language is inextricably intertwined with science and mathematics learning. When teaching second language learners, who are navigating a change in the LOI midway through their basic education, the interdependencies of language and science learning have their own dynamic. Sometimes it involves eliciting and making connections to common-sense knowledge articulated in a familiar language. However, eliciting and connecting to scientific knowledge expressed in the registers of primary school science is equally important. We have expanded our repertoire of strategies for supporting students to read, write and articulate their ideas about science in English and have a strong appreciation of the value of learning resources matched to students' language ability and subject-language demand being placed in the hands of teachers and learners. One of the most significant steps we have taken as a community of teacher educators is to switch from viewing language in education as an insoluble policy problem beyond our domain of expertise to approaching it as a pedagogic problem relevant to all of us. As such, it is firmly within our domain of expertise and through conversation with our language education colleagues we can take steps to strengthen learning despite the policy context.

We do not yet know to what extent the enthusiasm generated in the last three years will be sustained or whether the spread of the innovation through networks that link teacher education institutions and schools will continue. However, the practice has to varying degrees, been institutionalized within the five participating teacher education institutions. Curriculum changes to subject methodology units in the Bachelors in Science Education programmes of the two universities have been approved and assessments modified. These courses now include content on recognizing and using language supportive materials, designing activities that develop understanding of science concepts along with developing the language skills to write about them. Seminar time has been extended or lecture time displaced by interactive teaching and micro-teaching. Inquiry into and take up of LSP has spread beyond the project boundaries. LSP has been introduced into a Kiswahili teaching methods and a nurse education course. Bachelors and masters students, who have no direct connection to LSTT are undertaking dissertation studies on LSP. Communications Skills tutors have an awareness of the language demands of science subjects and education programmes. In teachers colleges, understanding and appreciation of the value of LSP extends across all teaching staff. In two of the colleges, the legacy of LSTT is layered onto and reinforces that of *Baseline*. In their micro-teaching and demonstration lessons, students are expected to take into account the range of language proficiencies in a secondary school classroom and pay attention to vocabulary; they are urged to download audio dictionaries onto their smartphones and use these to check the standard pronunciation of subject specialist terms.

The outcomes of the project have not, however, been uniform across the five participating teacher education institutions. Each institution, and each individual, has strengthened their practices and discourses according to their capacity and degree of engagement. The University of Dodoma made significant curriculum changes and made these the most quickly. St. John's University of Tanzania made some similar changes but was slowed by staff turnover. The teachers colleges had less autonomy, so changes to teaching and learning were more incremental, were limited to changes in pedagogic practice and did not extend to changes to curriculum documents. The two teachers colleges that had benefited most from participation in previous projects concerned with pedagogic improvement were better able to appreciate, adopt and adapt the new ideas LSTT introduced. There was however, a sustained and enthusiastic engagement with problems of adapting pedagogy for learners not proficient in English across all five institutions. In the next section, we offer some reflections on the process of scale up as professional learning.

Reflecting on the process of scale up

After three years of implementing LSP in teacher education, we have established a community of practice, a form of learning partnership within which science and language educators collaboratively negotiate subject-language integrated practice (Farnsworth et al., 2016). There is within the partnership an enthusiasm to continue the process of professional learning and to expand the membership of the community of practice into schools. There are individuals who have taken the lead in the continued development of LSP as a practice, extending the repertoire of teaching and learning activities. As illustrated by the examples of lesson-study team innovations above, the direction of change has been towards greater participation by student teachers and the democratization of classrooms. Hence, tutors on the subject-methods courses have found attention to language opens up new pedagogic possibilities compatible with their long-held commitment to active student learning.

Others have focused on dissemination, taking a lead in designing training for in-service teachers, introducing LSP to schools and projects concerned with professional development. Their efforts, still in the early stages, have taken the form of workshops, which combine theory, demonstration and opportunities to experiment with the pedagogy through designing teaching and learning activities and lesson plans. This is quite a different professional learning process to the lesson-study methodology through which LSP has spread across the five partner teacher education institutions. Over the last three years, LSP has taken root not as a static recipe for classroom practice to be replicated, but rather as an open-ended process of collaborative inquiry. A more promising approach would be to support interdisciplinary teams of teachers within and across schools to implement elements of LSP collaboratively and reflexively through a process of professional inquiry adapted to their contexts.

LSP, or other versions of MLE, cannot be scaled up as a static idea or set of practices to be replicated but as a process of professional learning. Neither is it helpful to be prescriptive about the form and organization of the process of professional learning. The adaptation of lesson study that worked well in teacher education institutions may not work so well in schools. Reflecting on our experiences, we identify six features of the process as central to its success so far. The first two relate to the readiness and ability of teacher educators to engage with a process of pedagogic change. First, LSP allowed teacher educators to build upon and extend their theories of learning. Participating teacher educators already had a well-developed understanding of pedagogy and a commitment to participative pedagogies based in social constructivist theories of learning. They both recognized the need to address language learning explicitly in their courses and were sympathetic to the theoretical precepts of the language supportive approach. Second, teacher educators were able to change their practice. They had the autonomy, particularly within universities, and professional expertise to digest new ideas and make changes to their practice. Taken together these two reasons suggest that an approach to nurturing communities of practice should take into account and build upon teachers' theories of learning and expertise as practitioners. The next two reasons for success derive from the organization and membership of the lesson-study teams. Third, cross-disciplinary collaboration, bringing together science or mathematics educators with language experts, created the potential to innovate and provided collegial support for changing practice that individual lecturers might have resisted implementing independently. Fourth, whilst teams were based within institutions there was also networking across institutions, including engaging with the two UK-based researchers and with research literature. Sharing of ideas across institutions can help to inspire and sustain the energy for change within institutions.

The last two reasons relate to the lesson-study design. The fifth reason is to do with allowing time for professional learning. Understandings of LSP were more restricted in the first year and teachers' practices were more fragile. It was only with continued inquiry and practice over a second, and in some instances a third, annual cycle that teacher educators became secure in the approach. Cycling over successive years also allowed teams to move from replication to innovation, an essential step in internalising an innovation. In the first year, teams were more dependent on guidance and more uniform in how they conducted their inquiry and the changes they introduced into their practice. In the second year, teams embedded these changes. Some teams also began to explore aspects of their students' learning in more depth following tutors' own research interests or focusing on learning areas that tutors regarded as important for their subject. Sixth, the lesson-study design directed attention to student learning, so changes to the curriculum and learning activities were focused on strengthening student teachers' development as teachers. The attention to student learning ensured the relevance and effectiveness of innovations introduced.

Conclusion

Taken together, the six reasons for LSTT's success allowed for endogenous development of multilingual education. Endogenous knowledge, Hountondji (1997, p. 17) explains, is "an internal product drawn from a given cultural background," and is to be contrasted with imported knowledge drawn from elsewhere. Endogenous knowledge can, however, be inspired by interaction with ideas from outside. Borrowed ideas are assimilated to the point of being "fully mastered and integrated" (ibid., p. 17). Hountondji goes on to characterize endogenous innovation as a dynamic, "never ending process of interiorisation" (ibid., p. 18). Pedagogies for multilingual education may share much in common but need to be developed and adapted for specific contexts. This includes adaptations responding to the language proficiencies of learners, the languages in which learners are accustomed to talk, write and read about science as well as the common pedagogic practices, expertise, versatility and professional freedoms of teachers. Patience with the pace of professional learning as a situated process may in the long term prove more sustainable than the common approach of cascade training neatly designed by external experts. In the words of Freire:

> For apart from inquiry, apart from the praxis, individuals cannot be truly human. Knowledge emerges only through invention and re-invention, through the restless, impatient, continuing, hopeful inquiry human beings pursue in the world, with the world, and with each other.
>
> (Freire 1993, p. 72)

For us, learning about language in science education continues to be an ongoing open inquiry. What we have learned so far raises just as many questions as have already been answered and opens up as many new pedagogic possibilities as we have already explored in our practice. The gradual expansion of a community of practice through a process of professional learning and travelling along preexisting networks within education systems is not an all-encompassing solution to the longstanding problem of the language barrier in secondary education in Tanzania. It does however hold out promise for embedding aspects of multilingual education that strengthen secondary school subject teaching even within the constraints imposed by a longstanding and seemingly intransigent monoglossic policy environment.

Acknowledgements

We would like to recognize the contribution and creativity of all participants in the LSTT project at the University of Dodoma, St. John's University of Tanzania, Butimba Teachers College, Morogoro Teachers College and Mpwapwa Teachers College. They are too many to mention by name but without their professionalism, creativity and generosity with their time LSTT would not have existed. We are grateful to colleagues at the University of Bristol, who read and commented on this chapter as well as the blind reviewer.

References

Barrett, AM & Bainton, D 2016, 'Re-interpreting relevant learning: an evaluative framework for secondary education in a global language', *Comparative Education*, 52(3), pp. 392–407.

Barrett, AM, Kajoro, P & Mills, M 2014, 'Strengthening secondary education in practice: Language Supportive Teaching and Textbooks in Tanzania (LSTT)', Pilot Study Report, Language Supportive Teaching and Textbooks, UNESCO Learning Portal. https://learningportal.iiep.unesco.org/en/library/strengthening-secondary-education-in-practice-language-supportive-teaching-and-textbooks-in

Cakir, M 2008, 'Constructivist approaches to learning in science and their implications for science pedagogy: A literature review', *International Journal of Environmental and Science Education*, 3(4), pp. 193–206.

Cenoz, J 2017, Translanguaging in school contexts: International perspectives, Special Issue: Breaking away from the multilingual solitudes in language education: International perspectives', *Journal of Language, Identity & Education*, 16(4), pp. 193–198, DOI: 10.1080/15348458.2017.1327816

Clegg, J & Afitska, O 2011, 'Teaching and learning in two languages in African classrooms', *Comparative Education*, 47(1), pp. 61–77.

Coleman, H (ed) 2017, *Multilingualisms and Development: Selected proceedings of the 11th Language & Development Conference, New Delhi, India 2015*, British Council, London. www.langdevconferences.org/publications/2015-NewDelhi/MultilingualismsandDevelopment-Coleman-ed-completepublications.pdf

Coyle, D 2007, 'Content and Language Integrated Learning: Towards a connected research agenda for CLIL pedagogies', *International Journal of Bilingual Education and Bilingualism*, 10(5), pp. 543–562.

Dembélé, M & Lefoka, P 2007, 'Pedagogical renewal for quality universal primary education: Overview of trends in Sub-Saharan Africa', *International Review of Education*, 53 (5-6), pp. 531–553.

Doig, B & Groves, S 2011, 'Japanese lesson study: Teacher professional development through communities of inquiry', *Mathematics Teacher Education and Development*, 13(1), pp. 77–93.

Duarte, J 2018, 'Translanguaging in the context of mainstream multilingual education', *International Journal of Multilingualism*, 22(2), pp. 1–16.

Eriksson, I & Osaki, K (eds) 2018, *School Development through Teacher Research: Lesson and Learning Studies in Sweden and Tanzania*, Mkuki na Nyota, Dar es Salaam.

Farnsworth, V, Kleanthous, I & Wenger-Trayner, E 2016, 'Communities of practice as a social theory of learning: A conversation with Etienne Wenger', *British Journal of Educational Studies*, 64(2), pp. 139–160.

Flores, N & Beardsmore, HB 2015, 'Programs and structures in bilingual and multilingual education', in WE Wright, S Boun & O García (eds), *The Handbook of Bilingual and Multilingual Education*, Wiley Blackwell, Oxford, pp. 205–222.

Freire, P 1993, *Pedagogy of the Oppressed*, Continuum, New York.

García, O & Wei, L 2015, 'Translanguaging, bilingualism, and bilingual education', in WE Wright, S Boun & O García (eds), *The Handbook of Bilingual and Multilingual Education*, Wiley Blackwell, Oxford, pp. 223–240.

Guzula, X, McKinney, C & Tyler, R (2016) 'Languaging-for-learning: Legitimising translanguaging and enabling multimodal practices in third spaces', *Southern African Linguistics and Applied Language Studies*, 34, pp. 211–226.

Halliday, MAK 1993, 'Towards a language-based theory of learning', *Linguistics and Education*, 5, pp. 93–116.

Hountondji, P 1997, *Endogenous Knowledge: Research Trails*. CODESRIA, Dakar, Senegal.

Juma, ZR 2015, 'Exploring the development of biological literacy in Tanzanian junior secondary school students', Unpublished PhD thesis, University of Wellington.

Komba, SC & Mohamed, HI 2017, 'Towards re-defining communication skills courses at Sokoine University of Agriculture: Lessons from selected African universities', *International Journal of Research Studies in Language Learning*, 6(2), pp. 55–67. https://pdfs.semanticscholar.org/4f15/4251322a18064666la8ad4978de3773fdd54.pdf

Lemke, JL (1990) *Talking Science: Language, Learning, and Values*, Ablex, Norwood, New Jersey.

Lin, AMY & He, P 2017, 'Translanguaging as dynamic activity flows in CLIL classrooms', *Journal of Language, Identity & Education*, 16(4), pp. 228–244.

McKinney, C & Tyler, R (2019) 'Disinventing and reconstituting language for learning in school Science', *Language and Education*, 33(2), pp. 141–158.

Ministry of Education, Science and Technology 2018, *Education Sector Development Plan (2016/17 – 2020/21), updated 2018*, Government of the United Republic of Tanzania, Dar es Salaam, viewed 2 March 2020, <www.globalpartnership.org/sites/default/files/2019-04-gpe-tanzania-esp.pdf>.

Mkonongwa, LM & Komba, SC 2018, 'Enhancing the quality of teaching and learning in Tanzania through improved English language teaching and educational management skills', *International Journal of Research Studies in Language Learning*, 7(2), pp. 1–14. https://doi.org/10.5861/ijrsll.2017.1705

Moate, J 2010, 'The integrated nature of CLIL: A sociocultural perspective', *International CLIL Research Journal*, 1(3), pp. 38–45.

Msimanga, A & Lelliott, A 2014, 'Talking science in multilingual contexts in South Africa: Possibilities and challenges for engagement in learners' home languages in high school classrooms', *International Journal of Science Education*, 36(7), pp. 1159–1183.

Mtana, NJ & O-saki, KM 2017, 'Empowering the marginalised through language supportive pedagogy in Tanzanian secondary education', in Coleman, H (ed) *Multilingualisms and Development: Selected proceedings of the 11th Language & Development Conference, New Delhi, India 2015*, British Council, London, pp. 169–180, viewed 3 March 2020, <https://issuu.com/britishcouncilindia/docs/multilingualisms_and_development>.

Mwinsheikhe, HM 2009, 'Spare no means: battling the English/Kiswahili dilemma in Tanzania secondary school classrooms', in B Brock-Utne & I Skattum (eds), *Languages and Education in Africa: A Comparative and Transdisciplinary Analysis*, Symposium, Oxford, pp. 223–234.

Ottevanger, W, de Feiter, L, O-saki, K & van den Akker, J 2005, 'The TEAMS Project in Tanzania: From intervention to capacity building', *Journal of International Cooperation in Education*, 8(1), pp. 111–123.

Probyn, M 2015, 'Pedagogical translanguaging: Bridging discourses in South African science classrooms', *Language and Education*, 29(3), pp. 218–234.

Qorro, MAS 2009, 'Parents' and policy makers' insistence on foriegn languages as media of education in Africa: restricitng access to quality education - for whose benefit?', in

B Brock-Utne & I Skattum (eds), *Languages and Education in Africa: A Comparative and Transdisciplinary Analysis*, Symposium, Oxford, pp. 57–82.

Rea-Dickins, P, Yu, G & Afitska, O 2009, 'The consequences of examining through an unfamiliar language of instruction and its impact for school-age learners in sub-Saharan African school systems', in L Taylor & C Weir (eds), *Language Testing Matters: The Social and Educational Impact of Language Assessment*, Cambridge University Press, Cambridge, pp. 190–214.

Samoff, J, Dembélé, M & Sebatane, EM 2013, 'Scaling up by focusing down: creating space and capacity to extend education reform in Africa', in L Tikly & AM Barrett (eds), *Education Quality and Social Justice in the Global South: Challenges for policy, practice and research*, Routledge, London, pp. 121–138.

Scott, P, Asoko, H & Leach, J 2007, 'Student conceptions and conceptual learning in science', in SK Abell & NG Lederman (eds), *Handbook of Research on Science Education*, Routledge, London, pp. 31–56.

Setati, M, Adler, J, Reed, Y & Bapoo, A 2002, 'Incomplete journeys: Code-switching and other language practices in Mathematics, Science and English language classrooms in South Africa', *Language and Education*, 16(2), pp. 128–149.

Shoba, JA & Chimbutane, F (eds) 2013, *Bilingual Education and Language Policy in the Global South*, Routledge, New York.

Stuart, JS 2002, 'College tutors: A fulcrum for change?', *International Journal of Educational Development*, 22, pp. 367–379.

Sumra, S & Rajani, R 2006, *Secondary Education in Tanzania: Key Policy Challenges*, Hakielimu, Dar es Salaam.

Terra, S 2021, Bilingual education in Mozambique: A case-study on educational policy, teacher beliefs, and implemented practices, *International Journal of Bilingual Education and Bilingualism*, 24(1), pp. 16–30, DOI: 10.1080/13670050.2018.1441803

Tang, K & Danielsson, K (eds) 2018, *Global Developments in Literacy Research for Science Education*. Springer, Dodrecht.

Tibategeza, E & du Plessis, T 2012, 'Language-in-education policy development in Tanzania: An overview', *Language Matters: Studies in the Languages of Africa*, 43(2), pp. 184–201.

Valdés, G, Poza, L & Brooks, MD 2015, 'Language acquisition in bilingual education', in WE Wright, S Boun & O García (eds), *The Handbook of Bilingual and Multilingual Education*, Wiley Blackwell, Oxford, pp. 56–74.

Wright, W, Boun, S & García, O (eds) 2015, *The Handbook of Bilingual and Multilingual Education*, Wiley Blackwell, Oxford.

Index

Note: Figures are shown in *italics* and tables are in **bold** type. Endnotes are indicated by the page number followed by "n" and the endnote number e.g., 246n1 refers to endnote 1 on page 246.

Printed in Great Britain
by Amazon

32465694R00170